W9-BHU-101

WHY GOVERN- MENT FAILS SO OFTEN

WHY GOVERN- MENT FAILS SO OFTEN

And How It Can Do Better

PETER H. SCHUCK

Princeton University Press
Princeton and Oxford

Copyright © 2014 by Princeton University Press

Published by Princeton University Press, 41 William Street, Princeton, New Jersey 08540

In the United Kingdom: Princeton University Press, 6 Oxford Street, Woodstock, Oxfordshire OX20 1TW

press.princeton.edu

Jacket photograph: DC Capitol Dome courtesy of Thinkstock
Jacket design by Faceout Studio, Charles Brock

ISBN 978-0-691-16162-4

British Library Cataloging-in-Publication Data is available

This book has been composed in Minion Pro

Printed on acid-free paper ∞

Printed in the United States of America

10 9 8 7 6 5 4

This book is dedicated to our federal officials—civil servants and political appointees alike—who struggle against great odds to make our government work.

Contents

Acknowledgments

Writing a book of this kind is inevitably a solitary undertaking. Nevertheless, I am indebted to a number of individuals and institutions. Some read portions of earlier versions of the manuscript—in a few cases, all of it—and provided me with useful comments, criticisms, and bibliographical suggestions. These include Henry Aaron, Lynn Chu, Martha Derthick, John DiIulio, Dick Fallon, Amihai Glazer, Judy Gueron, Judd Kahn, Mark Kleiman, Walter Lafeber, Bob LaLonde, Bob Litan, Ken Manaster, Jerry Mashaw, David Mayhew, Shep Melnick, Geoff Miller, Pietro Nivola, Rick Pildes, Ricky Revesz, Nancy Rosenblum, Steve Sugarman, and Cliff Winston. Many other people, not named here, kindly answered specific questions. Shortly before his death, James Q. Wilson commented on my original outline, assuring me that such a book was needed. Three formidable groups of scholars—my Yale Law School colleagues and those at the Brookings Institution and the Manhattan Institute—kindly convened workshops to discuss the work in progress. Two institutions supported my work, each in its own ways: Yale Law School, where I am a longtime faculty member; and the New York University School of Law, which has generously given me an office, library and administrative support, and intellectual fellowship during the past fifteen years when I have lived in New York City. At various points I benefited from the able research assistance of Yale Law School students Mathew Andrews, Josh Handell, Charlie Hauch, Steven Kochevar, Ted Wojcik, and Jacob Goldberg who prepared the index. Finally, I have enjoyed the enthusiastic support of Princeton University Press, especially its fine director Peter Dougherty, his associate Beth Clevenger, production editor Mark Bellis, and copy editor Brian Bendlin.

—New York City, November 2013

WHY GOVERN- MENT FAILS SO OFTEN

Introduction

O ur political system has long been admired and wondered at by Americans and outsiders who marvel at its ability to govern for 225 years a remarkably dynamic, diverse society. Yet most Americans today believe that our government is failing to deliver what it promises, and they have lost confidence in its effectiveness. Herein lies a deep and dangerous dilemma, one that this book seeks to explain and perhaps to help solve.

Consider some of our government's past successes—many of commission, some of restraint. Since the Civil War, the U.S. political system has been extraordinarily stable and durable, experiencing no deep crisis of regime legitimacy and requiring only a dozen additional amendments to our eighteenth-century Constitution, most of them of only historical significance. Our polity and civil society have accepted and integrated a vast number of immigrants of diverse races, religions, languages, and cultural backgrounds, most with relatively low education levels, transforming them into patriotic Americans and loyal permanent residents. Our competitive, resilient economy leads the world in technological innovation and has given us the highest standard of living in the world. (Despite recent setbacks, it still vies for that distinction with oil-rich Norway and tiny tax haven Luxembourg.[1]) Having rescued our allies in two world wars, the United States has exerted hegemonic military, cultural, diplomatic, and economic power (for better and worse) for seven decades. It has extended civil rights for racial and religious minorities, women, gay people, and the disabled. It reduced poverty significantly between 1960 and 2010, with much of that decline occurring since 1980.[2] Its civil society is the world's most robust and creative, with a vibrant religious and civic culture that supports a bewildering variety of philanthropic, religious, and social service activities. Among liberal democracies, Americans are by far the most patriotic people; almost 90 percent completely or mostly agree with the statement "I am very patriotic"; most claim to engage in patriotic activities.[3] Our natural environment, highlighted in its national park system and vast tracts of unsettled territory, is stunning. The U.S. demographic structure and fertility rate are the envy of faster-aging Western democracies. A deep norm of tolerance leaves the United States as one of the few advanced democracies without a nativist or xenophobic political party. Its formidable military establishment poses no threat to civilian politics. Its response to 9/11 was largely effective in avoiding subsequent attacks on the homeland. It maintains a stable currency that helps support the global economy. Some of its domestic policies and programs are highly successful (see chapter 11).*

This is the good news. The bad news is that Americans have a dismal opinion of the federal government's performance, one that is only getting darker.[4] Significantly, this growing antipathy is not antigovernment generally (see chapter 4). Instead, it targets *only* the federal government; respect for state and local governments is both high and stable. Nor is this hostility toward the federal government in Washington a partisan matter. Instead, it is expressed by a majority of Democrats as well as Republicans.[5] And perhaps most revealing, this disaffection long preceded the current political gridlock in Congress that many pundits see (wrongly, as I shall show) as the root of the problem.

In both 1997 and 2010, a Princeton Survey Research Associates/ Pew survey reported that only 2 percent of respondents believed that the federal government does an "excellent job" in running its programs; 74 percent of respondents said that it did only a "fair" or "poor job."[6] In 2011, 79 percent said they were "frustrated" or "angry" with

---

*A *policy* is a statement of goals; a *program* is an instrument for implementing a policy. Generally, I use the terms interchangeably. Policy makers are those who design, adopt, and implement policies. Again, I shall use the generic term except where it seems important to distinguish among them.

the federal government. (In 2007, before the recession, that total was 74 percent.) Again, Obamacare's initial website breakdown, unexpectedly low enrollment by the young and healthy, and the constant regulatory maneuvers necessitated by these factors have probably magnified this deep discontent.

In 2010, only 36 percent thought the government "often does a better job than it is given credit for." Fully 83 percent thought that federal programs' performance was "getting worse" or "staying the same." In 2011, 64 percent thought that "big government" was the biggest threat to the country in the future; only 26 percent identified "big business" as the biggest future threat, even only five years after the economic meltdown.[7] In 2010, only 4 percent had "a lot of confidence" that when the federal government decides to solve a problem it will actually be solved. In July 2013, a *Wall Street Journal*/NBC News poll reported that 83 percent of Americans disapprove of Congress's performance—the highest in the poll's history.[8] And, perhaps most ominous, a Harvard Institute of Politics poll published in April 2013 found that among voters under thirty, traditionally the most optimistic and idealistic demographic group, trust in the president and in Congress is at low levels and declining.[9] Not surprisingly, both parties are finding it harder to induce attractive, ambitious candidates to run for the U.S. Senate.[10] Even the public's approval rating of the Supreme Court, which it traditionally revered, has declined significantly since the 1980s to just 44 percent.[11]

Consider the responses to a question that pollsters have asked for more than a half century: "How much of the time do you think you can trust the government in Washington to do what is right?" In 1958, 73 percent said "just about always" or "most of the time"; in 2011, only 10 percent did so.[12] In April 2013, only 28 percent of Americans had a favorable opinion of the federal government; even among Democrats, who controlled both the White House and the Senate, it fell to only 41 percent, down ten points from the previous year.[13] Indeed, even the Democrat leadership decries failures in many programs, while insisting that it can rectify them with more money, greater fairness, and smarter administration.[14] The public evidently disagrees. A

2011 Rasmussen poll found that a record-low 17 percent of voters felt "the federal government has the consent of the governed" and 38 percent (a plurality) wanted the federal government to become "inconsequential" in American life.[15] In 2013, the Brookings Institution found that even *56 percent of Democrats* believe the government is "mostly or completely broken."[16] And this was *before* the government shutdown and failed Obamacare rollout on October 1, 2013, which of course aroused even greater public disgust! Even liberalism's century-old flagship, the *New Republic*, now despairs.[17]

In short, the public views the federal government as a chronically clumsy, ineffectual, bloated giant that cannot be counted upon to do the right thing, much less to do it well. It does not seem to matter much to them whether the government that fails them is liberal or conservative, or how earnestly our leaders promise to remedy these failures. Failure is also common in the private sector, of course. Most new firms go out of business within their first five years,[18] and the performance of leading private firms have often been abysmal and sometimes criminal[19]—for example, the "big four" accounting firms that audit brokerage safety and performance,[20] the top bond rating companies,[21] stock exchanges,[22] and the major financial institutions.[23] The leading heart organizations' new set of cholesterol guidelines was discredited within days. But whereas consumers dissatisfied with private providers can usually take their business elsewhere (as Blackberry and other companies have discovered), discontented citizens are stuck with the government they have, until the next election.

Why, then, do most members of such a successful society so disparage their government? (Interestingly, Europeans' faith in *their* governments appears to be even lower!)[24] This is an urgent, complex question, to which I offer five answers that are consistent with the social science evidence.[25]

The most straightforward answer is that *the federal government does in fact perform poorly in a vast range of domestic programs.* (As explained below, this book focuses exclusively on *federal domestic* programs.) This is amply demonstrated by the large body of evidence compiled by the nation's leading social science analysts and public administration scholars,[26] evidence that I prefigure later in this chapter and in detail in part 2. A competitive party system and an attentive, critical media get the word out on these failures, and the public naturally takes notice.

Second, and equally conspicuous, *our legislative process is highly dysfunctional by almost any standard.* "Even in some of the worst years of partisan gridlock," *New York Times* reporter Jonathan Weisman reports, "a deadline has meant something to Congress—until 2013."[27] The title of a recent book by two leading scholars of Congress is telling: *It's Even Worse Than It Looks.*[28] And as with the survey evidence just discussed, these professional judgments were rendered *before* both the latest government shutdown, the Obamacare website fiasco, and the impending debt limit crisis.

Third, *Americans perceive a gap between "the democracy of everyday life" and democracy as practiced in Washington,*[29] between how well their neighborhoods and religious communities generally function, and the federal government's often dismaying performance.*

Fourth, *prosperity may have raised public expectations and demands.*† This could explain why voters from wealthier countries like the United States tend to criticize their governments more than those from poorer ones do, and also why they direct their discontent not at democracy per se, which still enjoys very strong support in all industrialized countries, but instead at their governing institutions and leaders. Some analysts ascribe this discontent to "postmodern" attitudes that erode respect for authority;[30] people want to know, "What have you done for me lately?"

Finally, *Americans harbor the conceit that we the people are not responsible for the government's failures, which are instead caused by*

*The main exceptions are one-off existential situations in which goals are clear and normal politics is largely suspended (as was the case in World War II), and the relatively few but important domestic program successes discussed in chapter 11.

†Brookings Institution economist Scott Winship shows that growing inequality is a doubtful explanation. See Winship, "How Much Do Americans Care about Income Inequality?" April 30, 2013, http://www.brookings.edu/research/opinions/2013/04/30-income-inequality-winship; and Scott Winship, "How Much Do Americans Care about Income Inequality? Part II," May 15, 2013, http://www.brookings.edu/research/opinions/2013/05/15-do-americans-care-about-inequality-winship.

alien forces in Washington. In this self-justifying view, those politicians are shortsighted, selfish, partisan, lazy, and hypocritical, but we citizens are not. We do not acknowledge the role played by our inattention, apathy, cynicism, ignorance, and demand for many more government services than we are willing to pay for.* Failure produces more finger-pointing than blame acceptance, as president John F. Kennedy noted after his own failure at the Bay of Pigs: "Victory has a thousand fathers; defeat is an orphan." Walt Kelly's cartoon character Pogo uttered another version of this truth: "We have met the enemy and he is us."[31]

DEFINING FAILURE AND SUCCESS

Assessments of policy or program effectiveness necessarily depend on how I (and the analysts whose work I synthesize) define and measure failure and success. Because these judgments are contestable, I use chapter 2 to explore these definitions and measures, answering questions like: Failure and success compared with what—an unregulated market? What about programs that are successful in some respects but not in others? How can one assess a program's performance? Since even ineffective ones create *some* benefits for at least *some* people, how can we assess them *overall?* Chapter 2 presents my answers to such questions. I note there that the main index of a program's performance should not be its durability or its enthusiastic defenders,† which may reflect political inertia protected by

---

*Former congressman Barney Frank reportedly once told a group of complaining constituents, "We politicians are not great shakes, but you voters are not a day at the beach either." Such candor is as rare as it is true. Most politicians flatter the voters, as when, in 1974, then presidenial candidate Jimmy Carter called for "a government as good as its people." Our framers had no such illusions, placing their faith not in individual virtue but in institutional arrangements. As James Madison wrote in "Federalist No. 51": "If men were angels, no government would be necessary. . . . A dependence on the people is, no doubt, the primary control on the government; but experience has taught mankind the necessity of auxiliary precautions."

†Social Security and Medicare, our largest federal programs, are so popular that anyone who proposes to reduce their benefits risks political defeat. This is why president Barack

strategically positioned beneficiaries, but instead its *cost-effectiveness*. I explain there what this means, how it can be assessed, and why many such assessments are controversial. We shall see that it is much harder to assess government failure than market failure, and to conclude that particular public programs do or do not "work."

As the analysis proceeds, readers should keep in mind several points that subsequent chapters will exemplify. Even the most successful programs (see chapter 11) exhibit flaws, some of them serious, and even failed policies confer some benefits. Sometimes the benefits are immense, but they are delivered at much higher costs than necessary. (This is why I do not count Medicare a success, as I explain in chapter 11.) All such assessments are *relative*—both to the criteria of success presented in chapter 2 and to how effective the program might be if its shortcomings could somehow be remedied. And although people often blame government failure on powerful interest groups, campaign contributions, and partisan polarization, the causes are almost always much deeper—and most of them, as we shall see, originate in Congress! In fact, interest groups (discussed throughout, especially in chapters 4, 5, 7, 8, and 11) are the lifeblood of a vibrant democracy like ours; their effects are large but widely misunderstood. Campaign contributions play a smaller role than most people think, as we shall see in chapter 7. And political polarization merely shows that the country is deeply divided; indeed, it has been from the very beginning and at times even more than now. But it does not explain policy failure.

Understanding government failure, then, presents complex challenges. Its funders, consumers, and ultimate appraisers—"We the People"—are more disgruntled than ever, and the social scientists who assess the evidence most rigorously find that these appraisers' disapproval is amply warranted. In a consent-based polity, so damn-

Obama, even with the political latitude afforded by his reelection in 2012, hesitates to offer specific proposals to alter these programs, and why the proposals of bipartisan, blue-ribbon commissions from Breaux under president Bill Clinton to Simpson-Bowles under Obama have largely been ignored.

ing a verdict by both generalist citizens and policy specialists should be a cause for grave concern.

THE SOCIAL STAKES IN IMPROVING GOVERNMENT PERFORMANCE

Advocates of federal regulation can point to many social gains in recent decades—declining auto and airline accident rates, public health advances, legal rights for minorities and women, environmental protection, and the like—that they ascribe to public policy. Many policy analysts applaud the gains but are skeptical that the government is responsible for most of them. They argue that market and other factors produced most of the gains, and that more effective policies could have yielded gains that were larger, less costly, or both. I present evidence bearing on the competing claims in chapters 5–8. Skeptics concede that entitlements like Medicare and Social Security—where the big money is—have succeeded in redistributing wealth progressively, but think that much of the redistribution is unfair (to young people) and poorly targeted (to well-off Americans), and that some entitlement programs like food stamps and unemployment compensation create too much moral hazard (discussed in chapter 5). No serious analyst denies that the projected growth path, if unchanged, is unsustainable and eventually ruinous, but no one expects future policy makers to let that happen.

Reasonable people differ intensely over the proper *scope* and *size* of the federal government—that is, the areas of activity in which it should intervene, the projects it should undertake, and the means it should employ. Historically, the federal government's size—and, more importantly, its responsibilities—have been hotly, sometimes violently, contested issues from the earliest days of our republic. Its role has waxed and waned in the wake of various crises or national emergencies. Notably, however, its expansion in the last half century—quite apart from national defense and other public goods—has been strikingly steady, ratcheting ever upward, with only the *rate* of increase varying.[32] Public administration scholar Paul Light has distilled from the federal statutes enacted between 1943 and 2000 a list of the government's most important missions. The list demonstrates the remarkable growth in its programmatic ambitions during this period, a growth that even president Ronald Reagan could only slow, not reverse. Light also shows that various techniques that *every* modern president has instituted in order to eliminate bad programs, reduce wasteful spending, narrow the agenda by devolving authority to the states, and "starve the beast" (a phrase often used by small-government conservatives) through deep tax cuts have failed to turn the tide.[33] Historian Niall Ferguson notes that the *Federal Register* has grown two and a half times faster than the economy over a long period of time, and that the ratio of final rules issued by federal agencies to laws passed by Congress in the last decade has been 223 to 1,[34] not counting "Obamacare" (and many Dodd-Frank Act) regulations still to be promulgated. Political scientist John DiIulio shows that the expansionary dynamic is largely irreversible.[35] And other leading political scientists concluded in 1997 that "the realm of policy knows no conceptual bounds."[36] And this was *before* the government embarked on No Child Left Behind, expanded Medicare to cover prescription drugs, adopted vast new regulation of the financial system, and enacted the remarkably ambitious Affordable Care Act (not to mention waging two wars).

Today, federal domestic spending is at the highest share of gross domestic product (GDP) since the end of World War II (albeit still well below European levels). A larger share of Americans receive entitlements than ever before; the federal government now backs 90 percent of new mortgages (up from half before the financial crisis), and 93 percent of student loans (a share that will approach 100 percent, with private lenders now excluded from the market). The number of regulatory agency staff members has ballooned, and these staffers churn out more and costlier rules than ever before.[37] Much of this increased spending since 2008 was due to the Great Recession, but its link to the business cycle has attenuated as administrations propose more spending even in a growing economy. Reasonable people differ, of course, on the merits of a more interventionist government. My point for present purposes is that its growth increases the urgency of understanding its endemic failures.

Policies that don't work pose many risks to social well-being, but in this introduction I shall mention only four: (1) wasting scarce social resources; (2) suffering on the part of those Americans who most depend on government; (3) reducing future economic growth; and (4) threatening the government's legitimacy.

Wasting social resources. In 2011, the federal government spent approximately $3.8 trillion. Even if we set aside the $768 billion in defense spending as sacrosanct (which it isn't, as was evident in the budget decisions negotiated at the end of 2011), this leaves more than $3 trillion of annual nondefense federal expenditure (almost 95 percent of total outlays) whose value depends on how well the government spends it.[38] Politics and ideology aside, the conventional justification for this immense expenditure is that the money is better spent by the government than by the private taxpayers from whom it is exacted. If and to the extent that this justification is false—if the government in fact spends it less wisely and generates less social value than taxpayers spending the same amount would—then the difference in that value represents sheer waste to society (what economists, usually when referring to certain market inefficiencies, call a deadweight loss).

This waste could occur for several reasons. First, taxpayers could derive more value from spending the same amount of money than even a perfectly executed government program (whatever that might mean) would generate. Second, the government program may perform less effectively (i.e., produces less social value) than it should—most obviously in waste due to duplication, overlap, and fragmentation of programs. (I discuss this problem in chapter 6.)[39] Although the first reason is no doubt important with respect to many government programs (I shall provide examples later on), my argument in subsequent chapters will focus primarily on the second.

Those who depend most on government. Every American is affected by federal programs; they are simply too ubiquitous to avoid. Even the wealthiest citizens, for example, benefit from public goods such as clean air, the Centers for Disease Control and Prevention, national parks, and the federal courts. But taxpayers also support a host of subsidy programs that seek to extend access to education, housing, nutrition, and a host of other "merit goods."*

In contrast, tens of millions of Americans, especially those who are permanently disabled, and unemployable, are now utterly dependent on the government for the essentials of life: food, shelter, basic health care, and other protection against hazards for which they are not responsible and which they cannot absorb without great suffering. (For the purposes of the present discussion, the normative value and design of these programs and their effects on recipients and society are beside the point; I will discuss them later.) Precisely because such public provision is life sustaining, it is immensely valuable to the recipients—and also to those better-off citizens, evidently a majority, who want the government to provide for the indigent. For that reason, poor government performance—inefficiency, unjust distribution, mistargeting[40]—harms the putative recipients and dismays their public-spirited fellow citizens.

Future economic growth. The achievements of the United States that I described earlier constitute a record unparalleled in world history. But precisely because of our successful legacy, some question the nation's ability to maintain, much less extend, these accomplishments in the face of remorseless challenges: global competition, implacable demographic changes, periodic financial and economic recessions, and rising public demands for more government intervention. Curing our daunting, interrelated pathologies—an embedded underclass, weak family structures, fiscally unsustainable entitlement programs, persistently mediocre (or worse) elementary and secondary education, growing inequality, a deteriorating infrastructure—demands many changes, some of which government policy alone cannot effect. But what we can and must demand of government is that its policies be cost-effective, a theme taken up in chapter 2. (Such discipline is not merely a domestic policy imperative. Mike

*The concepts of public and merit goods are discussed in chapter 3. I discuss the effectiveness of programs to provide them throughout the book, especially in chapter 8.

Mullen, then chairman of the Joint Chiefs of Staff, said that "the single, biggest threat to our national security is our debt."[41])

Is the United States capable of reforming its system in these ways? I think so (otherwise I would not have written this book) but, in truth, many informed, sympathetic observers harbor serious doubts. Consider for a moment just the business environment. The *Economist*, generally a staunch admirer of American economic institutions, notes that growing legal restrictions on financial transactions are making it "so difficult to list shares on an American stockmarket that firms increasingly look elsewhere or stay private. America's share of initial public offerings fell from 67 percent in 2002 (when the Sarbanes–Oxley Act passed) to 16 percent last year. A study for the Small Business Administration, a government body, found that regulations in general add $10,585 in costs per employee. It's a wonder the jobless rate isn't even higher than it is."[42] Quoting comments by Harvard Business School faculty and alumni, the *Economist* observes, "The US government is failing to tackle weaknesses in the business environment that are making the country a less attractive place to invest and [is] nullifying some of American's most important competitive strengths. . . . 71% [of HBS alumni] said that American competitiveness would decline in the coming years."[43] In June 2013, Niall Ferguson cited the United States' dramatic decline since the mid-1990s in World Governance Indicators for voice and accountability, government effectiveness, regulatory quality, and control of corruption.[44] Subsequent chapters will express similar doubts about many other aspects of government performance (or passivity, which of course is itself a policy).

Many commentators insist that the problem is partisan bickering and congressional paralysis. I have my doubts. Incivility in politics is a long American tradition,[45] and many of the greatest governmental achievements of the past—the transcontinental railroad, the Hoover Dam, the interstate highway system—were accomplished only fitfully and after protracted disagreements, often appalling corruption, and political skulduggery.[46] Partisan polarization, I think, is not so much a *cause* of our problems as a *consequence* of a central political reality that has its virtues and its vices: the American people, from whom the partisan politicians take their cue, disagree fundamentally about many of the substantive directions that they want policy and institutional change to take—though as we shall see in chapter 4, this polarization is often exaggerated. To some extent, moreover, public division over which policies to support and in what forms reflects the fact that the problems are so difficult even to comprehend, much less to solve. Until the public somehow reaches greater consensus on these difficult policy issues—something that politicians even in the recent past have occasionally managed to forge for a time—we will be mired in a status quo that can only be altered by effective government reform of one kind or another. This, of course, is easier said than done—but it *has* sometimes been done in the past. Chapter 11 provides some precedents for reform, and chapter 12 discusses some possibilities for today.

Threats to government legitimacy. The opinion data cited earlier indicates that the American people have dramatically less confidence and trust than they used to in the federal government's propensity to do the right thing. This is very bad news not only for those who advocate new and innovative public initiatives but also for those who want to reform or repeal existing policies. It seems to bespeak a genuine feeling that the government cannot or will not do much well or right. (I say "seems" because the questions posed in these surveys do not usually invite respondents to distinguish in their misgivings among different policy choices.)

Does this widespread and growing mistrust of governmental morality (doing "the right thing," whatever that might be) amount to a loss of its legitimacy? The answer to this important question depends on definition and degree. Some years ago, I cautioned against overuse of the concept, noting, "For many legal [and other] scholars, the invocation of legitimacy is not merely a handy rhetorical trope. It also serves as an indispensable prop, a kind of all-purpose, gap-filling, *deus ex machina* that we often use to rescue arguments that lack much empirical support or merely reflect our deeply-felt preferences.

We can all readily agree that any sound democratic regime must be perceived as legitimate in the sense that those subject to it accept and feel bound by its law *because* it is its law, quite apart from whether they agree with its merits." In the specific context of affirmative action policy, I argued that when its advocates "insist that the policy is necessary to democratic legitimacy, what they really mean is that they feel very strongly about it. Their opponents, of course, feel just as strongly, yet this fact does not render laws authorizing [or prohibiting] affirmative action illegitimate."[47]

At some point, to be sure, growing public suspicion of the government's morality, motives, or competence might well produce widespread feelings of illegitimacy. This was illustrated most vividly in the public outrage over the abject failures of the Federal Emergency Management Agency in response to Hurricane Katrina.[48] In my view, however, public doubts about the government's effectiveness and ability to do the right thing,[49] and do it reasonably well, do not yet amount to a perception of illegitimacy (although some astute commentators disagree[50]). Nevertheless, it does pose a growing danger, like rising floodwaters threatening to breach a levee. It is also sobering to recall, as Paul Light does, that there have been two periods in recent history—during the administration of president Ronald Reagan, and in the months following 9/11—when trust has rebounded but then fallen back.[51] Today, as noted above, trust in the federal government is lower than ever before. Given the unusually difficult political and policy challenges that it faces today and for the foreseeable future, such trust will be difficult, though not impossible, to regain. A relatively new development that supports this downbeat prediction is this: presidents and other elected officials on both sides of the aisle (albeit more often Republicans) no longer content themselves with merely disparaging this or that public policy; they now lead the chorus of systemic criticism of government competence and capacity.[52] More speculatively, increasingly well-educated, well-traveled, and technologically sophisticated citizens may be more receptive to such systemic criticisms of government as they hold it to ever higher standards of professional ethics, wise policy making, and efficient administration.

Even if the current level of dissatisfaction falls short of widespread loss of legitimacy, it still constitutes a serious challenge to effective governance. It means not only that citizens hold low expectations of the government (which, after all, should be easier to satisfy), but also that the public is less willing to provide government with the authority, support, resources, and patience that effective policy making may require. Political scientist James Morone has chronicled the historical cycle of public dissatisfaction with government performance: discontent, demands for reform, and enactment of new policies, followed by fresh disappointment. He argues that the public's chronic suspicion of governmental power, a signal feature of American political culture going back to colonial times, has engendered a self-fulfilling prophecy: suspicious voters resist providing the government the power and resources that are necessary, in Morone's view, for the kind of successful, effective programs that could have reversed this mistrust and disrespect of government.[53]

There is little doubt that the perpetual despair–reform–despair cycle that Morone describes has confirmed, and likely increased, public resistance to large new policy initiatives. President Barack Obama's signature Affordable Care Act of 2010, far from refuting this claim, actually confirms it. In a heavily Democratic Congress, it survived a filibuster by one vote and its popularity began to plummet practically before the ink from the presidential pens was dry. As I write more than three years later after an election that returned Obama to office with a Senate controlled even more firmly by his party, many states continue to resist the new policy by failing to establish the mandated insurance exchanges and Medicaid expansions,[54] and public opinion about the act grows increasingly negative as full implementation unfolds.[55]

This resistance to grandiose public initiatives seems endemic to our time. *New York Times* columnist David Brooks has contrasted the New Deal era, when a desperate public actually believed that the federal government could solve big problems, with the current public's weary cynicism.[56] As noted earlier, a large majority of Americans view big government as a larger threat to the country's future than even big business—and this only a few years after misconduct by major financial firms brought the economy to its knees.[57] This state of mind could be fatal to the kind of "public spirit" that political scientist Steven Kelman thinks is essential to sound policy making.[58] In short, all citizens have a vital stake in improving government's performance, but none more so than liberals and progressives deeply committed to bolder public undertakings.

Tellingly, federal policy intervention has increased over the same period during which public mistrust of government has risen. Contrary to what growing public disaffection might imply, the threshold for intervention is markedly *lower* today than it was as recently as fifty years ago. Long before the Dodd-Frank and Affordable Care Acts were passed, political scientists James Q. Wilson and John DiIulio noted the change:

> The Old System had a small agenda. . . . When someone proposed adding a new issue to the public agenda, a major debate often arose over whether it was legitimate for the federal government to take action at all in the matter. . . . For the government to take bold action under this system, the nation usually had to be facing a crisis. . . . Each succeeding crisis left the government bureaucracy somewhat larger than it had been before, but when the crisis ended, the exercise of extraordinary powers ended. . . . The New System . . . is characterized by a large policy agenda, the end of the debate over the legitimacy of government action (except in the area of First Amendment freedoms), the diffusion and decentralization of power in Congress, and the multiplication of interest groups. . . . Under the Old System, the checks and balances made it difficult for the government to *start* a new program, and so the government remained relatively small. Under the New System, these checks and balances make it hard to *change* what the government is already doing, and so the government remains large.[59]

These institutional and attitudinal changes, then, place far greater demands today on a government already prone to policy failure and lacking the public's confidence. As we shall see, the deep, systemic causes of programmatic failure cast great doubt on the claim by commentators like Morone that more authority and resources would enhance governmental performance commensurately.

Indeed, the trajectories of public confidence and federal expenditures have moved in opposite directions. More specifically, the decline in public confidence has paralleled a large growth in the share of federal expenditures devoted to safety net programs, especially for health care.[60] This correlation is a strong and consistent one. Whether the correlation between more government and less public confidence is causal is harder to say: Medicare, for example, has accounted for much of that budgetary growth, yet it enjoys very widespread public support. Likewise, as columnist Ezra Klein observes, the decline of confidence in government seems unrelated to the increase of money in politics (discussed in chapter 7).[61]

What is clear, however, is that the federal and state governments have grown steadily (the former is now more than five times as large as it was in 1960, in real terms, and the latter's growth during this period is even greater), that total government spending per capita in the United States is now greater than in France, Germany, and the United Kingdom, and that it grows in both good times and bad. Our debt-to-GDP ratio not only exceeds that of most European democracies but also the average for Latin America.[62] This growth in the federal government is obscured somewhat because it has largely taken the form of private contractors, nonprofit grant recipients, and state and local government implementers rather than federal employees per se. (I discuss this obscuring phenomenon further in chapter 10.) This fact probably explains why so many people, including many who should know better, still believe the antiquated notion that the United States has a relatively small public sector. As DiIulio put it in an important 2012 article, "Big government is here, and it isn't going away."[63] All the more reason, then, to demand that the giant become more effective.

The rest of this introductory chapter does five things: (1) it defines the scope of the analysis; (2) it presents general conclusions about government's performance by leading social scientists; (3) it distinguishes optimistic and realist stances toward this performance; (4) it introduces the central role of markets in policy effectiveness; and (5) it provides a road map to the rest of the book. I then conclude with a paragraph about my own policy background and political orientation.

THE SCOPE OF THE ANALYSIS

My analysis concerns only *federal domestic programs*. Thus, I do not discuss foreign, military, or national security policies. The criteria, measures, and expectations of effectiveness in these areas are simply too controversial and opaque.[64] Nor do I consider state and local programs. This has nothing to do with their significance in American life. Indeed, as I discuss in chapter 4 under the rubric of localism, state and local governments perform highly important functions, especially in education, criminal justice, and land use regulation. They constitute roughly half of the nation's public sector, and have expanded their workforces far more than the federal government has. Federal policy vitally affects state and local governments in many ways—for example, through enforcement of federal laws against state and local police forces and other programs,[65] or federal mandates (funded and unfunded). Including them here, however, would be an unmanageable undertaking. Even so, the analysis in the chapters that follow will shed considerable light on lower levels of government because many of the same systemic forces that shape federal performance also apply, mutatis mutandis, to them.

By the same token, the performance of foreign governments is outside my ken here.* Many of our government's defects are also found elsewhere—see, for example, *The Blunders of Our Governments*, a 2013 book about British failures[66]—but again, this book

---

*Such comparisons, however, would hardly be reassuring. A comparison of our progress on seventy-five separate objectives with that of other leading democracies up to the mid-1990s found that it has been below average in roughly two-thirds of the cases and at or near the bottom in approximately half. See Derek Bok, *The Trouble with Government* (2001), table 2.

does not analyze governments in general. The term *exceptionalism* points to many unique features of our public and private orderings;[67] some are highlighted in chapters 3 and 4. Comparisons between our government's effectiveness and that of other advanced liberal democracies might yield valuable insights, but they would suffer from severe data and comparability problems, which is why they are rare.[68] In certain areas, however, foreign experiences may have much to teach us—for example, about bureaucratic organization (chapter 10) and the war on drugs (chapter 8). I shall draw upon them where they seem useful and reliable.

My analysis focuses on the *actual performance of government programs that are already in place.* I do not discuss the more abstract theoretical, philosophical, or ideological claims about the nature, role, and scope of government under one or another political theory. Library shelves already groan with weighty tomes on the origins of government, the various forms that it may assume, the a priori arguments concerning its proper purposes, and the sources and nature of political obligation, legitimacy, and power. All societies have grappled with these fundamental questions, and every political philosopher since Aristotle has reflected on them, often brilliantly. But exploring them would distract from my narrower purpose here. Accordingly, I shall finesse them, with apologies to (and disagreement with) those who believe that one cannot assess and explain government performance without resolving these core philosophical and theoretical questions. Instead, I shall for the most part take the current configuration of government programs as a given and try to answer questions of the following sort: What kinds of programmatic tasks has the government set for itself, and how well does it perform them? Why does the government fail so often in discharging those tasks, and which factors best explain its occasional successes? How might we do better?

These questions are dauntingly difficult—even conceptually. This probably explains why no one has taken them on in *systematic* fashion. By *systematic,* I mean an analysis that (1) applies to a broad range of specific public policies; (2) focuses on the structural, endemic forces that shape government performance rather than the contingent and partisan ones; (3) rests on empirical evidence of government performance rather than intuitions or deductions from political theory; (4) invokes economic analysis where relevant (as it often is) but goes beyond it; (5) has no partisan, ideological, or interest-based ax to grind and no programs to defend; and (6) is conducted in a pragmatic, moderate, meliorist spirit.[69]

SOCIAL SCIENCE EVIDENCE ON GOVERNMENT PERFORMANCE

Systematic studies of government performance exist, but they are rarer than one might think. Peter Orszag and John Bridgeland, top budget and policy officials in the administrations of presidents Barack Obama and George W. Bush, respectively, write, "Based on our rough calculations, less than $1 out of every $100 of government spending is backed by even the most basic evidence that the money is being spent wisely," which is hardly surprising given that in the hugely costly health care area, "less than $1 out of every $1000 that the government spends . . . this year will go toward evaluating whether the other $999-plus actually works."[70] And those studies that are conducted are narrow in scope. Alan Gerber and Eric Patashnik report that political scientists—our most thoroughgoing students of government—publish four times as many works on distributive issues than on studies of government effectiveness.[71] (They imply here that if more studies were conducted, more failures would be documented.) Political scientist Terry Moe, reviewing the public choice scholarship that has dominated the field in recent years (more on this in chapter 4), observes, "The question that has traditionally been at the heart of public administration . . . the effectiveness of the bureaucracy—is given no serious attention."[72] (This is not quite true. Chapter 5 shows that even flawed public choice theories can shed useful light.)

Microeconomic studies provide the best evidence on programs' effectiveness, and I shall rely heavily upon them in the chapters that follow. As Wilson explains, social science is at its most rigorous when conducting retrospective studies of existing policies that can "tell people in power that something they tried did not work as expected."[73] In this introduction, I merely canvass more general evaluations of programs' performance by leading social scientists.

Noted sociologist Peter Rossi, writing in 1987 after many years of experience in evaluating government programs, formulated the following "metallic laws" of program effectiveness:

The Iron Law of Evaluation: The expected value of any net impact assessment of any large scale social program is zero. The Iron Law arises from the experience that few impact assessments of large scale social programs have found that the programs in question had any net impact. The law also means that, based on the evaluation efforts of the last twenty years, the best a priori estimate of the net impact assessment of any program is zero, i.e., that the program will have no effect.

The Stainless Steel Law of Evaluation: The better designed the impact assessment of a social program, the more likely is the resulting estimate of net impact to be zero. This law means that the more technically rigorous the net impact assessment, the more likely are its results to be zero—or no effect. Specifically, this law implies that estimating net impacts through randomized controlled experiments, the avowedly best approach to estimating net impacts, is more likely to show zero effects than other less rigorous approaches.

The Brass Law of Evaluation: The more social programs are designed to change individuals, the more likely the net impact of the program will be zero. This law means that social programs designed to rehabilitate individuals by changing them in some way or another are more likely to fail. The Brass Law may appear to be redundant since all programs, including those designed to deal with individuals, are covered by the Iron Law. This redundancy is intended to emphasize the especially difficult task faced in designing and implementing effective programs that are designed to rehabilitate individuals.

The Zinc Law of Evaluation: Only those programs that are likely to fail are evaluated. Of the several metallic laws of evaluation, the zinc law has the most optimistic slant since it implies that there are effective programs but that such effective programs are never evaluated. It also implies that if a social program is effective, that characteristic is obvious enough and hence policy makers and others who sponsor and fund evaluations decide against evaluation.[74]

Rossi, a highly sophisticated analyst with a tart tongue in his cheek, surely did not mean that his "laws," iron or otherwise, are certainties, only that they are exceptionally strong tendencies. And while his reference to "expected value" of zero implies that some assessments might be more positive, it also implies that at least many will be negative rather than simply have "no effect."

Two books published in 2006 by the predominantly government-friendly Brookings Institution tend to support and extend Rossi's iron laws. One is a collection of articles whose authors analyzed the effectiveness of four large, costly, and important federal policy undertakings.[75] In a case study of a particular arthroscopic surgery undergone by millions of Americans at federal expense, the authors find this procedure often unnecessary, usually no more valuable than a placebo, and subsidized by the government without any good evidence of effectiveness.[76] The vast majority of federal spending on urban mass transit goes to transit workers (at above-market wages) or equipment suppliers, with just 25 percent used to improve transit and to lower fares.[77] Federal rental housing programs are dominated by unit-based assistance when recipient-based assistance would be far more cost-effective: "Even the smallest estimates of the excess costs of unit-based assistance imply that shifting ten families from unit-based to recipient-based assistance would enable us to serve two additional families."[78] And the federal special education program both creates incentives to include many students who are not truly disabled and underserves those who are.[79]

The second Brookings book, authored by regulatory economist Clifford Winston, reviewed *every published scholarly study he could find* of the actual microeconomic policy effects of federal programs designed to correct three types of conventional market failure: market power, information inequalities and externalities, and public goods.* (In chapter 2, I explain the notion of market failure; chapter 5 discusses nonmarket or government failure.) I detail many of Winston's specific program evaluations in chapter 8, but here I simply present his conclusion that "policymakers have attempted to correct market failures with policies designed to affect either consumer or firm behavior, or both, or to allocate resources. Some policies have forced the U.S. economy to incur costs in situations where no serious market failure exists, while others, in situations where costly market failures do exist, could have improved resource allocation in a much more efficient manner."[80]

These scholarly critiques of government performance are echoed in program-specific studies by government agencies and think tanks, and in peer-reviewed academic analyses. In 2012, I and two research assistants canvassed all of the assessments published since 2000 by the Government Accountability Office, the Office of Management and Budget, the center-left Brookings Institution, the center-right American Enterprise Institute, and two conservative think tanks, the Cato Institute and the Heritage Foundation. (The Congressional Budget Office conducts only prospective, predictive assessments of proposed policies, so its reports were not useful for my purposes.) The results were stunning. We found more than 270 such assessments, some of which will be cited in later chapters. Only a small number of these assessments could be considered positive; the vast majority were either clearly negative or showed mixed results.

This scorecard, of course, is not decisive. Critics might raise three objections—selection effect, unrepresentative examples, and "success is in the eye of the beholder"—which I have endeavored to meet.

---

*Clifford Winston, *Government Failure versus Market Failure: Microeconomic Policy Research and Government Performance* (2006). Winston largely eschewed studies conducted by the government, agreeing with regulatory economist Robert Hahn that such studies "can be biased, inconsistent, and technically flawed because they have not been subject to review by appropriate scholars. Hahn even suggests that some government agencies do not appear to trust the numbers produced by government assessments of their own policies" (9).

A selection effect could occur in two ways—either if assessors were more likely to evaluate programs of doubtful effectiveness, perhaps in order to help policy makers improve them or replace them with better ones, or if assessors were motivated by an antigovernment bias. A selection effect under which putatively weak programs are more likely to be assessed is plausible, but it is also plausible that those who support particular programs will want them assessed in order to demonstrate their merit to skeptics and to the public. A priori, it is hard to know which tendency dominates in any particular situation.* As for ideological bias, it is not confined to conservative opponents of public programs but can also be found among liberal-progressive defenders of more active government. The only practicable way to assure analytical balance is to rely on studies published in peer-reviewed academic journals by professionally qualified researchers from mainstream institutions. My own approach to these questions is summarized in the final paragraph of this chapter.

A representativeness critique would argue that the policies whose assessments I report here constitute but a small fraction of those that fill the pages of the United States Code and the *Federal Register*, and that they are not representative of the much larger set that I do not discuss. Without assessing all programs, no one can say for sure whether the ones I do discuss are representative, and because programs differ from one another across so many dimensions—substantive content, animating theory, legal requirements, leadership talent, bureaucratic talent, public and congressional support, interest group dynamics, market conditions, implementation obstacles, funding, and many others—no sampling technique could possibly meet rigorous social science standards. What I can say is that the programs I do discuss are particularly important by reason of their budgetary size, prominence, durability, and political support. Because the structural

---

*Winston, focusing on the academic studies that he canvassed, concedes the possibility of such a selection bias but adds that "academics, especially economists, are contentious individuals who are unlikely to shy away from the opportunity to challenge other researchers' findings simply because they will be identified as supporting government policy." Winston, *Government Failure versus Market Failure*, 11n3.

factors analyzed in part 2 evidently impair the performance of so many important programs, and because these factors are present in one form or another in virtually all other programs, I can think of no reason why the patterns that I shall describe would not also apply to them. Accordingly, the burden of proof should now shift to those who deny the accuracy or representativeness of the evidence that I shall adduce, or the inferences that I shall draw from it concerning the policy effectiveness of particular programs.

The "eye of the beholder" critique—the notion that a program's effectiveness is nothing more than a subjective judgment on the assessor's part—assumes that more objective assessment criteria of success and failure are unavailable. This critique is discussed and refuted in chapter 2.

OPTIMISTS AND REALISTS

Policy analysts can be broadly grouped into two camps: optimists and realists. Optimists look at the many national achievements that I listed early in this chapter and insist that the government had a lot to do with these gains. In one variant of this optimism, political journalist E. J. Dionne thinks, contrary to what I argue below, that government would succeed more often if public expectations were higher, not lower.[81] Kelman is another prominent optimist, noting, "Government performs better than its reputation, but not well enough. . . . Government organizations take millions of young children every year and teach them to read. . . . A government organization gets millions of old people a pension check every month. Government organizations enforce environmental laws, and the air gets cleaner. The wilder tales of government waste and incompetence generally turn out to be grossly exaggerated upon closer examination. Furthermore, just as new government programs can fail, so too can new products from private firms fail because of the inability to create organizational capacity to make them succeed."[82]

Part 2 will show that Kelman's optimism is excessive and misguided. He vastly underestimates the barriers to more effective government; some are remediable (see chapter 12), but many are too structural for significant improvement. He assumes that government is responsible for producing environmental and other social gains; we shall see, however, that the government's causal role in producing some gains—relative to other factors—is often debatable, and that some outcomes are not gains at all but have made matters worse (see examples in chapters 5, 8, and elsewhere). His assertion that both government and markets can fail is true but misleading as it implies a false equivalence: failed products quickly exit the market; failed programs, like diamonds, are forever.* To cite but one of countless examples: the Davis-Bacon Act, a perennial target of policy reformers because of its wastefulness, was passed in 1931 and shows no sign of departing.[83] Were Kelman to review—as a hard-eyed analyst, not a dewy-eyed idealist—the mountain of empirical evidence presented in part 2 on the ineffectiveness of program after program, he would probably have to abandon his optimism; there simply is too little basis for it, except perhaps for straightforward redistributions like Social Security and a few other areas like voting rights (see chapter 11).

Realists believe that optimists are, well, unrealistic. One group—call them the *stoic* realists—holds that government failure is an inevitable product of the human condition in a fallen world populated by Immanuel Kant's "crooked timber of humanity,"[84] where politics and self-interest, narrowly conceived, contaminate everything. The stoic would point out that the "good enough for government work" indictment is equally true of flawed families, religions, markets, popular culture, universities, friendship, sex, sports, and everything else that matters to us. In this world-weary, tragic view, the best advice to the disappointed citizen is "get over it."

As will become clear, I am a different breed—call me a *melioristic* realist. I emphasize the deep, recurrent reasons for widespread

---

*See James Q. Wilson and John J. DiIulio Jr., *American Government: Institutions and Policies, 12th ed.* (2011), 463: "Policies once adopted tend to persist, whatever their value. (It is easier to start new programs than to end old ones.)" Congress does occasionally kill programs, but not remotely as many as it creates; Bok, *The Trouble with Government*, 91.

government failure analyzed in this book, believe that most of them are endemic to our system, and note that policy makers can have at best a severely limited knowledge of the opaque, complex social world that they seek to change, and meager tools for changing it—a point to which I return in the book's final pages. Nevertheless, as chapter 12 demonstrates, I am convinced that important policy-making improvements are possible in many areas if demanded by a public that is better informed about how human nature operates in the political realm, about how government works and doesn't work, and about what it can and cannot realistically deliver. I return to this melioristic realism in chapter 13.

A PREFACE TO MARKETS

Markets cast long shadows across *all* policy making. Although they receive separate and lengthy analytical treatment in chapter 7, their effect on government performance is so great that I introduce them briefly here by way of introduction. Markets protected by property rights and the rule of law advance many precious human values: liberty, decentralization of power, competition, individual choice, productive incentives, prosperity, a robust civil society, and crucial information about costs, benefits, and desires that cannot be obtained as quickly, cheaply, and accurately in any other way. Markets have improved the standard of living of billions of people, particularly during the last few decades with the rise of China, India, and many other developing economies. In that vital sense, markets have also reduced inequality in those countries and strengthened many other civil society institutions on which the quality of community life ultimately depends.

At the same time, any particular market can exhibit defects ("market failures," schematized in chapter 2) that reduce efficiency in that market and may also yield distributive outcomes that society deems unacceptably unfair. As detailed in chapter 8, much policy making seeks to ameliorate these market failures, whether real, exaggerated, or imagined. It is hard to know whether a particular market's failure is large enough to warrant policy change, and whether government interventions of one kind or another can improve matters over the market baseline. These questions are partly theoretical, partly empirical, and partly normative; reasonable policy makers and citizens tend to disagree about them. But as chapter 2 will show, they are the *right* questions. Later chapters offer two types of convincing answers: general, systemic analyses identifying the conditions that presage policy failure or success, and specific policy assessments marshaling empirical evidence that reveals how effective those policies actually are.

Markets are fueled by self-interest, which is one reason why many Americans mistrust them.[85] For centuries, critics have viewed this as a moral problem, identifying self-interest with materialistic excess, exploitation, and absence of the gentler virtues. Many public intellectuals and religious people claim that market-driven commercialism crowds out more communitarian, moral, and aesthetic values.[86] On the other side, many have argued, at least since Charles de Secondat Montesquieu and Adam Smith, that the values that markets esteem and reward—liberty, attention to others' needs and preferences, risk taking, cooperation, gains from trade—underlie and promote conventional morality and generate valuable forms of solidarity.[87] Markets also facilitate environmentalism, cultural preservation, philanthropy, and other desirable practices—even religion, whose vitality in the United States has been stoked by fierce market competition for congregants.[88]

What is incontrovertible is that American society, more than perhaps any other on earth, favors markets as the strong default condition. The United States defers entirely or partly to market actors to perform many of the functions that in other advanced societies are reserved almost exclusively for government—for example, health care, pensions, low-income housing, education, social services, and bail bonding. We are far more likely than others to believe that market outcomes reflect hard work and talent rather than luck; one-third of Americans think that our fate is determined by outside forces, not personal behavior, while nearly two-thirds of Europeans think this.[89] Americans, to be sure, often support regulation to reform markets, producing far more of it today than even a decade ago, especially in health care and financial services. But even in the "new system" described above by Wilson and DiIulio, we also demand special justification to overcome the promarket and civil society defaults for solving perceived problems. Indeed, when Congress does intervene to reform markets, it often relies on private entities or public-private hybrids like Fannie Mae and Freddie Mac to get the job done rather than solely public administration. Such preferences dovetail with some other aspects of our political culture (see chapter 4).

This promarket default, which the New System has weakened, reflects three sturdy national values and a common misconception. The values are a highly individualistic, capitalism-friendly ideology, materialistic consumerism, and a chronic mistrust of centralized governmental power. It is striking indeed that even corporate power, which has aroused populist movements and popular indignation throughout our history—the public protests against the post-2007 economic meltdown, scandals, and officials' solicitude for large financial interests are only the most recent example—tends to arouse less suspicion than governmental power. The misconception is that our political economy is divided into two separate spheres—government and civil society (which includes markets)—whereas in reality they are hybrid, highly interactive forms fundamentally shaped by each other.

Although chapter 7 focuses on markets, their complex relationship to public policy plays an important role in *every* chapter's analysis. In each case, I shall approach markets pragmatically: markets tend to work well compared both with the government's own performance and with much of the regulation that tries to control them, but they are not sacrosanct. If a strong case can be made for improving on markets in the interests of greater fairness or efficiency, reformist politicians will eagerly take up the gauntlet and many voters will support them; otherwise, not. But this public philosophy still leaves us with the two questions that this book seeks to answer: how effective are government policies (including those that hope to improve or use markets), and why is failure so common?

In this introduction, I have presented enough preliminary evidence of widespread government failure and public dissatisfaction to support (only provisionally, to be sure) the two general hypotheses advanced earlier: first, the public's dissatisfaction is well-founded, amply justified by the government's record of poor performance; and second, the root causes of this endemic policy failure are structural and thus largely inescapable under present policy-making conditions. A corollary is that government failures do not merely reflect poor implementation of sound policies—although implementation obstacles are indeed a major cause of failure, as we shall see in chapter 8—but are built into the system and thus that much harder to rectify. In chapter 12, I propose remedies for this endemic failure with this caution clearly in mind.

Hopefully, this introduction will induce readers to hang in there to consider the more substantial evidence, both theoretical and empirical, presented in the rest of the book. In lawyers' jargon, I want at this point merely to survive an early motion to dismiss by readers who assume that government usually succeeds in achieving what it sets out to do. If so, I can then proceed to the "discovery" stage, where I present the existing evidence about its *actual* performance. By book's end, I hope to persuade you, the jury, that I have proved my case. As the saying goes, everyone is entitled to his own opinion, but not to his own facts.[90] And the facts about government performance are damning—and vital to our efforts to do better in the future.

A ROAD MAP OF THE BOOK

This book consists of thirteen chapters, divided into three parts. Part 1 (chapters 2–4) provides the context in which policy making occurs. Part 2 (chapters 5–11) constitutes the book's core, presenting an immense body of empirical findings on the effectiveness of an extraordinarily broad range of federal domestic policies. Each chapter analyzes a discrete cluster of endemic sources of government failure that are deep, structural, and systemic. As such, these problems cannot easily be remedied but they can be mitigated. Part 3 (chapters 12–13) explains how this might be done. Because these sources of failure are multiple, interrelated, and often occur simultaneously, the topics treated in part 2's chapters are not as analytically discrete as the chapter titles might suggest. They inevitably overlap to a degree, and even my many cross-references to other chapters cannot completely alert this fact to the reader.

Part 1

Chapter 2 presents the methodology of policy assessment. It addresses questions on which any analysis of governmental effectiveness must turn: how should we define failure and success, with what bases of comparison in mind, and how can we assess the performance of particular programs in light of those criteria? Because no crisp, wholly satisfactory answers to these questions are possible, I suggest a number of approaches that converge enough to support the book's hypotheses about why government fails so often.

Chapter 3 provides the necessary background on how public policy making works. It is divided into five parts: (1) the different *functions*—some indispensable, most matters of policy discretion—that the government performs; (2) the *processes* of policy formulation; (3) the *missions* that agencies are assigned to perform; (4) the diverse *instruments* that can be deployed in pursuing these missions; and (5) the most important *institutions and practices* that constrain government performance. Readers who already possess a sophisticated knowledge of political economy and of how policy making works may want to skip this chapter—although it emphasizes aspects of policy making that even the cognoscenti may overlook.

Chapter 4 probes the unique political culture in which our policy-making system is embedded. It focuses on ten elements of this culture: (1) constitutionalism; (2) decentralization; (3) protection of individual rights; (4) interest group pluralism; (5) tolerance for inequality; (6) religion and political moralism; (7) social diversity; (8) populism; (9) public opinion; and (10) civil society. These values and attitudes animate and constrain policy makers at every turn.

Part 2

Chapters 5 and 6 analyze the most fundamental characteristics that shape the substance of public policy, afflict its performance, and distinguish it in kind or in degree from most private decision making. Chapter 5 explores two of these characteristics: the incentives of policy makers and of private actors who policies affect (including policy-induced moral hazard), and the irrational aspects of policy makers' decisions. Chapter 6 considers four others: (1) information deficiencies; (2) the inflexibility of the policy system; (3) its credibility problem with those whose cooperation is necessary for success; and (4) mismanagement encouraging fraud, waste, abuse, and related conduct.

Chapter 7, as already noted, focuses on how markets affect policy performance. It is long, as befits the importance of the topic. I show that the powerful incentives, logic, hydraulics, and political influences of markets are difficult to control and tend to undermine the effectiveness of many public policies, including those explicitly designed to correct market failures. Although market-savvy Cassandras often predict policies' ineffectiveness, their warnings, like those of their classical namesakes, usually go unheeded until it is too late and the policy misfires. After showing how markets compete with government for participants, administrative talent, and performance, I discuss nine reasons why markets tend to confound the effectiveness of policies that seek to perfect them: (1) speed; (2) diversity; (3) informational demands; (4) price and substitution effects; (5) transjurisdictional effects; (6) political influence; (7) obstacles to policy enforcement; (8) "informal" markets; and (9) the lack of good substitutes for market-based ordering. (Two other reasons, moral hazard and black markets, are discussed in chapters 5 and 7, respectively.) In the chapter's final section, I explain how innovative policy makers have sought to exploit market forces for policy purposes (especially environmental protection) rather than trying to subdue them. While I generally support this innovative approach, I show how it too is hobbled by implacable market forces.

Chapter 8 analyzes the problem of policy implementation—the obstacles that invariably litter the path between policy design and real-world outcomes. Policy makers can and often do try to anticipate these implementation problems, but their efforts almost always fall short—and for identifiable, predictable reasons. These reasons may include a flawed social or causal theory, faulty program design, naïveté or ignorance about the force of the relevant market(s), political-bureaucratic impediments, and a host of other unforeseen, often inchoate developments including Murphy's Law ("anything that can go wrong will go wrong"). Given the indeterminacy of precisely which factors cause which particular policy failures, I use the term *implementation* to refer to any or all of them. After using a particularly well-documented example—the Oakland Project—to illustrate how these factors interact to produce policy failure, the chapter reviews the empirical evidence on the effects of a large number of specific programs across a broad range of public policy domains. I organize this large body of evidence around nine broad categories of policy goals directed at markets: (1) perfecting; (2) supplementing; (3) suppressing; (4) simplifying; (5) subsidizing; (6) redirecting; (7) reintroducing; (8) midwifing; and (9) recruiting for regulatory purposes.

Chapter 9 is concerned with law—the vocabulary and grammar in which almost all public policies (except for the policy of inaction) are expressed—and particularly with its inherent limits. I focus on six of these limits: (1) law's ubiquity; (2) the inescapable trade-offs between simplicity and complexity; (3) its linguistic ambiguity; (4) the discretion necessary for it to function; (5) its costly procedural apparatus; and (6) its inertia. These inherent limits, I suggest, preordain much of the government's failure.

Chapter 10 discusses the growing pathologies of the civil service bureaucracy that, depending on the policy instrument being used, typically implements the policy at the governmental end and monitors and enforces it when the private sector acts on it.

Chapter 11 is about policy success. Given the dismaying portrait of endemic government failure that I paint in the earlier chapters, it is reassuring to know that some programs have been relatively successful. I discuss some of the most important ones, and analyze what conditions, systemic and otherwise, seem to account for their success.

Part 3

Chapter 12 advances a guardedly optimistic reform agenda, discussing three approaches to reform. Two of them—policies to promote cultural change that might in turn produce better outcomes, and changes at the most basic level of constitutional design—are almost certainly nonstarters, but I take them (especially the latter) seriously. This prediction reflects my sense of political reality, my respect for the remorseless law of unintended consequences,[91] and my conviction that cautious, carefully tested reforms often produce better outcomes than more radical ones do. Accordingly, I devote most of the chapter to a third, far more promising approach—cross-cutting reforms that seek to reduce the dysfunctional aspects of the policy systems diagnosed in part 2. I illustrate these reforms by imagining how they might improve some specific programs that are now failing us.

Chapter 12's proposed reforms will strike some readers as merely incremental. This incrementalism will disappoint more radical reformers who deride it as both unimaginative and not going to the root of the problems. I nevertheless defend incrementalism there as a wise, honorable, efficacious, and profoundly moral concession to our cognitive limitations, our complex social systems, and our diverse views of what constitutes good policy.[92]

Ironies abound in the struggle between incrementalists and more audacious reformers. Small, cautious changes, for example, sometimes cumulate over time into far-reaching reform, as with food stamps, which grew from a small temporary program in the 1930s to one serving nearly 45 million low-income Americans today (see chapter 11). At the other, root-and-branch end of the policy spectrum, relatively comprehensive reforms often come a cropper, which fuels disillusionment and may even discredit the progressive project. Thus, campaign finance regulation, which its advocates claimed would "take the money out of politics," has done pretty much the opposite and fueled fury at the Supreme Court's protection of core political speech (see chapter 7). In such cases, disappointed reformers will often insist that a more radical reform would have worked—a counterfactual that, conveniently for them, can be neither proved nor refuted. Finally, opposition to modest gains may doom reform altogether. For instance, president Richard Nixon's family assistance plan, which liberals rejected as inadequate, would have installed their long-sought principle of income guarantees for the poor, thus opening the door to future expansion.

Chapter 13 sums up, presenting the major themes that emerge from the analysis. All Americans have a strong stake in understanding why government's failures are so endemic, and what might be done to improve matters. For liberals, poor performance both discredits activist government and swallows up the precious resources needed to sustain and extend it. Once conservatives accept that an activist state is here to stay, they can focus on improving programs' effectiveness, not just quixotically demand wholesale repeal. Centrists must learn enough about the true causes of failure to propose moderate solutions. If we do not do so—and soon—our great experiment in self-government may itself come to be seen as a failure. In an era of fiscal cliffs, pallid enforcement, special-interest pandering, and growing public disgust with politicians, this warning is not hyperbole.

For better *and* for worse—and it *is* both—we are largely stuck with the government that we've got along with many of the cultural legacies, institutions, processes, and values that have shaped and inspired it for two and a quarter centuries. Reform is both essential and within our reach. But more radical transformation—if it be desirable, which is harder to predict, the more radical it is—must await a new political dispensation whose contours are not yet visible and whose consequences are thus even more speculative.

Finally, a few words about my own bona fides. I am a political independent, a self-styled militant moderate who has always voted for Democrats for president (except for a protest vote in 1968).[93] I served as a former policy planning official in the Department of

Health, Education, and Welfare during the administration of president Jimmy Carter, and am as committed to social progress (properly defined and suitably pursued) as the most interventionist reformer. I support many public programs, and as a citizen I take no pleasure (indeed, I am dismayed) in finding how often my government fails, as I dutifully report in the chapters that follow. I do take heart from the important successes to be discussed in chapter 11 but, regrettably, they are too few and far between. However, they can help us understand the reasons for the far more numerous failures.

PART 1

The Context of Policy Making

CHAPTER 2

Success, Failure, and In Between

It is tempting to think that government performance, like so much else in life, is simply in the eye of the beholder. Where you stand, as Miles's Law puts it, depends on where you sit.* After all, supporters of a program often perceive great success where opponents see abject failure. The truth may lie somewhere in between, as the cliché has it, but how can we know when that is so? Moreover, in between covers a vast territory, and it matters a great deal where particular programs fall within that wide spectrum.

Like investors who assess their portfolios periodically, conscientious citizens should assess their government's performance from time to time—even though the latter is a much more difficult task, with fewer clear objectives and benchmarks. In any event, as we saw in chapter 1, the citizenry has already passed judgment on the federal government's performance, and it is one of sharp disapproval. If the customer is always (or even frequently) right, then the government's programmatic failure must be common indeed.

But if citizens are to make such judgments accurately, they will need help from policy analysts who systematically assess programs' effectiveness. In an earlier book, I and a coauthor sought to provide such help by analyzing certain dynamics of social programs directed at unfortunate, disadvantaged people whom we called "bad draws."

*Claims about policy effectiveness, which I use as a synonym for success, sometimes cite statistics, much as the devil cites Scripture. I shall often do the same, while being mindful of Thomas Carlyle's warning, "Statistics are the greatest liars of them all," and Benjamin Disraeli's cynical quip, "There are three kinds of lies: lies, damned lies, and statistics."

We focused attention on one criterion of policy success—how well or poorly programs *target* their scarce resources on recipients—and on two groups of recipients: "bad bets" (those who are unlikely to gain much from the program relative to others) and "bad apples" (those whose misbehavior prevents other bad draws from benefiting from the program).[1]

I have identified numerous general categories of "bad policies," a term that reflects certain normative judgments (including poor targeting) that I shall explain later in this chapter. I list the categories here simply in order to orient readers to the many examples of success, failure, and in between that they will encounter in later chapters. These categories, which are a mix of design and performance failures, include those that are so poorly enforced as to subvert their own goals; those that entrench an inefficient or unjust status quo and retard innovation; those that permit officials to continue programs that the private sector can do as well or better and at lower cost; those that reduce or even bar competition in private goods; those that create uncertainties that discourage beneficial investment and other welfare-enhancing transactions; those that give officials too much discretion; those that give officials too little discretion; those that threaten constitutional values; those that increase moral hazard for private actors or for governmental actors*; those that encourage self-destructive behavior by those who can least afford it (an extreme version of the previous category); those that are costly relative to the marginal effect that the policy seeks to promote (as with bad bets); those that indirectly harm the poor by wasting resources on bad bets; those that directly harm the poor by allowing bad apples to stigmatize otherwise worthy programs; those that invite fraud and abuse; and those that redistribute wealth regressively.[2]

This chapter consists of three parts. I first discuss the criteria for assessing policy effectiveness—that is, for assessing what does and does not work. I then present the most important methodology for

---

*Moral hazard—the propensity to take on more risk when one knows that one will not bear much of the expected cost of that risk—is discussed, with many examples, in chapters 5 and 12.

policy assessment: cost-benefit analysis (CBA). Finally, I provide the prescriptive context for applying CBA to actual policy decisions by elaborating fourteen normative guidelines or principles for policy makers and those who would assess their decisions.

CRITERIA OF EFFECTIVENESS

A policy, it has rightly been said, is based on a theory (often only implicit) about a causal chain linking initial conditions and future consequences.[3] A policy works to the extent that it produces outcomes that meet appropriate standards of effectiveness. This chapter develops the standards that I shall use. By the same token, a policy does not work to the extent that it falls beneath these standards. As just noted, a policy may fail for many reasons: a flawed theory or design, costs that exceed benefits, erratic enforcement, muddled implementation, unforeseen consequences,* or political compromises that undermine its efficacy either at its inception or as it plays out in the real world. These definitions of success and failure are tautological, of course; they beg all of the important questions about policy success and failure that I discuss in this book.

Even before addressing those questions, however, some complications must be recognized. First is *the "compared to what?" question.* Public policies should not be held up to impossible standards, and I shall not do so. Instead, I shall advance conventional, time-tested criteria which in principle are hard to dispute (though their application to specific cases, as we shall see, is often more debatable). They consider whether a policy's benefits exceed its costs and whether it is cost-effective. This is likely to be true only if two other conditions are met: it improves on market outcomes, and is also well targeted on those who need the benefits most. These restrictive criteria are feasi-

*An interesting current example, though local rather than federal, is evidence that San Francisco's ban on plastic grocery bags on environmental grounds has led to an increase in bacteria-caused illness from reusable bags, the main substitute for the plastic ones. Jonathan Klick & Joshua D. Wright, *Grocery Bag Bans and Foodborne Illness*, University of Pennsylvania Institute for Law and Economics Research Paper No. 13–2, November 2, 2012.

ble, unlike the pie-in-the-sky "Nirvana fallacy" that I criticize at the end of the chapter.

Second, *all policies succeed in some respects and fail in others.* We must not let the perfect be the enemy of the good. For our civic purposes, imperfect policies should suffice (or "satisfice," in Herbert Simon's decision science vocabulary[4]) if, but only if, it is the best that the system can reasonably do under the circumstances. We citizens have a right to demand that our policies work in this pragmatic sense. Policy effectiveness is all a matter of degree: even the best are not as good as they could be, and even the worst confer *some* benefits on *some* people, who may therefore consider it a success.* The reader should understand, then, that *success* and *failure* are relative terms that I shall use as a shorthand. In a democracy like ours, judgments about efficacy are ultimately rendered by those whom the policy affects as politicians, taxpayers, or otherwise.† As we shall see in part 2, and especially chapter 8, on implementation, what policy makers hope and promise for their programs may bear little resemblance to how well those programs actually turn out. For lots of reasons—some good, some unfortunate—the vast majority of voters do not follow these things closely. This inattention creates "political slack" that affects how policies get made, assessed, and reformed (see chapter 5).

Third, *policy assessment requires systematic goal clarification, fact gathering, and analysis.* Even for the well-informed, it is not simply a matter of common sense, practical wisdom, or inference drawn from a program's durability. In their seminal book on program implementation (discussed in detail in chapter 8), political scientists Jeffrey Pressman and Aaron Wildavsky noted the tendency to infer, incor-

---

*For example, Milton Friedman once said, "If you put the federal government in charge of the Sahara Desert, in five years there'd be a shortage of sand." But as Friedman would surely concede, this shortage would benefit sand suppliers!

†An estimated 46 percent of American households did not pay federal income taxes in 2011, although many paid federal payroll, excise, and other taxes (a qualification that candidate Mitt Romney failed to make in his infamous "47 percent" remarks in a taped briefing of his donors). See Chuck Marr & Chye-Ching Huang, "Misconceptions and Realities about Who Pays Taxes," http://www.cbpp.org/cms/index.cfm?fa=view&id=3505.

rectly, that because most federal programs persist, they must have been successfully implemented and are working. As they note, "Adaptation to the environment must have been achieved; otherwise, by definition, programs would not exist. No genius is required to make programs operative if we don't care how long they take, how much money they require, how often the objectives are altered or the means for obtaining them are changed. Indeed, the law of averages would suggest that, given sufficient new initiatives, some of them must grow and prosper in the world, though the flawed adult may bear scant resemblance to the promising child."[5]

Political support, while necessary to establish a policy, is insufficient to make it work. Political compromises before enactment or during implementation are often essential to the program's very existence—and may also promote credibility and stable expectations, which are policy virtues discussed in chapter 6—but they can sow the seeds of policy failure. Moreover, much failure, as we shall see, is due not to these political compromises but rather to systemic reasons of the sort that I analyze in part 2. The political and systemic reasons why many policies don't work are not distinct categories conceptually and are even less distinct empirically, so disentangling their effects in any particular case is very difficult. In addition, different programs mix these reasons in different proportions.

Fourth, *reasonable people will disagree about how to assess a policy.* Unanimity is not to be expected or even desired. People differ, among other things, in their predictions about what the likely effects of a policy will be; how they evaluate those effects; what relative weights they attach to them (i.e., the tradeoffs); how they discount the flow of the beneficial and costly effects over time; whether they optimize or merely "satisfice";[6] and the values that they ascribe to the particular decision *processes* by which a policy is determined and implemented. In addition, as we shall see in chapter 3, Congress often assigns agencies several, sometimes even conflicting, missions. Part 2 presents many examples of programs having multiple purposes that may be in tension with one another. This diversity of individual preferences and policy purposes means that any effort to characterize, measure, and then integrate them into a single "social welfare function" (as economists call it) is bound to be arbitrary. Indeed, such a function is "impossible" in the sense that it cannot satisfy even minimal standards of consistency in most circumstances.[7] As discussed later in this chapter, the field of welfare economics can help us to assess consequences through the techniques of cost-benefit and cost-effectiveness analyses, but in the end, normative choices among preferences are inescapable.*

Finally, *process norms are no substitute for policy effectiveness.* This normative diversity makes it tempting to search for more cognitively and normatively manageable standards for identifying the criteria for assessing policies, and to find them not in substantive criteria but in less controversial process norms. (As chapter 3 notes, much judicial review of legislative and administrative actions reflects this same understandable urge to focus on process instead of substance—or at least to appear to do so.) In this spirit, public policy scholar Steven Kelman advances two standards for evaluating policy making, both of them procedural: Does the policy-making process tend to produce good public policy? Does the process itself build our dignity and our character? Renouncing any effort to define "good public policy" in substantive terms (doing so would be "excruciatingly difficult"[8]), Kelman focuses instead on the "public spirit" and dignitary and character-building qualities of the process. These qualities, however, are obviously conclusory and subjective. Most important, they elide what the public ultimately cares about most: what works.

Contrary to Kelman's view, I shall defend assessment criteria defined not by the policy-making *processes*, which tend to be the same whether the policy turns out to be good or bad, but by its *substantive* effectiveness, defined in terms of three normative features: its *efficiency* (its margin of benefits over costs and its cost-effectiveness); its

---

*Welfare economics' basic efficiency criteria—Pareto superiority and Pareto optimality—exclude situations, which are universal in the policy realm, when a change makes even one person worse off than before. A Kaldor-Hicks-efficient policy, defined as one that generates net benefits such that gainers *could* compensate losers (even if they don't do so; hence the term *potential Pareto*) calls for CBA, discussed below. See Edith Stokey & Richard J. Zeckhauser, *A Primer for Policy Analysis* (1978).

equity (the fairness, by some criterion, of how those benefits and costs are distributed); and its *manageability* (the ease of implementing). As we shall see in part 2, these normative criteria alone will cast doubt on a distressingly large number of existing programs.

Of these three criteria of effectiveness, I shall most emphasize efficiency. All reasonable people should agree that an inefficient policy should either be improved or abandoned; this efficiency is conventionally assessed according to the familiar CBA technique discussed immediately below. Equity can often be addressed under the rubric of *target* efficiency, which finesses some difficult normative disagreements by asking not what is fair in the abstract (a judgment on which people will naturally differ) but instead whether a policy in fact maximizes *whatever* fairness goal it has adopted. I now turn to CBA and include a discussion of target efficiency. Manageability is the subject of chapters 6 and 8.

COST-BENEFIT ANALYSIS

Cost-benefit analysis posits that policy A is more desirable than policy B if and to the extent that the net benefits (i.e., benefits minus costs, including opportunity costs) that flow from A are larger than the net benefits that flow from B. So stated, CBA is simply rationality in the service of sound policy, a call for policies that maximize net benefits, a principle to which seemingly no sensible person could object. *It does not demand that policies be perfect, only that they be more beneficial on net than alternative policies, including the status quo.* Nevertheless, genuine technical, conceptual, and normative objections to CBA do exist, and its implementation in the real world of complex, politicized policymaking can be highly controversial.

CBA is a welfarist decision-making tool, focusing on the actual consequences of policies for human well-being.[9] It has gained steady support among American economists and policy experts. (It is far less accepted in Europe, where even impact assessment is viewed as relatively novel.[10]) In the 1930s, Congress required that CBA be used to assess federal water projects, and it has been widely used by government agencies ever since. Indeed, every president from Ronald Reagan to Barack Obama has mandated its use to analyze proposed government regulations through a succession of executive orders, which established the Office of Information and Regulatory Affairs (OIRA) in the White House's powerful Office of Management and Budget, and prescribed in some detail how OIRA is to administer the CBA process in the executive branch's regulatory policy making.[11] A large literature on CBA by academic economists and lawyers has elaborated and refined its normative justifications, valuation techniques, empirical findings, and political effects.[12]

Despite CBA's long-standing provenance and widespread acceptance and deployment, government's use of it often arouses intense opposition. Some criticize the very idea of using CBA to analyze programs designed to protect values such as human life and health, biological diversity, and environmental purity that are difficult even to measure, much less price. Indeed, many argue that the very effort to quantify such values itself debases them and offends basic morality.[13] Others, such as policy scholar Mark Moore, show that performance measures can be developed and applied in CBA even for goals like education, policing, and public health.[14]

Some criticisms of CBA are more technical or methodological in nature—that certain benefits are harder to quantify than some costs, for example. This is surely true in some cases. Thus, the reasonable accommodation requirement of the Americans with Disabilities Act of 1990 has imposed substantial, measurable costs in terms of infrastructure retrofitting, yet the benefits of inclusion to both the disabled and everyone else are difficult if not impossible to measure. Of course, the reverse may also be true. Regulations often create important, hard-to-quantify costs, such as rules that make it harder for new firms to enter. They also can harm young, unskilled, inexperienced jobseekers who are excluded from the labor market by minimum wage increases but who may not realize that those mandated increases limited their job opportunities.* Indeed, CBAs seldom include a rule's

---

*I term such people "invisible" or "silent" victims when, as is often the case, the policy's causal responsibility for their harms is opaque. I say more about invisible victims below.

job-displacement effects, apparently on the assumption that such workers will find other jobs.[15] Another quantification challenge is how to value a life (often called the value of a statistical life, or VSL) that a particular regulation might save or sacrifice—a valuation that, like the discount rate discussed immediately below, can determine the outcome of the CBA. Again, a large literature exists on how this should be done.[16]

CBA is most useful in evaluating policies in which one can plausibly hold other factors constant for purposes of the analysis than for policies that will create significant changes in factors that therefore cannot be held constant.[17] A CBA's results may turn on significant variables whose valuations are arguably arbitrary and results-driven. Two such variables are the VSL and the social discount rate; the latter measures our willingness to forgo welfare now or in the near future welfare in exchange for more time-distant benefits, and is highly sensitive to assumptions about future economic growth and policy impacts and more significant to the extent that a policy's costs are immediate while its benefits will come (if at all) in the future.

One much-debated approach to the discount rate is the "precautionary principle," a highly risk-averse norm that urges a correspondingly low discount rate in calculating the present value of future benefits and costs—including those that will affect future generations—particularly those that flow from avoiding or suffering potentially catastrophic risks such as climate change.[18] An important policy question is whether the precautionary principle and CBA are compatible. Some analysts believe that they are, especially if the analysis can be tweaked to take into account diverse risk preferences, opportunity costs, loss aversion, autonomy values, and other complications. In one sense, the principle simply prescribes a very low discount rate for those policy proposals being assessed by CBA. Still, it would be wrong to underestimate the principal's potential effect on policy assessment outcomes. In the case of climate change, for example, it could (depending on the precise discount rate used) condemn policy proposals that would increase (now or soon) the carbon burden on the environment—that is, many projects that a CBA using a higher discount rate might approve.

But the precautionary principle raises another, deeper question: Is there something about certain kinds of harms imposed in certain circumstances on certain groups of people (e.g., the unborn) that makes it socially reasonable to accord to harm avoidance more weight than a standard efficiency analysis such as CBA might give it? Although there are plausible arguments for this,[19] no clear, explicit consensus on this question has yet emerged. Even without such a consensus, particular policy assessments implicitly answer it in one way or another. In some cases, agencies like the Food and Drug Administration put an analogous thumb on the scales by building a "margin of safety" into their standards.

Many other objections to CBA arise. The data on which such assessments depend may be poor or even nonexistent, thus requiring extrapolations that may also seem arbitrary. Attributing benefits or costs to a policy often begs elusive questions such as which factors cause which effects, the baseline conditions from which gains and losses can be calculated, whether an outcome constitutes a benefit or a cost or both, which consequences are taken into account, and so forth.[20] Greater consumer choice, for example, can both provide new options and paralyze decisions. More generally, the choices that underlie the numbers plugged into a CBA may leave much discretion to those conducting the analysis, so that the process generating these choices may be vulnerable to political influences.

Some oppose CBA because of its essentially utilitarian methodology, which treats all preferences the same. It gives no special weight to social values that are not expressed in people's preference functions. It ignores the distributional effects of the policy being assessed, quantifying benefits and costs without regard to which particular groups of people receive the benefits and which ones bear the costs. It takes all preferences at face value even if they are distorted by inadequate information or other reasons. The intensity with which preferences are held—a crucial factor in coalition building, logrolling, vote trading, and other forms of political decision making—are measured in CBA by people's *willingness* to pay. Willingness to pay, of course, is a function of *ability* to pay (i.e., wealth) and also depends on whether one factors in other variables that affect preferences such as attitudes toward risk and felt obligations to future generations—and if so, how they are to be measured.

These criticisms and complexities of CBA reflect the inherent limitations of its methodology and data sources. All have some force; a CBA that does not take them seriously is to that extent incompetent and objectionable. Fortunately, conscientious CBA practitioners can mitigate some of these limitations. They can conduct sensitivity analyses to reveal the extent to which using different data or assumptions would affect the CBA's outcome, and then lay out alternative scenarios based on these differences. They can specify their level of confidence in the controversial propositions that they advance. They can assure a transparent process, be explicit about the many assumptions on which the CBA rests, solicit competing assumptions and data, and respond to criticisms leveled at preliminary CBAs. They can acknowledge the fact that despite the analysts' best efforts, at least some unanticipated consequences are inevitable, consequences that might yield a different set of conclusions. Perhaps most important, they can call attention to the normative and empirical uncertainties that no CBA can authoritatively resolve. (All of these cautions will be especially important as the Obama administration proceeds with regulations on carbon reduction, as estimates of its public health and other benefits [as well as the control costs] vary widely.[21]) CBA should be seen not as a decision *rule* but as a decision *tool*, one with distinctive capacities and limitations that must be compared with those of other decision tools.

To put the point differently: if factors that are less tractable to a CBA are nevertheless deemed relevant to the policy decision, then CBA cannot itself dictate the best policy, but it can at least identify these other unanalyzed factors so that decision makers can somehow take them into account. Moreover, any policy option that fails either the CBA or the cost-effectiveness analysis (its less demanding cousin, discussed above) is presumptively undesirable, leaving it up to those who accord great weight to these unanalyzed factors to overcome that presumption.

That said, even the use of these "best practices" of CBA will not forestall vehement objections to its use for decisions that affect ineffable values such as human dignity (which OIRA itself has recently sought to highlight more, as with a Centers for Disease Control and Prevention rule allowing HIV-positive people to enter the United States),[22] the interests of future generations, or other aspects of particular assessments. After all, the greater CBA's influence over the decision, the higher the stakes in how the CBA is conducted and the greater the possibility that any particular set of contestable assumptions in the analysis will influence the outcomes. This is altogether fitting; the contestation may well improve the quality of both the CBA that officials ultimately use and the larger decision process of which it is only a part. (Even desirable contestation may impose delay and other costs on the process, but its capacity to improve the decision may override this consideration.)

Even with all of these concessions to the legitimate concerns about CBA, some will doubtless still object in principle to using it in government decisions. But the ultimate answer to these principled objections is that CBA, conscientiously conducted with due regard for its problematic features, is probably the best that we can do to assess the efficiency merits of policies. What other decision modes are available to us in deciding among policy options? Good intentions, intuition, caprice, political power, abstract philosophical theories, or coin flips are not acceptable bases for sound policy making, although all of them (especially good intentions and political power) surely affect some decisions. As environmental economist Bjorn Lonborg has put it, CBA "is a far more effective and moral approach than basing decisions on the media's roving gaze or the loudness of competing interest groups."[23] To recalcitrant objectors, then, one must respond in the spirit of Winston Churchill's quip about democracy: CBA is the worst decision tool except for all the others that have been proposed so far.

No informed, sophisticated analyst could deny that some CBAs are conducted more rigorously and convincingly than others, depending on whether the analyst's assumptions, data, and techniques were the best available. My point is that *this*—the competence, transparency, moral scrupulosity, and persuasiveness of a given CBA—is what the argument *should* be about. The argument *should not* be about whether CBA is a legitimate, desirable, and arguably indispensable technique for policy assessment. When well-conducted, CBA is each of those things. A CBA should not necessarily be deemed dispositive of a program's effectiveness, but if it meets the objections reasonably well, it should at the very least shift the burden of proof to those who would challenge its conclusions.

GUIDELINES FOR INTEGRATING CBA INTO POLICY DECISIONS

Cost-benefit analysis is the central tool of policy evaluation, but policy makers need some additional normative principles in order to guide its effective use. Here are fourteen such principles.

1. Policy makers should intervene only when it will correct a significant market failure. For reasons deeply rooted in the American political culture (see chapter 4) and economic system (chapter 7), market competition and provision are public policy's strong default conditions. Like any default conditions, these may be—and often are—overridden by some government intervention that is usually rationalized as one that will cure the kinds of standard market failures discussed in chapter 1. In order to overcome the default and justify the intervention, policy makers should have to answer four relevant questions in the affirmative: (1) Does an actual market failure exist? (2) Is that market failure large enough to justify an intervention, given the costs that it will impose on actual or potential market actors and on taxpayers? (3) Are substantial public values at stake that the market default cannot adequately advance? (4) Is the intervention likely to succeed, given the possibility that the intervention may itself constitute a government or "nonmarket" failure (discussed in chapter 5) that could not readily be corrected or dislodged?

Many public policies, especially those designed to correct market failures, do not satisfy these tests. According to Brookings Institution economist Clifford Winston, assessments relying on detailed empirical analysis are a relatively recent development in policy studies, and they have led to a damning verdict: "Thirty years of empirical evidence on the efficacy of market failure policies initiated primarily by the federal government but also by the states, suggests that the welfare cost of government failure may be considerably greater than that of market failure." On a brighter note, Winston finds that some of the more egregious *government* failures have been rectified and that such failures may therefore be more avoidable in the future.[24] (Many of the policy assessments to which he refers are detailed in chapter 8.)

2. *A program should maximize net benefits and also be cost-effective.* To be considered successful, a program must at a minimum pass a cost-benefit test—it must yield more benefits than the costs it entails—and if it is one of two policies that pass this test, the policy maker should choose the one that *maximizes* net benefits, all other things being equal. This principle is straightforward and incontrovertible. As discussed above, however, some of its normative assumptions and especially its application to particular programs can be matters of intense debate. A somewhat less demanding and less controversial criterion of effectiveness demands that a program that produces net benefits also be cost-effective. This simply means that *whatever a program's purposes* are and *whatever level of benefits it actually produces*, these purposes and this level should be attained at the lowest possible cost—and, correlatively, that at any given level of cost it should produce as many benefits as possible. In other words, whether one holds constant the actual cost or the actual benefits of a program, it should maximize the benefits or minimize the costs, as the case may be.

Because this criterion accepts whichever benchmark (its existing costs or existing benefits) the program chooses to hold constant, I can think of only one plausible objection to it in principle: that cost-effectiveness analysis compares the actual performance of an existing program to the imagined performance of a hypothetical alternative, ignoring the implementation difficulties that could well afflict that alternative if it were instituted in the real world—difficulties that are analyzed in chapter 8. This, however, is less a principled objection to cost-effectiveness analysis than an important reminder that the analyst must strive to anticipate those difficulties.

3. CBAs should be conducted for different levels of benefit. Although Mae West opined that "too much of a good thing is *wonderful*," the same is not true in the policy world. For any given policy under assessment, diminishing returns are likely to set in at some point of benefit generation. That is, the cost-benefit ratio almost certainly will vary across different levels of benefit, with the ratio increasing as the policy approaches 100 percent achievement. Because reaching the highest levels of benefits tends to be much more costly per unit of benefit than at lower levels of benefit, the CBA will generate different outcomes at different levels of benefit achievement: gaining 90 percent of the benefits may be cost-effective, while getting to 95 percent—much less 100 percent—may not, as the last increment may be far costlier.[25] Before joining the Supreme Court, Stephen Breyer, then a regulatory reformer, argued that policy makers' "tunnel vision" often blinds them to this essential and far-reaching constraint of diminishing returns in regulation and indeed in all policy efforts.[26]

4. A program should be target-efficient. Target efficiency—the notion that resources should be allocated to where they can do the most good, given the program's purpose—also logically follows.[27] But knowing where they can do the most good can be difficult because the policy maker lacks information about key facts, such as the extent to which program resources will produce desired policy outcomes. Certain normative judgments may also be disputed. For example, we usually want a program to target its resources on individuals who are disadvantaged relative to others who might claim the resources. But not always. The public, for example, may think that the neediest people the program could target will not use its resources wisely or effectively, or are capable of being independent without the government's resources, or are needy only because of some sort of misconduct or other personal failings. In this spirit, the public often distinguishes between the "worthy" and "unworthy" poor in considering which programs to support and how they should be designed and funded.[28] In practice, moreover, the target efficiency criterion is applied only in discrete policy domains.*

Despite these complications, resource scarcity makes target efficiency a compelling policy criterion with considerable bite—and a sound default rule, at a minimum. Indeed, it indicts many programs that will be discussed in part 2—most farm subsidies, for example—and universal entitlements even more so. Because initial enactment necessitates adding enough beneficiaries to assemble a winning political coalition, policy makers tend to sacrifice target efficiency—until perhaps decades later, when cost control needs become compelling and, as in today's debates over Social Security, Medicare, and food stamp reform, they are faced with the much harder challenge of denying benefits to some in the previously successful coalition.

5. A policy may be cost-ineffective because it uses the wrong tool. Chapter 3 will discuss many different policy instruments—subsidies, taxation, regulation, tort law, market incentives, competition, and many others—that might be deployed individually or in combination to reach the policy makers' goals. Each, of course, entails characteristic features, advantages, and disadvantages, so the choice among them is seldom straightforward—and, despite political rhetoric to the contrary, is never as simple as a choice between "government" and "the market." Nevertheless, this choice will significantly affect the relative success or failure of a program. Which tool is "best" for a given

---

*Ideally, policy makers would look across the government as a whole in asking where taxpayer dollars would do the most good. In principle, the government's overall budgetary process—conducted in the congressional budget committees, the Congressional Budget Office, and the Office of Management and Budget (OMB)—is designed to encourage such synoptic decisions. In practice, however, the key decisions are anything but synoptic. Orchestrated by Congress's substantive and appropriations committees (whose membership is determined with a view to their narrow constituency interests), the OMB's sectoral program offices (which divide up the budget by program and function), and the executive branch's individual, subject-matter-oriented departments and agencies, the process instead focuses narrowly on discrete programs and policy areas. No one actually takes responsibility for target efficiency in the government as a whole.

purpose will usually depend on a number of factors, and analyzing this question can be difficult.

For example, much of the criticism of federal environmental policy during the past four decades has readily conceded the need for regulation but maintained that the precise regulatory *form* that the Environmental Protection Agency has often used—command and control rather than market incentives–based—is misguided and far more costly than alternative forms would be. As explained in chapter 8, this economic critique is largely accepted today among regulators, theorists, and environmentalists, as is the fact that the two approaches often appear in hybrid forms. Nevertheless, the use of command-and-control forms of regulation still dominates in many regulatory systems, including some environmental programs; indeed, some environmental statutes also reject the use of CBA. As a result, much environmental regulation, while producing public health and other benefits, fails a cost-effectiveness test.

6. Special efforts must be made to identify "invisible victims" and consider their interests in the analysis. Many people whom a policy will make worse off are not aware of this fact until the policy is operative—and often not even then. Policy makers will not attend to the interests of these cost bearers unless they make a special effort to identify, analyze, and weigh them. Such cost-bearers, which I call invisible or silent victims, are systematically neglected by policy makers whose programs adversely affect their interests. These costs ordinarily gain little recognition because they are small at the individual level and because the causal link between the policy and these costs is difficult to trace, even or especially by its victims. Thus, they will not organize politically to protest those interests even though the costs may be quite large when aggregated across all of the invisible victims. Invisible victims include, for example, those who will not get a job opportunity because a new regulation, higher minimum wage, or litigation-averse employer chills job creation. Other examples include those whose food prices rise somewhat because biofuel requirements increase the demand for corn (chapter 8), and low-income people who do not receive the medical care to which they are entitled under Medicaid because of the program's rigid, inadequate reimbursement rates (chapter 6). Policies will systematically ignore or undervalue these interests unless analysts make special efforts to take them into account and urge policy makers to do so.

7. *CBA should be used to retrospectively analyze the effectiveness of existing policies, not just proposed ones.* Such systematic retrospective reviews are indispensable. The predictions of programs' sponsors are singularly unreliable guides to policy assessment. Because public funds are always scarce (even in a federal budget approaching $4 trillion in 2013), a program that is perfectly defensible and successful at one level of cost may be undesirable and thus unsuccessful at a higher cost. Politicians, interest groups, and bureaucrats often have a powerful incentive to predict costs and benefits by minimizing the former and maximizing the latter. (This bias is explored in chapter 5, and helps explain why government cost overruns are endemic.*) The only constraint on this incentive is politicians' need to devise a way to pay for it—in this sense, they are buyers of their own legislative product—but the complexity and obscurity of the legislative process (to outsiders) and their ability to hide costs weaken this constraint. Later chapters discuss this problem, emphasizing the need for greater accountability both before and after the fact. Thus, minimizing policy makers' incentives to underestimate costs and exaggerate benefits is one of the most challenging and urgent tasks of a democratic polity. (If voters and other participants fully and accurately discounted these distorted estimates of costs and benefits, then perhaps no harm would occur; but this is implausible, especially among voters.) Unfortunately, holding them accountable when later assessments show their estimates to have been wrong is an insufficient constraint on such chronic underestimates.

*They are not universal, however. NASA's Mars Rover turned out to be faster, cheaper, and better than projected. Some cost overruns are more avoidable than others. In the case of agricultural subsidies, unpredictable weather conditions may affect what the government must pay. When a procurement agency purchases weaponry or other products or services, it may demand costly design changes or an accelerated production schedule after the initial contract cost was signed.

Research by psychologist Philip Tetlock finds systematic failures both in experts' predictions and in their "postdictions" (explanations of the past). He explains why we cannot rely on the "marketplace of ideas" to flush out bad policy ideas quickly enough to avoid serious damage in the meanwhile, and why "lots of nonsense [can] persist for long stretches of time." Competition among information providers will not suffice if consumers are unmotivated to discriminate among competing claims, are themselves biased as to the information, or are unable to determine the truth of the matter.[29] These conditions, unfortunately, are commonly met in policy debates.[30] Government effectiveness, then, depends not only on ex ante predictions of these complex interactions, but also on ex post assessments of—and hence learning from—predictive and programmatic failures in programs already on the books. The value of this may be obvious, but OIRA is only now beginning to conduct the kind of retrospective reviews presented in this book (especially in chapter 8), and even then is doing so only on a limited basis.[31]

Another reason why retrospective assessment is so important is that the alternative is to rely on officials' post-hoc accounts of why programs did not meet expectations—for example, that the program did not have enough money to do the job right or was administered by unsympathetic officials. Although such claims may be true in a particular case, their implausibility as a general matter becomes evident once one understands the deep structural reasons for failure. These reasons, detailed in subsequent chapters, often combine to overdetermine program failure.

Tetlock's research has established empirically that experts are poor at predicting future events. Indeed, experts are actually worse at prediction than nonexperts, including nonexperts who choose more or less at random. In his experiments, both experts and nonexperts were highly intelligent, well-educated individuals who were asked to make more than 27,000 predictions over a large number of topics, regions, and time periods. The main difference was that experts were specialists in the areas in which predictions were sought while nonexperts were not.[32] These findings are consistent with what many other observers have concluded on the basis of less systematic experience and observation. Examples include elite law professors predicting Supreme Court decisions,[33] psychologists diagnosing mental illness and dangerousness,[34] and movie executives predicting film hits.[35]

Tetlock ascribes the large observed difference in predictive accuracy to the different cognitive styles that, drawing on Isaiah Berlin's famous distinction, he ascribes to expert "hedgehogs" (those who know one big thing and try to integrate the diversity of the world into a comprehensive and parsimonious vision) and to nonexpert, more eclectic "foxes" (those who know many small things and try to improvise solutions on a case-by-case basis).[36] Tetlock finds that who experts are (i.e., taking into account professional background and status) and what they think (i.e., whether they be liberal or conservative, realist or institutionalist, optimist or pessimist) are less important than *how* they think—their reasoning style. Specifically, he finds that "the tentative, balanced modes of thinking favored by foxes" predict better than "the confident, decisive modes of thinking favored by hedgehogs." Among other differences, hedgehogs are slower to change their minds as much as they should when they err. This is partly because they employ "belief system defenses" to avoid such revisions, including the belief that bad luck explains their predictive errors more than good luck explains their predictive successes: "their defiant attitude was 'I win if the evidence breaks in my direction' but if not, 'the methodology must be suspect.'" Both modes of thinking exhibit certain characteristic advantages and disadvantages, Tetlock finds, but "[t]he dominant danger remains hubris, the mostly hedgehog vice of close-mindedness, of dismissing dissonant possibilities too quickly."[37] More recent analyses by Nate Silver and Nassim Nicholas Taleb reach similar conclusions about experts' overconfidence in their predictions and their systematic underestimation of uncertainty.[38]

Quite apart from Tetlock's theory of the specific cognitive causes of predictive failures, many other studies have demonstrated how weak most predictive models are when they seek to forecast complex nonmarket phenomena.[39] As we shall see in later chapters, the success of federal programs depends on accurately predicting the interactions of autonomous individual actors and voters, bureaucracies, markets, other levels of government, and other factors. And, as we shall further see, these predictions are especially prone to error.

8. Ending a failed policy is a kind of policy success. Occasionally, government officials acknowledge that one of their long-standing policies has failed and should be abandoned. Such confessions of governmental error are to be strongly encouraged, of course, but they are usually belated and exceedingly rare. One example, discussed in chapter 11, is the Airline Deregulation Act of 1978, which repealed a forty-year old regulatory cartel that was egregiously inefficient, replacing it with a competitive system that has benefited the vast majority of consumers immensely.[40] Another example is the military's repeal of its "don't ask, don't tell" rules in September 2011. No less an expert on the subject than congressman Barney Frank supported the original "don't ask, don't tell" policy because he was convinced that it was a step forward and the best policy reform that could then be obtained. The fact that the military now believes that its policy was wrong is indeed welcome.[41] Gay policy entrepreneurs' vision, skill, persistence, and courage over a twenty-year period in agitating for the repeal of a misguided, unjust regime are remarkable and admirable. Compare this with the speed with which private firms that anger their customers often respond quickly to regain them—for example, the banks that had to revoke their debit card and swipe fees once consumers rebelled.[42] Occasionally, a legislative policy is quickly reversed when it proves very unpopular; the Medicare Catastophic Coverage Act of 1988, repealed less than eighteen months after enactment, is an example. Chapter 6 discusses policy rigidity in greater detail.

9. Policy-making demands appropriate organizational analysis. The success of particular programs will depend on the kinds of organizations in which they are embedded and the ways that their task structures constrain and shape their behavior. The late political scientist James Q. Wilson explored these design considerations in some detail, which I consider in chapter 7, on policy implementation, and in chapter 10, on bureaucracy.

10. Policy assessment requires an appropriate time frame. Historical contingency, timing, and plain luck may affect a policy assessment. A program that seems effective at time A may seem ineffective at time B, and vice versa. Hindsight, of course, is 20–20, but myopia is far more common. The time frame constraint has three aspects. First, after a program is enacted, its opponents may succeed in undermining its effectiveness. Embedding a policy so that it can resist attack is difficult; the 1986 tax reform failed to do so, and "Obamacare" faces an even stiffer challenge given unanimous Republican opposition in the Senate and the law's reliance on implementation by many recalcitrant states.[43] Only time can tell whether this will happen.

Second, the program being analyzed must have been in effect for a sufficient length of time to demonstrate both its desirable and undesirable effects. If, for example, one were assessing the government's 2009 bailout of General Motors solely in light of its consequences—that is, not in terms of whether such a policy is desirable in principle or in terms of its possible future precedential effect—then one should wait long enough to determine whether the company can be restored to profitability without huge losses to the government. (This will evidently be a long time. In September 2012, the U.S. Treasury, fearing that it would suffer an immense loss, once again rejected GM's pleas to sell its remaining stake in the company.[44]) At the same time, the bailout of American International Group was successful by many accounts,[45] although the government's cost-benefit calculations do not factor in the below-market rates that it charged the company (and other recipients of large bailout loans) at a time when liquidity was almost impossible to obtain otherwise.[46] In the case of Head Start (discussed in chapter 6), the policy's goal is to improve long-term education, social, and health outcomes for participant children as they reach adulthood, so assessment of its performance requires a suitable time frame to permit that reckoning. Some policies—the Safe

Streets and Crime Control Act of 1968, for example—may have far-reaching effects long after they are repealed.[47]

Third, the time frame should allow for the possibility that a policy that makes sense at time A no longer does at time B. The alternative minimum tax, for example, may have been a sound and successful policy when it was enacted in 1982 (a predecessor minimum tax was enacted in 1969), but a fair assessment today would properly consider the fact that because of inflation and bracket creep, it now applies it to millions of middle-income taxpayers who Congress never intended to subject to it.

11. Policy assessment requires competent and objective assessors. This precept is obvious, yet needs some elaboration. Any assessing organization has some characteristic perspective or orientation about government programs, even if it does not have any manifest political or ideological ax to grind.* Program evaluations are often costly and difficult to conduct, and none is likely to be immune from some criticism, so we must take them as we find them and then try to assess the assessments by applying to them professionally refined principles of analytical rigor with as much objectivity as possible. This can be challenging for outsiders not intimately familiar with the program data, but there really is no alternative if we take seriously the ancient poet Juvenal's query *quis custodiet ipsos custodies*—"who will guard the guards?"

12. The well-designed randomized controlled experiment is the gold standard for assessment. This methodology, discussed in chapters 11 and 12, is the only way to justify confidence on the part of policy makers that they know what they think they know about the effects of actual and proposed policies. But although it is now used to test policy innovations in business, political strategy, and many other areas, policy makers seldom use it.

---

*The ax may also be financial. For example, the main credit rating agencies for financial instruments (Moody's, Standard & Poor's, and Fitch Group) used by a number of government agencies and regulatory programs were paid by the companies that they were assessing. This not only constitutes a manifest conflict of interest but by most accounts contributed significantly to the financial crisis that erupted in 2007.

13. Policy assessments must take most of the existing social and institutional context as given. The assessment, to be useful, must take certain existing conditions as a baseline and then try to predict how outcomes would change if we altered some of those baseline conditions. We may consider some of these baseline conditions suboptimal in the sense that society would arguably be better off today had it made different choices in the past—indeed, if we didn't consider the status quo suboptimal, we probably wouldn't conduct the policy analysis in the first place—but we must hold them constant. For example, our society would be very different today—perhaps better in some respects, worse in others—had the United States invested in creating better rail networks instead of using the resources to build a national highway system. Nevertheless, when we consider policy proposals today on mass transit, we must take the highway system and its consequences as a given for purposes of conducting the assessment. This is not conservative; it is simply necessary for a coherent, accurate policy assessment. The policy implications of such an analysis, of course, may be conservative, radical, or something else altogether.

14. Avoid the "Nirvana fallacy." When one concludes that a policy has failed, one usually has in mind a better, more effective, reformed version of that policy. Fortunately, such reforms often do improve the program's performance. In making such comparisons, however, policy makers should not idealize the new version, for it will be vulnerable to many of the same structural factors that have promoted failure in the existing policy. Economist Harold Demsetz has called this seductive idealization "the Nirvana fallacy": viewing the policy choice as if it were one between an ideal program and the existing, flawed one.[48]

In conclusion, policy success or failure is *not* simply in the eye of the beholder. We have seen that good policy assessment rests upon a number of well-established, relatively uncontroversial criteria that are certified in analytic methodology and routinely used in government practice. Although the application of these criteria to particular policies might be contested, it turns out that the *results* of such assessments are *also* remarkably consistent—and consistently negative. Winston, who as noted in chapter 1 claims to have read all of the studies, finds,

> Notwithstanding the potential for methodological disputes to arise when microeconomic policies are evaluated, my assessment of the empirical evidence reveals a surprising degree of consensus about the paucity of major policy successes in correcting a market failure efficiently. In contrast to the sharp divisions that characterize debates over the efficacy of macroeconomic policy interventions, I found only a handful of empirical studies that disagree about whether a particular government policy had enhanced efficiency by substantially correcting a market failure. . . . Generally, my fundamental conclusions are not influenced by studies that use a particular methodology. In fact, researchers who used vastly different techniques to assess specific policies often reached very similar conclusions.[49]

Nor is Winston alone in this conclusion. Derek Bok's careful review of the evidence concurs: "Again and again, in field after field, the operative legislation is burdened by unrealistic objectives, inadequate funding, clumsy implementing machinery, and poor targeting of funds. The costs in terms of waste, frustrated expectations, and harmful side effects are virtually incalculable."[50]

CHAPTER 3

Policy-Making Functions, Processes, Missions, Instruments, and Institutions

Public policies are the product of five interacting factors. First, government must tailor its policy choices to the particular *functions* that it wishes to perform. Second, these policy choices are made through a variety of formal and informal *processes*. Third, policy makers assign *missions* to administrative agencies—indeed, often multiple and sometimes conflicting ones. Fourth, the policy that is chosen will pursue these missions by deploying some specific *instruments* rather than others. Fifth, public policies—when created and when implemented—are profoundly influenced by the *formal institutions* that surround and shape them. (Policy making's political culture—its *informal* institutions, in a sense—is discussed in chapter 4.) Here I describe each of these five factors in turn, prefiguring the analysis in part 2's chapters, which explore the reasons why, and the evidence that, government fails so often—and why it sometimes succeeds.

FUNCTIONS

The proper functions of government is a truly ancient question to which different answers have been given at different times by different commentators, including political theorists, economists, constitutional lawyers, and ordinary citizens. A conventional taxonomy of federal government activity recognizes three discrete, basic functions: production, regulation, and redistribution. *Production* entails the creation of goods and services for public consumption. The most important example is national security, but it also includes the provision of physical and cybernetic infrastructure, biomedical research, and so forth. *Regulation* entails the prescription of rules, licenses, and other influence mechanisms designed to shape private (and subnational government) decisions. *Redistribution* entails taxation and subsidy of various private-sector activities. (Production and regulation both have redistributive effects as well.) Each of these three functions, of course, requires different kinds of policy choices and is shaped by a different political context.[1]

A gauzier, less technocratic conception of government function would emphasize another, more communitarian, function: its ability to define how citizens are connected to one another in a common venture. One is struck, however, by the erosion of these connective tissues even as government has expanded to occupy more and more social space. This erosion is likely both a cause and a consequence of the apparent, much-lamented (but also disputed) decline of social capital in our communities.[2]

The common public school—the traditional site (along with the family) of civic education and socialization—is being challenged and in some cases replaced by private and hybrid educational institutions. Universal military service has been replaced by a wholly professional cadre that has less and less in common with the citizenry.[3] The U.S. Postal Service, formerly the hub of the national communication system, is in effect bankrupt, with most of its traditional functions now performed more efficiently by privately provided technologies. (In 2013, Britain decided to privatize its five-hundred-year-old Royal Mail.[4]) The management of water, power, communications, highways, and other community infrastructure has increasingly been privatized. The Department of Motor Vehicles, another site of government-citizen interface, is widely considered a parody of public service. The failure of so many of these connective institutions—partly due to technological changes—is likely both a cause and a consequence of public dissatisfaction with government. Increasingly, then, Americans are raising the most fundamental questions about the state: what are its essential functions, which of those must be performed by politically accountable agents, and which can be performed better by nongovernmental institutions? These questions about the state's functions are ancient ones; the answers have changed over time—and not in a unidirectional way. This inquiry leads to a third way to distinguish among governmental functions that I shall briefly discuss here. This approach asks whether in principle they are functions that government *must* undertake, that it *should* undertake, or that are *optional* (i.e., those that government might or might not be wise to undertake). I say "in principle" because the extent to which the government actually succeeds in any of these three types of activities depends on how it goes about designing and implementing them. As shorthand, I shall refer to these as *necessary, desirable,* and *optional* functions.

Necessary functions. Political economy theory identifies two absolutely necessary functions of government: the *production of public goods* and the *control of spillovers* (or "externalities"). (I do not discuss here a third necessary function—the control of natural monopolies—because it is comparatively rare and technical area of government regulation that many experts in the field of regulated industries believe would be best left unregulated).[5] Simply stated, public (or "collective") goods are goods or services that, once produced, are available to all in at least two senses: they can be consumed by all at zero marginal cost (they are "nonrivalrous"), and people cannot, at any reasonable cost, be excluded from consuming them (they are "nonexcludable"). If such goods are to be produced, government must produce them; no market actor would have an incentive to do so, as it could not exclude consumers and thus charge them for the goods' costs.[6] The classic public goods are national security, clean air, and standardization of weights and measures.*

---

*The rule of law is in many ways a public good; everyone benefits from it and none can be denied it (constitutionally). In fact, financial and other barriers exclude many people from accessing the justice system; these barriers have no obvious parallels to national security or clean air (except perhaps for very poor people trapped in a badly polluted environment).

Spillovers are different. *Negative* spillovers are produced when an actor has an incentive and an opportunity to impose on others some of the costs generated by its activity, or does so inadvertently. In either case, it will produce more of the activity than it would produce if it had to bear all the costs itself. Pollution is the paradigmatic example. In such cases, only the government can induce the polluters—through taxes, regulation, tort law, or other legal mechanisms—to internalize those costs so as to reduce them to a socially optimal level.*

Desirable functions. Positive spillovers occur in the case of "merit" goods—examples include education and public health—that confer benefits not only on those who directly consume them but also on other members of the public who do not. In such cases, the good's social value is not exhausted by consumers' demand for it, so less of it may be produced privately than is socially optimal. The government may intervene—through public provision, subsidies to private providers, or other legal techniques—to assure that more of it is produced than would be without government action, but these interventions will be subject to many if not all of the nonmarket (governmental) failures (to be discussed in part 2).[7]

Although even libertarians accept that government must correct for these market impediments to public and merit goods, there is much disagreement about their precise contours: how much should be spent on national defense, which military systems should be installed, how clean the air should be, how that level of environmental control should be achieved, and so forth. Government provision of merit goods is even more controversial, reflecting disagreement about which goods are meritorious, the size of their benefits and costs, how their benefits should be distributed, how their costs should be controlled, and in what forms they can best be supplied. Education and public health are generally considered the most meritorious of goods,

---

*Private contracts to reallocate the externality's costs and benefits more efficiently than these legal mechanisms do may be impeded by transaction costs or equitable concerns. Ronald Coase analyzes this aspect of externalities in "The Problem of Social Cost," *Journal of Law and Economics* 3 (1960): 1–44.

yet bitter disagreements exist over which kinds of educational or public health programs should be established (e.g., debates over contraception or, in an earlier day, the fluoridation of water), the precise programmatic forms they should take (e.g., public provision, vouchers, regulation), and so forth. Another merit good—consumer or voter information needed to overcome knowledge advantages held by producers or politicians—also raises disagreements over how the desired information should be compiled and presented.

In both principle and practice, the particular level of government at which these goods should be provided is a separate question. In some cases of public goods or externalities—national security or interstate pollution, for example—citizens will support government intervention at the *federal* level, usually for efficiency reasons or concerns about "races to the bottom" among states competing for tax base and budgetary savings, as with the food stamps program (now the Supplemental Nutrition Assistance Program,[8] which is discussed in chapter 11). In other cases, however, the public may prefer that the intervention be undertaken at lower levels of government, usually for efficiency reasons (e.g., with land use controls) or localism values (e.g., with public education).

Optional functions. Governmental intervention (if not its specific programmatic form) is almost universally accepted in the areas just discussed, but the same is not true of most other programs in which the competing advantages and disadvantages of politics and markets (and hybrid forms), and the soundness of particular interventions on a variety of policy grounds, provide an unending source of public controversy and partisan polarization. Here, the desirability of particular programs, and sometimes their very legitimacy (a slippery concept discussed in chapter 1), are highly debatable. For example, law-and-economics professor Saul Levmore argues, controversially, that government should sometimes regulate health and safety "internalities," situations in which people who lack sufficient self-control to stop, say, smoking or eating junk food want the law to help them precommit to change their future behavior.[9]

PROCESSES

Government policies emerge from decision processes, and the performance of those policies depends on the kinds of processes that produced them and how well those processes worked. Procedure and substance are inextricably linked, but in subtle ways that are often difficult to discern.

The discussion that follows seeks to reveal the nature of this linkage by identifying just a few of the many features of different policy processes that shape programs' ultimate effectiveness. Although there is an immense literature on policy processes and although politically sophisticated readers will find some of what I have to say familiar, my discussion will be highly selective, focusing on a relatively small subset of the linkages between policy process and program effectiveness that are less obvious, even to many sophisticates. The discussion here will also seek to minimize any overlap between this overview and the more pointed analyses in the chapters that follow in part 2.

Legislative process. Congress has the immense advantage (and vulnerability) of being the most directly accountable and geographically oriented branch—especially the House, with its two-year terms and smaller, less diffuse constituencies. Hence, its members possess relatively good information about the political support that a policy will have at the point of enactment. Its committee system, which depends heavily on a highly professional, permanent staff of subject-matter specialists, is capable of bringing considerable policy expertise to bear on legislation. Both the members and their staffs, moreover, are ever mindful of the more remunerative employment opportunities that await them in the private sector should they leave government. This keen careerist sensibility, although a potential source of corruption (discussed in chapter 6), has the advantage of making them especially sensitive to the real-world effects of their policy choices on their constituents and attentive interest groups. Congress also gathers a great deal of technical information in the course of its committee hearings, meetings with constituents and interest groups, and bill negotiation and drafting processes. Postenactment, members and their staffs receive a great deal of feedback from the field concerning how their policies are working in practice. Unfortunately, Congress has often exempted itself, in law or in effect, from having to comply with the policies it has imposed on others—despite enacting laws that on their face seem to demand full congressional compliance.[10] Such exemptions are objectionable, among other reasons, because they deprive Congress of one source of information on the costs that their fellow citizens bear.

On the other hand, members tend to have selective hearing, attending far more to the arguments, desires, and complaints of well-organized interests than to more diffuse ones. Business-oriented interests are far better represented in Washington than individual citizens—by a factor of eight to one, according to one recent calculation—and private-sector unions (representing only 7 percent of private-sector workers) are in sharp decline, in contrast to public-sector ones.[11] The attention span of members, moreover, is severely limited due to the hyperactive nature of most politicians, the fast-moving, fast-changing legislative calendar, and the inertia that must be overcome to return to a program after it has overcome the many obstacles to passage and is now in place. Absent a sunset provision requiring that a law be re-reenacted periodically, members are very loath to revisit it—and even sunset provisions are often extended or treated as pro forma. The legislative agenda is formed through a chaotic, adventitious, opportunistic process that is the very opposite of rational prioritization and problem solving.

Administrative process. Agency policy making also has comparative strengths and notable weaknesses, and although each agency has a distinctive, specialized policy domain and bureaucratic culture, they exhibit many important similarities such that one can speak coherently about the "administrative process." Nevertheless, the administrative agency occupies a peculiar position in our government, being not directly accountable to the citizenry, claiming the authority of expertise that the public does not readily grant, and often exercising vast, difficult-to-control discretionary powers to shape policies in ways that can affect the vital interests of all citizens. For these reasons, their democratic legitimation poses a perennial problem in American government.[12]

Agencies are conventionally divided into two categories: those that are in the executive branch and subject to presidential control, and those that are "independent" of such control. This binary classification is, however, both crude and misleading. First, many important agencies exist that lawyer–political scientist Anne Joseph O'Connell calls "boundary" organizations. Lying at the borders between the federal government and either the private sector (e.g., the Postal Service) or other levels of government (e.g., the National Guard, the Social Security disability program), this category also includes the many agencies that do not fit neatly within the executive branch/independent agency dichotomy.[13]

Second, actual distribution among federal agencies of these independence-affecting features is quite varied: removal protection, specified tenure, multimember structure, partisan balance requirements, litigation authority, adjudication authority, and centralized Office of Management and Budget (OMB) review of budget proposals, congressional testimony, and legislative proposals. A recent study of these patterns concluded that "there is no binary distinction between agency types. Indeed, there is no single feature that every agency commonly thought of as independent shares, not even a for-cause removal provision. Agencies fall along a spectrum from more insulated to least insulated from the President."[14] Except at an agency's very top level, any formal accountability to the White House is attenuated by the fact that agency officials are hard to remove or discipline. (If they are career civil servants, it is almost impossible, as discussed in chapter 10.) Indeed, presidents almost never remove an agency head for cause, even when the law empowers them to do so.

Nevertheless, even relatively independent agencies are not at liberty to do as they please. The president has a variety of informal ways—some more effective and politically costly than others—to influence all agencies, including the most conventionally (though not formally) independent of them all, the Board of Governors of the

Federal Reserve Bank (the "Fed").[15] Congress determines its legal authority and resources, and they are highly attentive to the informal interventions of individual members, especially those on the agency's authorizing and appropriations committees. Compared with the free-wheeling, entrepreneurial Congress, the agency's agenda and processes, which are governed by the Administrative Procedure Act of 1946 (APA), tend to be more centralized, regularized, rule-driven, and orderly, with fewer internal power centers to be accommodated.

Agencies employ a variety of formal and informal processes to make policy and provide guidance to those subject to their jurisdiction, but I shall focus on the two processes that are prescribed most closely by the APA: rule making and adjudication. These two processes are designed to operate very differently, and they do. Most rule making entails providing widespread notice of the agency's proposed rule, a period for public comment on that proposal, occasionally a public hearing, and issuance of the final rule together with an explanation of the reasons why the agency did what it did. Rule making resembles some attractive aspects of the legislative process in its use of technocratic expertise, openness to widespread public participation, explicit consideration of policy alternatives, dialogic back and forth, culmination in a rule of substantial generality, and highly deferential judicial review either before or after the rule goes into effect (pre- or postenforcement review). In contrast, agency adjudication resembles a judicial trial and exhibits some of a trial's features: application of a legal rule to specific parties and circumstances; due process guarantees, including rules of evidence and prohibition of ex parte contacts; trial before an independent "administrative law judge" with a decision based on a record; and issuance of an individualized "order" (not a general rule). For policy-making purposes, however, these procedural differences are smaller than they seem: almost every agency is authorized to use either procedure, exercise its discretion to choose which to use when (subject to very limited judicial review), and can usually accomplish its policy goals using either. (This is because the agency can draft a rule to apply very narrowly, while its adjudicative orders can be formulated in fairly general terms.)

Although agencies have succeeded in exploiting many of the strengths of the legislative and judicial processes (I discuss the latter below), they have not managed to avoid some of the weaknesses. Agency proceedings of both kinds can be very costly and protracted, especially if they are appealed to the courts and then remanded back to the agencies for further deliberation. Centralization of agency authority can introduce rigidity and politicization of policy making (although that is even truer of Congress). Agency bureaucratization, while assuring some degree of continuity and technical expertise, often produces predictable pathologies: tunnel vision, middling competence, limited imagination, fear of controversy, and obsession with process.

These institutional features and trade-offs are familiar to those who study the administrative process. But another exceedingly important one—the appropriate allocation of policy discretion between Congress and the agencies—has largely been conceived as an issue of constitutional law rather than as the fundamental, often pivotal issue of public policy design that it is. Accordingly, I shall give it some attention here.

The Supreme Court's "nondelegation doctrine," announced in its *Schechter Poultry* decision in 1935,[16] holds that under Article I of the Constitution, Congress possesses the exclusive power and responsibility to exercise "all legislative powers" and thus may not delegate to agencies the power to make the fundamental value and policy choices that legislation instantiates. Although the Court has sought through various statutory interpretation techniques (e.g., "clear statement" and "intelligible principle" requirements) to narrow the extent of broad delegations, it has essentially given up the effort and has not actually struck down a statute for excessive delegation since *Schechter Poultry* itself.[17] This judicial back of the hand to the doctrine has not stopped scholars from advocating its revitalization as a way of assuring that Congress remains accountable for what it has wrought and that only very limited policy discretion can be exercised by agencies.[18] And in 2011, the House passed the tendentiously titled Regulations from the Executive in Need of Scrutiny Act, endorsed by Republican presidential nominee Mitt Romney in 2012, that would require Congress to approve any proposed "major rule" before it could go into effect.[19]

For many reasons, which I have elaborated elsewhere,[20] the Court has been wise to leave to Congress the choice about how specific statutes must be. The particular aspects of a statutory delegation—its breadth, type, and level—are themselves among the most consequential policy choices. Indeed, these issues are almost always at the heart of the members' political debates over the content of particular pieces of legislation. Legislation is only part of the process of responsible policy making, and it is becoming a less important part relative to agency decisions.

The costs of participating at the agency level, where many of the most important policy choices are in fact made, are likely to be lower than the costs of lobbying or otherwise seeking to influence Congress. Moreover, an agency's institutional culture is likely more familiar to the average citizen, who deals with bureaucracies constantly and may well work in one (public or private), than Congress's exotic, intricate, unruly (and "unruley"), insider culture. An agency is often a more meaningful site for public participation than Congress is because the policy stakes for individuals and interest groups are most immediate, transparent, and well defined at the agency level.

One can scarcely exaggerate the importance of this consideration to the legitimacy of democratic politics and to the substantive content of public policy. After all, it is only at the agency level that the generalities of legislation are broken down and concretized into discrete, specific issues with which affected parties can hope to deal. It is there that the agency commits itself to a particular course of action; because only there does it propose the specific rate it will set, the particular emission levels it will prescribe, the precise restrictions on private activity it will impose, the exact regulatory definitions it will employ, the kinds of enforcement techniques it will use, the types of information it will collect, and the details relating to the state's myriad other impacts on citizens and groups. In short, it is only at the agency level that citizens can know precisely what the statute means to them; how, when, and to what extent it will affect their interests; whether they support, oppose, or want changes in what the agency is proposing; whether it is worth their while to participate actively in seeking to influence this particular exercise of governmental power, and if so, how best to go about it; and where other citizens or groups stand on these questions. God and the devil are in the details of policy making, as they are in most other important things—and the details are to be found at the agency level.

Finally, the agency is often the site at which public participation is most effective. This is not only because the details of the policy's impacts are hammered out there. It is also because the agency is where the public can best educate the government about the true nature of the problem that Congress has tried to address. Only the interested parties, reacting to specific agency proposals for rules or other actions, possess (or have the incentives to acquire) the information necessary to identify, explicate, quantify, and evaluate the real-world consequences of these and alternative proposals. Even when Congress can identify the first-order effects of the laws that it enacts, these direct impacts seldom exhaust the laws' policy consequences. Indeed, first-order effects of policies usually are less significant than the aggregate of more remote effects that ripple through a complex, interrelated, opaque society.

When policies fail, it is usually not because the congressional purpose was misunderstood. More commonly, they fail either because of faulty policy design or—what may amount to the same thing—because Congress did not fully appreciate how its purposes would be confounded as the policy ramifications became evident in the real world. (Implementation difficulties are discussed in chapter 8.) Often, however, this knowledge about future effects can be gained only through the public's active participation in the policy-making process at the agency level, where these implementation issues are most clearly focused and the stakes in the correct resolution are highest.

Judicial process. The courts are far less influential in the design and implementation of public policy than Congress and the agencies are. In principle, they are not to consider the merits of policies but only their legality. (In practice, they sometimes do, particularly in the Supreme Court.[21]) Nevertheless, judicial review can have substantial policy consequences.

Except in the rare case where an important public policy is challenged on constitutional grounds—the Affordable Care Act,[22] for example—the courts' main powers are to interpret statutes and regulations, and to assure that agency actions do not transcend the scope of the congressional delegation of authority. Judicial interpretations of statutes can elucidate their meaning, in some cases fundamentally transforming it. As political scientists have shown, the federal courts sometimes interpret ambiguous provisions to allow private enforcement of public law in ways that substantially alter the nature and meaning of the schemes that Congress has enacted and that agencies administer.[23] And judicial review of agency regulations sometimes changes agency policy,[24] although reviewing courts uphold the agency in the vast majority of cases or remand the case to the agency so that it can exercise its policy discretion under the correct legal standard.[25]

By and large, however, courts readily acknowledge in their opinions that as a matter of relative institutional competence and capacity,[26] they are in a poor position to second-guess congressional and agency decisions entailing technical judgments or normative trade-offs. Except in the rare case where constitutional values are at stake or when a statute invites closer judicial scrutiny, the most that reviewing courts are supposed to do is to ensure that the agency remains within its statutory authority and avoids "arbitrary and capricious" regulations. The courts' engagement with any particular substantive policy issue is only episodic and narrowly bound by the litigation's facts, which are often atypical, unrepresentative of the world in which policy must be implemented. For these reasons, moreover, the reviewing courts' principal remedy is a very limited one: to remand the matter to the agency to review the matter anew, sometimes several times in a back-and-forth that can stretch over many years.[27]

The difficulty of controlling discretion is not confined to administrative agencies. Concerns about widespread perceptions of excessive judicial discretion in criminal sentencing led Congress in 1984 to establish the U.S. Sentencing Commission within the judicial branch to issue sentencing guidelines that until 2005 were thought to be mandatory.[28] The commission's work has been contentious from its inception, with many federal judges opposing the guidelines in part because of the difficulty of regulating judicial discretion in this area given the large number of factors that judges have traditionally taken into account in their sentencing decisions, which in turn led to troubling disparities in the sentences meted out to criminals. One dramatic indicator of how difficult it is to control discretion through such regulation is that more than twenty-five years after the Sentencing Commission began its work, disturbing disparities remain.[29] Some thoughtful reformers like Philip Howard argue that improving government performance requires allowing policy implementers to exercise more discretion, not less.[30]

Other processes. Occasionally, Congress or the president will establish a special, usually bipartisan and professionally staffed, body to advise it on particular policy decisions; in some cases, this body's recommendations may even be made legally binding. This highly unusual arrangement is usually created when the policy decisions being considered are especially sensitive politically and Congress is willing to pass the decisive responsibility for these hot potatoes on to a special body. The most important successful examples of this institutional innovation are the National Commission on Social Security Reform, which reported back to Congress in 1983; the Base Realignment and Closure Commission, whose recommendations are by law difficult to overturn; and electoral redistricting commissions in certain states. Unfortunately, however, such committees are often unsuccessful—for example, the Kerry-Danforth Entitlement Reform Commission (1993), and the Breaux-Thomas Medicare Commission (1997). The Simpson-Bowles National Commission on Fiscal Responsibility and Reform (2010) has had little effect, although it may yet have some influence on future legislation. At a minimum, effectiveness requires that such commissions be used very rarely; in order to garner public and congressional support, the public must see them as very rare exceptions to the conventional policy-making process.

MISSIONS

Legislation defines, with more or less specificity, the mission that an administrative agency is to discharge. Traditionally, each agency was given a single mission—for example, protecting the integrity of securities markets, or promoting homeownership—to pursue. Since the 1960s, however, Congress has enacted five kinds of statutes that transcend this single-mission focus. First, it has established agencies to engage in "social regulation" promoting workplace safety, environmental protection, equal opportunity, consumer protection, and the like. This social regulation is applied across the board to *all firms* in the economy (unless exempted). The enormous diversity among these firms, vastly greater than among firms in a single industry subject to traditional economic regulation, has made these agencies' regulatory missions more difficult to achieve. Second, Congress has adopted laws that apply across the board to *all agencies* (unless exempted) and in effect multiply the number and variety of missions (or constraints) that each agency must discharge (or satisfy). These laws include the National Environmental Policy Act, the Paperwork Reduction Act, the Government in the Sunshine Act, the Federal Advisory Committee Act, the Regulatory Flexibility Act, the Civil Rights Act, and the Freedom of Information Act, among others. The OMB has added other such constraints, such as the cost-benefit analysis requirements discussed in chapter 2. Third, Congress often assigns multiple missions to a single agency. This inevitably divides the agency's limited resources, which may render both missions less effective. But the missions may conflict in a deeper sense: they may to some degree actually be inconsistent with one another. Many economists, for example, believe that Congress diluted the Fed's ability to single-mindedly pursue its original task of regulating monetary policy to combat inflation when it later required the Fed to also maximize employment, which can be inflationary. In another example, the centrality of the Justice Department's prosecutorial function arguably had made it a poor agency to administer clemency petitions.[31] Fourth, Congress sometimes assigns similar missions to multiple agencies— for example, dividing antitrust policy between the Federal Trade Commission and the Justice Department,[32] and dividing federal banking regulation among no fewer than five agencies (the Fed, the Comptroller of the Currency, the Federal Deposit Insurance Corporation, the Commodity Futures Trading Commission, and the Consumer Financial Protection Bureau). (Again, this does not include the extensive regulation of state-chartered banks by state authorities.) Finally, Congress sometimes establishes what one legal scholar calls "offices of goodness"—for example, offices for privacy and civil liberties in the Office of the Director of National Intelligence and the Department of Justice—in hopes of limiting the agencies' potential abuses of authority by providing various forms of advisory input into their decisions.[33]

For present purposes, the important point about this multiplication of missions (and constraints) is that it greatly complicates and protracts agencies' decision processes, increases the likelihood of interagency conflict and policy incoherence, and injects many more hard-to-resolve policy trade-offs into their policy choices. The impasse over the final version of the Volcker Rule, discussed in chapter 8, exemplifies these interagency difficulties.

INSTRUMENTS

Whatever the government decides to do can be done in many different ways by employing any one or combination of a variety of policy instruments. Each of these instruments involves a distinctive incentive system, imposes distinct informational demands, triggers distinct legal structures and operating procedures, exhibits a distinct dynamic of accountability, and generates a distinct constellation of political factors. Each possesses its own characteristic advantages and disadvantages, and thus entails a distinctive set of trade-offs.

So diverse are these instruments and so common are their deployments by policy makers today that this development, in political scientist Lester Salamon's words, is "a revolution . . . in the 'technology' of public action . . . not just in the scope and scale of government action, but in its basic *forms*. A massive proliferation has occurred in the *tools* of public action, in the *instruments* or means used to address public problems."[34] This revolution, Salomon notes, has shifted critical focus from the agency or the program to the instruments used by government to pursue its policy goals.[35] In an edited book, *The Tools of Government*, Salamon and his contributors distinguish more than a dozen distinct policy instruments that government can and does use.

1. Direct bureaucratic administration.[36] This is the delivery or withholding of a good or service by government employees. When we think of government programs, this is the paradigm that we almost always have in mind, yet it is an anachronistic image of what government typically does. In fact, direct bureaucratic administration accounted for only 5.2 percent of federal government expenditures in 1999; even if income transfers, direct loans, and interest payments are included as "direct government," it amounts to only 28.1 percent. Nor does this pattern simply reflect the privatization, contracting out, and reinventing government initiatives of the 1980s and 1990s. Even in 1982, direct government administration accounted for only 39 percent of government-funded human services, with over 60 percent delivered by nonprofits and for-profit firms.[37] Chapter 10 discusses the bureaucracy in detail.

2. Government corporations and government-sponsored enterprises.[38] A government corporation is a government agency owned and controlled by government, and is set up as a separate legal entity distinct from the rest of the government. It is often used for activities that are expected to be revenue producing and thus self-sustaining, so they are "off-budget"—not subject to the appropriations and budget limitation that restrict ordinary government agencies and thus not accountable to Congress in the same way. A government-sponsored enterprise (GSE), in contrast, is government chartered but privately owned. In return for certain statutory privileges, including tax benefits and regulatory exemptions, as well as reduced borrowing costs (because of an implied government guarantee), a GSE is confined by its charter to serving specified market segments through a limited range of services.

In recent years, the most important GSEs have been the two largest—the Federal National Mortgage Association (FNMA, or "Fannie Mae"), and the Federal Home Loan Mortgage Corporation (FHLMC, or "Freddie Mac"). They evolved from a small government agency created in 1934, to a large and powerful duopoly owned by private and public investors in the 1970s, to insolvency and federal conservatorship in September 2008, reporting to the Federal Housing Finance Agency in the Department of Housing and Urban Development. These GSEs, which enjoyed a line of credit at the U.S. Treasury, and thus a government guarantee, failed spectacularly after 2007, a development whose staggering policy significance is discussed in chapters 5 and 8.

3. Economic regulation.[39] This specialized bureaucratic process combines aspects of both courts and legislatures to control prices, output, and/or the entry and exit of firms in an industry—particularly those regarded as public utilities.

4. Social regulation.[40] This, too, is a specialized bureaucratic process that, in contrast to economic regulation, seeks to restrict behaviors that directly threaten public health, safety, welfare, or well-being, including discrimination on the basis of race, gender, religion, and so forth.

5. Government insurance.[41] Here, government undertakes to compensate individuals or firms for losses from certain specified events, charging a premium for this insurance. Examples are insurance against flooding, crop loss, and health care costs.

6. *Public information.*[42] Here, government disseminates information to elicit desired policy outcomes by influencing what people
think, know, or believe when they engage in the targeted behavior.

7. *Corrective taxes, charges, and tradable permits.*[43] These policy
tools use prices and other market mechanisms to create economic
incentives—penalties or rewards—for individuals or firms to induce
them to change their behavior in ways that reduce social harms or
secure other social benefits.

8. *Contracting.*[44] This is a business arrangement between a government agency and a private for-profit or nonprofit entity in which
the entity is paid to deliver, on the government's behalf and under
conditions specified in the contract, certain products or services to the
agency or to third parties (such as clients in a social services program).
One public policy expert calls this process, and the policy uses that
the executive branch can make of it, "the power of the purchaser."[45]

9. *Grants.*[46] These are payments from government to a recipient
organization (typically another level of government or a nonprofit
group) or to an individual. They are intended to either stimulate or
support some sort of service or activity by the recipient. The grants
can take the form of cash, land, or anything else of value.

10. *Loans and loan guarantees.*[47] In a direct loan, the government
borrows from the Treasury to lend money directly to borrowers, and
then services the loan and—if the borrowers default—forecloses or
otherwise attempts to collect. With a loan guarantee, a private lender
such as a commercial bank or mortgage lender makes the loan to the
borrower. The government agrees to make full or partial payment to
the lender in case the borrower defaults on the guaranteed loan. The
private lender originates the loan, secures the government guarantee,
and services the loan according to government regulations or minimum standards.

11. *Tax expenditure.*[48] A tax expenditure is a provision in the
federal tax law that usually encourages certain behavior by individuals or firms by deferring, reducing, or eliminating their tax obligation.
In this way, the government pursues its policy objectives not by
spending the tax dollars it collects but by allowing individuals or cor-

porations to keep and spend dollars that they would otherwise have to pay the government.

12. Vouchers.[49] A voucher is a subsidy that grants purchasing power in a certain amount, or as a percentage of some price, to an individual the government wants to assist in order to enable the recipient to choose among a set of goods and services (restricted according to the terms of the voucher program) whose consumption the government wants to encourage. By giving program beneficiaries the resource (i.e., the exchange value of the voucher), it gives them control over the consumption decision rather than placing that resource and control in the hands of providers of the vouchered good or service.

13. Private cause of action.[50] This policy tool gives a right to individuals or other entities to seek monetary compensation (damages) or injunctive relief through the judicial system for certain types of loss caused by the negligence, breach of contract, or other wrongful conduct of others. This right is ordinarily recognized or established by common law courts but may also be created by statute or, in some cases, by administrative regulation. As a mechanism for preventing loss, it can be a decentralized, privately initiated, privately processed alternative to other tools.

INSTITUTIONS

Policy making and implementation are conducted through formal institutions, and these institutions are suffused with their distinctive cultures. In this section, I make no attempt to introduce and explain the principal institutions that shape government policy, which is a huge undertaking best left to political science textbooks and one that many of my readers may not need. Instead, I shall briefly mention here four more or less formal or structural elements of the institutional landscape. (The more informal political culture that surrounds and shapes these institutions is discussed in chapter 4.)

These elements are: (1) separation of powers at the national level; (2) federalism; (3) parties, campaign finance, and plurality elections;

and (4) media. In discussing them, I shall stress their impact on policy effectiveness, which even otherwise well-informed readers may seriously underestimate or misconceive.

Separation of Powers. The federal government (and to a large extent its state government counterparts) is a theater of unending titanic conflicts among the executive, legislative, and judicial branches— and often *within* each of those branches. This system of "separate institutions sharing power" exhibits many virtues,[51] particularly the protection of what Isaiah Berlin termed "negative liberty."[52] These virtues are justly celebrated in liberal theory and in democratic practice. Another consequence of this system, however, is a veritable scrum of vigorously competing power centers that often produces public policies that, while interest-driven and democratically legitimate, are so (literally) compromised that they are ambiguous, hard to administer, and even incoherent. By incoherence, I mean inconsistency or illogic, a genuine problem for, or at least constraint on, public policy effectiveness. In the rough-and-tumble policy world, however, too much fastidiousness about coherence is probably unrealistic.[53]

Each of the three branches contributes to this policy free-for-all, which is rendered even messier by intrabranch conflicts simply by doing its constitutionally ordained job. The framers of the Constitution intended such conflicts, with the policy incoherence that such conflicts would tend to produce, in order to keep the federal government from infringing unduly on the powers of the states and the liberties of the people in civil society.* Sometimes, this policy free-for-all yields reasonably good outcomes when compared with policy-making processes, such as Westminster-type systems, that are designed to minimize executive-legislative conflicts. Pietro Nivola, for example, argues that America's superior post-recession performance relative to Europe's "may well have much to do with the actions that

---

*As James Madison's "Federalist No. 51" famously put it, "[T]he great security against a gradual concentration of the several powers in the same department, consists in giving to those who administer each department the necessary constitutional means and personal motives to resist encroachments of the other. . . . Ambition must be made to counteract ambition."

our system *impeded*, not just the actions that it permitted. Unlike the British parliamentary model—so admired for its capacity to act decisively—our separation of powers, with its sometimes frustrating checks and balances, blocked precipitous budget-cutting and tax increases."[54] Chapter 10 discusses how the separation of powers affects bureaucratic policymaking and implementation in our system.

At a time when the federal policy agenda was exceedingly limited by today's standards, albeit daunting enough—to prevent dangerous wars, maintain the fragile union, promote commerce, settle the vast interior, deliver the mail, and gain investment and forbearance from Europe—domestic policy confusion was the least of our problems. Today, when federal spending constitutes 22 percent of gross domestic product, we have vastly more reason to worry about such confusion. A striking example of this confusion occurred in the wake of the Newtown, Connecticut, mass school shooting when president Barack Obama vowed not merely to seek gun control legislation from Congress, which often occurs with highly controversial legislation promoted by either party, but to use his independent authority to accomplish administratively some of the same ends without congressional action. Many months later, few of the twenty-three executive orders he issued have been implemented, and his nomination of a permanent director of the key firearms regulatory agency—a position that has been vacant since 2006!—has not even been scheduled for a Senate hearing.[55]

Federalism. Like the "horizontal" separation of powers, the "vertical" separation, which we call federalism, was designed to protect state prerogatives and individual liberty, not to facilitate federal policy coherence. Indeed, when the Constitution was adopted, federalism was an entirely novel invention for so large a polity and was expected to inhibit federal programmatic initiative and performance. Even so, the relationship was complicated and unstable from the outset; federal commandeering of state officials for some federal purposes was widely endorsed in the early republic, only to be opposed later on.[56]

The expectation that the states would inhibit federal power has in one sense been turned on its head in the modern era: the states have participated in, and to some extent instigated, the vast expansion of national policy making since the 1960s, although resisting it in particular cases. The states play essential roles in the political support, substantive content, administration, and substantial funding of these (nominally) federal policies. As Nelson Polsby put it, numerous policy domains "cannot possibly be understood without a disaggregated look at the activities, policies, decisions, and inclinations within each of the fifty states."[57] I elaborate on this theme in chapter 4, under the rubric of localism.

For present purposes, however, the more important point is that these roles vastly complicate and confuse the policy system in ways that will become apparent in part 2. In emphasizing this, I certainly do not mean to disparage American federalism. Quite the contrary, it has succeeded admirably in making more workable than otherwise a federal policy juggernaut that the framers could never have imagined and would certainly have opposed. As Martha Derthick, a leading scholar of federalism, observes, "It takes a very large leap to imagine the United States with a unitary government, run from Washington with the help only of wholly subordinate units, and a still larger leap to suppose that such a country—it would of course need a different name—would be a better place to live."[58]

Parties, campaign finance, and plurality elections. The American party system is a creature of this federalism. At its inception, the Jeffersonian Democratic-Republicans and Hamiltonian Federalists were largely sectional parties—and this pattern (with name changes, and solidified by the Civil War) continued essentially until the New Deal. The party system today is experiencing remarkable changes. During most of the twentieth century, the two major parties were notably less programmatic and ideological, and far more heterogeneous demographically, than their European counterparts. Essentially bargaining entities, they were organized and administered largely at the state and local levels, coming together nationally only for the quadrennial presidential election. Polsby, probably the leading scholar of both the party system and the Congress, viewed "each of the two American major parties [as] in most respects a loose coalition of state parties.

These coalitions are not structured alike. Democrats are primarily a mosaic of interests making claims on government; Republicans are bound together much more by ideological agreement. . . . [It is] in its devolved aspect close to a one-hundred party system." Accordingly—and also because of numerous primary contests that the weak parties cannot prevent—many more (and longer) elections are held than other liberal democracies.[59]

In addition, these votes—particularly those for Congress and the presidency—tend to be more fiercely competitive between the parties than they were during most of the twentieth century, when the solid Democratic control of the South enabled that party to control the House (with two brief interruptions) from 1930 until 1994, and the Senate for most of that period. The periodic gerrymandering of House districts has reduced this competitiveness only slightly in recent years, and displaced much of it to party primaries.[60] These closely contested general and primary elections are both a cause and a consequence of higher campaign spending, which in turn has increased the reliance by parties and candidates on private campaign contributions and other forms of cash and in-kind support. This reliance, which parties and candidates regard with some ambivalence, has been heightened considerably by the recent emergence of Super PACs, 527 committees, and 501(c)(4) organizations that can engage in unlimited independent expenditures funded by individuals and groups,[61] and by Supreme Court decisions that allow corporations and unions to make unlimited independent expenditures.[62] These developments are deeply controversial for several reasons: their supposed threats to political equality; suspicions that these putatively independent expenditures are surreptitiously coordinated with the campaigns and candidates; and doubts about how effective (and constitutional) ostensibly equalizing legal reforms have been and would be in the future, having been crafted by incumbent politicians determined to disadvantage their challengers. The effects of the campaign finance rules are discussed in greater depth in chapter 7.

Less remarked but perhaps even more relevant to government performance is how this heavy reliance on private, independent campaign support reduces the control by candidates and parties of their campaign messages and strategies and thus their political behavior once in office. As candidates swiftly learn where their bread is now buttered, the new system encourages them to be freelance entrepreneurs rather than party loyalists, which weakens party influence over politicians. Moreover, the growing frequency, competitiveness, and cost of primary and general election battles have not only increased the level of conflict within Congress and between it and the presidency; they have also made elected politicians, and the agency policy makers they influence, more accountable and sensitive to shifts in voter sentiment—shifts that the parties are less able to mediate. Arguably, this more exquisite electoral sensitivity is a good thing; it certainly accords with the textbook model of democracy. (I say "arguably" because precisely how free politicians should be of constituent pressures even in a democracy is a perennially difficult question; Edmund Burke's letter to the electors of Bristol, November 3, 1774, is a classic discussion of this issue.) For present purposes, however, its most noteworthy effect is to render federal policy ever more unstable, mercurial, and inconsistent.

The future of the American party system is uncertain. The proportion of voters who eschew a party affiliation and call themselves independents was about 40 percent in 2011,[63] a record high. Although the share of independents usually drops in presidential election years, the May 2012 figure reached 44 percent (nine points more than at the same stage of the 2008 campaign) before dropping a bit. Nor is party decline peculiar to the United States; it is even more pronounced in Europe.[64] The reasons for this decline—and for the concomitant rise of what political scientist Russell Dalton calls "apartisan" voters—are complex and controversial, but one of the causes is the changing media, discussed immediately below.[65]

How this less representative party system will affect policy making is not yet clear, but several consequences seem likely. Deprived of strong, dependable party structures, legislative politics and public policy will probably be more volatile and unpredictable than before, which will reduce the credibility of government programs even further, a problem discussed in chapter 5. This greater uncertainty will affect party finances and thus campaigning to some extent, while rippling through the rest of the policy system in a variety of other ways.

The relationship between parties and policies is mediated by a distinctive institution: plurality elections (also called "winner-take-all" or "first-past-the-post"), which is the rule in almost all American elections, most notably in the Electoral College for the presidency. This institution profoundly affects politics, parties, and policy making. First, it encourages and fortifies a system of two broadly based parties. This contrasts with systems of proportional representation, common in continental Europe, which usually produce partisan fragmentation in the legislature with arguably more faithful representation of voters' views but greater instability in the governing coalition. Plurality elections also contrast with majoritarian elections, which award victory only to candidates who win more than 50 percent of the vote (either in the first round or after a runoff election). Second, the plurality system tends to reduce sharp ideological cleavages by inducing minorities to seek a home within the two major parties. These aspects of the system lead to more centrist policies, as the two parties seek to appeal to the "median voter." Plurality elections, like any electoral system, has its characteristic disadvantages, especially the "wasted votes" of those who either supported a losing candidate and have no party explicitly representing their views in the legislature, or whose votes exceeded what was needed to elect the candidate.[66] This feature also tends to reduce voter turnout and to encourage gerrymandering. Third, and perhaps most significant to policy substance, plurality-based two-party systems are much less likely—indeed, one-third as likely according to a study of seventeen large democracies—than proportional representation systems to elect center-left governments that will redistribute wealth to the poor.[67] All things considered, the United States has found that plurality elections' advantages—especially a stable two-party system that tends to absorb most social conflict, that both reflects and promotes political moderation in the electorate, and that therefore avoids extreme public policies—are compelling.

Media. Even the traditional American media, compared with that in other liberal democracies, is decentralized, locally owned (for newspapers), crowded (for radio and TV stations), competitive, wholly independent of government, and opinionated but largely non-partisan.[68] The "new" web-based media is even more so. Its technologies have rendered the traditional news cycle utterly anachronistic, vastly increasing the opportunities for public influence on policy making rapidly and in a variety of nontraditional forms. Feedback loops, once attenuated, are now almost instantaneous, giving sudden gusts of public opinion outsized influence over politicians' behavior, reducing officials' leeways. Using the media to build public support for policies has become more difficult given the public's greater skepticism about media accuracy and bias and given the media's greater negativity about politics and politicians.[69] These media-related changes may also have made it more difficult for politicians to negotiate compromises, lest they be attacked immediately by partisans in the media before the difficult bargains can be struck.

CHAPTER 4

The Political Culture of Policy Making

A government's political culture—the ensemble of institutions, practices, and attitudes that animate public policy—is in a sense its DNA. Political culture does not wholly predetermine policy outcomes, but it does create very powerful tendencies and constraints on which outcomes are possible and likely. This culture does change over time. The most important examples are attitudes toward ethnic minorities, gay people, and women, and the "new system" of policy making discussed in chapter 1. But absent an existential threat such as an all-out war or a deep economic depression, most changes in public policy occur over generations within limits and in forms largely dictated by the political culture.

In every sphere of human activity, of course, the gravitation pull of familiarity is immense. The comforts of routine, illusion, fear of the unknown, and self-satisfaction (even smugness) among most elites reinforce the social status quo. These conservative forces, however, are constantly being challenged and subverted by two related forces: technology and popular culture.[1] What primarily drives and exploits the relentless dynamism of these two forces is human ingenuity and motivation, expressed through market and nonmarket activity. Popular culture and technology are the spheres in which the passion for tumultuous change that foreigners have long associated with American life is chiefly to be found, and they then transform other, supposedly stable, areas of civil society such as religion.

Political culture could hardly be more different. Where popular culture is dynamic and subversive, political culture is stable and conservative. The former is irreverent and youth-driven, the latter venerates institutions and is cemented by the sheer electoral power of the elderly. Like popular culture, political culture does change, but the pace of that change is glacial, and when it does occur the change agents, exquisitely sensitive to the appeal of stability in this culture, tend to (mis)represent it as continuity. This misrepresentation is most self-conscious in the courts, where a common law tradition frequently creates new rules while concealing these innovations with citation of precedents, disavowals of invention, and other forms of judicial sleight of hand. Politicians have their own techniques for promoting change in the guise of a firm fidelity to the past.

This contrast between the extraordinary dynamism of civil society and the equally remarkable stability, even inertia, of government is by no means a contradiction. Disparate spheres of life often have different cultures and produce different identities; the culture of one's family life differs from the culture of one's workplace, political organization, consumer activity, religion, and so forth. This normative and experiential diversity, this protean character of our identity-forming, value-expressing contexts, is characteristic of modernism, which is itself a kind of transcendent metaculture. Our experience of modernism is both liberating (we can take on different roles and identities) and alienating (we struggle to achieve a rooted, integrated personality). Despite the ministrations of psychotherapy, religion, yoga, and other contending suppliers of meaning, it seems inescapable.

The unique culture that shapes our policy making is my chief concern in this chapter. I focus here on ten elements of the culture: (1) constitutionalism, (2) decentralization, (3) protection of individual rights, (4) interest group pluralism, (5) acceptance of social and economic inequality, (6) religion and political moralism, (7) social diversity, (8) populist suspicion of technical expertise and official discretion, (9) public opinion, and (10) civil society.* (Another cultural

---

*I put to one side, and have discussed elsewhere, other cultural factors—for example, demography and patriotism—that are highly relevant to policy making and distinguish the

sphere, the market, is so powerful and pervasive that I devote an entire chapter—chapter 7—to it.) These cultural commitments, I believe, help to explain why our public policies fail so often; they are in this sense a large part of the price that we pay for preserving these features of our culture.

Before proceeding, let me clarify the nature of my argument. I do not believe that these features of our political culture represent past choices that are now readily reversible. Quite the contrary: some of these cultural values are constitutionally inscribed and all are so deeply embedded in our national psyche that they are alterable, if at all, only slowly and at the margins, particularly since there is no evidence of any widespread popular wish to repudiate them. Nor do I contend here that these values *should* be abandoned, even on the doubtful assumption that they *could* be. To responsibly support such a change, one would first have to clarify and then assess the complex normative and empirical trade-offs. Such an analysis far exceeds this book's scope. What I do maintain is that our political culture is one important reason, along with others elaborated in this book, why the United States is a difficult nation to govern effectively.

CONSTITUTIONALISM

As countless commentators on American politics have observed, the Constitution is our civic religion, venerated and constantly appealed to by participants in public debate as the ultimate authority and source of fundamental principles that mark our faith as a people. For purposes of this particular discussion, the important point about the Constitution is that it is exceedingly difficult to amend and thus casts a shadow over policy innovations of certain kinds. For example—and for better or worse—the constitutional principles of federalism, while broadly permissive, limit what the federal government may require the states to do, how and what states may tax, and which judicial remedies they

United States from other modern liberal democracies in degree if not in kind. See Peter H. Schuck & James Q. Wilson, "Looking Back," in Schuck & Wilson, eds., *Understanding America: The Anatomy of an Exceptional Nation*, (2008), 627–43.

may provide. The First Amendment severely limits Congress's power to regulate campaign finance. The Seventeenth Amendment prevents states from imposing term limits on members of Congress. And so forth.

The constitutional restraints on government action influence how the economy, the bureaucracy, the legal system, and the mass media operate, all of which shape and significantly constrain policy makers' adoption, design, implementation, enforcement, and subsequent revision of government programs. First, the political system is presidential, not parliamentary, yet the Congress is almost certainly the most powerful legislature, both constitutionally and functionally, in the world. Most members of Congress are elected on schedules that are to some degree independent of the presidential election and come from states and districts where local issues often influence the outcome more than does presidential popularity. Congress can reject even the most important presidential proposals without causing a new election to be held, and when there is a new election, the support or opposition that legislative candidates receive from the president ordinarily counts for little, even when the presidential party controls the Congress. If the policy process produces failure, as it too often does, Congress is largely responsible.[2]

Second, the constitutional authority of the federal courts to constrain the actions of both agencies and legislatures—and in a real sense, to make law—makes the policy-making system remarkably accessible to the people. As discussed below, the Constitution—especially the Bill of Rights and the Fourteenth Amendment—strongly orients judicial power to the creation and protection of individual rights, usually at the expense of governmental claims.

Third, the constitutionally constrained system of administrative law delegates enormous power and discretion to federal agencies, but under political conditions that make it unusually difficult for them to establish the democratic legitimacy of their actions, especially when compared to their European counterparts. This, coupled with the fact that the constitutional system also leaves many of the most important political functions—education, land use, criminal justice, transportation, domestic relations, tort law, occupational licensure, and much more—in the hands of state and local governments means that federal policy makers' writs have limited reach.

DECENTRALIZATION

Hostility to centralized power has deep roots going back to the colonial period. As we saw in chapter 3, this hostility is institutionalized in a distribution of governing authority with both horizontal (separation of powers) and vertical (federalism) elements. Americans depend less on government—and hence on its effectiveness—than Europeans do. More skeptical of the gains that more government might generate, Americans are more intent on minimizing the harm that it can do. (Game theorists call this a "minimax" strategy.)

But the theoretical debate over the functional and power-diffusing values of decentralization (on which a vast literature already exists) is not my focus here. After all, state and local policy makers are not waiting for Washington to adopt those values; they are initiating their own programs to fill the policy vacuum created by federal failure and gridlock.[3] In this section, then, I focus on how they use localism and privatism, two aspects of decentralization, to resist federal policy controls.

Localism. By localism, I mean the commitment to the principle that if governmental power must be exercised, it should be exercised at the lowest level of government that can do so: the states and their localities (including special-purpose units of government).* This notion has several normative components. One is the claim that state and local levels of government are "closer to the people" and in that sense more democratically accountable. (In reality, most citizens know even less about their state and local governments than they do about the federal one, those elections are usually less prominent, and the quality of state and local officialdom, as measured by formal educational credentials and some performance criteria such as incidence

*This power allocation principle is widely accepted in Europe under the rubric of "subsidiarity," which is also a norm of Catholic teaching.

of corruption, is lower.) A second is the claim that state and local decisions can better reflect the diverse social conditions that pose such an immense challenge to federal policy making. A third claim is that localism assures that error costs of misguided policies will be low.[4]

Whatever the truth of these claims, the public clearly believes it. In a 2013 Pew Research Center poll, only 28 percent of respondents viewed the federal government favorably. This compared with 57 percent and 63 percent—and majorities of both Democrats and Republicans—who viewed their state and local governments favorably. This gap between views of federal and local government, Pew reported, has never been wider, yet the 63 percent favoring their local governments is unchanged in recent years. Even more striking at a time when Democrats control both the White House and Senate, only 41 percent of Democrats view the federal government favorably, down ten points from the previous year.[5] I speculate that this reflects their generally favorable perceptions of their local schools, police, and land use and other policies, as well as the negative attitudes toward the federal government summarized in chapter 1.

This pervasive belief in localism is reflected in several facts about American policy making that are remarkable, especially compared with other countries' governments. First, very few domestic programs that are both federally created and federally funded are administered exclusively from Washington; the most important examples are Social Security and defense. (Medicare does not involve the states, but it is mostly administered through carriers and intermediaries that are widely distributed throughout the country.[6]) Almost all other federal programs delegate federal funds and substantial policy-making authority to the states (and on occasion, directly to localities). Second, as noted above, many of the most important public functions are primarily creatures of state and local law, funded and administered at state and local levels. Third (and related to the first two), the state and local government collectively employ about seven times more officials than does the federal government's civilian workforce—19.8 million versus 2.8 million, respectively, in 2009.[7]

As a political matter, this results in programs' funding being divided into a relatively large number of smaller pieces—often too small for policy success, and inimical to economies of scale—as members of Congress insist that their constituencies receive some of the money. In 2008, for example, Congress created a special program to help local governments finance clean energy projects through conservation bonds, with Washington paying part of the cost. Four years later, few states and localities had participated because once the subsidy was spread nationwide, the amount available to each locality was too small to pursue projects.[8] This is true even of many experimental programs, such as Model Cities in the 1960s and Race to the Top in the current era of president Barack Obama, which were originally designed to achieve critical mass in order to demonstrate their potential or reward innovation but had to spread the funds too thin in order to satisfy each member of Congress.[9] From a policy perspective, this localism means that even programs that the federal government creates and largely or exclusively funds must almost always rely on 89,500 units of state and local governments not only to administer and enforce them but also to adopt state laws to authorize and implement the programs in those jurisdictions. This system of "cooperative federalism" (as it is optimistically called) aims to exploit the putative virtues of localism but often produces policy chaos and incoherence,[10] even in areas of great national importance. Part of the problem is that states may be unwilling to implement or enforce federal law, even when offered carrots to do so, and the federal sticks are far weaker and cruder than the law on its face might suggest.[11] The problem is typified by three high-priority federal programs: the No Child Left Behind Act, the REAL ID Act, and the Affordable Care Act.

No Child Left Behind, a program adopted by a bipartisan Congress in 2001 with high hopes in the glow of president George W. Bush's first year (before 9/11), has disappointed even modest expectations and, apart from its increased focus on school accountability, is fairly described as ineffective.[12] Such an indictment should acknowledge that the condition being addressed—inadequate student and school performance in disadvantaged communities—is among the most intractable of all social problems, but localism makes it that much harder for the federal government to solve. Even President Obama, who along with his secretary of education has firmly embraced the program, in effect conceded defeat in July 2012 when, more than a decade after the law's enactment, he exempted schools in more than half the nation from central provisions of the law. This followed years of fierce resistance by the states and Congress's repeated refusal since 2007 to reauthorize the law.[13]

The REAL ID Act, enacted in 2005 at the urging of the 9/11 Commission, was intended to reduce terrorism risks by requiring each state to assure that driver's licenses and identification cards that the state issues are reliable enough to be recognized as "official" under federal law. The act prescribed a May 2008 deadline for compliance, but when all fifty states demanded extensions of the deadline, Congress agreed. Many states explicitly refused to enact implementing legislation, and the federal government has granted extensions that now extend to 2017. In 2012—eleven years after 9/11 and seven years after enactment—the Government Accountability Office issued a report detailing many states' continued noncompliance and the federal government's failure to address persistent authentication problems.[14]

In the case of the Affordable Care Act, enacted in 2010, the law provides for state-based health insurance exchanges in which individuals and small businesses can shop for affordable, comprehensive health insurance plans. These exchanges are at the core of the federal scheme, yet by November 2013, only seventeen states and the District of Columbia had opted to run their own exchanges; by default, the federal government must establish and run the rest.[15]

Localism—specifically, the geographic mobility that it encourages—poses another obstacle to policy coherence and effectiveness. Geographic mobility by individuals varies significantly by education level. Almost half of college graduates move away from their birth states by age thirty, whereas 27 percent and 17 percent of high school graduates and dropouts, respectively, do so.[16] Firms, and to some extent individuals, can and often do respond to a policy that they oppose by relocating to a different jurisdiction or region with a more attractive policy mix. (This is known as the Tiebout effect.) Relocation is facilitated in a federal system in which different states or regions provide different goods, services, costs, and amenities. For example, firms often move to areas offering more congenial tax, labor, immigrant, regulatory, and other policies.[17] Individuals often move to find better schools, lower taxes, greater job opportunities, and more desirable public goods (or better weather; the evidence does not indicate that they move for more generous welfare benefits).[18] State and local governments may alter their policies to meet this competition—often a good thing for the public—but such adaptations take time, political will, and tactical skills, which are all hard to come by.

More to the point here, Tiebout-motivated mobility also frustrates *federal* policy effectiveness. Washington's efforts to promote integration in housing and schools, for example, are constantly being subverted by firms' and individuals' choices and geographical mobility. Such efforts often encourage white, and even middle-class black, flight that simply exacerbates the problem in the communities of origin.[19] Freedom of choice has race- and class-separating effects in many policy-relevant areas of social life, which puts it in tension with more egalitarian, integrative ideals. But so long as liberal America embraces individual choice as a paramount value—and there is no sign that its appeal is waning in residential location or any other area of life—federal policy makers cannot effectively prevent these effects but must instead focus on indirect policies of remediation in the now increasingly segregated communities of origin.

Privatism. Localism, in which power is delegated to (or retained by) state and local governments, hardly exhausts the valuation of decentralized power in our political culture. Indeed, decentralization is instantiated far more radically in the norms and forms of privatism, which holds that individuals, families, firms, and other civil society groups should exercise the dominant power over important decisions that in many or most other modern democracies have long been made primarily or exclusively by government. The list of such domains is very long, but even a partial one includes education, social welfare services, health care, low-income housing, museums and other cultural institutions, and much philanthropy. In the United States, even political parties (discussed in chapter 3) are treated as private organizations, and religious organizations are as a constitutional matter hands-off for government. This contrasts sharply with the tradition in Europe, where government supports parties and religions in various ways.

The arguments favoring privatism are both principled and functional. We value individual autonomy in its own right as an expression of human dignity and freedom. In terms of Isaiah Berlin's negative liberty conception, government intrusion on that autonomy is ordinarily an intrusion, a diminution of liberty. From a Kantian perspective, legally required actions not only infringe on liberty but deprive such actions of the distinctive moral quality produced by the exercise of autonomous wills. For libertarians, such requirements violate our natural rights to be free, within very broad limits, to do as we wish. The functional arguments for privatism are also appealing. As citizens are the best judge of their interests, their free choices will yield efficient outcomes. When government makes such choices for them, government will frequently make the wrong choices, and incur greater inefficiencies in the process, for all the systematic reasons discussed in this book. Citizens deprived of autonomous choice are infantilized to an extent, as their capacity for reasoned deliberation and initiative atrophies.

This insistence that individuals retain the right to make choices that in other societies the government would make for them has been exemplified recently by federal statutes allowing for defaults that individuals or their private delegates (such as employers) may select but that the government may not establish. Advocates of a "behavioral law and economics" approach to policy making, who emphasize that individuals often make irrational choices, have urged government to "nudge" them toward better choices by establishing default provisions that will govern individuals unless they specifically choose to reject them.[20] Christine Jolls notes that where Congress has done so— as in the Pension Protection Act of 2006—it has been careful to allow *employers* to establish a default for their employees' retirement savings plan rather than allowing the *government* to do so. Jolls observes, "Yet such a default was never even seriously considered in the American context. Instead, [Congress] chose an arrangement under which a private actor, not the government, selects among potential default contributions, a positive 401(k) contribution versus a zero 401(k) contribution." This is precisely the opposite of what other liberal democratic countries like New Zealand and the United Kingdom have done.[21] Nor is this a one-off instance of preferring private choice to government-set defaults; Jolls also shows that in the Dodd-Frank Wall Street Reform and Consumer Protection Act of 2011, Congress also rejected a legislated mortgage structure default. Strikingly, Congress was aware that both of the rejected defaults would almost certainly have benefitted the vast majority of citizens, but the privatism principle prevailed nonetheless.[22] The point here is not the merits of Congress's policy decisions but instead that the political culture prefers to respect individual choices, however irrational, to government-knows-better paternalism.

Such arguments also help to explain the trend toward "privatizing"—that is, contracting out to private profit or nonprofit providers—a growing number of basic functions traditionally performed by governments, such as corrections, waste management, charter schools, water and electric supply, revenue collection, some highway maintenance, and so forth. (As noted in chapter 1, market actors perform many functions that are governmental in other advanced societies.) Studies indicate that these services can usually be provided better and more cheaply by private groups due to competition, more access to capital, nonunion labor, technology, cost consciousness, and other efficiencies.[23] How accountable these privatized services are to taxpayers and consumers is another matter, for agency supervision through contract provisions, periodic monitoring, and other accountability techniques varies in its intensity, credibility (see chapter 6), and effectiveness. Abuses are most likely to occur when the target populations are poor, vulnerable to predation, and politically weak, and when oversight is lax. (Indeed, such abuses occur whether the providers are private or public.) Investigations by officials and journalists yield many blistering critiques and even some criminal charges, but one suspects that these publicized exposes are but the tip of the iceberg of abuse. Chapter 6, on managing fraud, waste, and abuse, discusses these problems more fully.

PROTECTION OF INDIVIDUAL RIGHTS

Long before Alexis de Tocqueville and ever since, foreign observers have been struck by Americans' faith—some view it as a naive and unwarranted faith—in the power of individuals to shape their own destinies through their exercises of freedom. Americans, far more than Europeans, believe that success in life is determined by their own efforts rather than "forces outside their own control." In 2012, according to the Pew Research Center, fully 77 percent of Americans feel that way; even in the United Kingdom, the European country that most felt the same way, only 57 percent took that view, as did 45 percent of the Chinese.[24] Compared with other peoples, Americans have especially cherished "negative" liberty, understood as freedom from government restraint, more than "positive" liberty, which imagines government as the source and shaper of moral community and guarantor of the resources necessary to develop individual capacity and social fulfillment.

This belief in individualism causes Americans to place an unparalleled emphasis on the notion of individual rights in every area of social life, defining public issues as matters of conflicting rights rather than of different preferences.* This emphasis also makes them correspondingly suspicious of group rights like affirmative action.[25] It also causes Americans to disparage their governing institutions, especially Congress (whose approval rating reached historic lows in 2013) and the bureaucracy, even as they revere the constitutional system that has created and sustained these institutions. When asked whether

---

*Ironically, according to recent research, "welfare rights" language was first deployed not by advocacy groups but by public agencies in the 1930s to justify expanded federal administrative responsibility for the poor. See Karen M. Tani, "Welfare and Rights before the Movement: Rights as a Language of the State," *Yale Law Journal* 122 (2012), 314.

they "completely agree" that the government should provide a safety net, only one-third of Americans say "yes," compared to 60 percent or more in most European countries. This ethos of individualism is manifested in almost all of the institutions and public policies discussed in this book. Religious pluralism, with a marked emphasis (even in Catholicism, to an extent) on decentralized administration, congregation-centered organization, and doctrines of individual access to Scripture and God, is probably the most important and historically continuous of these individualistic manifestations. But much of the same pronounced individualism is also true, mutatis mutandis, of the American economy, education systems, public administration, health care system, law enforcement, and much, much more.

This cultural commitment to individual rights is most evident in the extraordinary power of American courts, which the public esteems as the ultimate custodians and protectors of those rights. The link between this obsession with rights and the extent of judicial authority is stronger and deeper in the United States than in any other constitutional democracy—including countries such as Canada and Germany, whose judiciaries are already powerful and becoming more so.

This link goes far to explain several important features of our policy system. First, as legal historian Lawrence Friedman observes, "Other countries may have as much law as the United States, if we define law broadly enough. But they have much less lawyering. They are also less rights-conscious. They give more power and discretion to administrative agencies, and they make it harder to challenge these agencies in court. . . . Only the United States feels it is in the grips of a litigation crisis."[26] As James Q. Wilson put it, "we are not more litigious because we have more lawyers: we have more lawyers because we are so litigious."[27] Private lawyers and the clients and causes they represent thus play an outsized role in the policy process.

Second, the open-ended nature of most legal texts, particularly the Bill of Rights and the due process and equal protection clauses, both invites and demands judicial interpretation, which often amounts to judicial lawmaking. (The line between them is itself a matter of interpretation about which reasonable lawyers vehemently disagree.) This inevitably injects even deferential judges into the policy-making process.

Third, public law litigation, relatively undeveloped in other democracies' legal systems but widespread here,* empowers individual and class plaintiffs to increase individual influence on the policy-making process by getting courts to shape statutes and administrative rules and grant additional remedies. Almost all law-and-policy scholars who have carefully studied this policy-making-through-litigation phenomenon condemn the courts' policy incompetence, the collateral damage that their interventions have wreaked on the effectiveness of government programs, and the culture of "adversarial legalism" (in Robert Kagan's phrase) that supports it. These criticisms include: long implementation delays, increased regulatory costs, inconsistent interpretations by different courts, a rigidified decision process, technical ignorance, invading agency discretion, displacing agency expertise, ignoring or misunderstanding congressional intent, distorting regulatory priorities, advantaging certain political groupings over others, increasing policy uncertainty, elevating the interests of individual litigants over those of society at large, and many others—most of this in the name of protecting individual rights against official error.[28] These large, chiefly adverse consequences of policy making through litigation, then, may plausibly be seen as a disadvantage of our veneration of individual rights.

The rights obsession (not too strong a word) of Americans bears another disadvantage. Legal scholar Mary Ann Glendon argues that this pervasive "rights talk" impoverishes political discourse in a number of troubling ways. Citizens, she claims, see almost all social controversies as a zero-sum clash of competing rights instead of a field of competing interests in which accommodation is desirable. This discourse engenders litigation in which the courts often formulate rights

*A major exception is the Supreme Court of India, which entertains "public interest litigation" in which that court has required bureaucracies and legislatures to take actions that even activist American courts would not be so bold as to order. For some examples, see Peter H. Schuck, "Fixer-Upper," *American Lawyer*, December 2011, 78.

in absolute terms, making them difficult to compromise. Such a rights culture, she argues, emphasizes a radical individualism in place of social responsibility, self-assertion instead of dialogue and fellowship, and conflict rather than collegiality, creating a winner-take-all ethos that is "inhospitable to society's losers." Glendon, a prominent communitarian and advocate of Catholic social doctrine, finds the American approach to rights far less congenial in these respects than that of European polities.[29]

INTEREST GROUP PLURALISM

As in all democratic political systems (and even in some autocracies, like China[30]), vigorous competition among groups for membership and other resources, along with competition among these groups for influence over the shape of public policy, are central dynamics of the governmental process. The term *pluralism* hardly seems adequate to convey the remarkable number and diversity of these interest groups, or the extent of their influence on policy makers. James Madison called these groups "factions" and in his "Federalist No. 10" famously described how their self-interested activities could, in a large republic like ours, advance rather than paralyze democratic government.[31] Almost two centuries later, political scientist Theodore Lowi inveighed against their success at penetrating policy process and outcomes at the expense of the less organized public interest.[32]

Interest groups affect every stage of policy making: idea generation, information flows, agenda formation and prioritization, recruitment and selection of officials, public education and mobilization, the legislative and regulatory processes, budgeting, implementation, and even post-hoc evaluations of program effectiveness. The excerpt from James Q. Wilson and John DiIulio quoted in chapter 1 notes that the "new system" has coincided with, and to some extent been caused by, a substantial growth in the number of Washington-based interest groups; about 70 percent of them opened those offices after 1960, and nearly half did so after 1970. Wilson and DiIulio attribute this proliferation to four main factors: (1) economic changes that created

new interests and redefined old ones; (2) government encouragement of group formation; (3) organizational entrepreneurship; and
(4) the larger government agenda.[33]

Interest group political activity is a mixed blessing. As I have argued elsewhere, it is both inevitable and beneficial in a liberal democracy.[34] But it can also promote unjust, inefficient, and ineffective policies. Although generations of scholars have studied how interest
groups operate and what goals they pursue,[35] they cannot show con-
clusively how much these groups actually influence outcomes. Examples of apparent interest group political efficacy coexist with examples of the groups' failure to get their desired policies. Interest groups
dedicate most of their campaign contributions and lobbying efforts to
legislators they already agree with, helping them make their case; they
spend little time trying to persuade opponents.[36] Causality is almost
impossible to prove. All that the studies can tell us with confidence is
that "lobbyists often get at least some of what they want and more
than they would have gotten had they not entered the fray."[37]

Prominent among these interest groups—but often ignored by
commentators on interest group pluralism (including Lowi)—is the
government itself. The government, of course, is not a single entity;
rather, it is an almost unimaginably complex congeries of institutions
and actors each pursuing some combination of goals. To conceive of
the policy-making process as one in which the government magisteri-
ally sits above and presides over clashing interest groups is a fundamental category mistake. In reality, the discrete components of the
formal government—elected politicians, bureaucracies, civil servants,
legislative staffs, procurement officials, and many others—are active
participants in the political bargaining process, asserting their own institutional prerogatives and interests as energetically as private organizations do. Sometimes these government interests are closely—even
inextricably—allied with private ones, as with the "military-industrial
complex" of which president Dwight D. Eisenhower warned.

In the current economic crisis, public employee unions are among
the most powerful of these progovernment interests. Despite the limitations of the Hatch Act, the unions' political influence on both Con-

gress and executive branch policy makers is substantial, deriving from their numbers (especially in Maryland and Virginia, where many of them live and vote), their financial war chests, their lobbying skills, and their provision of many essential public services (as with air traffic controllers).[38] This influence has at least four far-reaching effects on government. First, these unions heavily support Democrats, who generally seek to expand government.[39] Second, their compensation, pension benefits, and work rules are among the major forces that raise program costs. The Postal Service is the most notorious of these political-fiscal battlegrounds at the federal level, but the conflicts are even more intense at the state and local levels, where governments are required, often constitutionally, to run balanced budgets.[40] Because their pension plans tend to be much more generous than private pensions (the richer ones are called "Cadillac plans"), they are at the center of bankruptcy risks in Detroit and other municipalities.[41] Third, the unions' opposition to the programmatic and budgetary reforms that are essential to the nation's long-term fiscal solvency makes those reforms very difficult to enact. Fourth, and most important, public employee unions are the strongest interest groups pressing vigorously for a larger government workforce and programmatic agenda. Their raison d'être, after all, is to increase the number, security, compensation, and working conditions of government jobs, thereby enlarging their membership and revenues. From the narrow perspective of their organizational self-interest, these goals will trump fiscal balance and policy effectiveness. We should not be surprised, then, to find the American Federation of Government Employees denouncing proposals to reduce federal prison overcrowding, to cut corrections budgets, and to privatize prison management.

Critics of the political process often focus on the fact that interest groups are unequal in the financial resources that they can bring to bear on it. A recent synthesis of the data on political inequality emphasizes the utter numerical dominance of lobbying groups favoring business interests, and the weaker turnout among lower socioeconomic status voters despite recent reforms facilitating voter registration.[42] This lower turnout, along with our first-past-the-post electoral system (discussed in chapter 3), seem to be important reasons why policies favoring the poor—welfare benefits, for example—are difficult to enact.[43] (Group turnout by blacks, however, was apparently higher than by whites in the 2012 presidential election.)

Academic and journalistic analyses alike show that business interests often get their way in policy disputes, especially when they can unite on a common position.[44] Money counts in politics, and mobilizing key political support (often aided by money) counts even more. Still, even well-heeled, well-connected, well-represented business interests often fail to get their way—particularly (but not only) from Democratic Congresses and administrations. Some other groups have less money but better organizational skills, name recognition or dynastic ties, a larger and strategically distributed voter base, superior contacts in Washington, more charismatic leaders and telegenic messages, broader and more supportive media coverage, stronger legal claims, the inertial advantages of a policy status quo, better arguments on the policy merits, and the most potent electoral asset of all—incumbency. These advantages are more important than ever, given the dramatically lower costs of mobilizing today through e-mail and social media. They often enable diffuse interests to overcome the remorseless "logic of collective action" explained in Mancur Olson's book of that name, discussed in chapter 5.

The business community, moreover, is anything but monolithic. It often divides sharply—for example, between exporters and importers on trade policy,[45] between manufacturing and service industries on tax issues,[46] between large and small companies on tax policy,[47] and among employers, providers, and insurers on health care cost control. The Obama administration's bailout of General Motors and Chrysler was opposed by Ford and foreign car makers. Also, some business interests will coincide with those of consumers, taxpayers, or labor interests—for example, policies favoring deregulation (discussed in chapter 11) or more cost-effective regulation; economic growth and innovation; price and quality competition; wider consumer choice; reduced health care costs; tax reform; and so on. To prevail, they may have to make large concessions to strategically placed adversaries.

The auto bailout, for example, could never have happened without the support of the autoworkers and allied unions in key presidential battleground states that received huge financial and pension protections in return.[48]

The political process is so complex and opaque, and the role of ideological zeitgeist such as environmentalism, gender equality, deregulation, civil rights, and market idolatry is so pervasive, that it is usually impossible—even after the fact—to know for sure how weighty each of the many politically relevant factors might have been in determining the policy outcome. Well-heeled groups often lose out to more impecunious ones; indeed, populist denunciations of corporate influence and moneyed interests are sometimes effective political weapons, as in the defeats of Mitt Romney, who was the business community's standard-bearer, and of Linda McMahon, who spent some $100 million in her 2010 and 2012 failed Senate bids. Corporate interests often refrain from political activity out of fear of retribution if their preferred candidate loses. One cannot plausibly explain in simple materialistic terms the countless legal and political victories of environmental, disability, minority, immigrant, gay rights, AIDS treatment advocacy, small business, proregulation, and other relatively low-budget interest groups. This more nuanced account does not mean, of course, that financial resources are not valuable and sometimes decisive, only that otherwise strong candidates attract much financial support, that financial advantages are often outweighed by other political weaknesses, and that gauging how influential they might have been in any given case is very difficult.

By the same token, claims that regulatory agencies are "captured" by powerful business interests are common but often beg the most important questions: What does capture mean? What are the underlying merits of the dispute? Is there an objectively discernible "public interest" in the matter, or are there instead merely competing conceptions of what constitutes sound public policy? Are there plausible public interest arguments for the positions that the industry advocates and that the government adopts, or are those positions only in the industry's self-interest? If the industry wins, does that necessarily mean that the public loses? Are the regulated firms monolithic such that we can speak intelligibly about "the industry," or are there conflicting interests among these firms that contradict the notion of a single industry position? Can private enforcement litigation constrain regulatory capture? And most important, how often do concentrated interests actually get their way?[49] Unless we can answer these questions with confidence, how can we know what regulatory capture means when it has actually occurred, and how it bears on the merits of any particular policy issue?

Any satisfying answer to these questions, I believe, must bring together two related and mutually informing kinds of inquiries, one empirical and the other theoretical. The first draws upon data about the actual performance of particular policies, assessing their effectiveness in light of the criteria discussed in chapter 2. The second draws upon a rich body of social science analysis to identify and elaborate the deep structural reasons why public policies fail so frequently, why they occasionally succeed, and why they often fall somewhere in between failure and success. Part 2 will integrate the empirical evidence and the theoretical explanations. Chapter 5, for example, analyzes policy makers' incentives, which include their need for interest group support and for policy-relevant information, some of which can be obtained only from such groups. Chapter 7 analyzes how well-functioning markets, which business organizations often claim to promote, tend to impair policy effectiveness. Chapter 8 draws on empirical assessments of many specific programs, including related interest group activity, to show how and why policy implementation fails so often. Chapter 11 does the same for successful policies.

ACCEPTANCE OF SOCIAL AND ECONOMIC INEQUALITY

By most measures, inequality in the United States is rising and is now greater than in other comparable societies.[50] (Consumption-based measures, which focus on the goods and services that people actually have and use, show less inequality than pretax and even posttax measures.) Economists sharply dispute the magnitudes,[51] and especially the causes, which surely include growing educational disparities, particularly affecting men and minorities; assortative mating by high-income couples; competition in manufacturing from low-wage countries; immigration's effects on low-skill American workers; lower rates of marriage and of intact families; high incarceration levels; more economic gains from better education; and redistribution programs that benefit the elderly and well-off disproportionately to low-income families with children.[52]

Although Americans are deeply committed to the ideals of legal equality and equal opportunity, we evidently find current levels of *social* and *economic* inequality regrettable but not a high-priority issue, much less one that our government should do much about. A 2011 Gallup poll found that only 1 percent of Americans believed that it was our most important problem (a percentage even lower than for those who cited foreign aid). Other research finds that even a tutorial presenting inequality as harmful had little or no effect on attitudes but did reduce respondents' trust in government.[53]

Americans, moreover, find inequality more acceptable than Europeans do. Economists Alberto Alesina and Edward Glaeser have compared public attitudes and comment, "Europeans maintain a belief that birth determines status and the poor are trapped. Americans believe that they live in a land of opportunity where the people who stay poor are those who are too lazy to pull themselves up by their own bootstraps. . . . Across countries, places that believe that the poor are trapped are much more likely to redistribute than countries that do not have this belief. Across the United States, the states where more people believe that achievement is determined by family background are more likely to have more generous welfare payments."[54] They note (writing in 2004, before the financial crisis) that these distinctive American attitudes persist in the face of certain realities that might seem to refute them. For example, they cite data indicating that the poor seem to work as hard in the United States as in Europe, and that (contrary to the Horatio Alger myth) social mobility in the United States has stalled and (contrary to common perceptions among Americans) is no longer greater than in some other developed countries.

One possible explanation for this difference—that Americans are less generous toward the poor—is clearly false. Americans are vastly more charitable toward the poor and more generally. Social scientist Arthur Brooks has shown that this is mostly attributable to Americans' far greater religiosity; that most of this charity goes not to religious activities but to secular ones such as education, health, and social welfare; that low-income families give away a higher percentage of their incomes than do better-off families (especially if the former's income is from earned wages rather than government transfers); and that self-described "conservatives" are more likely to give, and give more generously, than self-described "liberals" with comparable incomes. Alesina and Glaeser present additional data consistent with Brooks's claim that Americans are more charitable than Europeans, and speculate that the "public provision of welfare (in Europe) in part crowds out private charity" and that "Europe's more generous provision of welfare does not stem from a greater innate endowment of altruism in Europe."[55] (In reviewing their work, I have argued that the United States–Europe comparison is more complex than they allow; in particular, they underestimate substantially the true size of the American welfare state, missing its most important feature: its reliance on private provision of certain benefits through policy instruments whose costs are not wholly reflected in public budgets.[56])

Equality, as legal scholar Peter Westen has explained, is an empty concept until one specifies the particular respect in which equality is being assessed and the variables that one is holding constant.[57] In American political ideology, equality is a founding concept gloriously inscribed in our Declaration of Independence. But for most Americans, the distinction that matters most in thinking about equality is that between equality of opportunity and equality of result. For most Americans, this distinction is a sharp one. (For many affirmative action proponents, it is *too* sharp.[58]) Be that as it may, the distinction is a cliché in political debates, one that few policy makers are prepared to repudiate—at least publicly. This cliché masks our unwillingness to define precisely what is meant by opportunity and result, and the difficulty of figuring out the empirical relationship between them.

Finally, political inequalities—surely an important cultural fact—tend to promote, or at least preserve, whatever economic inequalities the market generates. As political scientists Kay Schlozman, Sidney Verba, and Henry Brady show in a recent, compendious study of the subject, these class-based political inequalities are manifest and reinforce one another with respect to voter turnout, interest group activity, campaign finance, and other forms of civic participation.[59] These inequalities are deeply embedded in the political culture, reflecting both constitutional values limiting government regulation of campaign contributions and other efforts to "level the political playing field" and civic values that are more sympathetic to business interests than to labor unions,[60] although unions—despite their decline, especially in the private sector[61]—are very active in campaign finance and in politics more generally.[62] (Campaign finance's actual effects, discussed in chapter 7, are far more complicated.) Such inequalities, moreover, tend to be self-reinforcing, partly due to uncontrollable technological and macroeconomic changes, have few countervailing forces,* and seem morally acceptable to most citizens.[63]

RELIGION AND POLITICAL MORALISM

Policy debates in the United States are pervaded by religious convictions, some quite dogmatic, and are also inflected by other moral claims. This is hardly surprising; Americans are far more religious and patriotic than the citizens of any other liberal democracy and, as Tocqueville noted, our religions are "democratic and republican." (Scholars disagree about whether American religiosity is waning.[64]) This helps to explain why even secular political movements like civil rights, international human rights, unionization, and feminism often invoke religious themes.[65] The infusion of such moral energy invigo-

---

*Paul Starr perceives one such force, "the rise of politically oriented 'issue generalists' on the liberal side." See Starr, "Politics in the Orbit of Money" (book review), *New Republic*, September 13, 2012, 28, 31.

rates American politics and shapes our public policies, both domestic and foreign, in many profound ways.

What is most salient about this religiosity and moralism, for present purposes, is that it raises both the stakes and the heat in policy debates. As participants are determined to vindicate fundamental—even sacred—principles, and as they mobilize politically around these issues, compromise becomes more difficult. Religion also gives many ordinary policy disputes a constitutional dimension; the courts must expound principles under the First Amendment's free exercise and establishment clauses that even Supreme Court justices lament are opaque, inconsistent, and even unprincipled. Many disputes end up in court, with the relevant public programs having to abide the judicial decisions. Examples of these issues include the use of public funds to promote school choice, institutional dress codes, local zoning disputes, criminal law's application to exotic religious practices, military and prison discipline, and countless others. Moralism, then, not only animates policy making but is a wild card in the many policy debates that ensue.

SOCIAL DIVERSITY

America is probably the most diverse society on earth, with the possible exception of India.[66] This is true regardless of how one thinks about or measures diversity or which kind of diversity is under discussion. Diversity in the United States grows apace despite ostensibly homogenizing factors—national mass media, advertising, popular culture, frequent intermarriage—and sometimes *because* of them. It is growing even in areas like residential housing and elite sectors of the economy in which segregation long existed.

America does more than tolerate diversity. Today, it also views diversity as constitutive of the national mythos and underwrites this by welcoming roughly one million legal immigrants each year. (Canada, a vast, thinly settled land seeking more people, accepts many fewer, but they constitute a much larger share of its much smaller population.) According to sociologist (and immigrant) Orlando Patterson, America's embrace of diversity "finds no parallel in any other society or culture in the world today."[67] In truth, diversity has little support outside the United States and Canada; even inside them, acceptance of a diversity ideal is quite recent.

This social diversity is highly advantageous to the policy process, but it also increases political conflict and the difficulty of managing it.[68] Many of the policy advantages of diversity parallel those of markets. As we have seen, markets are highly responsive mechanisms for giving effect to individuals' diverse choices.* In a similar way, diverse groups competing for resources, status, and various forms of power benefit society by limiting undue concentrations of political and economic power, increasing accountability by elites, enhancing public participation in decisions that affect them, encouraging innovation, educating public officials about the consequences of their actions, and much more.

Diversity also increases a society's capacity to learn and to adapt swiftly and creatively to changing conditions.[69] (As discussed in chapter 5, government tends not to possess this adaptability.) Religious diversity, for example, fostered social learning such as the lessons that the Constitution's framers took from the long history of religious wars in Europe and intolerance in early America, the role of religions in easing immigrant assimilation, the social reforms for which religious groups campaigned to great effect, and the work of faith-based organizations in providing many essential public goods and social services, which in turn has helped make possible America's commitment to limited government.

Political diversity also advances social learning. The federal system, for example, both enables and encourages the states and localities to experiment with their own programmatic approaches to a

---

*There are exceptions. For example, in situations where interconnectivity and network externalities are significant (i.e., where an activity's value to individual participants increases geometrically as the number of participants increases, as with a telephone or computer network), market competition offering different service or connectivity standards may be less efficient than having the government mandate uniform standards. Adverse selection in insurance is another diversity-related impediment to market efficiency, one that has played a central role in the debate over the Affordable Care Act's insurance mandate and subsidies.

wide variety of public issues. Louis Brandeis's now clichéd view of the states as "little laboratories" of social learning is probably even truer today that it was in his time. State-level policy innovations now set the agenda for national debates in a host of policy areas. Examples include term limits, health care regulation, voter registration rules, recent antismoking efforts, gun control, the death penalty, working conditions, environmental standards, tax law, consumer protection, campaign finance, special education, energy deregulation, conservation, school choice, same-sex marriage, and bureaucratic reforms.[70] (Of course, simply extrapolating from the experience of one or a few states to the nation as a whole may be methodologically doubtful,[71] and there are other limits on the efficacy of the "laboratories" model.[72])

A particularly important instance of diversity-inspired policy learning was Congress's overhaul in 1996 of the welfare system, which many bitterly denounced when president Bill Clinton agreed to sign it, but is widely hailed as one of the great policy successes of recent decades.[73] This far-reaching reform, discussed in chapter 11, followed—both substantively and chronologically—several years of experimentation by several states with a variety of approaches. Some of these experiments became possible only after the Clinton administration granted waivers from federal law requirements that all state programs conform to uniform national standards. In Wisconsin and some other states, these experiments showed promising results in moving welfare recipients into jobs and in reducing their dependency without generating the increased homelessness, child abuse and abandonment, and other indicators of immiseration that most commentators had predicted. Although powerful political pressures would probably have ensured extensive welfare reform in any event, these experiments contributed greatly to the political viability and the specific programmatic content of the 1996 law. States' policy *failures* can be as influential as their successes in shaping national policy debates.*

---

*During the 2000 election campaign, for example, the Democrats were able to cite the inability of state programs to attract insurers into the market for prescription drug coverage for the elderly as evidence that could be used to discredit Republican proposals to extend that approach to the nation as a whole. This debate strongly affected the approach taken

For all its policy advantages, diversity can also be dysfunctional. It can adversely affect group performance in a variety of contexts by interfering with the ability of people to communicate, define common goals, and pursue them effectively. Indeed, the chaos of the Tower of Babel in Genesis made this nonobvious point long before social science confirmed it. Within any particular group—whether public or private, profit or nonprofit—the existence of conflicting views and interests, mobilized by strategic behavior opportunities, magnifies the costs of internal governance, decision making, and collective action. In the extreme, this produces organizational paralysis or failure. Research by political scientist Robert Putnam suggests that diversity can imperil what he calls "bridging social capital," encouraging people in ethnically diverse communities to withdraw from civic life.[74] Indeed, a diversity that is too widespread, too divisive, too inward-looking, and runs too deeply can narrow or dissolve the bonds that make collective action possible.

Pointing to party line voting in Congress, bitter Supreme Court nomination battles, budget impasses, government shutdowns, and a partisan media that has sundered our shared informational base,[75] many commentators conclude that the government has reached such a paralytic point. This dire conclusion, however, is highly doubtful. First, the current level of invective and character assassination pales before the politics of the early republic, the antebellum and Civil War eras, and many periods since then,[76] yet our political system has endured—indeed flourished—for more than two centuries. Americans' fervent patriotism, far deeper than in other Western democracies,[77] somehow transcends even sharp partisan divisions.

Second, the fact that Americans and their politicians and media are deeply divided on important public policy issues is neither surprising nor worrisome. Inherently complex problems such as sustain-

---

by the Affordable Care Act of 2011. Another example occurred in the aftermath of the 2000 election itself, when the failure of Florida's electoral machinery and the likelihood of similar failures in other states spawned a political groundswell in support of national legislation in hopes of remedying the problem. In the event, that legislation has proved quite ineffective.

ing Medicare, Social Security, and other entitlements in the face of unprecedented demographic and fiscal challenges,* do and should engender competing approaches and sharp conflicts. The compromises that are ultimately struck—and they *will* be struck—are inevitably messy, unsatisfying, and, in a sense, inevitably unprincipled. This says more about the difficulty of the issues than about any political pathology.

Third, some prominent political scientists, led by Morris Fiorina, reject what they call "the myth of a polarized America"; the public, they find, is not more polarized than before.[78] Other scholars disagree.[79] Many voters do live in more ideologically homogeneous communities,[80] and the parties and politicians are somewhat more ideological in recent years, but this does not mean that the citizenry as a whole is more sharply divided.

Finally, the nation is more difficult to govern today than in the recent past. This fact, however, has far less to do with social and political diversity than with government's inability to muster the resources discussed in chapters 5 and 6—incentives, rationality, dynamism, and credibility—that are essential to government's ability to deal effectively with an ever more complex social and policy environment.

POPULIST SUSPICION OF TECHNICAL EXPERTISE AND OFFICIAL DISCRETION

American history and society are laced with populism—the belief that ordinary people, more than elites, are to be trusted with important political decisions. In the United States, and indeed in mass democracies everywhere, bitter resentment and suspicion of powerful groups—banks, large corporations, exclusive universities, "inside the Beltway" politicians and agency bureaucrats, and "establishments" of every kind—always has some political resonance. This resentment sometimes assumes darker conspiratorial tones, as with movements against the putatively powerful: Masons, Jews, the Catholic Church,

---

*The term *entitlement* is something of a misnomer, as Congress can always alter or abolish them. See *Flemming v. Nestor,* 363 U.S. 603 (1960).

"outside agitators," the "striped pants" State Department, foreign powers, and even the New York Yankees in their juggernaut days.

Populism can have far-reaching policy significance, some of it desirable, much of it undesirable. What is desirable is the faith in democratic self-governance, the conviction that ordinary people can do extraordinary things, and a healthy suspicion of elites. Unfortunately, populism can also go too far. Almost 90 percent of judges in the state systems face some kind of popular election, with thirty-eight states putting all of their judges up before the voters. Almost no other country in the world has ever experimented with the popular election of judges, and there are good reasons to think that judicial elections, particularly in their current form, are an inferior mode of selection than appointments.[81] Obviously, however, reasonable people (and states) differ on this question.

More worrisome are populist attacks on public health advice by technical experts. Stephen Breyer, before ascending to the Supreme Court, wrote a fine book defending such expertise and analysis in the face of what he saw as widespread mistrust of it in health and safety regulation,[82] only to find it being used against him in the name of populism during his Senate confirmation hearings. More recent and alarming examples are bogus conspiracy theories and fraudulent claims that encourage parents not to immunize their children against the risk of cervical cancer, a leading killer of women, and against the risks of measles, mumps, and rubella, despite unequivocal science supporting use of the human papilloma virus and MMR vaccines, respectively.[83]

But the targets of populist suspicions go far beyond scientific expertise and technical analysis; they extend to the exercise of official discretion more generally. Indeed, this hostility to official discretion has always been a major motif in American public law, distinguishing it sharply from European policy making, and is by no means confined to those with populist attitudes. Elites harbor it as well. The history of public law is in substantial part a search to domesticate and legitimate the growing administrative state by instituting various kinds of techniques (many discussed in chapter 3) to control official discretion.

This perennial search has had mixed results: greater public participation, more complex and protracted decision processes, and the subordination of expertise to political and judicial controls, among others.[84]

There are other valid concerns about populism. It can flatter intuition or what passes for simple common sense about public issues that are in fact highly complex, issues that can only be apprehended through careful study and analysis. Politicians are often tempted to pander to this populist strain in our public life; indeed, the trope of "the people against the interests" is a prominent one in almost all political campaigns, even when the candidates who employ it are themselves exceedingly wealthy elites. Finally, populist demonology is often used to divert attention from the substantive merits of policy proposals to their provenance. This tactic encourages the use of ad hominem arguments in which all one really needs to know in order to appraise a position is who is advancing it on behalf of which group. The idea that we are known by the company we keep may be better advice to our children than it is to those wishing to seriously assess policy proposals. Such mental shortcuts are tempting, of course—like any simplistic process, they reduce decision costs—but sound policy making requires more complex analysis.

PUBLIC OPINION

In 1922, journalist Walter Lippman wrote an influential reflection on the emergence of public opinion as the most powerful force in politics.[85] His analysis was prescient, but he could not possibly have anticipated the explosion of media through which public opinion is now both influenced and expressed, nor could he have predicted the far higher level of education and sophistication about public affairs that exists today.

As discussed in chapter 3, the policy-making process is a complex and protracted one, replete with opportunities for public participation, especially that mediated by interest advocacy groups. Public opinion is more powerful today not only because of the much-noted instantaneous, real-time news cycle facilitated by new technologies but also because the gap between the education level of the citizenry and policy makers—and the greater deference to the latter that this gap once commanded—has shrunk. For these and other reasons, public opinion exercises more control over decision makers in the United States than in Europe. Although public opinion in the United States and in, say, France on a number of controversial issues—capital punishment and abortion, for example—is similar, U.S. policies seem to cleave more closely to public opinion than French policies do. Our government's greater responsiveness to public opinion may reflect its more limited powers compared to those of governments in European parliamentary systems (especially France's).* Coupled with the power of new technologies to cheaply and quickly mobilize opinion to pressure politicians on hot-button issues, this heightened responsiveness means greater caution and volatility in policy making, which in turn reduces the credibility of particular policies, as discussed in chapter 5.

CIVIL SOCIETY

Civil society refers to the vast, extraordinarily diverse array of private entities—both nonprofit and for-profit—that stand between the government and individuals. (It may stand outside of government proper, but a key part of it, nonprofit organizations, is highly dependent on the public fisc for its funding; one-third of all nonprofit dollars come from government grants or contracts, with grants nearly tripling in real terms in the last quarter century.[86] It is also the domain in which almost all people conduct the most important activities and cultivate their most meaningful relationships of trust and cooperation—what Robert Putnam and others term "social capital,"[87] and what Nancy Rosenblum calls the "democracy of everyday life."[88] This is particularly true in a liberal democratic nation like the United States, which

---

*An apparent exception is the Senate's rejection of gun purchase background checks in April 2013—checks that the overwhelming majority of Americans seem to favor. This may say more about the nonmajoritarian nature of Senate representation and cloture rules and the unusual power of the gun lobby than about U.S. politics in general.

as we have seen emphasizes individualism, voluntary associations, and limited government.* (Because I discuss private interest groups and markets—both central elements of both civil society and politics—in chapter 7, I do not consider them further here.)

Consider religion.[89] Surrounding and shaping America's political and popular cultures is a remarkably strong religious tradition and an inventive though sometimes repellent popular culture of religiosity. The relationship between religion and both popular and political culture is a complex and generative, socially beneficial one on the whole. Although measures and estimates of American religiosity vary, no scholar disputes the fact that we are much more deeply involved with religion than are Europeans. Church leaders and their flocks have led almost all of the great reformist causes in American history: abolition, women's suffrage, temperance, civil rights, opposition to unpopular wars, environmentalism, and "choice" and "life" forces in the abortion debate. Some mainstream religious groups tend to support liberal candidates and policies. Many others now support conservative presidential candidates, but this is only a recent development. Moreover, these conservative groups are divided politically by quarrels over abortion, gay rights, stem cell research, foreign policy, and many other issues. One reason for this pronounced religiosity is that creating and sustaining churches was never in the hands of the federal government and only briefly in those of the first states; instead, religious development was promoted by spiritual entrepreneurs engaged in competitive marketing, vigorous proselytizing, and doctrinal and liturgical innovations. Immigration, moreover, has fortified this religious commitment throughout American history.

Private philanthropic giving from and to nonprofit groups—to secular as well as religious causes—is unmatched anywhere in the world not just in absolute terms but also as a share of income and

---

*Perhaps the most striking, and disturbing, aspect of American life is that its civil society is extraordinarily robust in every respect—*except the most important one, the family*. This, of course, is no small exception. On the state of the American family, see Linda J. Waite & Melissa J. K. Howe, "The Family," in Peter H. Schuck & James Q. Wilson, eds., *Understanding America: The Anatomy of an Exceptional Nation* (2008), chap. 11.

wealth.[90] Private charity, operating with varying financial and other relationships with the government, including strong tax incentives to donors, supports a vast array of civil society organizations—schools, universities, hospitals, nursing homes, child welfare agencies, ethnic advocacy groups, amateur sports, museums and the arts, and a host of others—that provide diverse social services to the needy and other members of the public. Local, regional, and national voluntary associations form constantly to pursue a bewildering variety of private and public interests, providing many more avenues for citizen participation in larger collective endeavors.

Civil society groups play an immense role in the implementation of government programs, performing many of the social functions that in Europe are largely reserved for government. These organizations are in a mutually dependent relationship with government. On the one hand, government depends on them for much policy implementation, yet they often stress religious and other values that a liberal government may not want to promote officially or is constitutionally barred from supporting. This often causes significant conflicts affecting (and often limiting) policy effectiveness. In 2012, for example, a serious crisis, with constitutional litigation in its train, arose when Catholic hospitals refused to implement the Affordable Care Act's mandate of full coverage of contraception services.[91] Other clashes arise over religiously sponsored child welfare agencies that challenge public policies imposing requirements that reflect more secular moral ideologies.[92] On the other hand, these groups have become financially dependent on the federal contracts. Organizations like Planned Parenthood, AARP, the Urban League, and La Raza receive large sums from Washington; more than half of Catholic Charities' budget comes from there. Not surprisingly, such groups are now major advocates for expanded programs.[93]

The remarkable achievements of the ubiquitous nonprofit sector, and the public's relatively high degree of confidence in it, have prompted policy makers to initiate a large number of programs seeking to draw on the distinct advantages of both public authority and private incentives and innovation. These public-private partnerships operate in many different fields, including housing and community development, scientific research, environmental protection, the integration of immigrants, public safety, and many areas of regulatory policy.

The results of such collaborations, however, are not always benign, particularly in the area of social services. Government programs funded by taxes can "crowd out" nonprofit providers that must rely on private donations, and may also alter the nature of the interactions and relationships between providers and clients, substituting more bureaucratic, rule-bound, and morally ambiguous service modalities for those that more religion-inflected private agencies provide.[94] This crowding out phenomenon is discussed more extensively in chapter 7.

PART 2

The Structural Sources
of Policy Failure

CHAPTER 5

Incentives and Collective Irrationality

D iscussion of the quality and effectiveness of government activity often emphasizes budgetary factors. When programs fail, the argument goes, it is usually because a good policy was not adequately funded. Doubtless this is sometimes true, but more typically the real causes lie elsewhere—and far deeper.

Policy success depends, at a minimum, on six attributes of a policy that have little or nothing to do with its budget. First, *incentives* must be capable of eliciting the desired behaviors both of the policy makers and of the actors they must influence in order for the policy to work. Second, the policy makers must be *rational* in selecting appropriate instruments for policy implementation. Third, the *information* on which policy makers rely must be accurate, unbiased, and up to date. Fourth, programs must be *adaptable* to the dynamic environments in which they will operate, overcoming the strong inertial forces endemic to political decision making. Fifth, the policy must be *credible* to those who must be induced to invest their own resources for it to succeed. Finally, programs must be *managed* well enough to avoid, at a minimum, the unholy trinity of fraud, waste, and abuse. Some of the relatively successful programs discussed in chapter 11 exhibit many of these attributes.

For deeply structural reasons, all six of these features are in shorter supply in government than budget is. To show why, I contrast government with markets that, for all their well-known imperfections, earn high marks for incentives, rationality, information generation, adaptability, credibility, and management. In contrasting government and markets, I emphatically am *not* making a general claim that markets should substitute for government programs. (One could only advance and defend such a claim based on empirical and normative analyses of particular cases.) Rather, I mean to use the features of well-functioning markets to highlight the systemic conditions that doom so many government policies to failure.*

This chapter discusses the first two features so lacking or deformed in government: incentives and rationality, at both the individual and especially the collective levels. Chapter 6 discusses the other four: information, inflexibility, incredibility, and mismanagement.

INCENTIVES

Policy effectiveness is powerfully affected by three categories of incentives—those that animate *policy makers*, *citizens*, and *private actors* whose interests a policy might affect. Private incentives are also explored in chapter 6 (on government credibility) and chapter 7 (on markets).

For decades, social scientists who study government have carefully explored two fundamental questions: What do government officials and other political actors do, and why do they do it? The "what" question is descriptive; it can only be answered by direct observational studies and other more indirect methods.[1] The more intriguing "why" question—our principal concern here—is more elusive; true motivations can only be inferred based on some theory. Officials' motives may have been more straightforward up until the early twentieth century when many officials could charge the government for some of their official acts (e.g., prosecutors earned a fee for each conviction) rather than receiving salaries.[2]

---

*For an (unpersuasive) argument that political markets are as efficient as economic ones are, see Donald A. Wittman, *The Myth of Democratic Failure: Why Political Institutions Are Efficient* (1995).

Generally speaking, there are two theoretical approaches to this "why" question. The first takes officials at their word. They usually are proud of what they do and invoke a high-minded reason for action such as the desire to do what the law or the "public interest" requires.* Steven Kelman insists that this "public spirit is important in public behavior and that therefore the dolorous results for the policy-making process that result when one assumes self-interest do not occur simply because self-interest fails to dominate the way advocates of the public choice approach believe it does."[3] In reality, however, Kelman's claim is little more than-wishful thinking and cannot possibly be verified. But even if it were true, the more important point is that his preoccupation with officials' motivation is quite irrelevant. What matters, or should matter, to the citizenry is the actual performance of officially administered programs on the ground, yet this performance may have little or nothing to do with how public-spirited they are. Indeed, just as speed is a bad thing if one is going in the wrong direction, so officials' zeal may in some situations actually exacerbate program failure.

One must distinguish between two uses of the "public interest": the normative and the positive. Almost all who speak of the public interest invoke it as a standard that all public policies *should* satisfy; indeed, it is one to which all but the most benighted and misanthropic can repair.† But as a positive account of how political actors actually behave, the public interest is a hollow, dangerously naive explanation. (This cynicism is *especially* common among self-styled "public interest" advocates on both the left and right who criticize most political behavior [other than their own] on precisely this ground.) The central difficulty is that the public interest is not self-defining. Even the most scrupulously public-regarding citizens, not to mention the many more narrowly selfish ones, tend to view the pub-

---

*Obviously, such formulations beg the question of what the law or the public interest actually does require, but that question is irrelevant to our central concern here, which is what motivates officials, not the particular actions that their motivations dictate.
†I presume that all citizens behind the Rawlsian veil of ignorance would do so. See John Rawls, *A Theory of Justice* (1971).

lic interest through their own particular lenses, investing their own preferences with broader justifications. Indeed, few political actors will concede, at least publicly, that their actions do not conform to the public interest. Whether the public interest conceit is delusive or something else, it is probably almost universal.

Government officials, like most trained people, tend to believe in what they are doing and that their programs serve the public interest. Is this inconsistent with the central hypothesis of "public choice theory" (discussed in chapter 4), which holds that officials' behavior is best predicted by assuming that they are motivated by self-interest? The answer depends, of course, on what one means by self-interest. As we shall see, public choice theorists define an official's self-interest not as her pride in advancing a public interest goal but more narrowly as her pursuit of individual or institutional power over budget, discretion, and other resources that are useful in attracting political support.

The competing answer to the "why" question posits that officials pursue their self-interest through rational, utility-maximizing choices and that their decisions can best be understood and predicted in light of that motivation. The body of scholarship that advances and seeks empirical support for this rational-actor model is known as "public choice" (or "rational choice") theory; its architects are largely economists and economics-oriented political scientists. It claims to show that these utility-maximizing policy-oriented actors—individual voters, politicians, other officials, interest groups, policy entrepreneurs, and even courts[4]—produce policies that tend to be inefficient and cost-ineffective, and to benefit discrete, well-organized interests at the expense of the diffuse general public, especially taxpayers. This bias can create many "invisible victims," an often large but politically ineffectual group discussed in chapter 2.

Public choice scholars also claim—both theoretically and empirically—that the smaller, better-organized policy-oriented actors purposefully embed their self-interest in "deals" negotiated by politicians to create and preserve governmental institutions and practices—congressional committees, judicial doctrine, administrative agencies, the

Administrative Procedure Act, seniority rules, and much more—that project these deals far into the future, protecting these arrangements against opposing interests that would undo them.[5]

Such an account encourages cynicism (many will call it realism) about politics and public policy, as chapter 1 showed. Whether this cynicism/realism harms the body politic, or instead provides a healthy antidote to both the frequent malignity of political self-seeking and the perils of credulous idealism, is of course a matter of profound disagreement between statist liberals and their more conservative, limited-government opponents. There is surely some truth to the public choice account of official decision making. This book is replete with examples of inefficient policies that seem consistent with a public choice explanation. Many published studies, reviewed in chapter 8, ascribe policy failure to the distortions introduced by interest-group politics. Even so, it is hard to know just how true the public choice account is. After all, these outcomes are also consistent with other explanations in which the self-regarding incentives of officials and private groups combine with other motives that are harder to define or model.[6]

Public choice theory has drawn many perspicacious critics, and its difficulties—exaggerated claims to universality, fragile empirical foundations, tautological use of "self-interest," excessive focus on collective action problems, reductive accounts of human intentions, and inability to exclude competing explanations—have been well-developed in the social science literature.[7] For example, if utility maximization were the only goal of political actors, one would be hard-pressed to explain why individual citizens bother to vote. After all, the burdens of voting far exceed the vanishingly small chance of affecting the electoral result and thus the voter's favored policy outcome. It follows that people vote for reasons other than rational utility maximization—expressive, idealistic, and reputational reasons, for example—but these other reasons are harder to model rigorously. One might call these other reasons self-interested, of course, but that renders the public choice explanation essentially meaningless: *any* action is self-interested at least in the minimal sense that the actor wants to achieve *something* for herself, but this tautology gives us little or no predictive power.

Another problem with public choice theory is that ideology evidently plays a significant role in much political behavior, yet ideology often suppresses or overrides narrow self-interest. One can describe ideology as self-interested to the extent that it provides the actor with a coherent, satisfying account of the world, but again this claim would render the theory wholly circular and nonfalsifiable. By explaining everything, the self-interest hypothesis would explain nothing. These question-begging aspects of public choice theory also make its claims somewhat vague, rendering its empirical predictions vague as well.

Still, this is hardly a fatal indictment; after all, no theory is perfect. The critical question for any theory is whether it explains and predicts the phenomenon of interest (here, official behavior) better than its rivals do.* My answer to this question consists of four propositions, which the evidence and analysis in the chapters that follow will amply support.

First, as a positive matter, public choice theory's rational actor model explains and predicts far more observed official behavior than its main rival, public interest theory. Second, public choice theory's defects—chiefly its ambiguity, resistance to rigorous empirical testing, and circularity—apply even more strongly to public interest theory. Third, public choice theory is most effective in explaining and predicting how a policy will be *implemented* once it is adopted (the subject of chapter 8). Finally, although both theories are flawed in some respects, both do contribute to our understanding of public policy.

This last proposition may come as a surprise, given my claim that the "public interest" account of politics tends to be vacuous and dangerously naive as a positive account of policy making. Properly defined and documented, however, it often has some explanatory

*Another possibility is that every theory of political action is worthless, as it can explain and predict nothing, presumably because political action consists simply of random events exhibiting no regularities. I reject this notion.

power. Consider the Airline Deregulation Act of 1978 (discussed in chapter 11), whose legislative history has been carefully documented and which expert analysts generally consider a great policy success.[8] The law was enacted through a combination of (1) self-interested lobbying by some members of the industry, would-be entrants, opportunistic politicians, and consumer groups seeking to benefit their supporters, and (2) reform advocates whose support for deregulation is best explained by their genuine belief that it would better serve the general public and most communities in medium- to long-run reform. These advocates included senator Edward Kennedy, Alfred Kahn (chairman of the agency that would be abolished by the act), Stephen Breyer (then counsel to Kennedy and now a Supreme Court justice), academic policy analysts, and even some regulators who would expect to lose their jobs under deregulation. In short, public-regarding motives, not just politicians' self-interest, animated the enactment of this important reform.[9] Likewise, the project to search for the Higgs boson and other cosmological esoterica is not easily explained in terms of our politicians' self-interest; the chief beneficiaries seem to be widely dispersed cosmologists, highly specialized equipment manufacturers (not all American), and construction workers in Europe, where the hugely costly CERN facility is located, spanning across the border of France and Switzerland.[10] Another example is the National Ignition Facility, a giant laser fusion project that is widely considered a failure and has already cost taxpayers $5 billion, with continuing operating costs of $290 million per year.[11] Congress's continued willingness to fund it might simply reflect pork barrel politics, loss aversion, and the sunk-cost fallacy, but it might also reflect a public interest bet that the project will produce low-cost power in the future. It is hard to know for sure.

However one may interpret these decisions, rational self-interest (as the actor perceives it) unquestionably drives most political behavior most of the time. Only the cloistered idealist will regard this as altogether pernicious. Self-interest, after all, is among the most powerful motors of human action and thus of the civic conduct and participation on which a vigorous democracy depend. Idealized images of the Athenian polis to the contrary, citizens are unlikely to undertake the burdens of this participation—time, study, inconvenience, frustration—unless they believe that it will advance their private interests as well as their more public values. James Madison's insistence on the need to design government in light of "the defect of better motives" and the fact that we are not "angels" confirms the fact that citizens are primarily self-interested when they venture into the larger, more impersonal world beyond their family circle and a few other small, moralized, interactive, and intimate collective enclaves.[12] Field studies by Nobel laureate Elinor Ostrom has confirmed how differently people think and behave in these disparate kinds of settings.[13]

If self-interest fuels much or most democratic participation and is in any event ubiquitous and inescapable, what are its effects on the shape, content, and effectiveness of public policy? Public choice theory propounds a number of hypotheses of midlevel specificity that empirical studies have been able to substantially confirm. Again, these hypotheses do not specify absolute rules; they merely predict strong tendencies. Here are a few of the findings that seem most relevant to predicting the effects of public policies. As we shall see in what follows, these structural regularities—political axioms, if you prefer—tend to produce policy failure. And as we shall also see, assessments of actual policies tend to confirm these predictions.

Ordinary citizens have little or no rational incentive to participate actively in political activity. More than a half century ago, Anthony Downs published *An Economic Theory of Democracy*, in which he applied simple cost-benefit analysis (CBA) to a citizen's decision whether to vote and to otherwise participate in government. He showed that, as noted earlier, no ordinary rational individual would do so given the costs of registering, traveling to the polling place, informing herself about the relevant issues, and so on, compared with the benefits of doing so, which are practically nonexistent because of the unlikelihood that her vote would affect the outcome. Other forms of participation are even more costly. This implies that those who do participate in politics will disproportionately have large, focused stakes that can be protected by joining to form an interest group with others who also have relatively large, focused stakes.

The manifest fact that a large number of Americans not only vote but join environmental, civil rights, pro- or antiabortion, religious, or other politically active voluntary groups does not mean that they are irrational. Instead it means that they seek through these activities to advance values that are not self-interested in the narrow, conventional sense but are more broadly self-fulfilling. This claim is not tautological; it rests on vast empirical evidence. That is, citizens report that they derive ideological, social, participatory, or expressive satisfactions from such activities, and they are willing to sacrifice some of their leisure and other resources to gain those satisfactions. In these ways they also signal to others in their community that they have certain types of values and commitments and are in that sense good, reliable people meriting respect and reciprocity.[14] Finally, and most important, these efforts often succeed not only in mobilizing disparate citizens for political action but in winning particular policy battles— outcomes not predicted by the dominant theory of collective action, discussed just below.

Political actors design policy-making institutions and processes to advance their self-interest. Legislators are for the most part professional career politicians who seek to maximize their chances of reelection. This requires, among other things, attracting financial, media, reputational, and other forms of support from those groups with the incentives and ability to deliver this support and that also have a special interest in the resources that legislators control: access, status, legislation, valuable information, favorable publicity, government subsidies, regulatory supervision by friendly officials, and much more. Legislators deploy their broad-ranging powers to enact statutes; shape the agendas, discretion, staffing, and budget of administrative agencies; manipulate appropriations; hold hearings; seek publicity and credit; and use countless other influence-enhancing techniques in order to position themselves to deliver what favored interests and supporters—those who are in a position to secure their reelection—

want. Congress organizes its internal rules and its committees' jurisdictions and assignments so as to serve members' electoral interests. Similarly, members use their party connections and other influence over state legislators who control the redistricting process to maximize the electoral prospects of their parties and themselves.

Agency officials, for their part, use their delegated authority in ways that, consistent with their legal duties, are calculated to increase their political and budgetary support and their future earnings, professional status, and job security. Federal judges, who enjoy life tenure and thus need not pander to voters or politicians, tend to interpret the law in ways that advance their own conceptions of justice and policy, which tend to correspond closely (though not entirely) with the policy preferences of the president who appointed them and the one who might promote them.[15] (The nature of legal reasoning and adjudication renders judges' incentives more obscure than those of other officials, but the literature on judicial decision making supports this general claim.)

The political effectiveness of a group depends, among other things, on its ability to manage incentives so as to overcome structural obstacles to collective action. Not all interest groups manage to sustain themselves, much less succeed in being politically effective. In a seminal book, *The Logic of Collective Action,* economist Mancur Olson explains why some groups manage to succeed more than others. In order to have even a chance at success, a group must attract the resources—financial, social, skills, and so forth—that it needs to do its work while minimizing its organization and maintenance costs. The organization costs for groups are higher to the extent that they are vulnerable to various cost-increasing opportunistic behaviors on the part of potential members. The most important of these behaviors, the "free rider effect," encourages those who might contribute such resources to try to benefit from the group's efforts without contributing to them. Two other impediments to collective action are opportunistic behavior by holdouts, whose strategic position enables them to extract an especially high price for their cooperation, and informational asymmetries that encourage exploitation.

Groups may be able to solve these collective action problems by tailoring incentives—with free riders, for example, by providing members with valuable benefits, such as group insurance or trips, that can be withheld from nonmembers. A group's vulnerability to such collective action problems depends on factors such as the distribution and heterogeneity of information, costs, and benefits among its members. Thus, groups whose members have low, diffuse stakes and information tend to wield less political influence than those with concentrated, high-stakes, well-informed memberships. Although the sheer number of a group's members matters in achieving policy influence, these other factors count for more because they affect the group's unity and ability to act collectively at low cost. Nevertheless, a group's diffuseness by no means dictates its political destiny. That disadvantage can and often is outweighed by other political assets—an important point discussed in chapter 3 (under "interest group pluralism").[16]

Officials have powerful incentives to provide voters and interest groups with short-term benefits and to hide the long-term costs that must pay for those benefits. Politicians have short time horizons tied to the electoral cycle and to their need to "do something" in the presence of a crisis, such as the 9/11 attack, the 2008 financial meltdown,[17] the protracted "fiscal cliff" imbroglio of 2012–13, and the government shutdown of October 2013. Radically present-oriented, their incentive is to devise ways to quickly bestow benefits on their constituents, exaggerating those benefits while hiding the costs. Various tried and true cost-hiding techniques are available.[18] They may simply *ignore* the costs, pretending that their constituents are getting a free lunch while hoping that no powerful interest will blow the whistle and reveal the deception. They may treat a resource as if it were *free*. The Federal Communications Commission, for example, wants to expand broadband by "repacking" areas of spectrum used by TV broadcasters to free up and then auction other frequencies for broadband use, despite the broadcasters' fears that this will degrade signal quality.[19] Another cost-hiding technique is for elected officials to delegate the tough, costly decisions to agencies, to which they can later deflect blame when the costs prove unpopular. They may disguise the costs, concealing them as off-budget programs like Fannie Mae, explicit or implicit loan guarantees, or "tax expenditures" like the home mortgage interest deduction. They may defer the costs, as with deficit financing whose interest obligations will not come due for decades. They may use unfunded mandates and pork barrel projects to shift the costs disproportionately to nonconstituent taxpayers and state and local governments. I discuss other policy consequences of policymakers' short time horizons in chapter 6's discussion of inflexibility and in later chapters.

The political dynamics of a public policy depend on how it distributes its benefits and costs among voters and groups. In *The Politics of Regulation* (1980), political scientist James Q. Wilson distinguished four types of politics, which he associated with four different distributions of costs and benefits. (He was writing about regulation, but the taxonomy applies also to other types of policy making.) Where the policy concentrates both the costs and the benefits on a relatively small number of people or groups, it will be characterized by what Wilson called "interest group politics" in which both sides—the putative beneficiaries and cost-bearers—can readily mobilize to advance their interests (in maximizing benefits and minimizing costs, respectively). Examples include rate regulation like that between well-organized shippers and carriers, and public-sector wage bargaining. Where both the benefits and the costs are widely dispersed among the population, "majoritarian politics" will prevail in which political entrepreneurs will make broad-based appeals to the public interest. Where the benefits are dispersed but the costs are concentrated, "entrepreneurial politics" prevails, in which a "public interest" advocate launches a crusade against, say, the tobacco industry, enacting a smoking ban or raising cigarette taxes. And where the benefits are concentrated but the costs are dispersed, we will find "client politics" in which the relatively small group of beneficiaries—say, an industry and its workers protected by import barriers—will be able to exploit their Olsonian advantage over the diffuse, unorganized interests of consumers who will each have to pay only a tiny bit more for the industry's product. Politicians who promote this kind of policy are duly rewarded by its winners, while its far more numerous losers will each bear a cost so small that they may not even notice it, much less organize to defeat it. Politicians are adept at designing policies that exhibit this incentive structure—for example, choosing "carrots" over "sticks" in programs designed to shape private behavior.[20] Such policies in turn tend to generate political rewards. This behavior is so endemic and so indifferent to the general public's more diffuse interests, that it has created what Jonathan Rauch calls "demosclerosis," a deeply pathological condition.[21]

Much political activity consists of narrow-interest logrolling at the expense of taxpayers. I noted in chapter 2 that differences in the intensity of preferences among voters and groups can be a potent source of political leverage. A small minority (A) can gain majority support for its favored policy by trading its votes on an issue about which another minority (B) is passionate but on which A is relatively indifferent, in exchange for B's votes on the issue about which A is passionate. These minorities may be very small; indeed, Olson's theory of collective action suggests that the smaller the group, the easier and cheaper it will be for it to organize itself for political action, other things being equal. The incentives-driven logic of this logrolling means that small and narrow but intense and well-organized groups are able to form coalitions that can gain majority political support for policies whose benefits will be enjoyed disproportionately by the coalition but whose costs will be borne disproportionately by the vast majority of unorganized, often unaware taxpayers.[22]

In this classic dynamic, a member of Congress strategically placed on the right appropriations subcommittee can gain approval for "bridges to nowhere"—projects that would clearly fail a CBA or cost-effectiveness test but create jobs, contracts, and favors of value only to locals, although it is unwitting taxpayers across the country who pay the bill. But this logrolling strategy is by no means confined to wasteful (in a CBA or cost-effectiveness sense) projects, nor are its results always condemned. Indeed, the essence of this strategy—trading votes according to different levels of preference intensity—underlies many politically successful coalitions, with the variables being the narrowness of the beneficiary class and the distribution of costs and benefits. For example, the food stamp program (discussed in chapter 11) exists because of a bargain struck by politicians from urbanized, high-poverty districts and those representing rural areas eager to sell agricultural products.[23] Indeed, this bargain has benefited liberals far more than they could have imagined back in the 1970s, when only one in fifty Americans received these benefits. Today, one in seven receives them; their value constitutes some 80 percent of the subsidies under the farm bill.[24] The 2013 law that funded benefits for the victims of Hurricane Sandy contained a number of costly earmarks for favored constituencies, including $1.7 billion for highway construction, most of which will go to areas unaffected by Sandy, and $247 million for Coast Guard spending in the Bahamas and the Great Lakes.[25]

Moral hazard is a major source of incentive-based programmatic failure. Congress has long sought to manage risks of all kinds through laws that spread, shift, or reduce them.[26] In doing so, these programs often generate moral hazard—the propensity to take on more risk when one knows that others will bear much of the expected cost of that risk—which may create new risks that may be even worse and harder to manage. Found in both market and nonmarket contexts, moral hazard encourages rational, incentives-driven conduct that increases the risk of loss, other things being equal. In one kind of moral hazard, an actor takes on more risk because he knows that the costs of that riskier behavior will be borne in whole or in part by someone else: government/taxpayers, an insurer, parents, or another ultimate risk-bearer. Moral hazard may occur where information about risk and the ability to reduce it is asymmetric so that potential risk-bearers cannot readily predict, monitor, or control the risk-taker's choices. When a risk-taker knows more about a risk's nature, level, costs, and benefits than the risk-bearer does, the latter cannot optimally manage the risk by accurately pricing or otherwise controlling it. As we shall see, moral hazard also occurs when a program creates incentives for an actor to behave in a way that is advantageous to him but perversely undermines the program's intent.

Increasing moral hazard can be sound policy when it is part of a coherent risk management strategy. In 1970, for example, Congress imposed a fifty-dollar cap on consumers' liability for unauthorized credit card use. Although this protection surely makes us somewhat less careful than if we remained at risk for large losses from credit card theft, it also reassures us about the safety of Internet shopping—a huge social gain—and shifts the risk of unauthorized use to credit card issuers, who are in the best position to efficiently monitor it.[27]

Unfortunately, this happy outcome is not true of the vast, egregious moral hazard created by programs to benefit financial giants, higher-income individuals, and students. Fannie Mae and Freddie Mac—dubbed the "toxic twins" by critics—engineered home mortgage policies and markets that systematically created vast moral hazard, ostensibly for the popular purpose of expanding homeownership.[28] (For all their efforts, homeownership in the United States is not particularly high when compared with other nations; it ranks twentieth, just behind the United Kingdom.[29]) After exhaustively reviewing the data on housing finance markets, economists Dwight Jaffee and John Quigley find that none of the rationales invoked to justify the agencies' policies—especially the need to preserve the long-term, fixed-rate mortgage—is valid. Quite the contrary; they were detrimental to that goal.[30] In addition, these agencies helped inflate the housing bubble by pressing lenders to make subprime loans to high-risk borrowers who, when the bubble burst, had irresistible incentives to walk away from their underwater mortgages. This left lenders—themselves often insured or hedged in ways that increased moral hazard in *their* lending decisions—and ultimately the government (moral hazard's chief victim) to bear the immense losses, with catastrophic damage to the larger economy. The Treasury estimates that Fannie and Freddie bailouts could amount to $200 billion by the end of 2015. This estimate takes into account some paybacks (actually, reduced loss reserves) generated by the recovering housing market, paybacks often mischaracterized as "profits" that may tempt Congress to preserve the agencies rather than reform them.[31] It does not take into account, however, the opportunity costs of these subsidies—an omission that an expert on subsidies says "would not pass Economics 101."[32] As chapter 8 notes, the Federal Housing Administration is now replicating these moral hazard–stimulated losses on a somewhat smaller but still massive scale—despite the searing experience of Fannie and Freddie. In addition, the regulators seem likely to weaken the traditional 20 percent down-payment requirement, a key bulwark against moral hazard in home mortgages.[33] Finally, quite apart from the moral hazard issue, a policy to subsidize people to own rather than rent homes can actually be harmful.[34]

The government seems to have learned the wrong lesson from this fiasco. The Dodd-Frank reform act has actually increased moral hazard by broadening Wall Street's safety net—and thus taxpayers' exposure—in at least two ways. First, it classified some of the largest financial institutions as systemically important financial institutions (SIFIs), which many experts think is tantamount to "too big to fail" status and gives them new marketing and credit advantages. Indeed, a recent Bank of England study finds that these advantages currently increase the profits of the twenty-eight SIFI banks around the world by some $500 billion—substantially more than their combined profits![35] Regulators' demand for "living wills" for these institutions is unlikely to be effective.[36] In speeches in July 2013, both the Treasury secretary and the Federal Reserve chairman expressed frustration and concern about the government's failure to end "too big to fail" among SIFIs.[37] Yet at the same time, regulators proposed to *extend* SIFI status (and thus "too big to fail" status) to *nonbank* entities such as insurers. (This raised a related policy issue: whether it makes sense to treat such entities like banks given their very different risk portfolios, incentives, and regulators.[38])

Second, Dodd-Frank creates a system for "orderly resolution" of insolvencies that may actually make future bailouts more likely.[39] The Federal Reserve's policy of keeping interest rates so low for so long, and of not raising margin requirements since 1974, invites excessive borrowing, speculation, asset bubbles, and future inflation (while harming savers).[40] Economists will have to puzzle out whether the policy was justified by the slow recovery from the Great Recession, or instead delayed the recovery and set the stage for more insolvencies and crises.

Other examples of moral hazard abound. Under a 1990 law, Congress *requires* the massive federal credit programs to systematically and significantly underestimate and misrepresent their true costs by accounting for loans through essentially ignoring default risks. This practice, denounced by the Congressional Budget Office (CBO) most recently in March 2012,[41] creates *two* kinds of moral hazard: it encourages government to lend too much by treating its loans as virtually risk-free, and it encourages high-risk borrowing by those who will default. The distorting effect of' this combination on policy is evident in the enormous but concealed default-driven costs of the student loan programs detailed in chapter 8.

The Pension Benefit Guaranty Corporation (PBGC), which guarantees employers' unfunded defined-benefit pension debts under certain conditions, sets firms' premiums far too low to underwrite their true risks of default. This tempts firms, especially those in bankruptcy, to shift their obligations to the PBGC, producing a $26 billion deficit in 2011, which could rise to $35 billion if American Airlines succeeds in offloading its pension obligations onto the agency.[42] Similarly, the National Flood Insurance Program (NFIP) run by the Federal Emergency Management Agency (FEMA) encourages homeowners and businesses to locate and build in the flood plain and beaches initially and then to return and rebuild there once the floodwaters recede—a form of moral hazard that Congress reinforced in its Hurricane Sandy legislation in 2013. Alert to this moral hazard, private insurers have fled the flood insurance field, leaving the government to pay the claims with premiums that are far too low to cover the true risk of loss. Indeed, the Hurricane Sandy aid bill enacted early in 2013 bailed out the NFIP for $9.7 billion. Worse, half of all NFIP policyholders apparently cancel their coverage after only three or four years, thinking that it isn't worth even the subsidized cost,[43] and Congress is under great pressure to increase the subsidies now that a 2012 law raising the rates has kicked in.[44] Finally, the Affordable Care Act increases moral hazard risks by encouraging the young and healthy to delay buying even subsidized coverage until they are ill, given the very low penalty for not buying insurance, their right to buy it later despite preexisting conditions, and their access to cheap or free (to them) emergency room care in the meanwhile.

Numerous other instances of government policies that encourage excessive risk-taking can be cited. This likely contributed to the savings and loan crisis in the late 1980s, in which the Federal Savings and Loan Insurance Corporation bailout cost taxpayers over $160 billion.[45] Large new subsidies to FEMA in 2012—it borrowed $18 billion from the Treasury to cover the 2005 and 2008 hurricanes, and will have to borrow even more to cover the Hurricane Sandy losses—impose huge, growing losses on taxpayers while preserving most of the moral hazard by owners that invited such losses.[46]

In similar fashion, federal drought insurance programs are replete with moral hazard. A recent study by agricultural economist Bruce Babcock finds that the programs, which are also discussed in chapters 6 and 8, are especially costly because they guarantee farmers, regardless of their wealth, a portion of their projected income rather than simply paying them for their damaged crops, so farmers buy more coverage than otherwise. As a result of the subsidies, which cost taxpayers over $6 billion a year, many farmers made more money from insurance payouts during the drought than they would have made from healthy crops! Further multiplying the program's egregious moral hazard, taxpayers cover about 62 percent of the costs of this insurance, which is sold by fifteen private insurance companies which keep the profits while receiving a federal guarantee against any underwriting losses.[47] Henry Olsen, former vice president of the market friendly American Enterprise Institute, calls this "obscene," utterly inconsistent with free markets.[48] To make matters even worse, it also induces excessive development in arid areas, which in turn produces more subsidized insurance and cost-ineffective water projects.[49]

Other programs induce moral hazard by encouraging the government to make "bad bets."[50] Again, the politically popular student loan programs, detailed in chapter 8, confer entitlements rather than screening for ability to succeed at school or to repay the loan, with the predictable result being high and rising default rates. And as Jack Donahue has noted, the government's own policy and management failures have spawned a different type of moral hazard, in which large aerospace and other contractors derive almost all of their business from the government, feeding on and enabling its chronic weaknesses.[51] The obvious psychological analogy is to the codependency of addicts and their enablers.

Unemployment insurance, which has been expanded on relatively easy terms, discourages workers from seeking or taking new jobs until their benefits run out, a delay that makes it less likely they will find new employment.[52] (Pending proposals to bar firms from considering applicants' unemployment in hiring decisions would likely have the same effect.) Government health insurance programs increase moral hazard when they reduce the costs of self-destructive behavior—for example, by subsidizing costly treatments for emphysema, which is almost always caused by smoking, of organ transplants for heavy drinkers, and of obesity-related diseases for reckless overeaters.

Moral hazard is common in government programs targeted at the poor, as one usually can receive benefits only by remaining poor.[53] If one's income rises too much, benefits either phase out or stop abruptly (called a "notch"), which means a very high, work-discouraging marginal tax rate. Indeed, the effective marginal tax rate on the thirty-eight million households receiving benefits from at least one federal welfare-entitlement program in 2011 averaged from 36 percent to over 50 percent (where additional income made them ineligible for Medicaid).[54] But difficult policy trade-offs involving moral hazard are almost inevitable in programs designed to help people in difficult circumstances. Discharging bankrupts' debts, for example, invites irresponsibility but also gives them a fresh start.[55] But some programs can be structured to reduce moral hazard. The Earned Income Tax Credit, discussed in chapter 11, does so by providing wage supplements to low-income workers; those without jobs are not eligible. Benefits for the elderly, the widowed, and the seriously disabled entail little or no moral hazard, either because the beneficiaries have no way to affect either the likelihood or the magnitude of the compensable event (old age, spousal death) or because the compensable event (serious disability) is so debilitating that no rational individual would significantly risk it. The Veterans Administration, however, also increasingly defines disability to include minor conditions, including common age-related ailments such as hearing loss, lower back pain, and arthritis. This helps to account for the nearly 900,000 backlogged disability claims, which are discussed in chapter 6.[56]

Most social programs adopted during the New Deal era hoped to minimize moral hazard by targeting individuals whose misfortunes occurred through no fault of their own. Since these misfortunates were common, the risks of such losses could be reduced or socialized by being spread among a much larger pool of individuals. This helped to justify the transfer of resources to those unfortunates who turn out to be what have been called "bad draws."[57] It also made these programs actuarially feasible, once they matured. Rational risk-averse voters, not knowing whether they would be lucky or not, would likely favor such a system—and the American public has emphatically agreed.

To the extent that most poor people are eager to escape poverty even if it means losing their benefits, programs that help them do so mitigate moral hazard but not completely, due to what Charles Murray calls "the law of unintended rewards: Any social transfer increases the net value of being in the condition that prompted the transfer."[58] Nicholas Kristof, a *New York Times* columnist and ardent supporter of antipoverty programs, notes some tragic examples of this in Appalachia.[59] Parents, he finds, often pull their children out of literacy classes to make them more likely to qualify for a monthly check from the federal Supplemental Security Income program for being mentally disabled. Young people don't join the military, a traditional escape route from poverty, because they can more easily get food stamps and disability payments (discussed just below). Antipoverty programs' incentives tend to reduce marriages, which in turn tend to reduce poverty. Kristof fails to mention a far more fateful, socially destructive example: poverty programs have encouraged some unmarried women to drop out of school or the workforce to have children that they could not otherwise afford. (The 1996 welfare reform, discussed in chapter 11, reduced this incentive but did not wholly eliminate it.) Cash transfer programs also encourage low-income mothers to leave unhappy marriages, which may improve their own lot but damage the life prospects of their children—especially boys.[60]

Sometimes moral hazard applies to government units that seeks to maximize federal dollars at little or no cost to themselves (depending on the federal program's cost-sharing formula). States, for example, have powerful fiscal incentives to expand food stamp eligibility as much as possible because the federal government pays 100 percent of the costs, which helps to explain, as discussed in chapter 11, why the states are partly responsible for the program's dramatic expansion in recent years far above what one would have expected from the Great Recession. Local governments encourage homebuilding in fire-prone areas, knowing that federal taxpayers will bear most of the fire-fighting and cleanup costs.[61] The vast inefficiencies of urban transit spending, detailed in chapter 8, also reflect the practice of federal matching dollars that make local projects seem far cheaper than they really are. Medicaid, under which the federal government has borne a much smaller share of costs than in these other programs, thus has weaker participation incentives for states. This largely explains why many states resist its expansion.[62] (Whether the Affordable Care Act can change this calculus will depend on whether the states believe Washington's promise to pay almost all program costs in the long run–a credibility issue discussed in chapter 6.)

This same intergovernmental incentive structure, added to the moral hazard of individual beneficiaries, helps to explain the explosion in the costs of the federal disability insurance (SSDI) program.

States pay for a laid-off worker's temporary welfare and unemployment benefits, but if they can get him instead on the disability rolls, the federal government pays 100 percent—indefinitely.[63] For the worker, the average annual SSDI benefit level is only $2000 less than the full-time return to a minimum-wage job, and Medicare benefits kick in after two years on SSDI. Moreover, over half of SSDI's beneficiaries now qualify because of easily claimed conditions like mood disorders and back pain, and the program makes it easy to stay on the rolls. Not surprisingly, SSDI has higher claim rates and lower return-to-work rates than comparable private disability insurance.[64]

These incentives help to explain why SSDI recipients have *tripled just since 1990 despite a much healthier working age population*; much of the expansion occurs among young people. The CBO finds that the program expanded nearly sixfold since 1970 to 8.8 million in January 2013 (10.9 million, including benefits to their spouses and dependent children), and that the SSDI trust fund will be exhausted in 2016, only three years hence.[65] Nicholas Eberstadt, a leading demographer, has analyzed the reasons for this stunning growth. First, the ratio of workers to those receiving disability benefits has plummeted from 134:1 to only about 16:1 (or, by another measure, 11:1). Second, the age at disability has dipped significantly. In 1960, about 6 percent of beneficiaries were in their thirties or early forties; by 2011, over 15 percent were that young. As Eberstadt dryly notes, "more Americans [seem to be] making the securing of disability status their life-long career." Third, over 15 percent are now granted disability for "mood disorders," and another 29 percent for musculoskeletal and connective tissue conditions—both of which are almost impossible to disprove and lend themselves to fraud.[66] Fourth, little of the increase in disability awards is caused by the Great Recession. Between 2001 (also a recession year) and 2011, private nonfarm jobs rose by 828,000 while beneficiaries increased by over three million.[67] According to leading students of the program, "It is difficult to overstate the role that [SSDI] plays in discouraging employment among these young people."[68] Fortunately, we do not lack for promising reform proposals.[69] Other federal disability programs also create moral hazard.

Thus, the Railroad Retirement Board waited five years to terminate disability benefits based on fraudulent medical evidence—and did so reluctantly.[70] Rapid expansions of food stamps, Pell grants, and other benefit programs have also reduced labor force participation beyond the recession's effect (although Pell Grants may improve recipients' long-term employability).[71]

The usual remedies for moral hazard are for potential *risk-bearers* to improve their information about the risk (at some cost) so that they can manage it better, or to make potential *risk-takers* bear some or all of the costs of their risk-taking through contract or public policy, which will increase their incentives to do so. But government finds it harder than private insurers to do these things. To woo beneficiaries, it is less likely to use co-pays, deductibles, and other provisions to assure that the insured has enough uninsured exposure to loss ("skin in the game") to act in risk-reducing ways. It is also less likely to gather and analyze information in order to quantify and monitor risks so that they can screen out those who pose high risks of claiming or defaulting, and can charge risk-related premiums for coverage. Knowing that the insurer (the taxpayers) will pay for losses in the event of default, they have even less reason to weigh risks and benefits carefully. Sometimes a program seeks to benefit precisely those who it thinks are too poor to share the costs, or it wants to avoid political flak for charging those who could afford it for its risk-bearing service. Moreover, officials eager to expand a program may soft-pedal the risks posed by the new participants.

The Mental Health Parity Act of 1996, for example, requires that insurance coverage for federally funded mental health services be treated like physical health coverage even though mental health claims tend to be harder to verify than physical health claims and, for a variety of reasons, are more prone to moral hazard.[72] A similar mandate now applies to all policies regulated under the Affordable Care Act.[73] The Medicare Prescription Drug Improvement and Modernization Act of 2003, which provides a prescription drug benefit for seniors under Medicare Part D, is another costly expansion of programmatic moral hazard by inducing excess use of low-benefit drugs.

Nonmarket failure, like market failure, is a systematic, incentives-based tendency of government policies. Charles Wolf, an economist at RAND, has elaborated a theory of "non-market" failures to supplement the better-developed theory of market failures.[74] Government is not the only non-market entity that exhibits such failures but it is certainly the most important, so I shall (as his theory does) focus on it. Wolf begins by identifying the four most salient differences between the supply and demand characteristics of government outputs (i.e., the effects of programs) and of private market outputs. On the supply side: "the 'products' of nonmarket activities are usually hard to define in principle, ill-defined in practice, and extremely difficult to measure independently of the inputs which produce them." Evidence of output quality is elusive, in part because the information that in the market would be transmitted by consumer behavior is missing. (I shall defer discussion of the information factor until the next section of this chapter.) Government outputs are almost always produced, often by legal mandate, by a single agency provider, eliminating competition. These outputs are also hard to evaluate because no profit criterion or other reliable mechanism exists for assessing their effectiveness, as there is with markets. On the demand side: politicians' electoral incentives and short time horizons lead them to support government programs with infeasible objectives and rising costs as a response to (or instigation of) public dissatisfaction with the shortcomings of market outcomes.

In light of these features of government activity, Wolf develops a typology of nonmarket failures that very roughly parallels the set of market failures cited in standard economic theory. The most important category of nonmarket failure is what he calls "internalities" (corresponding to the "externality" problem in private markets). Internalities are the private goals that apply within nonmarket organizations to guide, regulate, and evaluate the performance of agencies and their personnel. These goals are "'private' . . . because they—rather than, or at least in addition to, the agency's 'public' purposes—provide the motivations behind individual and collective behavior. This structure of rewards and penalties constitutes what Kenneth Arrow refers to as 'an internal version of the price system.'"

The most obvious internality conducing to government failures and distortions is budgetary growth, which substitutes for the profit criterion as a measure of performance. The dynamics that conduce to budgetary growth include not only bureaucratic self-interest but also external political pressures to expand the coverage of benefits and the bureaucratic capacity to deliver them. This is not always the case—government sometimes reduces benefits, especially those for politically impotent groups, and agencies occasionally seek to limit their responsibilities so as to protect their core mission—but bureaucratic expansion is a very powerful tendency indeed even when, as often occurs, it actually impairs the agency's effectiveness (for example, by diluting its resources and management focus or by saddling it with conflicting incentives). I shall return to this point in the last section of this chapter, which discusses government credibility.

Perhaps the most pervasive and dangerous internality, however, is the disconnect between a policy's public costs and private costs. The true cost of a government program is not limited to that which appears on the program's budget, which is a notoriously misleading document (except to the cognoscenti). Among other gimmicks, a vast amount of government cost and debt is kept off-budget, especially the activities of the government-sponsored enterprises (GSEs) like Fannie Mae, Freddie Mac, Farmer Mac, the Federal Home Loan Banks, the Farm Credit institutions, and some others. The true costs also include the *private costs* that private compliance with the programs requires. These costs may vastly exceed the public outlays, yet they do not appear on any public budget and thus are unlikely to be fully considered by federal officials—unless officials are somehow forced to do so. The significance of this obvious fact for the design and cost-effectiveness of public programs can hardly be overstated. Indeed, if we assume that these private costs produce *any* positive benefit for the official's program, her incentive is to ignore the private costs that produce that benefit regardless (perhaps literally so) of how large those private costs may be. A public budget that does not include these private costs encourages policy makers to neglect them. Only by compelling systematic attention to the private costs of public programs through the kinds of analytic requirements discussed in chapter 2 can we accomplish this. Alternatively, we might imagine that the private cost-bearers will mobilize to demand attention before the policy is in place and the damage is done is, but their ability to foresee and measure those costs before the policy is fully elaborated and implemented is likely to be severely limited. (This timely knowledge-of-private-costs problem may help to explain why industry claims about the effects of proposed rules often seem reflexive, poorly supported, and lacking in credibility.)

Another type of nonmarket failure is what Wolf calls "derived externalities" unanticipated side effects, often in an area remote from that in which the public policy was intended to operate. Derived externalities are exacerbated by government's tendency to operate through large organizations using blunt instruments. The last nonmarket failure category worth mentioning here is a maldistribution of influence and power, which must be compared to the maldistribution of income and wealth that private markets often generate.

We shall see in later chapters that Wolf's theoretical account of nonmarket failures helps to explain a regrettably large number of government failures. This account, however, cannot itself determine whether the market or government (or some hybrid form) can best deal with perceived social problems. Each kind of system has some advantages and disadvantages relative to the other. As Wolf puts it, theory provides no clear bottom line: the answer will depend on the specifics of particular cases.

Incentives can distort policymaking in other ways, which we can get at by asking the question: why, or how much, would an official actually care about the soundness of policy? Political scientists Alan Gerber and Eric Patashnik, whose work was mentioned in chapter 1, provide one approach to an answer in their notion of "zero credit policymaking." They first review some of the significant obstacles that any conscientious policymaker would confront, such as convincing others that some objective social condition constitutes a "problem" requiring governmental intervention; overcoming disagreement over the best solution to that problem; deliberating, bargaining, and compromising to develop a politically viable proposal; seeking to create public demand for the policy; and so forth. They then consider what happens if this political effort and creativity begin to bear fruit:

In a commercial setting, such an investment often enjoys legal protections such as patents and trademarks. In a political setting, however, there is nothing to stop an opportunistic opponent who observes the changes in public opinion produced by a rival's hard work from proposing a substantively similar proposal of his own. If this effort at political mimicry is successful, the policy innovator will capture, at best, a small share of the credit for the results of his efforts. Worse, the second politician, by hanging back until political conditions become more favorable and observing how opinion unfolds, may generate more support for his alternative scheme, a copycat plan better tailored to public opinion. In the ruthlessly competitive world of democratic politics, the policy innovator could end up worse off for his effort. . . . [A "zero-credit policy" is] a government intervention or activity that offers no captureable political returns even though it has large social benefits. . . . If policy innovators anticipate that the political benefits from proposing novel solutions to public problems will be quickly appropriated, the effect will be to discourage the entrepreneurial investments in the first place.[75]

Their point, of course, is not that policy makers never invest in costly policy innovation. They sometimes do, as exemplified by the inspiring, successful policies discussed in chapter 11. Yet the fact that they are always trotted out suggests how rare such breakthroughs are. (Another successful change, the 1983 Social Security reform, was politically easier because it would "bite" only decades later.) The authors' structural point is that zero-credit policy making makes such investments risky and thus less probable.

The far-reaching effect of zero-credit policy making is perhaps best illustrated by the stimulus legislation of 2009, the American Recovery and Reinvestment Act. Since president Barack Obama desperately needed some Republican votes in the Senate to avert a filibuster, the Republican leadership had a great deal of bargaining power. It made a strategic decision not to cooperate with the administration on the bill, even though it contained some provisions that Republicans strongly favored. Its theory was that if they helped the bill to pass and the stimulus then succeeded, Obama would get all the credit, whereas if the stimulus failed, the Republicans could tell the voters "we told you so."[76] The bill ultimately passed; the assessment of the program's effects is controversial and ongoing. Although the stakes in this case were perhaps uniquely high, one could cite numerous other examples of the immobilizing politics of zero-credit policy making.

Another incentives-based source of policy failure is a feature of many administrative agencies or subagencies—what sociologist Philip Selznick in his classic study of the Tennessee Valley Authority described as "tunnel vision," or the propensity of administrative units, particularly those with a single mission, to narrow their cognitive focus so as to promote that mission and that mission only.[77] (Chapter 3 discussed multi-mission agencies, noting there that OMB now assigns even single-mission agencies other, sometimes conflicting policy goals or constraints.) This narrow focus perversely blinds them to other factors that should be relevant to their missions. (Congressional committees and subcommittees, which by political design are also highly specialized to serve their members' electoral needs, exhibit— indeed, nurture—this same parochial tendency.) A recent Brookings Institution analysis sees this tunnel vision operating in certain environmental policies where "fuel efficiency and energy efficiency matter, but nothing else does. In effect, government officials are acting as if they are guided by a single mission myopia that leads to the exclusion of all concerns other than their agencies' mandates."[78] A related phenomenon is for agencies to pursue their dominant mission at the expense or to the exclusion of all the others.[79]

IRRATIONALITY

Rationality is one of the most contested ideas in social science and philosophy. But almost regardless of how one defines it, two things are clear. First, individual rationality can produce collective irrationality. Voters, for example, have a poor grasp of numbers and consistently overestimate the amount of government spending on key programs, the foreign-born share of the population, the number of illegal aliens in the country, the relative shares of the budget going to education and prisons, and the share of the population on welfare.[80] Second, individuals often make irrational choices. This is no paradox, nor is it confined to Prisoner's Dilemma or other game theoretic situations in which individuals' inability to communicate with each other in order to further mutually advantageous cooperation may induce decisions that leave each of them worse off.* The more general transformation of individual rationality into collective irrationality is endemic to politics and thus to policy making. The brief shutdown of the federal government in 1995 and 1996 is a dramatic example. The product of tactical choices and familiar bargaining ploys by president Bill Clinton, House Speaker Newt Gingrich, and other congressional leaders that they considered eminently rational, the shutdown was egregiously irresponsible and accomplished nothing for the public (unless a brief boost in Clinton's power qualifies as useful). This judgment seems likely to apply to the October 2013 shutdown as well.

There are strong reasons to believe that collective choices are less rational than individual choices in competitive markets, although there are exceptions.† Markets are driven and disciplined by self-interested (broadly defined, as discussed earlier) decisions by individuals transacting voluntarily with one another and weighing costs and benefits at the margin. Absent coercion, fraud, or other market

---

*Kenneth Arrow's impossibility theorem is sometimes called the "voting paradox" (John B. Taylor & Akila Weerapana, *Principles of Microeconomics*, 6th ed. [2009], 453), but that is only because the theorem seems to violate common-sense assumptions about logical decision making. As explained below, however, irrationality in politics, far from being paradoxical, is commonplace. For an explanation of the Prisoner's Dilemma and its erstwhile solutions, see Robert Axelrod, *The Evolution of Cooperation* (1984).

†Markets can be distorted by a crowd psychology that produces bubbles and panics that seem (especially, but not only, in retrospect) manifestly irrational. The housing bubble that burst in 2007 and the Asian panic of 1997 are recent examples. Even such markets, however, produce a winner for every loser, and actors are disciplined by playing with their own money, not that of the taxpayers.

failures, these transactions cannot occur unless they make at least one of the parties better off and none worse off (known as a Pareto-superior move). And intense competition from other markets and actors means that they fail unless they become more efficient.

This account of market rationality does not deny that markets sometimes experience panics, bubbles, and other forms of herd mentality. But whereas markets severely punish irrationality, politics does not; indeed, it magnifies it. As Nobel Prize laureate Kenneth Arrow famously demonstrated, there is no agreed-upon social welfare function that can transform individual voters' preferences into a collective decision without violating certain elementary rules of logic. (The actual policy significance of this "cycling" phenomenon is disputed.) The Pareto-superior condition is never possible in politics; public policies invariably make some citizens better off at the expense of other citizens who are made worse off. Government seldom competes against other providers; this monopolization (as Wolf also emphasized) encourages inefficient provision whatever logic might dictate.

Political actors—voters, politicians, officials, interest groups—are often influenced by strong emotions, self-deception, and other factors that may suppress or deviate from their rational interests. (Again, markets harshly penalize such deviations.) Perhaps the most pervasive of these factors is *ignorance*, particularly among voters. (I discuss policymakers' ignorance in the next chapter.) For more than fifty years, studies of how much voters know about the political system, their own representatives, and the important issues of the day have invariably found appalling levels of ignorance about the most basic facts. (The theological ignorance in America, perhaps the most religious of the advanced western democracies, is equally remarkable.[81]) Reviewing these studies, Vanderbilt University political scientist Larry Bartels explains that a number of analysts, while conceding this inattention and ignorance, have dismissed these findings on various grounds: that voters' ignorance is actually rational in that they use "information shortcuts" such as party identification, endorsements by opinion leaders, and other cues to decide whom to vote for; that the most ignorant citizens don't bother to vote at all; that aggregating large numbers of voters substitutes the "wisdom of crowds" for the ignorance of many (Condorcet's jury theorem); that they vote the same way they would vote if they were better informed; that they are well enough informed about how well they are doing to vote rationally; and that even if none of these explanations produces rational voting, their irrationality does not affect electoral outcomes. Bartels refutes each of these "rationalizations" of irrational voting behavior and shows that such behavior affects many important election outcomes.[82]

Numerous other empirical studies by leading social scientists have established additional sources of predictable irrationality on the part of individuals, both as voters and in other settings. Four are of special interest. First, in widely cited experimental work that earned a Nobel Prize, Daniel Kahneman and Amos Tversky showed that individual decision making is commonly distorted by recurrent, recalcitrant cognitive patterns and logical errors—some forty-five of them! Some of these "heuristics and biases" include the "availability effect" (we tend to exaggerate phenomena that are easy to remember); "anchoring" (we tend to rely too heavily on one trait or piece of information); "loss aversion" (in assessing an objectively identical risk, we tend to strongly prefer avoiding losses over making gains); the "planning fallacy" (we tend to underestimate how long things will take even when we have prior experience with them); the "representativeness heuristic" (we assess the probability of an event according to how representative we think it is to some other event rather than by how likely it is); the "optimism bias" (we assume that we are less at risk of some negative outcome than others are); and "status quo bias" (we prefer the current state of affairs even when it is irrational to do so).[83] Other researchers have identified a "projection bias" (we exaggerate how much our future preferences will be like they are today).[84] In a book aptly entitled *How We Know What Isn't So*, social psychologist Thomas Gilovich distinguishes cognitive distortions in everyday reasoning ("something out of nothing;" "too much from too little;" "seeing what we expect to see"), as well as motivation and social ones ("seeing what we want to see;" "believing what we are told;" "the imagined agreement of others").[85] Future research will surely uncover more such irrationalities, but how they actually interact and affect human decisions in the real world will likely remain controversial.[86]

In a second body of irrationality research, legal scholar Cass Sunstein and his research colleagues (including Kahneman) have shown that people often make what they call "predictably incoherent judgments" in a wide variety of situations mainly because of two cognitive difficulties: they use category-bound thinking even when it leads them astray, and they cannot readily translate moral judgments into the metrics of numbers and years, as jury decisions and CBA often require.[87] In a more counterintuitive finding, they also noted empirical support for a "group polarization" theory: when groups deliberate over a decision (such as juries, interest groups, and legislative committees), their decisions tend to be more extreme versions of their predeliberation views.[88] Sunstein and colleagues have also proposed that policy makers deploy "soft paternalism" in the form of disclosures, warnings, and defaults (which individuals can reject, albeit at some cost) in order to "nudge" the public toward more rational decisions on pensions, fuel economy, and the like.[89] This approach assumes, of course, that officials will make systematically better choices in establishing these defaults despite two factors discussed above: their own biases and their poor information. It also assumes that the architecture of the nudge approach will better protect against the psychological sources of irrational choices than more intrusive regulatory forms.[90]

A third area of irrationality research has established the phenomenon of "cultural cognition"—people's propensity to assess objective evidence in ways that try to maintain consistency with their preexisting cultural or ideological commitments, such as individualism/hierarchy or communitarianism/egalitarianism. Led by my Yale Law School colleague Dan Kahan, these interdisciplinary studies find that this bias affects the public's views of a large number of policy issues that pivot on assessments of risk.[91] Through cleverly designed statistical studies, they also show that people on both ends of the ideological spectrum (not just those who possess what one writer dismisses as "the Republican brain"[92]) resist scientific findings that they think contradict their strongly held political or social values. They find no significant differences between liberals and conservatives as to their amount of ideological bias on controversial scientific questions—even for those on both sides who most engage in "cognitive reflection" rather than heuristic or intuitive forms of reasoning—but they find enough on both sides, as Kahan puts it, "for everyone to be troubled and worried."[93] For every conservative skeptical of climate change, it seems, there is a liberal who is convinced of the repeatedly disproved link between vaccines and autism,[94] who denies the health and environmental benefits of genetically modified foods,[95] and who insists that public school teachers are underpaid.[96] The fourth body of research, by social psychologist Jonathan Haidt, extends Kahan's findings by identifying six "moral modules"—care/harm; fairness/cheating; loyalthy/betrayal; authority/subversion; sanctity/degradation; and liberty/oppression—that evolutionary struggles have bequeathed to us, that shape our political values (among other things), and that cause us to reject evidence and arguments that contradict our existing moral commitments, usually by interpreting them to accord with those commitments.[97]

Does this voter ignorance and irrationality produce failed public policies? Bryan Caplan, a George Mason University economist, argues strongly that it does.[98] One can imagine several ways that voter ignorance and irrationality might be palliated. Legislators animated by a Burkean ethos of independence from and fiduciary responsibility to their constituents could vote in ways (hopefully more rational) that contradict constituents' desires. Irrational laws could still provide better-informed administrators with enough discretion to improve the legislators' irrational choices. Caplan shows, however, that even if these were realistic possibilities, they would not fully solve the problem of ignorance-driven policy.

Is this not a troubling paradox? On the one hand, most voters fail the minimal test of knowing enough about candidates and public issues to rationally decide which candidates will best promote their interests. On the other hand, America is in most respects a highly successful, if flawed, democracy. Caplan proposes two resolutions to this paradox. First, data show that the median voter can make more rational political choices than the median nonvoter, largely because education correlates with both economic literacy and voter participation. Even if the mass of citizens fail minimal tests of knowledge and rational judgment, those who actually vote perform somewhat better. Second, voters' outcome preferences are not necessarily the same as their policy preferences: as with the North American Free Trade Agreement, they want the economy to prosper even if they oppose the policies that make it prosper. This places policy makers in a tough situation but also enables them to enact wiser policies than the median voter prefers. *If* these policies can generate quick enough results for politicians to gain credit from satisfying voters' outcome preferences, they can ignore or finesse voters' policy preferences.[99]

This is a big *if*. After all, many sound policies will prove effective only in the medium or long term. Even if one accepts Caplan's underlying analysis, then, his resolution of this paradox is not entirely convincing. Yet my analysis in the succeeding chapters only deepens it. Chapter 12 offers some possible remedies.

CHAPTER 6

Information, Inflexibility, Incredibility, and Mismanagement

I n this chapter I extend the analysis of policy failure beyond incentives and irrationality to consider four other sources of ineffectiveness: (1) poor information; (2) rigidity where flexibility is needed; (3) lack of the credibility needed to secure the cooperation of other actors; and (4) mismanagement, particularly in the forms of fraud, waste, and abuse. These impediments to policy success are alike in their deep, structural, endemic nature.

INFORMATION

In addition to the problem of incentives (discussed in chapter 5), much government failure reflects the fact that information is costly—to gather, verify, contextualize, assess, deploy, and keep up to date. As we saw in chapter 1, markets are much more efficient than government in mobilizing the information needed for decisions. Unless protected through contract or intellectual property law, information is a nonexcludable good. That is, once it is produced it is available to all, which means that those who incur the costs of producing it cannot garner for themselves its full value, so we get less of it than we want. Accordingly, it becomes even more valuable but less available.

The public policy implications of this simple fact about information are enormous. First and most obvious, sound policies require good information—about the existence, nature, and causes of a problem, about the costs and benefits to the affected public of various possible solutions to the problem, and about the effectiveness of current policies. This information is hard to come by under the best of circumstances. More than a quarter century after Congress made control of the nation's southern border a high priority and poured enormous sums of money into new surveillance technology, patrol staff, and the building of a border fence costing about $16 million per mile, the government still does not know enough about which conditions have caused the recent decline in illegal entries—economic and demographic changes in Mexico, criminal gangs in border cities there, a beefed-up Border Patrol, the fence, and so forth—to make rational budgeting decisions.[1] Nor does the government even have goals and measures in place for this purpose.[2] The world is not organized in ways that make such information transparent, much less readily accessible by government. Rather, it must often be mined from resistant materials at great cost.

This point is vividly illustrated by information that the government requires sellers to disclose to consumers—ostensibly a relatively straightforward problem. Such policies are designed, among other things, to help consumers make rational choices in the market; they are discussed and assessed in some detail in chapter 8. Most policy experts consider such information disclosure to be a relatively straightforward, uncontroversial regulatory technique carrying a relatively low risk of error, compared with more interventionist and prescriptive policy approaches like command-and-control regulation or even decentralized market-based schemes (also discussed in chapter 8). A second implication of information costs relates to political information that is pivotal to effective policy making but that only insiders possess. Such information is often difficult to acquire and assess in a reliable form because of political actors' opportunistic production and use of it. It includes, among other things, how intensely different groups feel about the proposals, which coalitions can be formed for and against them, how politicians are likely to align themselves, how the internal politics of the relevant policy-making institutions will work, how bureaucrats are likely to use the discretion Congress would give them, how the courts will react to the proposals, how the proposals will affect other levels of government (and even foreign countries), how effectively they can be implemented in the real world (the subject of chapter 8), how long the adoption and implementation processes will take, and so forth.

A third implication of information costs relates to markets— foreshadowed in chapter 1 and the focus of chapter 7. How markets will react to a policy proposal is as elusive as it is important. A policy that the markets condemn is probably doomed to failure— regardless of its political feasibility and theoretical merits. President Bill Clinton's budget proposals, which angered many of his own supporters, reflected Wall Street–sensitive calculations driven home to him by Treasury secretary Robert Rubin, an aficionado of capital markets. But because markets reflect and respond to myriad influences that often confound predictions,* market movements are often difficult to explain even *after* the fact (postdiction). Years after the financial crisis of 2007–8, the most sophisticated analysts are still arguing about the precise causes,[3] yet policy makers have proceeded as if they knew the answer.

Fourth, information is seldom self-evident, self-defining, or self-authenticating. To the contrary, its uses and meanings often are ambiguous and require interpretation, which inevitably means competing interpretations. Much policy debate is about the epistemic, political, and moral implications of such ambiguities. This is why additional information seldom resolves political disputes, and indeed often inflames them.

Fifth, the distribution of information is markedly unequal. Members of Congress are far better informed about the specific policy issues that they deal with (on their committees and otherwise) than are

---

*As just one example, consider how Facebook, one of the most successful business ventures in history, failed—by a large margin—to accurately predict the market for its public shares despite the best expert Wall Street advice that its billions could buy.

the vast majority of the voters who sent them to Washington. Typically, career administrative officials are even better informed than both their congressional masters and their own politically appointed superiors. This is most clearly true as to the more technical and data-dependent aspects of the relatively narrow policies for which they are responsible, but political information in the policy areas in which officials have long worked is skewed as well. Another problem with information inequality is the common situation in which market actors possess the information that policy makers need but have an incentive not to reveal it. Congress can demand or subpoena information it wants from private actors, but this remedy is costly and protracted, and its committees often do not know what information they need.

Steven Kelman's detailed study of federal procurement of computer systems from private vendors vividly exemplifies this problem. To reduce vendors' opportunities to corrupt procurement officials, the process mandates an "open competition" among potential vendors that severely limits officials' ability to work with vendors during the contract negotiation stage to obtain the detailed information that the officials need to figure out and specify in the contract precisely which systems and service they should purchase; this also prevents the officials from rewarding the best-performing vendors by promising to buy from them in the future. This informational imbalance, coupled with a process that aggravates it, produces contracts that are costly, ill-informed, and difficult to enforce ("stupid" contracts, as one reviewer put it).[4]

Sixth, informational gaps about social problems mean that policy makers often direct their efforts at the symptoms of social problems, not their root causes—and so the underlying problem may persist even if some of the symptoms have been addressed. This is not necessarily because they fail to recognize the difference between a symptom and a cause, but for two other reasons: either they do not know what the root causes are, or they know (or think they know) what the root causes are but for one reason or another they cannot deal with them. Crime is a good example.[5] Even today, despite billions of dollars spent on criminological research, we do not know what ultimately *causes* crime—as distinguished from some of the social factors that are correlated with various crimes. Nevertheless, many criminologists believe that they know the root causes of crime, and that these causes are to be found in family life and the (anti) socialization process. But even if they were correct about this, and even if they could pinpoint those aspects of family life and socialization that cause crime, it is unlikely that public policy could do much about them because family life is considered largely a private matter, absent parental neglect or abuse, and because there may be legal, even constitutional, limits on how government may intrude. My point is not that policy makers should never focus their efforts on symptoms—indeed, they are often wise to do so because that may be the best that they can do under the circumstances[6]—but only that our ignorance about ultimate causes often requires this decidedly second-best approach.

A seventh reason why information costs confound sound policy making is not simply that the data systems that government demands of the private sector often misfire—Medicare's troubled, overpromoted digitalized medical records program, discussed in chapter 7, is just one example—but that its *own* data systems are so poor, often undermining federal policies. As the Affordable Care Act geared up to begin operations, the government so despaired about the integrity and coordination of the essential databases that it had to abandon a main safeguard against fraudulent applications. Thus, it ruled that if these databases could not verify within one day the income and employment information needed to prove eligibility for the Act's insurance and subsidy provisions, the government must approve them based on mere personal attestation.[7] This is no isolated example. An agency created by the Dodd-Frank law found the models used by officials to assess risks taken by regulated financial institutions to be simplistic and fundamentally flawed.[8] The Federal Housing Administration's outdated information systems have impaired the accuracy of its data, helping to distort its disastrous loan programs—*even long after the mortgage crisis had erupted.*[9]

Gun control is an even more tragic example, involving failures in the data systems of *two* agencies—the FBI (in the Justice Department) and the Bureau of Alcohol, Tobacco, Firearms and Explosives (BATFE, part of the Treasury Department). A *New York Times* analysis found that although Congress began requiring background checks for gun buyers almost two decades ago, the FBI's spotty database of criminal and mental health records allows thousands of people to buy firearms every year whom the law should bar from doing so. Because of these data gaps, the FBI often cannot use the three-day waiting period to verify personal histories, thus enabling violent felons, fugitives, and the mentally ill to buy firearms. Since 2005, the *Times* found, 22,162 firearms—including nearly 3,000 in 2012 alone—have been bought after the waiting period by people later determined to have been disqualified by their criminal and mental histories.[10] As for BATFE's gun control program, Congress has assured its failure by barring it from maintaining an effective database.[11] In a particularly perverse demonstration of Congress's determination to bar essential policy information, it acted—only months after the school shootings in Newtown, Connecticut, and other mass killings by gunmen that inspired public fury and demands for reform—to make *permanent* several earlier provisions preventing BATFE from compiling the database needed for effective enforcement.[12]

Poor information systems have also hobbled immigration enforcement and policy making. For decades, Congress has chastised the immigration enforcement agency for continuing to rely on paper-based files on aliens and then often misplacing them, and also for repeatedly bungling its computerization efforts. Sometimes, the government's ignorance is willful and self-inflicted, as with Homeland Security's decision not to comply with a congressional demand for a reliable metric for assessing border security, a political sine qua non for a deal on immigration reform. According to the *New York Times*, officials resisted producing it "because the president did not want any hurdles placed on the pathway to eventual citizenship for immigrants in the country illegally."[13]

These examples, important as they are in policy terms, are merely the tip of the iceberg. Numerous federal agencies have neither digitized nor managed their own information systems competently, much less coordinated them with those of other mission-relevant agencies and databases at all levels of government.[14] (The computer system's failures as Obamacare operations began, discussed later in the chapter, are merely the most notable, far-reaching example.) These obstacles to well-informed federal policy are vastly magnified by the centralization in Washington of most key decisions, despite the fact that the information needed to formulate and implement them is located a universe away—in 320 million Americans whose needs, intentions, desires, and behaviors are remarkably diverse and opaque to even the most well-intentioned officials. How can central policy makers gather and aggregate all of this vastly dispersed information into effective policy?

The short answer is, they can't—however smart they are and however hard they try. The famous Austrian economist Friedrich Hayek developed this simple fact into a body of work that, along with his more technical work on the business cycle, won him a Nobel Prize in 1974. In *The Constitution of Liberty* and other books, Hayek showed that officials' efforts to centralize this dispersed information and then massage it into coherent policy was doomed to failure. Only markets, he argued, could elicit and process this immense amount of information and convert it into a workable "spontaneous order." Centralized decision making would invariably, inevitably, and tragically (for the people subject to it) get it very wrong. Frustrated by the calamitous social consequences of these errors and determined to bend society's complexity to their will, officials would need to increase their power so as to control and rationalize this disorder (as it seemed to them), which would only further distort and suppress what was in fact a stubbornly diverse and opaque complexity that is unknowable ("illegible," in political anthropologist James Scott's terminology) to any centralized intelligence.[15]

Hayek famously depicted this cycle of centralized control, failure and frustration, redoubled efforts at centralized control, then further failure and frustration as "the road to serfdom," and Scott's analysis of the failures of grand state-driven "schemes to improve the human condition" (his book's subtitle) lends empirical support to Hayek's road map to dystopia. (Hayek had experienced this firsthand as a refugee from the Nazi *anschluss* of Austria in the late 1930s.) Although this woeful cycle, this fateful journey to statist repression, has occurred in many societies, it is by no means inevitable—despite some conservatives' hysterical hyperbole to the contrary. The growing power and reach of states—their often laudable but sometimes feckless efforts to improve the human condition—will never lead to anything remotely approaching serfdom in the United States or any other liberal welfare state in Europe. The slope may be slippery, but our political and social systems, our constitutions of liberty, provide many sturdy and deeply embedded footholds.*

Nevertheless, Hayek's analysis of the dynamics of information in complex societies remains true and profoundly important. In the remainder of this section, I shall briefly describe some applications of his analysis to our policy-making system.

Members of Congress, at the summit of our system, receive a veritable tsunami of information, but much or most of it is highly biased and selective. Their main sources—lobbyists, party organs, and staff—are self-interested, partisan, precommitted, and result-oriented, not objective problem-solvers. Members' positions on many important issues are predetermined by their party affiliations and campaign pledges, and are usually not open to significant revision in light of new or better information. Preternaturally busy people, they typically spend most of their time on fund-raising, campaigning, subcommittee work, and constituency-tending. Consequently, they have little time to read or think deeply about issues, and in any event politicians are seldom drawn to such passive activities. Instead, they rely on cues, party and staff summaries, and various politics-specific heuristics and routines for processing information and voting. Some of Congress's institutional staff organizations—the Congressional Budget Office, the Library of Congress, and the Government Accountability Office (GAO)—do provide objective, high-quality research support and anal-

---

*Based on an informal talk by Hayek that I attended in 1979 when he was 80, I venture to speculate that Hayek, who was a great admirer of the United States, agreed.

ysis, and indeed I propose in chapter 12 to expand their resources, but members' scarce attention is usually elsewhere.

Finally, an increasing amount of legislation is bundled into enormously complex omnibus bills often covering diverse subjects. This practice, which the majority ordinarily uses to advance its political-tactical purposes, can facilitate enactment of spending and other bills, but it adversely affects members' ability to inform themselves about the legislation they are considering. (Most state legislatures limit this practice through single-subject rules.) It reduces their ability to focus on particular portions of the omnibus measure, to deliberate fully and knowledgeably, and to raise penetrating questions and make useful amendments.

Administrative agencies, in contrast, can conduct more systematic information-gathering, careful deliberation, and detailed analysis of policy issues.[16] Their staffs, at least, tend to be more technocratic and apolitical in their training and orientation. Moreover, some agencies fund a great deal of policy-oriented research. As noted in chapter 3, they also are usually the best loci within the government of fine-grained policy analysis, reflecting their more detailed focus and ability to elicit input on the writing and implementation of regulations from the interests that will be most significantly affected.

That said, several factors severely constrain agency information-gathering and analysis. As Charles Wolf noted, even the most systematic of agencies lack the quality and quantity of policy-relevant information that the supply and demand side of markets quickly, cheaply, and automatically generate, integrate, and assess. Instead, as also noted in chapter 3, agencies must rely for their policy information on adjudication (notoriously slow and narrowly confined to the particular parties and facts in the litigation), on rule making (usually better at generating valuable policy information, but also so protracted that the information often becomes stale before the policy makers can actually deploy it), and on staff research efforts (limited by budget and narrow peripheral vision). And although agencies are required to collect performance data by laws like the 1993 Government Performance and Results Act (GRPA) and the 2010 GPRA Modernization

Act, these reports often remain unused and irrelevant, perhaps because those laws did not take into account the wide diversity of agency operations and because agencies seldom collect performance data in a systematic fashion—a failure much criticized by the GAO itself.[17] Especially lamentable is the dearth of information about the performance of government-funded medical procedures, where the now conventional call for evidenced-based medicine almost always goes unanswered.[18]

Relatively well-organized and well-funded private groups are ordinarily in the best position to generate the information, much of it self-interested, that Congress and the agencies need to do their policy work. These groups operate at the core of civil society—ordinary people, business firms, media, communities, scientists, markets—and thus know more about the diverse sources of valuable policy-relevant information "out there." Even environmental, consumer, and other "public interest" groups that are not well-funded often command other valuable resources that can influence agency policy makers and policy outcomes, including a patina of widely shared ideals, an image of selflessness, and access to important politicians, information, and media. This may be the best explanation for why Head Start, an immensely popular and well-connected program, has flourished politically for so many decades. Its budget grew from about $400 million in 1968 to almost $8 billion in 2011, including under Republican administrations.[19] Yet many carefully conducted studies have consistently found that its initial beneficial effects largely dissipate within a few years; some effects do not survive the summer breaks. According to the Brookings Institution's educational policy center, a government study published in 2010 demonstrated that children's attendance in Head Start has no significant impact on measureable outcomes such as their academic, socio-emotional, or health status at the end of first grade.[20] When the government then extended the study to third graders, it found the same dissipation of benefits.[21] (Nobel economist James Heckman's research may help to explain why; it suggests that even Head Start begins years too late to help disadvantaged children.[22] Preschool programs in other countries have also had mixed results, with no clear patterns explaining why some succeed more than others.[23]) Nor is Head Start alone in these dismal results for such efforts: the Even Start Family Literacy Program failed to improve child and parent reading, at a cost of over $1 billion before it was finally defunded; the Scared Straight programs that bring at-risk youngsters into prisons to learn about what might await them actually increase their criminal behavior; and 21st Century Community Learning Centers fail to improve academic outcomes but increase suspensions and other forms of discipline, yet receive more than $1 billion a year in federal funds.[24] A July 2013 Brookings research report on pre-K programs finds little or no success in random assignment studies.[25]

At the bottom of the information chain are judges, who typically know little or nothing about the policy considerations, technical concepts, and political values that underlie the legal texts that they review. As lawyer-generalists, they are untrained in such matters. They instead rely almost entirely on their common sense, their inexperienced law clerks, and especially the tendentious briefs that opportunistic lawyers on each side submit, briefs that are often designed to conceal information damaging to their client's cause rather than call attention to it. This ignorance by federal judges is especially worrisome because they increasingly use preemption and federal common law doctrines to shape legal and policy domains that were always governed by state law and informed by states' in-depth expertise and experience. Examples are domestic relations, intergenerational wealth transfers, insurance, and torts, to name just a few.

This account of information flow to policy makers bears a disturbingly close resemblance to the theoretical predictions made by Hayek and Wolf about the poor fit between the complexity of social facts and the simplistic, distorted information that officials in Washington rely upon for their decisions and propagate to the public. The classic example of this problem is the official poverty index, devised back in 1963 for a different purpose and one that all experts agree, regardless of their differing views on other issues, overstates the poverty rate substantially, which misinforms the public and distorts policy choices. Experts also largely agree on how to revise the index in line with recommendations by a National Academy of Sciences task force in 1995. Yet the government, fearing strong objections from groups whose policy positions the 1963 index favors, will probably never abandon it.[26]

This inability or refusal to update the misleading poverty index after a half century provides an excellent segue to the problem of governmental inflexibility.

INFLEXIBILITY

The technological, economic, political, and normative conditions that generate and define tough policy problems are not static; they often change, sometimes rapidly and dramatically. To achieve or maintain policy effectiveness, policy makers who wish to avoid irrelevance— or worse, perversity—must adapt their goals, instruments, or both to these changes. Nassim Nicholas Taleb calls this approach "antifragility," emphasizing its special importance in complex systems.[27] The government, alas, is especially ill-equipped to do this.* Although it may be able to act nimbly in a genuine crisis situation,† government (fortunately) seldom makes policy under such conditions.

Public policy is driven by public expectations, which are often created and reinforced by politicians and interest groups. Having accumulated over a long period of time, these expectations are now so deeply embedded that they seriously constrain policy choices, often predetermining outcomes that maintain a socially undesirable status quo. One example is the expectation of cheap energy, particularly gasoline and home heating fuel, resulting from our historically abundant supply of oil and natural gas. Indeed, presidential popularity ratings are far more highly correlated with gasoline price levels than with unemployment rates.[28] Politically, it is almost suicidal to propose

---

*I distinguish this desirable purposive or functional adaptability from the kinds of spasmodic, unpredictable shifts in government direction and commitment that impair its performance by undermining its credibility—a special problem discussed in the next section.
†The Federal Reserve's innovative course since the financial meltdown of 2007–8 may be the exception that proves the rule. After all, as noted in chapter 3, the Fed is the most independent of all agencies.

raising federal gasoline taxes, despite strong policy reasons to do so; they have not been raised since 1993 (although some individual states have raised them).

Public expectations about the most popular—and highly regressive—"tax expenditures" are also deeply embedded and, at least so far, politically untouchable. These include the deductions for home mortgage interest, charitable contributions, and state and local taxes, as well as the exclusion of employer-provided health insurance benefits from income.[29] Although eliminating these provisions—or at least limiting their regressivity—would go a long way toward solving the nation's fiscal crisis, simplifying the tax code, and making it fairer, no major-party presidential candidate within memory has even proposed doing so. (During the 2012 campaign, Mitt Romney gestured in this policy direction, but steadfastly refused to specify which provisions he would change. President Obama did not even go this far.)

This is not to say that public expectations and the policies they engender can never be changed. The most courageous and talented politicians are skilled at managing and gradually altering those expectations, as was the case with president Lyndon Johnson and civil rights legislation.[30] Until recently, laws authorizing homosexuals in the military, women in the Marines, and same-sex marriage would have been unthinkable. It is telling, however, that same-sex marriage has been instituted mainly by state courts, not legislatures, and that federal acceptance of it at the state level may also come about only through judicial action (by invalidating the Defense of Marriage Act). Not surprisingly, unelected judges with lifetime tenure are sometimes more willing than politically accountable legislators are to override public expectations.[31]

The challenge of policy adaptability, which would be difficult under the best of circumstances, is vastly magnified by the short time horizon of almost all elected politicians, which causes them to focus on the here and now, especially in response to crises, rather than on the longer term. In the jargon of policy analysis, they apply a very high discount rate to the future, focusing on the present and the short-term and minimizing or ignoring longer-term effects. This myopia reflects their incentives, political needs, perceptions, and personal rhythms, which are largely dictated by the election cycle. Even senators with six-year terms are caught up in a permanent campaign.[32]

Although career civil servants have longer time horizons, they must look for leadership and policy guidance to their politically appointed superiors whose tenure in office, as detailed in chapter 10, tends to be even briefer than that of elected officials—only three years on average (fewer in executive agencies, more in independent regulatory agencies)[33]—and whose time horizon is correspondingly short.[34]

These truncated time horizons have several distorting effects on policy. Government may act precipitously, as when policy makers are in a hurry to make a splash before some political or fiscal deadline.* Instead, as with entitlements reform or stopgap financing measures, it may do the opposite—temporizing in hopes of not having to make difficult choices or leaving them to others to pay the political price. These incentives to either lurch or delay render longer-term policy planning impossible or irrelevant. As the next section shows, this radical present-orientation undermines the credibility that the government must have in order to induce others to make the long-term investments in reliance on government promises—investments that are often essential to policy success. Instead, programs are designed in order to address only current and short-term political needs.

Nothing better demonstrates this than the Budget Control Act of 2011, passed only days before Standard & Poor's downgraded the government's credit rating for the first time in our history. Designed to avert the public fury that would follow another government shutdown, the act deferred all of the tough policy reform and budgetary decisions to the lame duck Congress after the 2012 elections, thus creating paralyzing and costly uncertainty (a problem discussed more generally below) and fiscal and regulatory "cliffs." At that point, federal officials once again kicked the can down the road to what they expected would be an action-forcing event—a procrustean sequester

---

*An example is the Oakland Project, detailed in chapter 8, in which officials acted hastily lest the appropriated funds revert to Congress.

on March 1, 2013. Seven months later, the government still had not made those hard decisions.

This reckless brinkmanship is only the most recent and dramatic instance of harmful inflexibility due to policy myopia. Alas, other troubling examples are more typical.

The US Postal Service, authorized by the Constitution,[35] boasts a storied past going back to the beginning of the Republic with important technological advances along the way.[36] It boasts an iconic brand name, universal service, and some efficiency advantages in package delivery. In recent decades, however, it has been heavily burdened by notorious inefficiencies. Congressional mandates, largely reflecting the power of federal employee unions, the relevant subcommittee members, and rural interests that fear restrictions of service and loss of patronage, have forced the Postal Service to run huge annual deficits. (So large are these deficits that it seems almost churlish to mention the $40 million that it wasted sponsoring Lance Armstrong's doped cycling team.[37]) The deficits have now reached crisis proportions: the postmaster general projects no cash or borrowing capacity. For appearance purposes, Congress has insisted that these deficits be off-budget, but has also required that Postal Service employees' health and retirement benefits—which are extraordinarily generous compared with those of private-sector counterparts—be prepaid for future employees, a requirement that has no private-sector analogue and has forced the Postal Service to default on these prepayment obligations.[38] Congress has also prevented it from installing far more efficient technologies, ending Saturday mail services at a saving of $2 billion a year,[39] closing unneeded post offices, and substantially reducing its workforce. At the same time, private postal services such as Fedex and the United Parcel Service (UPS), as well as e-mail, have flourished because of their vastly superior efficiency, innovativeness, and quality of service. Labor represents 80 percent of the agency's expenses, compared with 53 percent at UPS and 32 percent at FedEx, which have utilized technology more efficiently.[40] Some of the Postal Service's higher costs are also due to its obligation to serve rural communities that are unprofitable for the market to serve. Yet it would still be far cheaper and more effective for Congress to subsidize those services directly, if necessary, as it did with communities deprived of service by airline deregulation.*

The No Child Left Behind Act of 2001, a pillar of federal education policy, clearly requires a thorough overhaul, as both parties have conceded. Yet the immediate political needs of policy makers have stalled any renewal legislation for more than five years, leading the administration of president Barack Obama to waive some of its most important mandates for thirty-nine states and the District of Columbia (as of July 2013), which many commentators believe essentially nullifies the law.[41] Another example is Social Security, discussed in chapter 11. Analysts largely agree on four facts about the program. Relentless demographic changes are making it fiscally unsustainable in its present form (barring an almost unimaginable long-term economic boom). A few relatively manageable policy fixes can protect the scores of millions who depend on it. These reforms must and will (in some combination) eventually be adopted. And the longer they are put off, the more costly and difficult implementation will be, and the more uncertainty they will inject into beneficiaries' life plans and expectations. (Much the same is true of Medicare, except that its reforms are more politically controversial and more difficult to design and implement.) Yet both parties have refused to adapt the program to the demographic and fiscal trends whose general parameters have been obvious since the baby boomers were born and the economic growth rate began to decline.[42] Again, a solution will surely be found, but at a time when the adjustment and transition will be more problematic.

Countless other instances of anachronistic policies burden society. Many farm subsidy programs, which originated in the days of the

---

*In a similar vein, it has been estimated that subsidizing private taxi service for the disabled would have been far less costly than requiring cities to retrofit their public transportation systems (as distinguished from making new facilities accessible). Some disability advocates argued, with apparent success, that although this approach could save money, it would violate the equality principle, turning the disabled into second-class citizens. This debate is reviewed in Robert A. Katzmann, *Institutional Disability: The Saga of Transportation Policy for the Disabled* (1986).

Dust Bowl and the New Deal, are now egregiously bad policy—distributively perverse and cost-ineffective[43]—yet their congressional support makes them relatively invulnerable.[44] Much the same is true of the deductions for employer-provided health insurance and for home mortgage interest.[45] By the same token, politicians often use the status quo's inertial force to terminate or truncate programs that seem effective, as with a pilot voucher program for the famously dysfunctional District of Columbia school system.[46]

The tax code's definition of "family" is inconsistent with many new social realities—for example, over 40 percent of children are born out of wedlock, and same-sex marriage and civil unions are legal in a growing number of states. The formula in Section 5 of the Voting Rights Act had become so patently outdated because of the vested interests that had encrusted it that the Supreme Court in 2013 took the truly radical step of holding it unconstitutionally anachronistic (as discussed in chapter 11). The ethanol program (discussed in chapter 8) is perversely rigid in the face of market changes. The EPA set a maximum safe level of fluoride in drinking water in 1986, received expert recommendations in 2006 to reduce it by half, and seven years later had not yet changed it.[47] The Merchant Marine Act of 1920, better known as the Jones Act, requires that all shipments of cargo from one U.S. port to another to be carried on vessels built in the U.S., owned by U.S. citizens, and operated by a U.S. crew. (The same restriction applies to cargoes financed by the Export-Import Bank.) The domestic shipbuilding industry and labor unions traditionally cite national defense and security justifications (and some waivers are permissible), but the Act is a protectionist measure pure and simple. Senator John McCain, perhaps our leading national security hawk, rightly calls such arguments "laughable." A government study estimated that repealing it would have saved $656 million in maritime services in 1999 due to the vastly higher costs of building and operating ships in the U.S.[48] In 2012, for example, American ships moved oil from the Gulf Coast to the Northeast at a cost of $4 a barrel, compared with $1.20 for foreign vessels.[49] Yet almost a century of efforts to repeal the Act have been unavailing, so powerful are the interests and inertia that defend it. (The same study found that liberalizing all significant import restraints would have saved $14.3 billion in 1999.)[50]

Sometimes, the policy change that does occur is herky-jerky. The Treasury, Fannie Mae, and Freddie Mac initiated programs in the aftermath of the financial crisis to reduce homeowner and taxpayer costs through principal reduction, only to halt them before a CBA could be conducted to assess the results of this innovation.[51] (Those loan modification programs, moreover, helped far fewer homeowners than predicted while still resulting in 27 percent re-defaults.[52]) The agencies also failed egregiously to implement the Hardest Hit Fund for the most distressed homeowners.[53] Our patent laws, designed to *promote* innovation, appear to be *inhibiting* it by awarding over-broad property rights and tying up inventors in costly, tactically motivated litigation.[54] And in perhaps the most dramatic example of abrupt change, Congress created a major catastrophic coverage program under Medicare only to repeal it seventeen months later.[55]

As these examples suggest, much government policy inflexibility is caused by how Congress legislates—and fails to legislate. Consider the severe, costly, and universally unwanted travel delays resulting from the Federal Aviation Administration's furloughs of air traffic controllers early in 2013 that were necessitated (so the agency claimed) by the fiscal cliff sequester law. What is most striking to a student of policy rigidity is that the statute governing the FAA denied it the administrative authority to shift its funds from less urgent uses to traffic controller compensation. It required new legislation, enacted quickly under emergency conditions, to authorize this commonsense repurposing of appropriated funds to forestall a genuine crisis.[56]

Occasionally, some changes in the external environment can actually increase policy effectiveness by simplifying the problem or providing a solution. An example is the development of air bags, which promised to reduce the toll of highway accidents and have fulfilled that promise. But even changes that regulators consider cost-effective usually entail countervailing disadvantages. Thus air bags also increased the cost of new cars, motivating owners to keep their old, bagless ones longer, and also caused an increase in some types collisions and injuries even as they reduced the incidence of others. On balance, the air bag requirement passes any objective cost-benefit analysis (CBA) and must be counted a policy success.[57] Other examples of policy game-changers are technologies that enable police agencies to detect crime more quickly, accurately, or cheaply, and new information systems that, if properly implemented (a precondition discussed in chapter 5) could improve the government's record keeping, cost controls, and enforcement.*

Regrettably, such instances of social changes that increase government effectiveness are vastly outnumbered by changes that frustrate or impair it. This can happen for several reasons. New developments may render a policy anachronistic by altering the nature of the underlying problem and the means available for dealing with it. Consider two cases in point. The Delaney Clause, enacted by Congress in 1958, prohibited the sale of processed foods with any additive or pesticide—regardless of its concentration—that causes cancer in animals or humans. By the 1970s, analytical chemists armed with powerful new mass spectrometers could detect infinitesimal amounts of residues, which rendered the Delaney Clause unworkable and dangerous to the food supply and public health. Congress finally repealed it in 1996, long after it had become anachronistic.

A second example comes from the financial services industry. In the decade or so leading up to the economic meltdown of 2008, the industry created, traded, collateralized, securitized, and multiplied instruments so exotic, complex, and opaque that federal regulators could barely comprehend the intricacies of these new markets, much less assess their effects and how to control them.[58] Indeed, as I write in December 2013, more than three years after Congress enacted the Dodd-Frank law, the financial regulators finally managed, under immense White House pressure, to issue the Volcker Rule, only to retract part of it barely a week later. I discuss the rule in chapter 8.

*Unfortunately, according to the GAO, the government's implementation of such changes—discussed in chapter 8—has often been egregious, particularly with new information systems.

Another obstacle to policy adaptability is what political scientists call "policy inheritance." Policy innovation is severely limited by the policies adopted earlier, which leave current policy makers with limited freedom of action. This inheritance effect is particularly powerful if the older policies were instituted by members of the same political party, but it is not confined to such partisan continuities.[59] Indeed, as discussed in chapters 3 and 6, political inertia is built into the constitutional system and the policy process. Because of separation of powers and numerous veto points, new statutory (and even administrative) policies are difficult to enact, but once in place are difficult to dislodge. This inertia likely explains why it took years, and an experiment, to finally move Medicare to adopt competitive bidding for the medical equipment it buys.[60]

Social change can also confound existing policies by significantly altering the magnitudes of their benefits and costs and undermining the rationale for the earlier policy. Consider the tax subsidy for employer-provided health insurance. Originating as a relatively small temporary adjustment to World War II wage controls, it has become the single largest "tax expenditure," costing the Treasury more than $175 billion per year. In its current bloated form, this policy causes many large inefficiencies in the health care system while disproportionately favoring workers who already enjoy relatively high wages and fringe benefits. Most health reformers and budgetary hawks favor eliminating or severely limiting this subsidy, but it is so politically entrenched and union-friendly that it cannot be dislodged.[61] Another example of an old policy that makes far less sense today than it did at its inception is the impacted aid program, enacted in 1950 to provide formula-based federal assistance directly to local school districts serving students whose parents work for the military, are Native Americans, or are otherwise "federally connected." It now costs about $1.3 billion a year, but its original rationale—that such districts needed special assistance—has been undermined by the passage of numerous federal education and Native American assistance programs starting in the 1960s, and by the fact that the federal connection often is on balance economically advantageous to these districts rather than burdensome. Again, however, the program is politically bulletproof.

The federal statute books are replete with programs of this kind—programs for which the cost and other parameters have greatly increased while the original rationale for the policies has eroded, and which nevertheless remain, even many decades later, essentially impervious to fundamental reform or repeal. Indeed, they are as impregnable as Fort Knox. As one contemplates these programs, then, one is immediately reminded of the French expression *plus ca change, plus c'est la meme chose* (the more things change, the more they stay the same). The government's rapid, decisive responses to Pearl Harbor and Sputnik were exceptional. Far more typical is immigration policy, where adaptation to new conditions is far slower than in other countries like Canada and Australia whose more flexible systems compete with us for highly skilled immigrants. Indeed, our legal immigration policy still operates under strictures of the 1965 Hart-Celler law, which was updated only marginally in 1990 and before immense technological and labor market changes transformed the policy challenge.[62] As of June 2013, nearly a half century after Hart-Celler, it was still not clear that Congress would bring our system into the twenty-first century.

Some programs with enduring rationales—for example, entitlements like Social Security (discussed above and in chapter 11) and Medicare (also discussed in chapter 11)—have over time become fiscally unsustainable in their present forms, necessitating some combination of benefit or eligibility reductions or tax increases that policy rigidity makes difficult. In both cases, Congress and the president have failed the politically difficult test of putting them on a fiscally sound footing for the long term—a task that is much easier for Social Security than for Medicare.

Two final points about inflexibility deserve mention. First, the mobility of capital and people, which chapter 4 discusses in connection with localism, often constrains policy adaptability. Second, policy rigidity can be desirable to the extent that it fortifies the government's credibility and thus its ability to induce reliance and investment by others. I now turn to this subject.

INCREDIBILITY

Even before the Constitution was adopted, James Madison saw the danger of fickle policies, commenting that "no great improvement or laudable enterprise can go forward which requires the auspices of a steady system of national policy."[63] Government credibility is usually mentioned in analyses of foreign and national security policy, where promises and threats can only be effective if they are believed.

But credibility is at least as important for domestic policy effectiveness. Many programs can succeed only if the federal government induces private and other governmental actors to do things that they will not do if they doubt that it will honor its own commitments.* In order to do that, the government must radically reduce the amount of uncertainty that chronically plagues its decisions,† including what theorists call "primary ignorance"—when decision makers do not even recognize that they are ignorant of risks and thus court failure without even knowing that they are risking it.[64] Uncertainty both increases government's costs and raises costs to the private actors on whose decisions policy success ultimately depends. These costs are difficult to quantify, of course—three Stanford University and University of Chicago economists find that economic policy uncertainty is much greater today than in the past, estimating its drag on the economy at *$261 billion since 2011 alone.*[65] William Galston, a leading Democratic policy expert at Brookings, cites new Federal Reserve research consistent with these estimates; together, these studies show

*The credibility problem can also be seen as a problem of government incentives. Specifically, changed social or political conditions may cause its ex ante and ex post incentives to diverge, a prospect that entities dealing with government or making decisions in light of its policies will anticipate and take into account.
†Economist Frank Knight usefully distinguished uncertainty from risk. With risk, probabilities of alternative states of the world can in principle be determined in advance of an outcome. With uncertainty, such probabilities cannot even be reliably estimated. See Frank Knight, *Risk, Uncertainty, and Profit* (1921).

that policy uncertainty is having dire effects on the economy, especially on hiring.[66]

This credibility imperative creates a deep and inescapable temporal paradox: for a policy to be effective, people must believe that the government will discharge today's commitments in the future (usually in the medium or long term), yet the demands of democratic legitimacy and accountability require government to respond to changed conditions in that future in ways that will impair its credibility.* Economists Dani Rodrik and Richard Zeckhauser made this important point twenty-five years ago, providing a number of policy examples. The government may have good reasons to adopt an amnesty for tax evaders or undocumented immigrants, but unless it can persuade them that the amnesty is a one-time-only policy, it simply encourages more people to evade taxes or come illegally in hopes of a future amnesty, which is precisely what has happened in both cases. A public utility commission may want to induce a utility to construct a new power plant, but unless it can guarantee the utility that it will grant a future rate increase to cover the necessary investment, the utility will not make the investment.[67] Yet in both of these cases (and countless others), the government cannot credibly make the necessary commitments for two related reasons: (1) any rational person will doubt that it will fulfill them because (2) one knows that it will change direction if future conditions demand it. In economists' terms, the government's utility preferences will change intertemporally as conditions change. In time B, the government will act according to its new preferences. We must assume first that the government knows that this will undermine its credibility both in time 1 (because of others' rational expectations about how government will act in the future) and in time 2 (when it actually changes direction) and, second, that it takes this credibility problem into account in deciding what to do. Nevertheless,

---

*Some agencies such as the National Institutes of Health and the Centers for Disease Control and Prevention have achieved wide credibility, probably because they possess scientific expertise and do not exercise regulatory authority, thus avoiding the politicization that such authority inevitably entails.

a greater necessity—its obligation to voters in time 2—demands that it do what the conditions then require.

This credibility problem affects almost all public policies. Rodrik and Zeckhauser show that the reasons are structural, not just political, and that the problem is far worse for government than for private actors. First, as just noted, government has a moral and political obligation to meet its constituents' felt needs, which change over time. (Discharge of this obligation can take forms that create severe moral hazard [discussed in chapter 5], such as the 2008 bailouts of General Motors, AIG, and more than 700 banks. Five years later, AIG had repaid its debt but the Treasury was likely to lose billions on its investments in GM and the smaller banks.[68]) In contrast, a private actor may have an incentive to respond to changes in its market or other domain, but it has no such obligation to do so. Second, the more discretion officials have under the law, the greater their freedom of action to change direction in the future—perhaps by repudiating the existing policy, failing to enforce it, or deciding not to make the promised investment. Even if the change is justified on the merits, it also exacerbates their credibility problem. Third, long-term credibility is even more essential when the policy depends on inducing private firms and other entities and individuals to make long-term, asset-specific investments—that is, economic or other commitments whose value to them would be much lower if redeployed to a different transaction—because investors fear being held hostage to opportunistic governmental behavior. In the public utility case, once its investment in the new power plant is locked in, the commission's short-term incentive is to reject unpopular rate increases. Anticipating this, of course, the utility may not make the investment in the first place. Similarly, some states have resisted Obamacare's full-cost federal subsidy for expanding Medicaid, fearing that in three years when the subsidy decreases, they will be stuck with higher costs.[69] (One wag likened this to receiving a free baby elephant.)

The greatest structural impediment to government credibility, however, is that it has fewer ways than private actors do to commit itself to a particular course of action over time. It can bind itself by statute, but statutes can be repealed by future Congresses (think of the Bush-era tax cuts) subject only to constitutional principles that—in recognition of government's moral duty to respond to changed conditions—are not very constraining. It can bind itself by contract, but public contract law provides government with some special defenses and immunities that make enforcement against the government less certain and more costly than in private contract law. To be sure, future government actions that disappoint these statutory or contractual expectations will make any course changes more costly, which further reduces its credibility, but the government may decide that the advantages of changing course are worth that cost in credibility. And those who might do business with the government know all this, of course, and must factor its lack of credibility into their own decisions about whether to deal with it and under what terms.

Abrupt changes in policy are common. For example, president George W. Bush proposed a $1.2 billion program in research funding to develop a hydrogen-powered car. Only five years later, President Obama cut 80 percent of the funding for this program, proposing instead to place his money on electric-powered cars, leaving scientists and entrepreneurs who had invested in hydrogen-car research in the lurch. One must doubt that they and people like them will stake their own funds and careers on the next round of government promises. Indeed, a 2009 National Academy of Sciences report cited "lack of sustained policies" as one of the three top barriers to promoting renewable energy, and new evidence further demonstrates this effect.[70] Congress vastly expanded the National Institutes of Health, whose success depends entirely on attracting and retaining top scientific talent, only to lose much of that talent by cutting appropriations. In real dollar terms, the agency's funding has decreased by roughly 20 percent over the last decade.[71]

Occasionally, policy changes are convulsive enough to violate the Constitution. In the most dramatic example of this, the Affordable Care Act amended the Medicaid program, a huge share of the states' budgets, to sharply increase the costs to the states. A Supreme Court majority struck down provisions that would have eliminated all Medicaid funding for any state declining to participate in the now costlier program, calling this threat "a gun to the head."[72] The main point here is not that the Court was correct to invalidate those provisions (I have serious doubts, and four justices strenuously dissented) but that the government often reconfigures (or abandons) programs that it previously urged states and private interests to rely on and invest in. The need to avoid both the Scylla of abrupt policy changes that violate government-created expectations and the Charybdis of maintaining the status quo long after new conditions demand its reform is precisely the dilemma noted above by Rodrik and Zeckhauser.

Economist Amihai Glazer and political scientist Lawrence Rothenberg have analyzed the political economy of government credibility. Where government regulates a concentrated industry, the authors find, the credibility of its policies is especially low because the industry is better able to coordinate efforts to delay or defeat those policies—as when the auto industry was able to delay passive restraints and fuel economy standards for many years, thereby discouraging private investments in the necessary supporting technologies.[73] New evidence shows the same to be true of investments in renewable energy generation.[74] Glazer and Rothenberg make two other points about credibility. First, government cannot credibly ration services whose denial would be visibly life-threatening, as with health care.[75] Second, weak government institutions can actually increase credibility by making policy change more unlikely—that is, more rigid—and this may sometimes be more important than adapting to changed conditions.[76] Rodrik and Zeckhauser suggest how government might enhance its credibility—giving "hostages" and creating countervailing constituencies, for example—but such techniques involve trade-offs. Each would reduce a policy's effectiveness, increase its cost, or limit the government's responsiveness to new conditions (a special kind of cost).

One type of institution through which Congress seeks to increase government credibility is the statutory trust fund. The trust fund earmarks certain taxes for the fund's use, and it can only spend those revenues for specified fund purposes. Congress has used this device in more than 150 programs; the most prominent are Social Security, Medicare, and highway and airport construction. Other statutory precommitment arrangements include entitlement programs, independent agency status, and indexation formulas. Eric Patashnik's authoritative study of the trust fund device finds its propensity to increase government promise-keeping depends on a number of design factors, especially the extent to which the fund's taxpayers and beneficiaries are the same people ("reciprocity") and depend on the promises being fulfilled ("reliance"). Social Security and Medicare score highest on both reciprocity and reliance, and their commitments have (so far) been kept. For most trust funds, however, Congress has changed the rules so as to avoid having to keep the original policy promises.[77] To avoid a fiscal catastrophe, Congress must certainly change the rules for Social Security and Medicare as well—the only questions are when and how—and much of the public has lost confidence in the programs' ability to discharge their existing commitments.

For our present purposes, two key points emerge. First, the credibility of a trust-funded policy depends on its underlying political structure. Second, the device may increase a policy's credibility at its inception, but that enhanced credibility either is unwarranted (for most trust funds) or tends to erode over time. Even the most reliable ones, Social Security and Medicare, are undermined by policy makers' tendency—grounded in their electoral incentives—to overpromise benefits and undertax toward paying for them.

Although the weak credibility of public policies inheres in the government's duty to respond to changed conditions, the problem is greatly exacerbated by a number of other factors that cause government to actually magnify uncertainty. Two of them are discussed at length in other parts of this book: the nature of its institutions (chapter 3), and the political culture in which those institutions operate (chapter 6), including the growing politicization and protracted delays in Senate confirmation of key executive and independent agency policy makers (chapter 10). Still other factors include the long lag times between identifying a problem and implementing a policy response, and the political conflict that continues long after a policy's enactment. Examples of such government-exacerbated uncertainty abound, and some of them have exceedingly far-reaching negative effects. By almost all accounts, the uncertainty caused by the "fiscal cliff" that loomed in 2012 reduced private-sector spending and hiring at a time when both were desperately needed, with baleful economic and social results.[78] Much the same is true of the "regulatory cliff" that pushed off final action on a number of major costly regulatory actions until after the 2012 elections.[79]

The Affordable Care Act of 2010 is an even more revealing example of policy-driven uncertainty because the law has already been on the books for over three years. The act's implementation depends upon innumerable public and private decisions—to invest, to legislate, to establish exchanges, to coordinate databases, to insure or exclude, to contract, to organize, and countless other actions—and the effectiveness of its many different policies turn on when, how, and how well those decisions are made and integrated. Yet for more than three years, its very existence, not to mention its authoritative meaning and timely implementation, rested in the opaque, unpredictable, and formally unaccountable hands of the U.S. Supreme Court—of one or two "swing" justices, actually. This has created a mind-boggling level of uncertainty throughout the relevant industries and patient populations.[80] And even when the Court finally rendered its decision upholding most of the act,[81] it did so in a way that created new uncertainty about both the federal program and the continuing status of fifty state Medicaid programs for the poor. At the same time, the Republicans (and a few Democrats like Senator Joe Manchin) moved vigorously to repeal, delay, or seriously amend the Act at the first political opportunity. Their arguments were aided by the computer system's egregious failures in the first months of operations, failures that the Obama administration had struggled mightily to avoid.[82]

This uncertainty will not be resolved for years to come, yet a vast number of public and private insurers, providers, consumers, consultants, and other actors must quickly undertake make-it-or-break-it decisions based on speculative possibilities about which rules numerous officials in different federal departments and state agencies will negotiate among themselves and then issue.[83] In September 2013, only one month before the act's key provisions on insurance exchanges went into effect, even the major labor unions that had supported it expressed deep concerns about how the act could harm their members.[84] Here are just a few of the myriad questions that as of July 2013 remained unanswered (which also meant that the necessary computer systems could not be designed and field-tested):

> To comply with the law, companies needed rules for reporting data to the government each month, including the names and Social Security numbers of anyone who worked full-time for at least one month during the year, plus information on the insurance offered and its price. They have to calculate and report, based on individual worker incomes, whether the premiums offered are affordable. Among the questions the administration hadn't answered in time: should companies be required to report month-by-month details about who they employed? Should employers who already offer insurance be subject to the same rules? What happens if workers say they weren't offered adequate insurance but employers say they were?[85]

As of late November, even the President conceded that the initial rollout was terribly flawed. Other uncertainties abounded quite apart from the Republican's quixotic threat to repeal or fundamentally change the act. Most states were operating their own insurance exchanges. Many young, low-risk people on whom the law's viability depends might decide not to get insured at all or instead pay the low statutory penalty (the final rules were issued only a month before the insurance exchanges went into effect).[86] How strictly the government would enforce that penalty was unclear, as were the premiums that insurers would charge. Much, much more was still up in the air.[87] When the administration suddenly suspended the employer penalty provision for a year because it could not yet predict how employers, insurers, and workers would be affected and respond,[88] it not only cost an extra $12 billion, according to the CBO,[89] but it created yet more confusion: whether the individual mandate might also be delayed, how agencies would get the information they needed (and apparently still lacked) to implement the many interlocking provisions, and so forth. Tasting blood, the program's opponents began to press for additional suspensions.[90] The program's credibility was further damaged when, only six weeks before rollout, another important delay emerged—this relating to the rules limiting patients' out-of-pocket costs.[91]

If a landmark social policy (surely the most important since the New Deal, other than Social Security and Medicare) must contend with this level of uncertainty—if government promises about the act's content therefore lack credibility in the minds of insurers, providers, patients, state legislatures, and countless other stakeholders whose own commitments are essential for success—what does this portend for the act's ultimate, overall effectiveness? (I say "overall" in recognition that *some* of its popular goals—especially increasing coverage of those now barred by preexisting conditions or by high individual policy costs—will likely be realized, albeit at a greater-than-predicted cost.)

The question, alas, answers itself.

MISMANAGEMENT

Sound management is essential to policy effectiveness, and we must presume that much more of it exists than a scandal-hungry media tends to report. Indeed, an instance of good management can become newsworthy, a man-bites-dog story.[92] Nevertheless, the problem is not media bias but endemic federal mismanagement that can have terrible consequences. Consider three particularly appalling examples. First, as many as half of discarded kidneys could be transplanted if the federal Organ Procurement and Transplantation Network were not hobbled by an outdated computer matching program, red tape, overreliance on inconclusive tests, and even federal age discrimination laws.[93] Second, the Drug Enforcement Agency had to pay $4 million to a student who it mistakenly jailed for four days and who almost died as a result.[94] Third, the popular policy of providing generous benefits to disabled and ill veterans, our most honored citizens, is mocked by the Veterans Administration's long claims-processing delays, which even predated the 9/11 attacks. The VA's $140 billion budget has more than doubled during the last decade in real terms, and it has added thousands of claims processers. Yet as Congress keeps authorizing new benefits and makes eligibility easier, the backlog (now 900,000 claims) grows steadily worse due to the agency's continued reliance on paper records, its perversely designed production quotas that encourage employees to reach for the thin folders first, the numerous refiled and appealed claims after denials, and its lax definition of disability to include common age-related conditions.[95] The *New York Times* reported that even a routine pension claim, undisputed by the VA, took nearly two years to process, and only after a congressman's intervention. The VA's employees publicly, and at some personal risk, criticize their own agency as dysfunctional; the agency has decided to address the backlog through "provisional" rulings to old cases, which will likely assure payments with little or no scrutiny.[96]

Another form of managerial failure is program fragmentation and overlap—a problem largely originating with Congress. Bureaucracy expert Paul Light notes the duplication and overlap among programs with nearly identical missions but separate overhead, including the 53 designed to spur entrepreneurship, the 82 to improve teacher quality, the 160 to support housing, and the 209 to strengthen science, technology, engineering, and mathematics education.[97] A 2011 GAO report identified forty-seven separate federally funded job training programs administered across nine agencies in 2009. Almost all of these programs overlapped with at least one other program providing at least one similar service to a similar population; differences sometimes existed in eligibility, objectives, and service delivery.[98] Indeed, Congress apparently added two more such programs *after* this critical GAO report.[99] In 2008, Congress created a new US Department of Agriculture (USDA) office to inspect imported catfish, which is a low-risk food, duplicating a long-standing FDA seafood inspection program. By 2013, the USDA had spent $20 million to establish it and $14 million a year to run it, yet it had not inspected a single catfish.[100]

Endemic fraud, waste, abuse, and corruption are perhaps the clearest signs of mismanagement. These excrescences have an ancient pedigree, of course: the first inspector general to investigate a procurement scandal was appointed by the Continental Congress, and virtually all presidents have campaigned against them.[101] Government bears a special responsibility for them both as an enabler of private misconduct—and also as a chronic source of its own. The government often violates the same rules it imposes on others. Congress, for example, repeatedly violates clean fuel requirements,[102] and even the supposedly squeaky-clean Secret Service security force was caught in a sex scandal.[103] In August 2013, the leading federal appeals court upbraided an agency for flagrantly violating its own governing statute,[104] and the special intelligence surveillance court, usually so deferential to the National Security Agency, castigated it for massive constitutional violations.[105] The remainder of this chapter, then, is devoted to this particular form of government failure.

The Office of the Inspector General for the Department of Defense defines fraud, waste, and abuse as follows:

Fraud: "A type of illegal act involving the obtaining of something of value through willful misrepresentation."

Waste: "[I]nvolves the taxpayers not receiving reasonable value for money in connection with any government funded activities due to an inappropriate act or omission by players with control over or access to government resources. . . . waste relates primarily to mismanagement, inappropriate actions and inadequate oversight."

Abuse: "[I]nvolves behavior that is deficient or improper when compared with behavior that a prudent person would consider reasonable and necessary business practice given the facts and circumstances."[106]

These somewhat overlapping and strikingly ambiguous definitions, of course, encompass a broad spectrum of action (and inaction). Accordingly, the three terms are usually joined into a single
phrase rather than analyzed separately; the shorthand referent is
FWA. It is ordinarily used to refer to a host of improper and/or illegal
practices by or against the government, and to measure its inefficiency, its susceptibility to being gamed and exploited. Although the
GAO often refers to "improper payments" (those that were made incorrectly or for an improper amount, including both overpayments
and underpayments),[107] it explicitly cautions readers that improper
payments are not necessarily fraudulent. A February 2012 GAO report
noted that only 42 of 79 federal programs complied with OMB guidelines for reporting the causes of their improper payments; the remaining 37 programs, together accounting for 60 percent of the estimated
$115 billion in improper payments in 2011, did not analyze causes.[108]

By any plausible definition, FWA is a huge problem. (It is not
unique to the United States, of course, but international comparisons
are meaningless because of different methodologies.) In 2002, Congress passed the Improper Payments Information Act (IPIA), which
requires federal agencies to review their programs annually and identify those most susceptible to improper payments. By 2012, improper
payments were estimated at $115.3 billion, or between 4 and 5 per-
cent of the $2.5 trillion spent by agencies subject to IPIA reporting
requirement.[109] (It's important to note, however, that much of this rise
tracks with the implementation of better monitoring procedures
rather than with raw increases in improper payment levels.) The leading offenders were Medicare Fee-for-Service ($28.8 billion), Medicaid
($21.9 billion), the Earned Income Tax Credit ($15.2 billion), unemployment insurance ($13.7 billion), and Medicare Advantage ($12.4
billion). Of the thirty programs that the GAO annually designates
"high risk," seventeen (including Medicare and Medicaid) have been
so classified for more than a decade.[110] The ten most wasteful programs together accounted for $107 billion in improper payments in
2011, but improper payment estimates fell for the first time that year

and again in 2012, partly because of lower unemployment insurance outlays and efficiency gains in the Earned Income Tax Credit and Medicare Advantage programs. In 2012, the Justice Department opened 1,131 investigations against 2,148 potential defendants in the health care industry, disrupted 329 criminal fraud organizations, and won more than $3 billion in fraud judgments and settlements.[111] Yet the GAO finds Medicare and Medicaid actions to prevent overpayments to be chronically ineffective.[112]

The Department of Defense has long been pressed to improve its contracting practices, having paid out hundreds of billions of dollars to contractors engaged in fraud.[113] The Citizenship and Immigration Service found that 21.7 percent of H-1B visa petitions (for temporary highly skilled foreign workers) contained fraud or technical violations.[114] The GAO has found that USDA programs are rife with fraud, partly because the department's inspectors often fail to follow up on suspicious claims. The GAO reported that the USDA paid $22 million to more than 3,400 crop insurance policyholders who had been dead for at least two years,[115] that the $9 billion program's fraud rate is 5 percent, and that the $75 billion food stamp program's fraud rate has declined to "only" 1 percent. A crop insurance fraudster in just one scheme involving nearly $100 million told the Associated Press that "it's everywhere, all across the country" because the insurance adjusters rely entirely on what the farmers tell them.[116] The GAO finds that the VA pension program is riddled with FWA.[117]

Tax fraud—through identity theft, refund fraud, or tax-preparer fraud—has grown dramatically to the point where it ranks just behind Medicare, Medicaid, and unemployment insurance. Tax-identify theft has exploded in the last few years, with the Treasury's inspector general for tax administration reporting more than $5.2 billion in potentially fraudulent tax returns in 2011 alone.[118] The government has failed to collect either the $780 billion that Americans already owe in delinquent loans, fines, and penalties, or the additional $300 billion that they already owe in back taxes—including $1 billion owed *by federal employees* and $757 million owed by *federal contractors!*[119]

Documentary fraud is particularly rife in programs like immigration control, in which the costs of obtaining false documents and the probability of detection (upon repeated attempts, if necessary) are far lower than the benefits of gaining entry to the American labor market. Numerous GAO reports, select commissions on immigration reform, and congressional hearings have called for more effective enforcement against document fraud, which the law already penalizes heavily. The legalization programs enacted in 1986 experienced widespread fraud, particularly among "special agricultural workers," and the new legalization programs considered by Congress in 2013 will, if enacted, surely be vulnerable as well. Congress's steadfast refusal to require a secure national identity document practically guarantees this result.

FWA in federal programs takes many forms and surely has numerous causes, of which I shall note only a few that seem endemic to contemporary government. One important cause is *program complexity*. Medicare, Medicaid, and a host of other programs have tens of millions of beneficiaries, and their eligibility depends on whether they satisfy a variety of conditions specified in the statute, regulations, and other administrative issuances. Because their own life situations—income, employment, health, family structure, and a host of others—change regularly, so does their eligibility. Yet the government is in a poor position to keep up with these changes, a problem that is greatly exacerbated by its chronically retrograde, inferior information systems, as discussed earlier in the chapter. Most of these programs, moreover, are administered by state and local governments whose systems may be even more anachronistic and inefficient than those in Washington. In addition to inducing high error rates, this complexity and decentralized administration practically invite fraudsters to exploit complex programs through false claims—a temptation magnified by the often weak enforcement discussed in chapter 7.* Another

*Weak incentives to control incompetence presumably magnify its incidence. See, e.g., Devlin Barrett, "Marshals Lose Track of Encrypted Radios," *Wall Street Journal*, July 22, 2013.

source of FWA is *poorly designed reimbursement rules*. Such waste occurs when inadequate reimbursement, as with Medicaid's fee structure, causes providers to refuse to participate in the program, exacting its toll by *non*care for low-income people who are legally entitled to health services—another group of "invisible victims" discussed in chapter 2. A more visible kind of waste results from excessive reimbursement, exemplified by more than $500 million in overpayments to dialysis clinics that Congress recognized as such.[120]

FWA also occurs because *officials' incentives* to combat it are relatively weak. Any improper payments they recover likely go to the general treasury, not even to their agency, much less to their program budget. FWA prevention is costly, legal rules make it hard for the government to win criminal convictions, and the legal process is protracted and often inconclusive. And if the misconduct is not rectified, it is the taxpayers that stand to lose, not the officials. They are busy people with other programmatic responsibilities. They are working with other people's money. As noted in chapters 6 and 12, Congress has not funded sufficient enforcement personnel. Some incentives— their sense of professionalism, respect for the law, and fear of congressional criticism—do cut the other way, but evidently are insufficient. For example, only a *New York Times* front page report on its own investigation of major fraud in disability benefits paid by the Railroad Retirement Board, followed by repeated demands for action by the board's own inspector general, got it to cut off the benefits. It then quickly restored the benefits until outside pressure again forced it in July 2013 to renew the cutoff.[121]

Beyond the inadequate incentives to control and reduce FWA, there is the vital question of federal procurement officials' managerial competence. Steven Kelman, a scholar and former administrator of procurement policy, notes that contracting is now a core organizational activity. Indeed, many agencies spend more than half their budgets on contracted products and services (among them the Department of Energy, at 94 percent, and the Department of Defense, at 46 percent). Michele Flournoy, undersecretary of defense in the first Obama administration, describes the mismanagement problem in

DOD procurement thus: "Since 1960, the U.S. government has commissioned at least 27 major studies on defense-acquisition reform, and more than 300 studies have been undertaken by nongovernmental experts. Still, the Defense Department rarely achieves the expected return on its investments. Most major weapons programs run over cost and over schedule, costing American taxpayers billions more while delivering less capability than planned."[122] No wonder a front-page *New York Times* headline in December 2013 proclaims, "In Tech Buying, U.S. Still Stuck in Last Century."

Government contracting is especially vulnerable to FWA, Kelman argues, because procurement officers lack the necessary *management* skills—business savvy, in other words. Procurement work is usually seen as unglamorous; it is rarely assigned to higher-ranking or higher-performing employees. Kelman and Flournoy urge federal managers to redesign contract administration in a number of ways.[123]

Although I have focused on FWA in this section, other kinds of federal management failure are endemic. Indeed, the list of much-heralded administration task forces that have studied and reported on federal mismanagement—both across the board and in particular areas—is long. From president Franklin Delano Roosevelt's Brownlow Commission in 1937 to the National Performance Review headed by vice president Al Gore during the Clinton administration, high-profile reviews of management problems have produced thoughtful proposals for reforms, but without much evidence of significant improvement. In 2013, the Brookings Institution established the Governance Studies Management and Leadership Initiative to promote these reforms and develop others—even more evidence that federal mismanagement is a chronic problem at the very time when the ambition of national policies has swelled.

CHAPTER 7

Markets

O n September 15, 2013, the *New York Times* ran a front-page story with a two-page spread inside headlined "Wall St. Exploits Ethanol Credits, and Prices Spike." The *Times* reported that government regulators were shocked—shocked!—that banks and other financial speculators were buying up ethanol credits created by the Environmental Protection Agency in order to reduce air pollution by mandating the increased use of ethanol in gasoline, which had the effect of driving the price of these credits up twentyfold in just six months and increasing gas prices accordingly.[1] Chapter 8 discusses the ethanol program in some detail; I mention this here because it perfectly exemplifies the power of markets to undermine policies and even to render them perverse. The ethanol program is hardly an isolated example of this tendency, as we shall see.

Markets—the array of transactions in which people and firms voluntarily buy and sell goods and services from each other—are probably more powerful in the United States than in any other developed country. By "powerful" I mean several things. First, they are ubiquitous, society-shaping, and inescapable, influencing everything that government does, how it does it, and what it decides *not* to do. Paul Volcker, former chairman of the Federal Reserve Board, noted this fact when economist James Tobin asked Volcker why he didn't just lower the interest rate at a certain point, a potent weapon in the Fed's arsenal of formal economy-stabilizing powers. Volcker replied that he didn't set interest rates; the market did[2]—a point that Tobin, a Nobel Prize laureate, surely understood.

Volcker's observation about markets' potency relative to that of government is not limited to macroeconomic policy. For example, government has always tried to shape energy markets,[3] but those markets are so powerful that they tend to resist, distort, override, and marginalize such policies. Oil and gas prices are largely determined by global market conditions. These prices—driven in part by private investment in hydraulic fracking of oil shale, deep-water drilling, and other technologies—in turn affect energy consumers' consumption and efficiency far more than, say, mandatory fuel economy standards for automobiles (see chapter 8).[4]

Markets are also powerful in another sense, which is discussed in chapter 4 under the rubric of privatism. They are given freer scope to operate over more domains of legalized activity than in other countries because they enjoy greater public legitimacy here. Markets' individualistic premises dovetail with many other aspects of American culture, and the public strongly identifies these premises with American prosperity and the "American Dream." (Thus, it is unsurprising that a public furor arose, especially among business people, over president Barack Obama's statement [which his critics took somewhat out of context], "If you've got a business, you didn't build that. Somebody else made that happen.")[5]

Markets' cultural legitimacy in turn supports a political presumption—one that is rebuttable and often overridden—against government regulation. In a society as ideologically libertarian and diverse as ours, this presumption is unsurprising. Because the diversity of people's preferences is precisely what makes market transactions possible and mutually beneficial, the more diversity there is, the more beneficial exchanges can occur. Markets affect diversity in other complex and interesting ways—and vice versa.[6] The pursuit of comparative advantage and scale economies among producers leads to specialization of functions that engenders further diversification of skills, products, interests, and preferences. This specialization of functions, like the market itself, underscores the importance of the interdependencies among market participants, the self-interested value of cooperating with others, and the benefits attending to their interests as well as one's own. Paradoxically, markets are, as Adam Smith famously maintained, a civilizing, socializing, and pacifying process—even as they wreak "creative destruction" (as Joseph Schumpeter put it) with remorseless efficiency. In this way, markets make the toleration of differences an economic virtue not just a civic one, and they give their greatest rewards to those who know how to anticipate and promote differences for which people are willing to pay.

But the presumption favoring markets is often overcome. Our modern history exhibits periodic spasms of proregulation fervor.[7] Such arguments often prevail—most recently in the Sarbanes-Oxley and Dodd-Frank Acts, which extended government controls over the financial industry, and in the Affordable Care Act, which imposes numerous new requirements on the health care and insurance industries.[8] The notion that markets have intruded upon public morality to an indecent extent is a familiar trope of moral discourse.[9] Even so, the promarket default governs more strongly here than anywhere else.

This chapter neither extols nor criticizes markets—although there is much about them both to extol and to criticize. Rather, my concern here is to analyze the formidable obstacles they pose for policy effectiveness. Upending the common complaint by market enthusiasts that public policies distort markets, I focus here on the reverse: how markets distort government policies.

I organize this chapter around five different ways in which private markets interact with public programs: (1) they compete for participants; (2) they compete for administrative talent; (3) they compete in performance; (4) they compete to build reputation; and (5) markets frustrate market-perfecting policies. I devote most of this chapter to the fifth aspect because one can only understand how markets frustrate such policies by examining how this dynamic plays out in different policy settings. In chapter 8, which focuses on implementation, I extend this analysis by exploring many more examples of market-driven policy failure.

COMPETITION FOR PARTICIPANTS

People eligible for a government program providing a good or service can choose whether to participate in it or whether instead to remain in the market that provides the same or a similar good or service, and they will ordinarily make this choice by comparing the advantages and disadvantages of each alternative. This choice, while an individual one, has several far-reaching policy implications.

First, creating a government program or expanding an existing one is likely to have a "crowding out" effect in which people who previously purchased products in the market at some cost or would do so in the future will now opt instead to obtain them from the government program where they are cheaper or even free.[10] This means that the government is not expanding access nearly as much as it might seem if one simply looks at its participation numbers. Instead, many of the "new" participants in the government program will simply have shifted from their private providers to the cheaper public one. Presumably, this is a net gain for these participants; otherwise they would not have shifted. The flip side of crowding out, of course, is crowding in: just as government provision may draw consumers away from market providers (crowding out), it will draw those consumers in to its program (crowding in), producing more demand (and thus greater staffing need and budgetary cost) than it may have anticipated.

From a public policy perspective, the consequences of these shifts may be highly undesirable, even fiscally catastrophic. Taxpayers will now have to pay for participants who, absent the program (or its expansion), would have continued to receive those products or services in the private market at their own expense. This may increase taxpayers' political opposition not only to this government program but to others. The resulting crowding in of program participants within a relatively fixed public budget may degrade the quality of the product or service for participants. Scarce taxpayer dollars, which could have been used to provide more coverage for the poor or been spent on other things that the market does not provide to people who need them will have been wasted in this important sense.

Many government programs "crowd out" market or other forms of private provision; the effect of this is difficult to measure precisely and likely varies from program to program. The home loans promoted by Fannie Mae and Freddie Mac are among the largest and most important examples of crowding out—in this case, mortgage-backed securities with a low-cost government guarantee (first only implicit, now actual) replacing private activity in the same market. Dwight Jaffee and John Quigley's study, discussed in chapter 5, finds that "[i]f the government guarantee were eliminated, there is every reason to expect that private market activity would simply replace the activity of the government entity."[11] In fact, their analysis shows that the market would more than "simply" replace government activity; it would produce different, and sounder, underwriting decisions.

Another example is Social Security retirement benefits, which may crowd out private savings for retirement during the working years. If so, this would somewhat reduce private savings' net positive effect on seniors' living standards. Much depends, however, on how rational and future-oriented people are; myopia would tend to reduce preretirement savings and thus the crowding-out effect. There are other complications as well, such as whether retirees plan to use preretirement savings for consumption or for bequests to their survivors.[12]

An even clearer case of crowding out is Medicaid's effect on private insurance for long-term care expenditures, which is one of the largest uninsured financial risks facing the elderly today. A National Bureau of Economic Research study finds that

> the presence of Medicaid is sufficient to explain why at least two-thirds of all households would prefer not to purchase private long-term care insurance, even if there were no other factors limiting the size of the market. . . . Medicaid's large crowd-out effect stems from the fact that—because of its design (specifically, means testing and its status as a secondary payer)—a large portion of the premiums for private insurance for most individuals go to pay for benefits that are redundant given what Medicaid would have paid if the individual had not bought private

insurance. [The authors call this an "implicit tax" that Medicaid imposes on private insurance].

Finally, "since Medicaid itself provides far from comprehensive insurance, reliance on public insurance alone leaves most individuals exposed to substantial out-of-pocket expenditure risk."[13]

The vast expansion of Medicaid coverage for previously uninsured children and pregnant women with low incomes in the late 1980s to the late 1990s provides another example of crowding out. The study concluded that "for a given level of public expenditure on a coverage expansion, enrollment by those who would otherwise have private coverage reduces the potential number of uninsured people who can be covered."[14] Reducing this crowding out is hard for programs, often requiring substantial resources without any guarantee that they will be effective.[15] Predictably, the Affordable Care Act will cause many small businesses that now provide private health insurance to their employees to drop this coverage, knowing that the employees will be covered under the new program. (In November 2013, the program's severe database problems forced it to delay small business participation in the exchanges.[16])

A special form of crowding out occurs with government provision for the poor, which reduces private charity. Philanthropy expert Arthur Brooks estimates that a dollar in public social welfare spending displaces at least twenty-five cents in private giving and also reduces private volunteering.[17] Knowing that the government will provide food, foster care, or other social services, charities have less reason to use their own scarce resources to do so. This may even destroy their very raison d'être. This substitution may or may not be desirable, depending on how one views the role of government. One may think that recipients, as members of a political community, should enjoy these products as a matter of right rather than as private discretionary "handouts." Others may want civil society to cultivate the charitable impulse, already powerful in American life,[18] believing (along with Immanuel Kant) that benevolence has greater moral value if it proceeds from voluntary, autonomous goodwill rather than coerced taxation. One may also have different views about how public provision and private charity affect recipients. On one account, charities use diverse approaches to serve the needy, including some that emphasize, far more than government programs can, individual character development, higher behavioral expectations, and the value of reciprocal obligations. On another account, public programs can exemplify bureaucratic ideals: equal treatment, formal process, and legal entitlement.[19]

Finally, government competition for participants may *displace* the market—another form of crowding out—as private providers, unlike the government, cannot provide a service for free. If this discourages private providers from entering the market in the first place, as in the long-term care insurance example, it will increase costs and reduce competition, to the public's detriment.

COMPETITION FOR ADMINISTRATIVE TALENT

The effectiveness of government policies depends significantly on the quality of its personnel. Their intelligence, administrative skills, diligence, policy sophistication, problem-solving ability, and other relevant attributes depend on government's ability to compete for talent with potential employers in the private sector. The terms of trade between public and private employment are somewhat complicated. First, the two may not be functionally interchangeable. (How can one compare a U.S. Air Force pilot with a Delta Airlines pilot?) Second, federal employees enjoy more job security than their private-sector counterparts, fewer work hours, and often richer fringe benefits as well. (Public school teachers are local, not federal, employees, but a recent study finds that holding these factors constant, they are significantly overpaid relative to what their human capital would command in the private sector or indeed relative to comparable private school teachers.[20]) In chapter 10, I explore the federal bureaucracy's talent, morale, attractiveness, and status. The essential point for now is that private firms can outcompete government for the best workers.

COMPETITION FOR PERFORMANCE

The relative performance of government and private markets can often be readily assessed in situations in which they do essentially the same thing. The key phrase here is "essentially the same"; we must not carelessly compare government apples to market oranges. For example, government often serves low-income or high-risk populations—in public housing and public hospitals, for example—that private markets tend to eschew. But even though the contexts in which they act are not identical in every respect, comparisons may nonetheless be useful in illuminating some of the endemic sources of government's strengths and weaknesses. An important reason for examining such comparisons is that ordinary citizens often observe the differences and make comparative judgments, which presumably affect citizens' more general assessment of government and markets.

When one compares government and market provision of essentially the same service, the inescapable conclusion is that the market almost always performs more cost-effectively. One example, mail delivery, was discussed in chapter 6. Another is hospital care. Medicare Advantage encourages seniors to enroll in private health insurance plans rather than traditional, government-run Medicare; these private plans are run by managed care organizations emphasizing capitation payments rather than fee-for-service reimbursement. Medicare Advantage has grown steadily in popularity at the expense of traditional Medicare and now serves more than 25 percent of Medicare beneficiaries despite strong political opposition from traditional Medicare proponents. (The comparison is imperfect because Medicare has made a higher payment to the private plans, a disparity that the Affordable Care Act will largely eliminate, and the private plans may have attracted healthier patients.) Private-sector competition has also driven down costs in the prescription drug program added to Medicare in 2003.[21] And despite Medicare's claim to have less bureaucracy (defined as a lower ratio of administrative costs to health delivery costs) than private insurers, the reverse may be true—once one considers that Medicare covers older and sicker patients and that many of its most significant costs (e.g., tax and premium collection, and some overhead) are borne by other federal agencies and do not appear on Medicare's budget, while the program also enjoys other fiscal advantages (e.g., exemption from taxes paid on premiums and less monitoring for fraud or improper billing, even though stricter prepayment review would pay for itself twenty times over).[22]

Market providers can also make government providers of the same service more efficient in two ways—by forcing government to compete in cost and other service variables, and by providing examples of greater effectiveness that government can incorporate into its own programs. A study of public and private prisons in states that operate both, for example, found that the mere presence of private prisons reduced cost increases in the public ones.[23] This suggests that a public service need not be completely privatized in order for the competitive dynamic to improve the government providers' performance. Indeed, policy makers sometimes use privatization for reasons other than merely providing the same services more cheaply.[24]

COMPETITION TO CREATE REPUTATION

Law professor Jon Macey argues that the recent spate of misconduct by regulated financial institutions is partly a perverse consequence of expanded regulatory interventions that falsely assure the public that regulated firms are honest, reliable, and competent, thus reducing the institutions' incentives to invest in building their reputations for these qualities.[25] When the Federal Deposit Insurance Corporation (FDIC) insures a bank, for example, it signals to depositors that the bank is safe, so the bank need not invest in safety beyond what will qualify it for the FDIC's seal of approval. If statutory rating agencies have assessed the risks of default, debt issuers have less reason to invest more to win lenders' trust. In this way, agency assurances displace firms' credibility earned through market processes.

MARKETS FRUSTRATE
MARKET-PERFECTING POLICIES

Because markets are so powerful and ubiquitous, we should not be surprised that they affect government programs in countless ways. After all, market transactions comprise most of the economy, and they directly or indirectly affect virtually everything else that policy makers seek to influence. For better *and* for worse, markets even shape some of the most intimate spheres of social life—marriage, parenthood, sexuality, religion, and morality[26]—as well as other areas that we often hope, perhaps naively, can be isolated from market forces—for example, politics,[27] the fine arts,[28] the natural environment,[29] and amateur sports.[30]

Government depends on markets in an even more elementary way: they generate the wealth that government must tax in order to support its activities. Although this fact is perfectly obvious, it constitutes one of the most important constraints on policy making— namely, that policies must be carefully designed so as not to kill the goose that lays the golden egg. Macroeconomists often disagree, of course, about which policies will have what particular effects on economic growth and government revenues; these disagreements figure prominently in political and policy debates. (Macroeconomic projections are notoriously inaccurate; their failure to foresee the Great Recession is simply the most recent example. Their predictive failures are themselves predictable.[31]) That said, any policy that seriously threatens to reduce economic growth and thus tax revenues will likely fail, both politically and functionally.

The same markets that provide government with its sustenance at the macroeconomic level also undermine its effectiveness at the microeconomic level, even under the most benign conditions. The reasons for these "subversive tendencies" inhere in the very nature of markets, coupled with the government's ineffectiveness in identifying and correcting market failures. In this section, I shall discuss nine of these endemic policy-frustrating reasons: (1) speed; (2) diversity;

(3) informational demands on regulators; (4) price and substitution effects; (5) transjurisdictional effects; (6) political influence; (7) enforcement obstacles; (8) rational expectations; and (9) lack of good substitutes for market ordering. Two other important market-related reasons for policy failure are discussed in other chapters—moral hazard (chapter 5) and black or "informal" markets (chapter 8).

Speed. Markets move at lightning speed and change constantly. This reflects the powerful incentives that market suppliers have to meet the demands of consumers who are constantly being stimulated and sought by similarly motivated competitors. The instantaneous price movements produced by computer-driven electronic trading on stock exchanges constitute only the most iconic example of this dynamic. They have helped to improve financial markets in many ways; Floyd Norris, a *New York Times* reporter, notes that "trading costs, whether for small individual investors or large institutional investors, have declined sharply. The cuts going to middlemen are smaller, and many markets are deeper and more liquid than ever."[32] Yet this enhanced speed risks occasional but very costly (and apparently more frequent) glitches.[33] Policy makers seeking to influence or control these markets must aim at a rapidly moving target that assumes protean forms, and their weapons are akin to blunderbusses. The ability of large investors to move their capital anywhere in the world with the click of a mouse means that policies whose success depends on attracting asset-specific investments are harder and more costly to implement, as the opportunity costs for such investments—their sacrifice of asset mobility—rise.

Perhaps the best example of how markets' speed challenges policy makers is macroeconomic policy, for which the main tools—monetary policy, fiscal policy, and exhortation ("jawboning")—are inadequate to this extremely complex, opaque task whose parameters constantly change.[34] The Federal Reserve Board, despite its history of exceptionally talented leadership, has compiled a mixed record on controlling inflation and unemployment and maintaining economic growth. (In fairness, the "compared to what" rejoinder is appropriate here; there is only one Fed.) Its record in regulating the banking system and preventing asset bubbles has also been severely criticized, particularly during the post-2008 banking crisis. This mixed record partly reflects the inevitable tension among these goals but also shows that seeking to fine-tune interest rates by manipulating the money supply, whose composition constantly changes, is inherently problematic. Fiscal policy, which is the province of elected politicians, has manifestly failed, as evidenced by more than a decade of growing budget deficits as a share of economic output even in good economic times, deficits that will explode due to impending demographic changes and (relatedly) rising health care costs unless radical policy changes are enacted. In addition, the effects of fiscal policy changes ordinarily take twelve to eighteen months before they can affect the real economy. By that time, the rational expectations and anticipatory adjustments of market actors may have neutralized the new policy, or economic conditions may have changed in other ways that render the policy change inapt or undesirable when it takes effect. Jawboning has occasionally had some bite in the very short run (president John F. Kennedy's stance on steel price increases, for example), but is notoriously ineffective as a serious policy tool.

Diversity. Markets are as diverse as the preferences of the consumers whom they seek to attract and satisfy. There is no single market for, say, banking, food supplements, Internet services, consumer credit, or sports clubs; instead, there are a vast number of providers, each with a different business model, seeking to find or create a specialized market niche with a discrete subset of consumers. Government policies seeking to shape or regulate these markets almost always rely on wholesale, centralized techniques that this vast, uncoordinated, volatile, differentiated array of market actors tends to confound. (The reasons why government relies on such crude techniques are explored in chapter 9.) Indeed, as I have explained elsewhere, government and law are natural enemies of diversity, especially when they are most eager to create it.[35] (Antitrust and antidiscrimination law are possible exceptions to this—only "possible" because although both are diversity-enhancing in principle, particular enforcement policies in both areas can sometimes suppress it.[36])

Informational demands on regulators. Government cannot influence markets effectively unless it has access to timely, accurate, inexpensive information about market actors, dynamics, and strategies—information that is appropriately tailored to the immense market diversity just described. Yet the government repeatedly experiences systemic difficulties in efficiently managing information flows generated by private market actors at any reasonable cost. Some information management is easier than others. For the Social Security Administration to send pension checks to seniors, for example, it does not need much individualized data about them other than their names, ages, addresses, and the number of quarters during which they have been employed—all readily ascertainable from standardized public records. It is only a slight exaggeration to say that this part of the program is essentially a check-writing operation. Contrast this, however, with the same agency's disability benefits program, which must make individualized determinations of disability status under vague legal standards and with a complex process and uncertain evidence, while relying to some (uncertain) degree on earlier decisions made by other people and institutions that together largely determine outcomes: federal and state hearing examiners, private physicians, vocational rehabilitation agencies, and other actors beyond close federal supervision or control.[37]

The problem is illustrated by the Bush and Obama administrations' failed efforts to generate accurate clinical information by subsidizing providers to adopt electronic medical records (EMRs). As a *New York Times* article on the $6.5 billion program put it, EMRs "can make health care more efficient and less expensive, and improve the quality of care by making patients' medical history easily accessible to all who treat them."[38] A 2005 RAND Corporation study, which digital record vendors strongly promoted, induced policy makers to give billions of dollars in federal stimulus subsidies to induce providers to adopt EMRs, with scant concern for how this would be implemented.[39]

Yet implementation has been a costly fiasco. The RAND study was grossly overoptimistic, as the Congressional Budget Office predicted at the time. The new systems were so "clunky and time-consuming" that it slowed the public health system of a major California county to a crawl, with doctors and nurses seeing only half as many patients as usual. The systems have increased Medicare billings and even facilitated fraud by inviting providers to check boxes opportunistically. In November 2012, the inspector general of the department that administers Medicare issued a scathing report that Medicare's payment of incentives to providers to digitize their records has inadequate safeguards against fraud and abuse, despite the agency's promise to control overbilling.[40] As one internist put it, "reading the electronic chart has become a game of looking for a small needle of new information in a haystack of falsely comprehensive documentation and outdated, copied text. Why do we doctors do this to ourselves? Largely, it turns out, for the same reason most people do most things: money."[41] Years after the subsidy payments, EMR's ballyhooed promise of lower costs remains wholly hypothetical.[42]

Price and substitution effects. Government programs cannot escape the inexorable market-driving law of supply and demand, whose price effects in turn activates behavioral incentives in ways often unwanted by policy makers. Nevertheless, policy makers often ignore this basic fact of programmatic life in ways that undermine their policy goals.

If government builds more roads to alleviate traffic congestion, the lower congestion costs will attract more drivers to the roads, thus frustrating the policy. If it seeks to reduce the price of gasoline, the lower price will discourage producers from bringing new supply online, thus raising the price; the lower price will also increase demand, which will also push the price back up. Requiring more energy-efficient air conditioners may actually increase power consumption as consumers respond to the lower electricity costs by increasing their utilization. Requiring child-resistant packaging of drugs may reduce safety on balance by making them harder and slower (i.e., more costly) for adults to open.[43] If one must be homeless to receive free housing, then—*ceteris paribus*—more people will claim that they are homeless, and if the shelters are more attractive, they will tend to remain longer.[44] When the National Highway Traffic Safety Administration (NHTSA) mandated safety features for cars, drivers took more risks and the accident rate rose[45]—an example of the Peltzman effect, according to which people adjust their behavior to a regulation in ways that counteract the regulation's intended effect. Other examples of the Peltzman effect appear in chapter 8.

A related phenomenon is the substitution effect, in which raising a good's cost (or banning it outright) will induce its producers to find cheaper (or legally permitted) substitutes. This substitution is often socially undesirable on balance. Thus, when the Environmental Protection Agency (EPA) raised gas mileage standards, auto manufacturers complied by switching to lighter cars that did consume less fuel but were more dangerous to occupants in collisions.[46] (The price effect also encourages owners to offset the lower fuel costs by driving more.[47]) Banning DDT led users to substitute other insecticides that are even riskier or more costly (or both), like malathion. And if they fail to find and deploy a better substitute, the result may be disastrous, as with the countless malaria-related deaths that scientists attributed to the government's ban on DDT.[48] Some Occupational Safety and Health Administration (OSHA) regulations have also produced "regrettable substitution," in which employers replace one source of deadly fumes with an even more dangerous one.[49] The 2009 stimulus law sought to create jobs, but its provisions raised the cost of hiring workers (or reduced job-seeking) in several ways—for example, with easier access to food stamps, lengthened unemployment benefits, minimum wage increases, and retention of the labor-cost-inflating Davis-Bacon Act. Economist Casey Mulligan estimates that such measures caused a substantial part of the precipitous decline in labor force participation and hours worked from 2007 to 2011.[50]

The list of policies frustrated by these market effects on behavior is almost endless. All things considered, the new equilibrium that is produced once a policy's price and substitution effects work their way through the system may improve the situation overall—or it may make the situation much worse, especially for those with fewer choices. Dodd-Frank compliance is imposing vast new costs on banks—an estimated $34 billion a year—that the market has passed on to low-income consumers in sharply reduced access to credit cards, loans, and other forms of credit.[51] When products are banned, consumers may turn to more costly and less satisfactory ones, including more dangerous ones. As political scientist Aaron Wildavsky showed, laws that raise consumers' costs in order to improve their health also produce offsetting health risks by reducing their wealth. As he put it, wealthier is healthier.[52] We can safely predict that policies which fail to consider or underestimate these price and substitution effects will produce outcomes that are less effective, more costly, and sometimes the opposite of what they intended. Chapter 8, on policy implementation, presents many more examples.

Transjurisdictional effects. Although some markets (particularly those involving personal services) remain local even today, most markets today are broader than that: interstate, regional, national, or global. Widespread evasion of state excise taxes and other regulations—for example, on cigarettes,[53] liquor, and other products—is widespread, just as it is in Europe, where cross-border travel is simple and inexpensive. (Denmark's tax on fatty foods was so easily evaded by shopping in neighboring countries that it was quickly repealed.[54])

The federal government lacks extraterritorial jurisdiction to regulate many foreign markets, and even when it possesses such jurisdiction, it is constrained to allow or even encourage foreign competition, which is advantageous to domestic consumers and some commercial interests (importers, for example) even as it may disadvantage some domestic firms, at least in the short run. The more telling point about foreign market actors, however, is that their actions may subvert domestic policy goals. Banking regulators, for example, are finding it difficult to subject foreign banks with large U.S. operations to the Dodd-Frank law's capital, leveraging, and other requirements for fear of inducing evasive tactics that could harm the interests of American banks and consumers.[55] (A similar transjurisdictional problem exists among our states—where insurers risk systemic insolvency by exploiting regulatory differences across borders.[56]) Informal markets, discussed in chapter 8, can arise precisely to exploit this transjurisdictional problem.

The possibility that government taxes and regulations will encourage domestic firms to move some or all of their jobs, activities, and investments abroad—where those restrictions are less onerous—is a constant, serious constraint on domestic policy, one with political resonance that conservatives often exploit effectively to defeat such impositions. The Sarbanes-Oxley law, passed in the wake of the Enron fraud, made listing shares on U.S. stock markets so costly that firms increasingly looked abroad for capital or remained private. Not coincidently, the U.S. share of initial public offerings fell from 67 percent in 2002 when the law passed, to 16 percent in 2011.[57] Another constraint on policy is a concern that foreign firms will use U.S. law to compete against domestic ones. An example is the Jumpstart Our Business Startups Act of 2012, which Congress designed to create job growth in the United States by reducing the costs to new small firms of raising capital and to established firms of going public, partly by reducing their Securities and Exchange Commission (SEC) disclosure obligations. A recent assessment of the new program finds that foreign companies are using the law to compete more cheaply against American firms; this tends to reduce domestic job growth while enhancing growth abroad. Some foreign companies are also using the program to market to American investors with less disclosure than their domestic competitors make.[58] Such foreign competition may on balance be beneficial (or not) to the U.S. economy; my point here is that it often undermines Congress's more insular policy goals.

Political influence of market actors. For a host of reasons, market actors exert enormous influence over political outcomes and government policies. Indeed, compared with more centralized parliamentary democracies, our political system is relatively porous and responsive to private interests at multiple points in the policy process.[59] This is particularly true where a single government agency intensively regulates a market or related markets, such as the SEC, the Food and Drug Administration (FDA), the NHTSA, and the Nuclear Regulatory Commission. In such regulatory contexts, the mutual dependencies of regulator and regulated—for information, personnel, political support, and sometimes even revenues (as with the FDA)—are great. The hoary notions of agency "capture" by the regulated firms and of an "iron triangle" of agency, regulated interests, and congressional subcommittee beg a host of difficult questions, as noted in chapter 4. These notions, moreover, also vastly oversimplify a complex, opaque reality, as political scientists have consistently demonstrated.[60] Still, a subtler, less deterministic view of the populist critique is certainly correct: mutuality of influences and interests are fundamental aspects of regulatory politics that cause program performance to deviate, often greatly, from policy goals.

In regulatory contexts such as health and safety, the environment, and civil rights, the agencies regulate a broader, more diverse group of industries, and the industries' influence over them tends to be more diffuse. Examples include OSHA, the EPA, and the Equal Employment Opportunity Commission (EEOC). Here the interests among the industries and within an agency may conflict, as regulatory units primarily concerned with one industrial sector (as in OSHA) or with one risk medium (as in the EPA's solid waste program) compete for congressional attention, budget, legal authority, publicity, and political support. At the same time, the influence of "public interest" organizations demanding that the agency regulate more vigorously—labor unions (vis-à-vis OSHA), environmental groups (the EPA), and civil rights organizations (the EEOC)—is often considerable.[61]

This dynamic of mutual influence and support between market actors and government is not confined to regulatory agencies but extends to agencies charged with other kinds of missions. Aerospace companies, for example, exercise strong influence over the relevant government procurement agencies. Veterans groups shape the activities of the Veterans Administration. Scientific communities shape with the agendas and processes of the National Science Foundation and the National Institutes of Health. The Justice Department is attentive to the substantive views of the American Bar Association, with the ABA's influence waxing or waning with different administrations and different issues. (Republican administrations, for example, have come to be suspicious of the ABA's relatively liberal orientation in its assessment of judicial candidates.) Even a seemingly apolitical agency such as the Census Bureau attracts strong interest from industries, demographers, civil rights advocates, and other groups eager to shape its methodology and use its data.[62]

The political influence wielded by interest groups takes many forms. Industries and other advocacy groups lobby Congress in order to shape agencies' budgets, priorities, personnel, legal authority, and other aspects of their work in ways that will advance the advocates' interests. Much lobbying, moreover, is intended to shore up support among members who are already inclined to favor the group's position rather than to convince those inclined to oppose it.[63] Interest groups and their lobbyists organize grassroots support, launch educational and publicity campaigns, seek to install sympathetic individuals in office, recruit officials when they are ready to leave office, perform favors for officials without exacting the quid quo pro that might constitute criminal bribery, and use top former officials to advocate before the courts and their old agencies. (The tobacco industry team that challenged the FDA's power to regulate it included every living former FDA chief counsel![64]) To observers such as Joseph Stiglitz, a Nobel Prize laureate in economics, the concentrated power of corporate interests is both extensive in scope and pernicious in its effects, encouraging the rent-seeking that undermines social equality, democratic values, and a competitive economy.[65] Other prominent commentators share that assessment.[66]

All of these critics strongly condemn the corrupting influence of money in politics;[67] they assume, plausibly enough, that money drives public policy. But in focusing on the hydraulics of money in politics, they often overlook the fact that the causal arrow *also* points the other way: more powerful government draws more private money into the political system. Expanded public authority makes groups more vulnerable to policies that can seriously harm them, which raises the stakes in averting those harms through whatever sources of influence they can muster.

In fact, the actual policy significance of contributions to those running for Congress is far from clear despite much study by political scientists. Most contributions are well below the legal ceilings and go to legislators who *already agree with them*—particularly incumbents, and especially committee chairs, with already well-established views.[68] The contributions serve more to fortify than to persuade, to improve access rather than to strong-arm.[69] Often self-protective in nature, they seek to minimize the risk of incumbents' anger or retaliation. Although pundits often claim that campaign contributions spawn bitter partisan politics (ignoring that eminent political scientists have long urged a more polarized "responsible party government"[70]), the connection is opaque. As political scientist John J. Pitney wrote in early 2012,

> Big money is not necessarily ideological or even partisan. Some interest groups side with conservatives on tax issues, but others have a material stake in the expansion of government programs and thus may side with progressives. In passing his healthcare bill, President Obama built a broad coalition that included industry lobbying groups such as the Pharmaceutical Research and Manufacturers of America and the American Medical Association. Groups may switch sides depending on how they gauge their interests. The financial services industry favored Obama in 2008, and now seems to be leaning to Romney.[71]

In the wake of Obama's reelection, the industry quickly moved toward a new, more conciliatory stance.[72]

The Supreme Court's controversial *Citizens United* decision—which held that the First Amendment protection of political speech permits corporations and unions to spend their treasury funds for independent advocacy favoring particular candidates[73]—has aroused legions of critics, yet the decision's holding (as distinguished from its objectionably overreaching, loose analysis) is clearly correct on its facts. After all, First Amendment protection of freedom of the press surely extends to the nonprofit group that made the film attacking Hillary Clinton's candidacy just as it would protect a *New York Times* editorial attacking Mitt Romney.[74]

More important for present purposes, the decision's actual effects on policy—the main focus of its multitude of critics (former president Jimmy Carter has said the decision is "stupid" and allows "legal bribery"[75])—remain unclear. An analysis by *Times* political reporter Matt Bai, written shortly before the 2012 election, noted that as of June 2012, not a single Fortune 100 company had contributed to a candidate's Super PAC during the primary season, and less than 1 percent of the money raised by Republican Super PACs came from publicly traded companies; only 13 percent came from privately held companies. The flood of money into campaigns, Bai writes, has been unleashed not by *Citizens United* but by the Bipartisan Campaign Reform Act of 2002, popularly known as McCain-Feingold. That law, notes Bai, moved campaign expenditures "from inside the party structure to outside it. . . . What we are seeing—what we almost certainly would have seen even without the Court's ruling in *Citizens United*—is the full force of conservative wealth in America, mobilized by a common enemy for the first time since [McCain-Feingold]. . . . Liberals dominated outside spending in 2004 and 2006. And should Romney become president, they'll most likely do so again."[76] In any event, presidential campaigns are unique; the influence of moneyed interests is probably greater in congressional and state races. There, campaign contributions primarily work to further entrench *incumbents* of both parties, who already enjoy greater name recognition, influence over the districting process, the franking privilege, publicity, seniority, and other advantages.

Indeed, political scientists have wondered why so *little* is spent on campaigns, not only as compared to consumer expenditures on cosmetics and other gewgaws but also as a share of gross domestic product. In a 2003 article, Stephen Ansolabehere and colleagues show that this share had not risen appreciably in more than a century, and might have fallen—probably because campaign spending seems to have little marginal effect. They also show that individuals, not special interests, are the main source of campaign contributions, and that there is little relationship between money and votes once one controls for other vote-relevant factors.[77] (Ballot initiatives may be different.[78]) Political commentator Ezra Klein argues that money's influence is greatest on small issues that matter to narrow interests, whereas "the more likely Americans are to have actually heard of the bill, the less likely money is to be the decisive factor in its fate":

[The "headline clashes"] all go the same way: the Democrats vote with the Democrats, and the Republicans vote with the Republicans. That's true even when the big money lines up in favor of another outcome. In 2011, the Chamber of Commerce and the AFL-CIO joined together to call for a major reinvestment in American infrastructure. None passed. In 2010, most of the health care industry was either supportive or neutral on the Affordable Care Act, and if any one of them could have swung the votes of even a few Republican senators or congressmen, the desperate Democrats would have let them write almost anything they wanted into the bill. But not one Republican budged. In 2009, the Chamber of Commerce endorsed the stimulus bill as a necessary boost to the economy. Not one House Republican voted for it. Almost every major business group has been calling for tax reform and a big, Simpson-Bowles-like deficit reduction package for years now. But Congress remains deadlocked. . . . while moneyed interests are decisive in passing laws and influencing provisions that few Americans care about, they're much weaker on the issues where Americans are actually watching. But those issues are the ones that have convinced America that Washington is broken.[79]

In truth, the political power of market actors lies less in their campaign contributions than in the real economic and political interests that elected politicians think these interests represent to their constituents. Investment by these interests adds to communities' tax bases. Their employees are productive citizens, taxpayers, and consumers who also vote. Their businesses promise to increase growth, jobs, and productivity. Investments in them include the life savings of ordinary people, not just local notables. Their presence attracts to their communities still other businesses and perhaps their upstream and downstream entities. Politicians tend to thrive from these developments, have a strong self-interest in promoting and preferring them over competing communities, and would almost certainly do so even in the absence of campaign contributions. In a representative system with local constituencies and frequent elections, this is a large part of what politicians are supposed to do. These ramifying economic impacts on Main Streets throughout the country explain—probably better than lobbying by Citigroup, Goldman Sachs, and other financial titans—why the federal government's solicitude for Wall Street interests leads to huge bailouts, despite the moral hazard.

The key question about campaign contributions, then, is what is their *marginal* effect—that is, above and beyond the effect that these primary political considerations would have on legislators' behavior? This question has no clear answer, but the evidence suggests that this marginal effect is far less than the fierce critics of *Citizens United* claim. An econometric study of congressional races from 1972 to 1990 found that campaign finance had only a tiny effect: an extra $175,000 in spending would increase the final vote by only a third of a percentage point.[80] The 2012 presidential election seems to have confirmed this pattern.[81]

Obstacles to policy enforcement. The headlines about government prosecutions of this or that market actor for some violation should not be taken as an accurate representation of what happens to those who transgress government policies. Although federal sentences for economic crimes are at a historic high in terms of both number and length,[82] prosecutions of such crimes remain rare and often unsuccessful.[83] The vast majority of violations go undetected or, if detected, inadequately remedied. In the classic economic theory of crime and punishment, the potential violator compares his possible gains to the severity of the punishment discounted by the probability that it will actually be imposed, which is the joint probability that he will be detected, apprehended, prosecuted, convicted, and fined or sentenced. This joint probability should also be discounted by the length of time that will elapse before these bad outcomes occur.[84] This theory, together with the fact that the penalties imposed on miscreant market actors are low relative to firm size (indeed, sometimes less than what they gained from their misconduct), suggests that they are significantly underdeterred. Prosecutorial confusion also confounds enforcement, making optimal levels of deterrence or sanctions unlikely. Jurisdictional overlaps produce multiple prosecutions for the same course of conduct by different agencies—for example, the SEC, federal banking regulators, state banking regulators, federal and state criminal prosecutors, private litigation, and sometimes even a non-bank agency.[85] At least *eight* federal agencies are investigating a single major bank.[86] Not surprisingly, less than a quarter of the respondents in a Kiplinger survey believe that the SEC effectively polices the stock market.[87]

There are many reasons for limited, weak enforcement, not all of them bad. First, the optimal level of enforcement for most crimes and regulatory violations is likely to be well below 100 percent (unlike with, say, murder). Prosecutorial discretion is both broad and largely immune from judicial review—far too broad and immune, according to leading scholars of the criminal law system.[88] At a certain point in the process, this discretion also becomes immune from *political* review; by custom, the president must not interfere with prosecutorial decisions even by his own appointed attorney general and Department of Justice staff. (There have been exceptions, most famously the "Saturday Night Massacre" of attorneys general by President Richard Nixon during the Watergate crisis.)

Prosecutors and agency officials often consult on whether particular cases are worth pursuing and, if so, how they will be handled and what punishments will be sought.[89] The enforcement sequence—from investigation and detection to actual imposition of a penalty—is costly to the government, which must pay for investigators, lawyers, data systems, experts in the policy field, detention facilities, and many other services. Enforcement budgets are severely limited, often because the relevant congressional committees, which attend to commercial interests that might be targeted, want it that way. The standard of proof—guilt beyond a reasonable doubt in criminal cases, a lower standard for civil sanctions—is difficult to satisfy. (This may explain why OSHA investigated more than twelve hundred cases in which investigators concluded that workers had died because of "willful" safety violations on the part of their employers but prosecuted a mere 7 percent of these cases.[90]) Although the public understandably resents the fact that financial companies may not only be "too big to fail" despite Dodd-Frank (see above, and chapter 5) but also "too big to jail"—a phenomenon that even attorney general Eric Holder concedes[91]—the latter is more complex morally, economically, and legally. Criminally prosecuting corporations, as the government did with Arthur Andersen after the Enron debacle, is certain to punish many altogether innocent employees and others by forcing the company out of business, which reduces competition in the industry. Except with criminal enterprises, the pursuit of fines, regulatory sanctions, private claims, and other noncriminal remedies is likely to be a better strategy.

White-collar defendants are often represented by highly skilled attorneys who previously worked as prosecutors and know how to create "reasonable doubt" in criminal cases. Some violators try to cover their tracks by destroying evidence, intimidating hostile witnesses, and creating smokescreens by attacking the government. The government's evidence or tactics may be inadmissible or, as in the case of complex accounting and financial data, hard for the jury to follow. Juries uneasy about the government's tactics, such as relying on testimony by informers who are themselves convicted criminals, may sympathize with the defendant. This is particularly true if the defendant is a small fish compared with other offenders whom the government is not prosecuting for one reason or another.

Second, the officials who run the regulatory agencies tend to be mindful of the need—both political and bureaucratic—to cultivate and sustain the regulated industry; they seldom are militant opponents or radical reformers of that industry. In the rare cases in which they are aggressive critics—for example, Craig Becker, a recess appointment to the National Labor Relations Board (NLRB), they are not renominated. The formal confirmation process and the informal norms of reciprocity that surround it practically assure that top regulators will be cautious and compromising. The protracted battle over the nomination to the Federal Reserve Board of the superbly qualified Nobel laureate economist Peter Diamond, led him to withdraw his name in frustration and disgust. Republicans' refusal to confirm Richard Cordray, a former Ohio prosecutor, as director of the recently established Consumer Financial Protection Bureau caused President Obama to make a recess appointment of him, which took two years for the Senate to confirm. Recess appointments to the NLRB have been challenged in the courts.[92] Sometimes firms can in effect select their own regulator and supervisor. Banks, for example, may choose federal or state charters, and may decide (within limits) whether to operate as a savings institution or a commercial bank, subject to somewhat different regulatory schemes.

Third, congressional appropriations for enforcement, as already noted, tend to be woefully inadequate. This point is vividly illustrated by ineffective policing of the vast and politically powerful securities industry by the SEC and federal prosecutors.[93] Arthur Levitt, SEC chair from 1993 to 2001, claims that congressional overseers constantly threatened him with budget cuts if he was too aggressive.[94] The agency notes that while other financial regulators have close to parity between the number of staff and the number of entities they regulate, SEC staffing and funding have not kept pace with industry growth in recent years.[95] Congress and the courts, sometimes abetted by the agency itself, have limited the availability of private class actions and other legal remedies against market malefactors, remedies that could augment the agency's own meager enforcement budget and use the formidable self-interest of plaintiffs' lawyers to strengthen the enforcement process. Nowhere was this clearer than in the Private Securities Litigation Reform Act of 1995, in which Congress, while remedying some abuses in private securities class actions, also made it much more difficult for such actions to be brought at all.[96]

A fourth reason for weak enforcement is that the enactment and administrative implementation of regulatory statutes is always shaped by a process in which industry lobbying plays an important role. Lobbyists provide valuable services to legislators and their staffs—technical expertise about the industry; political intelligence; anticipating how particular provisions will operate; rebutting opposition arguments; drafting statutory language and speeches; proposing compromises; testifying at hearings; creating legislative history; and mobilizing political support through grassroots organizing, coalition building, public persuasion, and other forms of advocacy. In exchange, they expect the final version to protect their clients with language that will reduce the incidence of future violations, prosecutions, penalties, and private lawsuits. One example is the extensive participation by financial industry lobbyists in writing laws that regulate their clients.[97] Another is attorney-client privilege protection legislation, which the white-collar defense bar promoted to limit prosecutors' access to their clients' legal and financial transactions. When it bogged down in Congress, the Department of Justice agreed to incorporate much of it into its enforcement policy.[98]

Fifth, the specific regulations that agencies promulgate to implement such statutes (a process described in chapter 2) tend to be highly technical and intricate. They are drafted by the agency's policy specialists and lawyers, often after consultation with business lobbyists. The regulators try to anticipate their industry counterparts' evasive tactics by eliminating possible loopholes and foreclosing even low-probability evasions. Their adversaries, however, tend to be more highly trained and paid, better supported organizationally, and more knowledgeable about how their markets work, and are often a step ahead of the regulators. Ironically, for reasons discussed in chapter 9, regulations' complex architecture may actually make them easier to evade. Indeed, no level of detail can entirely eliminate ambiguities, which sometimes are inadvertent but which drafters, often guided by lobbyists, may insert intentionally to conceal policy conflicts or to give leeway to market actors or government enforcers. This process shaped the much-heralded rules issued by the Consumer Financial Protection Bureau in early 2013 to reduce the risk of future home foreclosures.[99] Industry lawyers can use these ambiguities to craft plausible arguments about the words' meaning and purposes, how they could and should be applied to specific situations, inconsistencies engendered by the larger text, and the way that different interpretations advance or retard putative policy purposes. These arguments, if plausible, make it harder for government lawyers to prove a criminal or even civil violation.

A sixth reason for weak enforcement inheres in the complex, protracted negotiations between the government and the target entities that may both precede and follow a decision to go forward with the case. The cost of government enforcement, and uncertainty about how judges and juries will assess the strength of its legal, factual, and policy arguments, often weaken prosecutors' negotiating position—a vulnerability that industry lawyers are trained to detect and exploit to great effect. For example, federal banking regulators, embarrassed by having paid more than $1 billion to consultants for a deeply flawed review of foreclosed home loans, accepted a settlement with major banks that reflected this weak bargaining position.[100] If the prospect of a protracted jury trial with an uncertain outcome daunts prosecutors more than their adversaries, it may accept a plea bargain in which the industry pays a fine but acknowledges no guilt.* Such pallid "go and sin no more" rebukes may in turn reduce deterrence of other possible violators. (Although this practice continues, some federal judges, led by Judge Jed S. Rakoff, have begun to insist that settling defendants in such cases acknowledges their guilt.[101])

Then there is the sheer force of incompetence, whose effect on enforcement should never be underestimated. The SEC's inspector general issued a scathing report detailing the agency's failure to investigate epic fraudster Bernard Madoff's $65 billion scheme despite complaints by securities experts going back to 1992 that raised red flags.[102] In April 2013, for another example, the Government Accountability Office (GAO) detailed a botched effort by the Federal Reserve and the Comptroller of the Currency to review the implementation of federally mandated payments by banks and other financial institutions to homeowners subjected to illegal and abusive mortgage foreclosures. The GAO report found that the regulators had designed a flawed review of the troubled loans, including requiring the institu-

---

*BP's record-setting criminal fines in the Deepwater Horizon disaster case were unusual, but represented only a small percentage of the company's profits in 2012. See Clifford Krauss & Stanley Reed, "BP to Admit Crimes and Pay $4.5 billion in Gulf Settlement," *New York Times*, November 15, 2012.

tions to hire independent consultants who then did delayed, shoddy work at very high fees and sometimes with conflicts of interest under contracts that were poorly designed, inconsistent, and unenforced. As a result, many homeowners did not receive the relief to which they were entitled.[103]

Finally, politicians sometimes seek to restrain enforcement against putative violators who are their constituents, allies, or favored interests. After the government has brought formal charges against a company, and perhaps even earlier, when an investigation is actively pending, such interventions or even subtler pressures may be unethical or possibly even constitute obstruction of justice, but they still sometimes occur.[104] Politicians, however, seldom need to go so far. They have other ways to signal both their intense opposition to an investigation or prosecution and their willingness to raise the political cost to the government of going forward with the case.

In sum, markets frustrate government enforcement efforts in their initial design (the proindustry frame of the authorizing legislation), their implementation (the forces that limit appropriations and enforcement authority), their senior staffing (the often politicized confirmation process), and their broad prosecutorial discretion (immunities from review). As a practical matter, a program cannot be effective, even in its own terms, unless two conditions are met: (1) almost all market actors voluntarily comply with its requirements, and (2) the relatively few violators are either brought into compliance quickly or punished sufficiently to deter future violations. To a great extent, condition 1 depends on condition 2 being fulfilled. These two conditions fail in some important programs. The Internal Revenue Service estimates that the incidence of noncompliance with the tax laws was about 17 percent, amounting to $385 billion in lost revenues in 2006 (the most recent year studied), the vast majority of which was personal income tax.[105] The failure to prevent widespread fraud in federal programs also undermines these two conditions.* Indeed, mas-

---

*Here are two of countless examples. GAO audits of Amtrak's food and beverage services found losses of $834 million since 2002, "largely because of waste, employee theft and lack of proper oversight." The GAO reported on this in 2005; seven years later, it was continu-

sive fraud, waste, and abuse by market actors, discussed in chapter 6, continue despite a host of independent inspectors general, government audits, congressional investigations, and perennial "get-tough" campaigns.

Rational expectations. The elaborate "dance of legislation,"[106] followed by the complex process of agency implementation described in chapter 3, combine to create long lags between the time when a legal change becomes likely and the time that it actually goes into effect. During this interregnum, market actors affected by the change can take steps to reduce the ultimate burden (or increase the benefit) that it will impose on them. Such law-anticipating, cost-reducing actions are ubiquitous, even routine (as with tax planning). Within days of the school shooting tragedy in Newtown, Connecticut, for example, gun sellers reported a surge of purchasers anticipating tighter regulations in the future.[107]

This exemplifies an exceedingly important phenomenon: what economists call "rational expectations." They posit not only that market actors will behave in profit-maximizing ways when government attempts to implement new policies (chapter 8 details such behavior), but also that the same will occur once they predict that changes will be adopted in the future. Economists who analyze, for example, market adjustments in anticipation of monetary policy changes by the Federal Reserve and fiscal stimuli proposed by other policy makers often disagree about the size, timing, and effects of such anticipatory market adjustments. To the extent that these adjustments do occur, however, they can seriously reduce the effectiveness of the impending policy change, sometimes even rendering the change counterproductive.[108]

Lack of good substitutes for market ordering. Social anthropology teaches that three kinds of institutions or practices are most useful for organizing and motivating human activity: legal rules, social norms,

---

ing unabated. See Ron Nixon, "Amtrak Losing Millions Each Year on Food Sales," *New York Times*, August 3, 2012. A federal audit finds that one in four nursing homes overbill Medicare $1.5 billion each year. See Thomas M. Burton, "Nursing Homes Said to Overbill U.S.," *Wall Street Journal*, November 12, 2012.

and markets. This chapter has analyzed why markets resist government controls, rendering many public policies ineffective. Social norms—the shared beliefs, common practices, and mutual expectations among members of a group—play an important, even essential, role in all social ordering. Informally and often unconsciously, they coordinate an immense amount of conduct and thought, including much market behavior.[109] Yet for reasons that I have explicated elsewhere, they are not realistic alternatives to markets.[110] This leaves law as the principal regulator of markets. Yet law's limitations—both the internal, structural ones to be analyzed in chapter 9 and the external, empirical ones detailed in the rest of the book—frequently render it ineffective under the best of circumstances.

CHAPTER 8

Implementation

The public policy world brims with interesting, provocative, often plausible ideas for improving social welfare. These ideas emerge from executive branch policy shops, congressional staff work, independent think tanks, lobbyists, economics and political science departments, public policy programs, law schools, business organizations, "public interest" groups, and other sources. Even judges sometimes get into policy-making-in-the-large when they find constitutional violations by government bureaucracies and then fashion unusual remedies—that is, those that go beyond simply awarding monetary damages or a simple prohibitory injunction—with the goal of rectifying those violations.[1] A very small percentage of these ideas successfully run the marathon political gauntlet and make it into the United States Code.

At this point, an even greater challenge looms for these new laws: they must be implemented in the real world outside Washington, D.C. The field consists of complex social, political, fiscal, market, legal, intergovernmental, bureaucratic, and institutional conditions that even the most seasoned policy makers in Washington cannot fully anticipate. Worse, even if the policy makers could foresee these conditions, they would have relatively little control over them.

Political scientists have spilled a lot of ink describing the recurrent kinds of implementation obstacles that impede a large number of federal programs. In the policy studies field, the leading study of this phenomenon is *Implementation*, a celebrated book by Jeffrey Pressman and Aaron Wildavsky, whose droll subtitle summarizes what they found: *How Great Expectations in Washington Are Dashed in Oakland; Or, Why It's Amazing That Federal Programs Work at All, This Being a Saga of the Economic Development Administration as Told by Two Sympathetic Observers Who Seek to Build Morals on a Foundation of Ruined Hopes.*[2] The book recounts in great detail the process by which, beginning in 1966, a grant from the Economic Development Administration (EDA) in the U.S. Department of Commerce of more than $23 million for public works projects in the port and city of Oakland, California, was implemented. The grant aimed to create infrastructure and provide three thousand new jobs to inner-city minority residents of the high-unemployment Oakland area. It was greeted with the great fanfare and high hopes that accompany such initiatives. Three years later, only forty-three jobs had been created as a result of the government's $1.08 million in business loans, and the Oakland antipoverty agency was deriding it as a "pretty big disaster."*

In chronicling this particular policy disappointment in Oakland, Pressman and Wildavsky did not merely recount what happened at each stage of this program's development as EDA officials sought to implement it at the local level. As distinguished political scientists deeply rooted in both theory and empirics, they had a larger objective: to draw from their detailed account of the program's failed implementation more general lessons about *why* so many promising, well-intended programs suffer the same fate. I now set the stage for these lessons by summarizing their rich, exhaustive chronicle of the Oakland Project.

Having explored the lessons of this case for policy implementation more generally, the chapter then turns to the empirical evidence on how a wide variety of other kinds of policies have been imple-

---

*The ineffectiveness of highly touted government programs targeted at creating jobs and getting low-skilled inner-city residents into the workforce, as in the Oakland Project, above, is an all-too-familiar story. Although politicians differed sharply in their predictions about how many new jobs the 2009 stimulus would create, subsequent reports suggest that the actual number was relatively limited. See Ianthe Jeanne Dugan & Justin Scheck, "Cost of $10 Billion Stimulus Easier to Tally Than New Jobs," *Wall Street Journal*, February 24, 2012 The research on these programs is briefly summarized later in this chapter.

mented, and with which effects. All of the policies examined here seek in one way or another to alter how particular markets function, thus extending the analysis in chapter 7. I shall discuss these policies under nine general rubrics, differentiated according to what the policies *aim to do to or with markets*: (1) perfect them; (2) supplement them; (3) suppress them; (4) simplify them; (5) subsidize them; (6) redirect them; (7) reintroduce them; (8) widwife infant markets; and (9) recruit them for regulatory purposes.

THE IMPLEMENTATION OF THE OAKLAND PROJECT

The EDA's principal mission was to aid the economies of rural areas and small towns, not cities like Oakland. An EDA internal evaluation noted, however, that the agency's leader was determined to use the agency to set up employment programs "where the action was," in cities, and he decided to concentrate its efforts on one city, apparently because he had to spend program funds quickly before the appropriation expired, and this could be accomplished by doing it in one city rather than dividing the funds among more of them. Oakland was selected for three main reasons: the EDA had experience and contacts there; it hoped that a jobs program there would head off a feared riot by unemployed blacks; and the city's Republican mayor could not go over the administrator's head to complain to the Democratic White House if something went wrong with the program.

The EDA, however, did not fully appreciate the obstacles to policy implementation posed by the nature of the Oakland city government, which would have to make key decisions if the program were to succeed. But the city government was fragmented into a number of municipal agencies that city hall could not control, in part because Oakland had a council-manager form of government in which the elected, part-time mayor was only one of nine city council members, and the full-time appointed city manager effectively ran the administration with staff, information, and financial resources largely under his control. Also, the lack of politically oriented interest groups and party activity meant that elected leaders could not mobilize relevant information or political support for policies they might wish to propose.

The EDA's program developed problems not only with its Oakland "partners" in the city government but within its own ranks and with other federal agencies. The administrator assembled a very talented group of young policy experts within the EDA to run the program for him, largely from Washington. Proud of their innovative energies and antibureaucratic values, and pressed for time by their other Washington responsibilities, they took shortcuts by disregarding prescribed bureaucratic channels. This, along with the priority that Oakland was demanding, aroused resentment in EDA headquarters, which had traditionally focused on rural development.

Other mission conflicts soon appeared. Business interests in Oakland wanted EDA funds to go to commercial development, which they predicted would create more jobs. But city officials doubted that the new jobs would go to the long-term and minority unemployed, so EDA officials designed an overall employment plan under which a board dominated by poverty group representatives would allocate program funds. Because the EDA wanted to get the funds committed quickly before the appropriation lapsed (which might cause Congress to reduce future funding), there was little time to conduct an extensive search for the best public works projects. Under these pressures, the EDA selected the Port of Oakland, the institution most adept at preparing federal applications. An EDA official explained, "EDA had to spend its funds by June of 1966. The port had the projects and the others didn't." The EDA ranked specific projects by expected job creation, and the funds were allocated to the ranked projects until the available funds ran out. The port, arguing that the EDA's stringent requirement that each project must recruit, train, and hire the local long-term unemployed would scare off potential developers, resisted the requirement but ultimately accepted it. Key EDA officials, consultants, and city personnel came and went. A new mayor took over in Oakland. The top EDA official and cheerleader for the Oakland projects resigned because, he said, the White House had decided that the

EDA should not be spending money in cities, and Vietnam was claiming more and more resources.

As program problems and danger signals appeared, officials eager to get the funds out tended to sweep the difficulties under the rug, saying that they were just glitches that did not affect developers' willingness to hire the long-term and minority unemployed. Some of these glitches, however, turned out to be far more consequential. For example, the port claimed that it could not proceed without advanced funding from the EDA for interim development and construction financing, advances that the EDA could not provide. A dispute over the quality of the fill materials on a terminal site arose, and the terminal's prospective tenant said it could not meet the program's stringent hiring conditions. The U.S. Navy's engineers complained that the construction would create both serious navigational hazards and threats to airplane safety, which brought the Federal Aviation Administration (FAA) into the dispute. When the port sought to begin dredging, the Army Corps of Engineers entered the fray, as did the Bay Area Rapid Transit District (BART), which claimed that the dredging would impinge on its operations. When the port requested changes in the plans (a larger restaurant), the EDA said this was major enough to require a new project application. The U.S. General Accounting Office (GAO) questioned the EDA's grants and loans, and the San Francisco Department of Public Works complained that the projects would interfere with water contact sports in the bay. The authors summarized the situation thus: "As 1968 ended and a new administration prepared to come to power in Washington, the future plans of the terminal lay in doubt. In the areas of dredging, filling, financing, design, and relationships with other governmental institutions, the technical problems surrounding construction of the marine terminal had proved to be formidable. What had appeared initially to be a relatively straightforward program now involved new and unforeseen participants—the navy, the GAO, local governmental bodies—whose agreement was necessary if the program was to continue."

The other major public works project—the aircraft maintenance hangar—was beset by even greater obstacles: a cost overrun of almost 50 percent in two years, delays caused by new rounds of bargaining among the various interests, divisions within the EDA about how to respond, and reports indicating that few new jobs were being created.

As the program bogged down, the EDA's leadership constantly changed, and bureaucratic units within the agency with differing perspectives jockeyed with each other for power. Meanwhile, the political situation in Oakland was changing, "becoming more strident, more polarized, more hostile" as black leaders sought to organize their constituents by attacking the mayor, who looked in vain for program support from the EDA—particularly when the EDA refused to pay for the huge cost overrun. With a new administration installed in Washington, new EDA policy makers coming on board, and both components of the Oakland Project—public works and jobs for the minority unemployed—floundering in delay, disarray, and unrealized promises, the EDA tried tightening the screws on the local players but to little avail.

Pressman and Wildavsky's verdict on the Oakland Project was a profoundly dismaying one. Five years after Congress had appropriated the funds and the EDA had committed them, projects and employment plans had been approved, but major obstacles to implementation remained. No final plan had been reached for the most important construction project, which was supposed to create twelve hundred jobs. The new small business loans program—targeted at inherently bad risks, replete with conflicts of interest, and competing with existing businesses—failed abjectly to create new jobs. The training programs that were to prepare the hard-core unemployed for jobs had become snarled in intergovernmental and interagency wrangling. And the EDA was having trouble enforcing its employment and affirmative action requirements even for those construction projects that were completed or underway. No one could be sure how many new jobs had been created, nor was it clear how many were filled by minorities and the hard-core unemployed, or how long they would last. (On the brighter side, one relatively small project, the West Oakland Health Center, seemed to have created 160 jobs, almost all of them for minorities.)

SOME GENERAL LESSONS ABOUT IMPLEMENTATION OBSTACLES TO POLICY SUCCESS

The failure of the Oakland Project implies that other programs are likely to fail for similar reasons, although the specifics of their failure will of course differ from Oakland's and from each other's. (See, for example, Derek Bok's brief account of the failure of the Comprehensive Environmental Response, Compensation, and Liability Act of 1980, commonly known as the Superfund.[3]) This implication is amply warranted because, as Pressman and Wildavsky emphasize, the Oakland Project was actually far easier to implement than most federal programs. The EDA sought "to avoid the institutional fragmentation, multiple and confusing goals, and inadequate funding that had characterized previous federal-city programs." It included

> just one federal agency in one city; there would be only one major local recipient, the Port of Oakland, whose tenants' performance could be bound by a written and signed employment plan; and there would be an immediate commitment of $23 million. . . . We are unlikely to get many programs that will be simpler in that they involve fewer participants or less complicated arrangements. Few programs would specify as clearly the benefits to the participants—cheap money, jobs, political credit— than this one. The difficulties that arose here, therefore, can be expected to afflict almost any new program. If we understand why this program ran into difficulty, we can hope to get at some of the underlying factors that make programs fail when there is no apparent reason why they should. . . . The apparently simple and straightforward is really complex and convoluted [because of] the number of steps involved, the number of participants whose preferences have to be taken into account, the number of separate decisions that are part of what we think of as a single one. Least of all do we appreciate the geometric growth of interdependencies over time where each negotiation involves a number of participants with decisions to make whose implications ramify over time.[4]

Pressman and Wildavsky offer some general principles to explain why even a program as straightforward and enthusiastically sponsored as the Oakland Project failed—and why other more complex and controversial ones can be expected to fail as well.[5] First, the many participants, like those in Oakland, are likely to have *different, often inconsistent perspectives* on the program. They may agree with its substantive goals yet oppose the means for effectuating it for any of a number of reasons: because their incentives differ; because the program conflicts with other, more compelling bureaucratic priorities; because they differ about the program's legal, procedural, or technical requirements; or because they lack the political or other resources necessary to wage an effective fight for it. The more complex the program, the more moving parts it has, the more agencies it involves, the less likely it is to succeed. (By this logic, the Volcker Rule, discussed below, seems destined to fail.)

Second, implementation must pass through *multiple decision points* (most of which may effectively be *veto* points), a number that only increases as the implementation process unfolds. In the relatively simple Oakland Project, the authors identified thirty separate clearances, involving seventy separate agreements, that were necessary before it could proceed. "The probability of agreement by every participant on each decision point," they conclude, "must be exceedingly high for there to be any chance at all that a program will be brought to completion." Moreover, the ability of each decision point to extract a price for its assent will cumulate into costs and constraints that deeply compromise the program's effectiveness.

Third, *delay* is a formidable barrier to implementation. Whether intentional or not, it can defeat, deform, and sap a program, while increasing its cost. Delay is a powerful weapon for those who either oppose the program or want to extract concessions from its proponents, and the greater their power and the intensity of their preferences, the more attractive and effective this tactic will be. By the same token, proponents' urgent desire to implement a program quickly—in Oakland, within the four months left before the congressional appropriation would expire—increases the leverage that those in a strategic position to delay implementation will have to extract programmatic concessions (or even bribes).

The Volcker Rule—named after a genuine hero of monetary policy making who has promoted it—illustrates this delay problem (as well as others). An integral part of the effort to implement the Dodd-Frank Act, the rule seeks to restrict banks' ability to trade in risky assets for their own accounts using funds that are federally insured or that might trigger a taxpayer-financed bailout in the event of the bank's insolvency. The protracted impasse over the rule delayed its final adoption until December 2013, two and a half years after the original statutory deadline. The delay was partly due to fierce industry opposition and disputes within and among the Securities and Exchange Commission (SEC) and four other regulatory agencies concerning its provisions.[6] But the delay, which will leave the banks little time to figure out how to comply by the thrice-extended enforcement date (now July 2015), also reflects the law's unprecedented complexity and its failure to draw clear lines among banks' different investment activities, including market making, risk hedging, underwriting, and proprietary trading. (As Alan Blinder, a former Federal Reserve vice chair puts it, proprietary trading "often fails the Potter Stewart test: you *don't* know it when you see it.")[7] It also reflects the law's failure to clarify the employee participation provision's scope;[8] the intricacies of the ever-evolving, increasingly arcane financial products that the banks often trade; the uncertainty about how different restrictions would affect their ability to compete with foreign banks operating under different legal regimes; and the definition of and interactions among the seventeen metrics that the banks would have to calculate each day and report to regulators each month. In designing the rule, the regulators have been stymied by all of the reasons discussed in chapter 7 as to why markets subvert policy coherence. The financial markets in question are extraordinarily complex and diverse, arguably beyond the ability of the rule drafters (far beneath the secretary of the Treasury) to fully comprehend, much less control. These markets are constantly evolving, in order both to exploit fast-changing market conditions and opportunities and to minimize the rule's anticipated costs. To implement the seventeen metrics, regulators must gather, process, assess, and act upon enormous quantities of transactional data, based on banks' answers to a myriad of opaque, hard-to-answer questions.* The banks and their elite lawyers, of course, are hard at work fashioning evasive strategies. No wonder president Barack Obama, more than three years after Dodd-Frank's enactment, publicly worried that it might not be properly implemented.[9]

Although the rule means to limit market-driven moral hazard, this outcome is doubtful because Dodd-Frank will actually *expand* the safety net.† Because it will only restrict U.S. companies, it will intensify international competitive and domestic political pressures that regulators can neither ignore nor alleviate without undermining the rule's bite. As already noted, the high stakes have elicited intensive industry lobbying and protracted delays in finalizing the rule, not to speak of implementing it. Its enforcement will be hobbled by all of the factors that, as we have seen, weaken government enforcement efforts generally. Its restrictions will engender black markets operating in its shadow. Nor is there any nonmarket substitute for these firms that the regulators might look to for guidance, as statist economies have invariably learned at great cost. Even setting aside the feverish politics surrounding the rule, it will be miraculous if at the end of the day the regulators get it right.‡

---

*The *Economist*'s February 12, 2012, briefing on Dodd-Frank used some numbers to capture this complexity. The Glass-Steagall Act, which governed the banking system from 1933 to 1999, ran 37 pages; Dodd-Frank is 848 pages. Five agencies weighed in on the Volcker Rule, which will be almost 1000 pages! Under the rule's then-version, firms were required to answer 383 questions, broken down into 1,420 subquestions, with compliance involving 355 distinct steps. The statute ordered the agencies to issue 400 rules; deadlines had already been missed for 40 percent of them; legal challenges to the rules were just beginning. It also mandated 87 studies, of which more than 40 percent had not been completed.

†The president of the Federal Reserve Bank of Dallas notes that Dodd-Frank gives the twelve largest banks—which account for only 0.2 percent of banks, hold 69 percent of bank assets, and are less accountable to shareholders—two immense and perverse advantages: a legal status of "systemically important financial institution" and taxpayer backing that make them in effect "too big to fail," and the lower borrowing cost that this status confers. By impeding the transmission of the Fed's monetary policy, these megabanks also reduce our economic growth. See Gretchen Morgenson, "How to Cut Megabanks Down to Size," *New York Times*, January 20, 2013.

‡Indeed, barely a week after the rule was finally issued, officials prepared to backpedal

Fourth, and most fundamentally, a *flawed theory* may doom a program. The success of any policy requires at a minimum that its designers and implementers know which factors and conditions are likely to cause which consequences, yet such knowledge—the policy's animating theory—is notoriously elusive when dealing with social behaviors. The problem, however, is even deeper than this because a policy's theoretical coherence is systematically undermined by the distorting factors analyzed in chapters 5 and 6: irrationality, skewed incentives, lack of reliable information, policy rigidity, lack of credibility with the other necessary participants, and mismanagement.

In the Oakland case, for example, Pressman and Wildavsky found that

> [t]he economic theory [animating the employment projects] was faulty because it aimed at the wrong target—subsidizing the capital of business enterprises rather than their wage bill. Instead of taking the direct path of paying the employers a subsidy on wages after they had hired minority personnel, the EDA program expanded their capital on the promise that they would later hire the right people. Theoretical defects exacerbated bureaucratic problems. Numerous activities had to be carried on—assessing the viability of marginal enterprises, negotiating loan agreements, devising and monitoring employment plans—that would have been unnecessary if a more direct approach had been taken.[10]

Chapter 7 explained how almost all public policies are embedded in one or more markets. As in the Oakland Project, policies cannot be effective unless they can solve the implementation problems that their surrounding markets engender. Such a solution requires, at a minimum, that the policy makers know how these markets work, whether and in what particular ways they fail (if they do), and how effectively, if at all, the government policy can manipulate them. In the case of embryonic or future markets, selecting an appropriate policy is even more delicate, as exemplified by the current status of commercial space travel.[11]

---

out of concerns about its adverse impact on small and midsize banks. Ryan Tracy, "Regulators Rethinking Rule on Bank Debt," *Wall Street Journal*, December 19, 2013.

We can distinguish at least nine different ways in which policy makers try to meet this challenge. Some attempt to *perfect* a relevant market by improving consumer information, controlling externalities, or increasing competition. Some *supplement* the market by providing public goods or infrastructure that make it more efficient. Some seek to *suppress* it, perhaps by banning or criminalizing certain transactions. Some try to *simplify* it by standardizing contract terms or product features. Some *subsidize* it in order to shape market actors' decisions. Some try to *redirect* it—for example, by trying to induce banks to lend in certain communities that they would not otherwise serve. Some try to *reintroduce* markets after they had been deregulated. Some try to *midwife an infant market*. And some try to *recruit* it to serve regulatory goals, as with pollution markets. None of these approaches can succeed unless policy makers have a correct, detailed understanding of how these markets actually work and possess the instruments to bend them to their will. In reality, however, the markets that surround policies are often so differentiated, detail-specific, dynamic, and opaque to centralized understanding and control that even the most sophisticated policy maker is apt to misunderstand the relationships among the markets' myriad moving parts. I shall use these nine approaches to organize the remainder of this chapter.

PERFECTING MARKETS

The most comprehensive, detailed analysis of existing programs designed to improve imperfect markets was conducted by Clifford Winston, who canvassed every scholarly article evaluating these efforts and whose overall findings in synthesizing this large body of research—that policy makers often exaggerated the extent of market failures, and adopted corrective programs that created government failures of greater magnitude—were briefly foreshadowed in chapters 1 and 5. His more detailed, program-specific findings, again based on the scholarly evidence, are as follows. (Market-perfecting policies focused on improving consumer information are discussed below in the section "Simplifying Markets.")

Antitrust policy. Finding no serious anticompetitive problems in the U.S. economy, Winston considered whether this might be due to antitrust policies directed at monopolization, collusion, and mergers. The cases in which a court accepted the government's monopolization argument "consistently found that the court's relief failed to increase competition and reduce consumer prices." In the landmark case that broke up AT&T in 1984, "antitrust policy was not necessary to restrain a monopolist from engaging in restrictive practices to block competition; rather it was necessary to overcome anticompetitive policies by another federal regulatory agency [the Federal Communications Commission]. In the absence of regulatory failure, the large costs of breaking up AT&T could have been avoided. . . . Given the protracted length of a monopolization case (some of the cases noted earlier took more than a decade to resolve), federal antitrust actions are likely to lag far behind market developments and thus be less effective than markets in stimulating competition." As for collusion cases, economists have yet to find that they have led to significantly lower consumer prices over a protracted period. Government challenges to mergers have not systematically enhanced consumer welfare, and have sometimes reduced it; indeed, mergers that were opposed by the regulators but consummated anyway "have often resulted in gains for consumers." Canvassing the empirical evidence on deterrence and the arguments of antitrust policy defenders, Winston concludes that "current policy provides negligible benefits to consumers that fall far short of enforcement costs."[12]

Economic regulation.[13] Beginning with the Interstate Commerce Act of 1887, the federal government regulated prices, entry, exit, and conditions of service in a number of industries, typically on the theory that their high fixed and low variable costs would produce ruinous competition and bankruptcies, producing monopoly power and exploitation of consumers. After a spate of deregulation during the 1970s and early 1980s, however, federal price regulations are now largely confined to agricultural commodities and international trade of selected products, neither of which involves a significant risk of monopolization.

Agricultural support programs, which date from the 1930s, are among the most inefficient and distributively regressive of federal policies. They are also a classic instance of the status quo bias (discussed in chapter 5) preventing policy adaptability to new conditions, which in the farm policy case include a vast reduction in the number of family farms, the rise of agribusiness, and farmers' significant off-farm employment, which helps make them wealthier than nonfarmers. These programs—direct payments, price supports, loans, subsidized insurance, environmental protection subsidies, acreage restrictions, and others—are exceedingly costly ($256 billion between 1995 and 2012), yet they generate large net welfare losses, disproportionately benefit the largest farms, and encourage excessive consumption of scarce water supplies.[14] (A number of farm-belt members of Congress are direct recipients of these subsidies.[15]) Between 1995 and 2010, fully 90 percent of direct and price-support payments went to the top 20 percent of farms; the vast majority of farms received nothing.[16]

The Freedom to Farm Act of 1996 addressed many of these problems and shifted American agriculture toward a free market system. It suspended the authority for income support based on market prices and ended planting restrictions. However, these reforms were short-lived. By 1998, commodity prices had fallen substantially, and Congress soon reinitiated direct payments to farmers. These "market loss payments" totaled $21.4 billion between 1999 and 2001.[17] Moreover, the government began to require farmers to enroll in subsidized insurance programs; by 2012, these crop insurance subsidies grew to $15.8 billion. Over this same period, the conservation requirements and environmental protections of the 1996 law withered away. Politically, much of this reversion to the status quo has been driven by Democrats and agribusiness lobbyists. President George W. Bush resisted the 2003 farm bill and vetoed the 2008 farm bill outright. Despite this opposition, both bills continue the long and damaging tradition of federal support for American agriculture.

International trade policy has produced some consumer gains through free trade agreements on many nonagricultural products,[18] but the remaining import quotas and tariff protections outweigh those gains. Synthesizing the published empirical studies, Winston shows that "trade protection has mainly generated gains to established U.S. industries that fall far short of the losses to consumers." (He also notes the large consumer losses created by the Jones Act, discussed in chapter 6.) These protectionist policies are bipartisan, as presidents of both parties succumb to them—most recently, George W. Bush on steel and Chinese clothing, and Barack Obama on Chinese tires.[19]

Another area of economic regulation, not mentioned by Winston, is immigration policy, which limits the number and type of people who may come to the United States to live and work and subjects them to a variety of legal conditions. Because immigration policy is designed to serve a number of different purposes—family unification; labor market expansion; economic growth; innovation and entrepreneurship; protection of human rights; source-country diversity; diplomacy; and others—assessment of its effectiveness is difficult. Historically, immigration has greatly enriched American life and promoted economic vitality, but recent policies have failed egregiously—a fact that has long been acknowledged by the leadership of both political parties. Border and interior enforcement, despite large and growing costs, have not prevented the illegal presence of an estimated ten to eleven million undocumented immigrants, nor has Congress enacted any substantial legalization of this population since 1986. A large number of families contain both legal residents and illegal ones, but there is no coherent policy to address the problems that these mixed-status families present. Policy makers have failed to meet the needs of employers in agriculture and firms in other industries seeking workers with skills in science, technology, engineering, and mathematics—workers who are eager to come to the United States but are increasingly being lost to competing nations with more flexible and responsive immigration systems.[20] By almost any measure, then, U.S. immigration policy has abjectly failed, with no remedy in sight.[21]

Regulation of safety. Safety standards regulation is a mixed bag. Standards mandated by the Consumer Product Safety Commission have produced little if any reduction in accident rates. The public health stakes are far greater in the Food and Drug Administration's premarket approval of drugs and medical devices, its regulation of advertising of health claims, and its prescription requirements. Regulatory effectiveness has been analyzed extensively with respect to the costs and benefits of different regimes of premarket testing, labeling, and postmarketing surveillance. Such assessments have also examined issues of consumer compliance with labels, regulatory delays in approving valuable new drugs, and consumer behavior that offsets potential regulatory benefits.[22]

Long delays in the implementation of firefighting technologies have contributed to huge losses of life and property from recent conflagrations. In July 2012, less than a year before the devastating Colorado fires, the *Denver Post* reported that the responsible federal agencies had failed to put in place the Fire Program Analysis system that they had heralded back in 2002 and had predicted would take five years to implement. This despite several earlier GAO reports criticizing the agencies' long delay and inadequate program.[23]

The benefits of National Highway Traffic Safety Administration standards have been affected by offsetting behavior, according to a number of studies using different methodologies. These behaviors include riskier driving induced by air bags, antilock brakes, and other mandated safety equipment. Analysts dispute whether such behavior has wholly erased those benefits, as the famous Peltzman study found,[24] or merely reduced them.

Risk expert W. Kip Viscusi found a similar "lulling effect" to explain why FDA-mandated child-resistant packaging of aspirin and other analgesics did not affect poisoning rates but sharply increased child ingestion rates, as parents assumed that the packaging reduced the risk and thus were more careless (e.g., leaving the caps off the bottles).[25] He also found no beneficial effects from Consumer Product Safety Commission regulation.[26] Winston's review of studies of workplace safety standards issued by the Occupational Safety and Health Administration (OSHA) and the Mine Safety and Health Administration concludes that they create few marginal benefits. Rather than the regulation reducing accident rates, the studies suggest, the decline mostly reflects workplace mechanization, independent market incentives to reduce accidents (e.g., workers' compensation premiums, lost work time, morality), weak enforcement, and inspectors' tendency to focus on easily identifiable and correctable hazards rather than more elusive but important ones such as employee turnover. Also, OSHA has largely neglected long-term occupational disease in favor of its spotty efforts at accident prevention.[27] A leading analyst of the program, John Mendeloff, notes that inspections in manufacturing have proved effective and some serious toxic exposures (e.g., to asbestos, lead, chromium) have been reduced. He observes, however, that the law's safety impacts have been limited, partly due to few inspectors in the United States compared with other countries, the difficulty of inspecting construction (a particularly risky industry), and poor data collection on causal factors.[28]

Regulation of externalities. Government has compelling reasons to regulate negative externalities—as with pollution, when one's activity imposes costs ("spillovers") on others without paying for them. Unless negative externalities are "internalized" (by making their producer pay for them), the activity will bear less than its full social costs; too much of it will be produced (an inefficiency), and others will have to bear those costs (an inequity). Winston's review of the assessments finds that some externality controls are "outright failures" in that their costs have exceeded their benefits.[29]

The most important category of externality policy is environmental regulation. Environmental conditions and public health have improved significantly since the early 1970s when the basic framework of federal regulation was established.[30] Still, it is hard to know the extent to which that regulation is responsible for this progress.* First,

---

*Some verdicts are relatively clear. Thus, the Magnuson-Stevens Fishery Conservation and Management Act of 1996 succeeded in returning many fish species to earlier population levels by limiting catches. Regulation also reduced dangerous lead levels. On the other side, some regulation has utterly failed. The Environmental Protection Agency's glacial pace in protecting endangered species is one example. See Michael Wines, "Coming Soon: Long-Delayed Decisions on Endangered Species," *New York Times*, March 6, 2013. Its non-implementation of the Toxic Substances Control Act of 1976 is another. See John M. Broder, "New Alliance Emerges to Tighten Chemical Rules," *New York Times*, May 25, 2013.

few ex post cost-benefit analyses (CBAs) of these laws exist, and none evaluates the field overall. This dearth of ex post CBAs contrasts with the abundance of ex ante predictions of whether particular environmental regulations will be cost-effective.[31] These ex ante evaluations are usually regulatory impact analyses (RIAs) prepared by the promulgating agency, submitted to the Office of Information and Regulatory Affairs (OIRA) for review (assuming that it is a "major" rule), and used for planning and implementation. RIAs are not legally binding, but OIRA would not clear such a regulation unless the RIA passed an ex ante cost-benefit test. Unfortunately, such analyses tend to overpredict both costs *and* benefits.[32] Indeed, a wide-ranging Office of Management and Budget review found that ex ante analyses often overstate both benefits and costs but especially benefits, which favors predictions of cost-effectiveness.[33] The most significant and comprehensive ex post analysis was undertaken by the Environmental Protection Agency itself—a 1997 retrospective CBA of the Clean Air Act (CAA) in which the agency estimated that the benefits from 1970 to 1990 vastly exceeded the costs.[34] Two more recent EPA studies reached similar conclusions.[35]

A second obstacle to analyzing the effects of environmental regulation is the difficulty of pinpointing which factors caused which outcomes. Before-and-after studies show that air pollution declined at the same rate before 1970, when the states were regulating it, and after 1970 under CAA regulation, suggesting that other factors may have been more causally important.[36] Another causal factor is technological change, which regulation affects in complex ways. For example, newer technologies tend to be safer than older ones,[37] yet regulation may not be responsible for emergence of those technologies. Indeed, although many programs seek to be technology-forcing, they sometimes *retard*, not promote, polluters to adopt cleaner methods by imposing tougher rules on new sources than on existing ones. Thus, many electric utilities continued to use their dirtier power plants because the CAA grandfathered them in, allowing them to operate under the old, lower standards while subjecting new plants to the more stringent, costlier rules.[38] This substitution effect (discussed in chapter 7) also explains why the Corporate Average Fuel Economy Standards (CAFE) program, despite changes that gave the auto industry more flexibility than before in meeting the standards, still induces car owners to continue driving their old, higher-pollution cars, significantly offsetting fuel economy savings.[39] Other complicating factors include consumers' expectations of future fuel prices, their behavioral responses to changes in fuel economy, automakers' technological and marketing strategies, and changes in used car markets.[40] These complications leave analysts uncertain, even after thirty years of studies, whether CAFE has raised or reduced social welfare.[41]

Another kind of causal uncertainty is exemplified by the 1990 amendments to the CAA. Previously, the law required plants to use the best available technology to control sulfur dioxide pollution.[42] The amendments, however, created an emission allowances market, which is detailed at the end of this chapter. While that policy change has generally controlled emissions more efficiently, economists maintain that unrelated factors, including railroad deregulation, have contributed significantly to the program's apparent success.[43]

SUPPLEMENTING MARKETS

The federal government has made an enormous investment in physical infrastructure, typically on the assumption that the private market would not or could not fund such costly projects. (Privately operated toll roads, airports, and communications networks do exist, but such exceptions constitute a very small fraction of the total.) A common theme in public discourse about this infrastructure—public lands and parks, roads, ports, airports, urban mass transit, intercity rail service, and the postal system (see chapter 6)—is its deteriorating quality and its inadequacy for a growing and spatially diversifying population.

Winston's review of the evidence on government performance in these areas leads him to conclude that public financing and management "have been extremely inefficient."[44] He finds vast opportunities for policy improvements in his very recent assessment of the performance of the U.S. transportation system—where total public and private spending comprised 17 percent of gross domestic product in 2007, equal to our health care spending; if congestion time costs are included, he notes, expenditures were more than $5 *trillion* a year.[45]

Policy on highways, vital social infrastructure with an estimated economic value of almost $3 trillion,[46] is replete with huge inefficiencies. Economists repeatedly note the failures by policy makers to remedy these inefficiencies through smarter road pricing for vehicles and assessing capital investments based on cost-benefit analyses. Federal and state gasoline taxes are insensitive to congestion and pavement damage factors, leading policy makers to opt for thinner, faster-deteriorating pavements that require more repair costs over time. Expanding highway capacity, they find, is a poor way to reduce congestion; on average, one dollar of spending in a given year reduces congestion costs to road users by only eleven cents in that year and only a few cents in subsequent years; this expansion strategy is also increasingly constrained by land limitations. Yet the vast inefficiencies persist.[47] In a new paper, Winston and his colleague Fred Mannering argue for an approach to circumvent these failures by using available, well-tested technologies to improve the efficiency of highway pricing, investment, and operations, which would improve travel speeds, reliability, and safety and reduce highway expenditures. The speed of private-sector development of driverless car technology sharply contrasts with the government's failure to exploit technology in the interests of more efficient highway construction, regulation, and financing.[48]

Winston and colleagues estimated back in 1989 that replacing gasoline taxes with marginal cost congestion tolls and pavement-wear taxes, and building roads to optimal pavement thickness, would generate a welfare gain of almost $24 billion a year; adjusting the tolls to protect low-income drivers would reduce these savings only insignificantly. Large efficiencies could also be generated by policy changes in the seriously compromised air traffic control system, and in airport pricing (most of which is locally determined).[49] A critical review of the Army Corps of Engineers management of waterway and harbor construction projects has revealed egregious inefficiencies reflected in negative benefit-cost ratios, vast cost overruns, political manipulation of estimates, and the like. During the Bush administration, the corps was required to suspend work on some 150 congressionally approved water projects until the corps' economic analyses could be improved.[50]

As for urban and intercity rail transit, Clifford Winston and Vikram Maheshri found in 2007 that, except for BART, every U.S. urban rail transit system actually reduced social welfare because of high capital and operating costs largely subsidized by taxpayers, underutilization except in rush hours, oversized vehicles, excessive labor costs, low labor productivity, lack of marginal cost fares, and inefficient service frequency.[51] (Including environmental and safety gains had little effect on these findings.) The National Railroad Passenger Corporation (Amtrak) has seen a large increase in ridership (55 percent since 1997) and now carries a record thirty-one million riders annually.[52] Its finances, however, are another story. Its political sponsors promised that it would become self-sufficient within a few years, but it has never even come close. Amtrak is a big money loser, partly because Congress requires passenger service in all but a few states, and many of those individual state services operate at big losses. After forty years of operation, Amtrak needed $4.4 billion in federal aid just in the last three years. Subsidies might be justified if it were a public good conferring large broad-based benefits unavailable through the market, but the benefits are localized. More than a third of its passengers travel in the relatively wealthy Northeast Corridor; it subsidizes operations elsewhere even more extravagantly. (Amtrak loses more than $80 million a year on its food/beverage service largely because of waste, employee theft, excessive salaries, and lack of oversight—despite Congress's requirement more than three decades ago that this service pay for itself.[53]) And even in the Northeast Corridor, Amtrak has not reduced travel times. As one analyst notes, it "isn't any faster than the same train route was forty years and $50 billion in federal subsidies ago. . . . Amtrak built its high-speed Acela system from Washington to Boston on the premise that it would get riders between major cities faster. Today, the Acela can get from Washington to New York in 2 hours 45 minutes at its fastest—or 15 minutes slower than the Penn Central Railroad could get a rider there in 1969 for an inflation-adjusted $102 per ticket."[54] Meanwhile, freight service, which was privatized in 1987, has flourished.[55]

One important reason why the kinds of federally funded public works projects discussed above are so much costlier than they should be is the Davis-Bacon Act, on the books since 1931, which requires that all project workers be paid locally "prevailing wages," which has usually been interpreted by the Department of Labor to mean union-level wages and benefits. A recent analysis finds that the act inflates the cost of federal construction projects by 9.9 percent over market wage levels; repeal would have saved taxpayers $10.9 billion in 2010 alone.[56]

Governmental management of the public lands is also inefficient, and perhaps even corrupt in some cases, given its sale and rental of those lands to farmers, ranchers, foresters, and others at prices below marginal cost and market value—and often free of charge. Winston cites a *New York Times* article reporting that a developer acquired federal land that the government valued at $763,000 and sold it the very next day for $4.6 million.[57] The National Forest Service's fire management practices have long been criticized by silviculturalists and ecologists for actually increasing explosive conflagrations by overcontrolling burn-offs on forest floors.

The U.S. Postal Service is our largest public enterprise, with annual revenues of $65 billion. As noted in chapter 2, the causes of its vast inefficiencies—especially excessive wage and benefit levels, political demands requiring unneeded facilities and personnel, a skewed pricing system in which first-class mail subsidizes the other classes, and many others—are well understood. It more than tripled its losses from 2011 to 2012 (only partly due to a large accounting adjustment), has exhausted its borrowing limit with the Treasury, and is in default on its mandatory payments for retiree benefits unless Congress bails it out.[58] Indeed, its losses are so large that it could probably subsidize e-mail services for residents of remote communities—a traditional justification for a public operation—and still save the taxpayers money. Fortunately, other advanced countries provide a rich array of experiences in fundamentally reshaping their postal services for a more competitive digital age in which the vast majority of physical mail is commercial. Indeed, virtually every country in the European Union has done so.

Labor markets are another area in which the government hopes to improve efficiency by subsidizing information, training, and the hiring of unemployed or underemployed workers. The GAO studied forty-seven such programs spread across nine agencies and spending $18 billion in 2009. Only five of them had assessed their impacts and only some of them demonstrated positive effects; these tended to be small, inconclusive, or restricted to the short term.[59] According to Robert La Londe, a leading expert on these policies, job search assistance programs are more likely than other employment programs to yield positive short-term impacts. The results for other programs is mixed, depending on the targeted groups. Classroom training has consistently generated modest short-term and medium-term benefits for economically disadvantaged adult women, but has just as consistently failed to produce gains for youths. For adult males, the results vary greatly across studies, partly because of methodological differences and sample sizes that are too small to measure program impacts with the same precision. On-the-job training programs have received less study. Some researchers find short-term benefits but with some doubt as to how long they persist. For reasons that are not altogether clear, private employers seldom participate in these programs, thus foregoing substantial wage subsidies available for hiring disadvantaged workers. A study of the Dayton Target Jobs tax credit during the 1980s suggested that these economically disadvantaged workers cannot overcome the labor market stigma of being classified as such.[60]

SUPPRESSING MARKETS

I now turn from the government's policies to perfect and supplement markets to its efforts to suppress or subdue them. As discussed in chapter 6, every market that the government regulates has a potential substitute: an illegal or "informal" (or "black") market that will provide a consumer with the same (or similar enough) product or service, presumably in a more attractive form than the legal market does (lower price, easier access, more convenient, etc.), even after one takes into account any additional costs of transacting illegally. (Where the law bars a product or service altogether—the sale of certain organs, for example—the informal market is all there is.) Other things being equal, the higher the cost of regulatory compliance, the more likely it is that market actors will decide to avoid it by instead transacting informally for a close substitute.

Other things, of course, are not always equal. Putting committed fraudsters to one side (discussed in chapters 6 and 10), we can presume that market actors are as law-abiding as anyone else; they will only consider informality when compliance costs exceed some moral or economic threshold. It may also depend on how compliant they think their competitors are, how they assess the risks of detection and sanctions, and so forth. Because informal markets are usually surreptitious, they tend to be more difficult to police. (Usually, but not always; unlicensed street vendors, buskers, gypsy cabs, drug dealers, prostitutes, and the like often operate in plain sight, quickly receding when they think that the police are about.) The benefits of evasion also tempt market actors to bribe officials who could blow the whistle on them but who for a price can be induced to look the other way.

Black markets of any size tend to undermine the legitimate government programs that they seek to circumvent, with potentially severe and perverse policy consequences. An example is the U.S. domestic and treaty law restricting the importation, sale, and use of certain coolants that damage the earth's ozone layer and contribute to global warming. Because of this restriction, the value of the illegal coolant HCFC-22 to those who need it to service existing air conditioners (which during a recession are used longer) has soared, and a large black market has sprung up to supply it at lower prices. This has increased its use, undermined the policy's environmental goals, and driven the production and marketing of the gas to Asia, where it is less regulated.[61]

The size of the informal sector in the United States is understandably uncertain but no economist doubts that it is immense. A study by Edgar Feige, a leading expert on our underground economy, estimates that Americans earned $2 trillion in 2012 that they failed to report to the Internal Revenue Service, and this number is increasing for reasons that are deeply embedded in the changing nature of the economy.[62] The size of the informal sector in developing countries with whom the United States must compete is also immense; for some goods and services, it dwarfs the legal market.[63] According to recent work by Robert Neuwirth, roughly one half of the world's workers work in jobs that are "neither regulated nor registered, getting paid in cash, and, most often, evading income taxes."[64] A comparative study of the size of the informal economies in 110 countries estimated that in 2000 it was 41 percent of the total economy in developing countries. Significantly, the informal sector was also very large in the most developed nations in which legal compliance is probably greatest: 18 percent in the countries of the Organisation for Economic Co-operation and Development, and 8.8 percent in the United States ($864 billion).[65] The expansion of the informal sector has coincided with the expansion of government regulation. There is every reason to believe that regulation is an important driver of informal markets, and also that these markets engender yet more regulation as officials desperately seek to control them by cracking down with new rules and more intensive enforcement. At the London Olympics, for example, the British statute that prohibited any secondary market in tickets—levying heavy fines for reselling tickets—yielded banks of empty seats even for some popular events because holders of tickets who did not want to use them for these particular events could not clear the market by selling the tickets to spectators willing to pay for them. Many spectators managed to circumvent this system in the black market, of course, but at a higher cost than necessary.[66]

Political entrepreneurship flourishes in policy making directed at "sinful" goods. Since there is so much money to be made in illegal markets for such goods—especially when policy and enforcement drive out potential competitors—unusual coalitions of "bootleggers and Baptists" can form in which the former earn higher profits (what economists term "rents") while the latter preach and organize against such practices.[67] Opportunistic police bureaucracies can then use these markets to justify expanded authority, personnel, and budget.

The futility and even perversity of enhanced enforcement against such markets is most evident with the so-called war on drugs, proclaimed by president Richard Nixon in 1969. It is surely the government's most hard-fought, long-lasting, and costly program of market suppression. Although some commentators argue that criminalizing the use and trafficking of abusable drugs is misguided, such drugs do create three types of genuine social problems—physiological toxicity, behavioral toxicity, and addiction—about which social policy is properly concerned.[68] Decriminalization could also have a devastating effect on disadvantaged communities.[69] That said, the war—by almost every account other than that of the Department of Justice, which has a proprietary bureaucratic interest in its perpetuation—has utterly failed on its own terms.* After more than forty years of intensive U.S. and Mexican government crackdowns on the illegal drug trade, efforts costing $20 to $25 billion a year and tens of thousands of lost lives in Mexico and Central America, the retail price of one gram of pure cocaine is now 74 percent cheaper than it was thirty years ago, and 16 percent lower than it was in 2001, with a similar drop for heroin and methamphetamine. (Only marijuana has not experienced a significant price decline.) These street prices have declined despite a significant increase in demand owing to the rising percentage of high school seniors who admit to having taken an illegal drug in the last year. Only 31 percent of Americans believed that the government is making much progress dealing with illegal drugs,[70] and this was

---

*Some of these costs have been exaggerated or misrepresented. For example, a recent review of drug policy finds that although the prisons and jails are full of people who use drugs and whose current sentence is not for a violent offense—the estimated number of drug offenders behind bars exceeded 525,000 in 2009—"people whose only offense is using drugs almost never go to prison and rarely spend much time in jail." Mark A. R. Kleiman, Jonathan P. Caulkins, & Angela Hawken, *Drugs and Drug Policy: What Everyone Needs to Know* (2011), 58.

before the Mexican government began to ratchet down its cooperation with our programs.[71] The surprise is that the percentage is not even lower.

While failing to achieve its most obvious and measurable goal, the government's war has also inflicted immense collateral damage on American society and on source countries, causing street violence, entrenching gangs and organized crime, facilitating illegal weapon flows to drug lords,* encouraging youths to leave school prematurely, destroying families, filling prisons (with little deterrent effect),[72] and much more. At the same time, experts have proposed many ameliorative policies, some of which are politically feasible—including legalization.[73] Deregulation of illegal drugs (and some other regulated industries) tends to be only partial, however, which leaves some of the same black market issues in place while also creating some new ones.[74]

SIMPLIFYING MARKETS

The most common form of market simplification is to provide consumers with better information in more standardized formats. Improved disclosure policies possess the political advantage that disparate political forces can often agree upon them; compliance costs seem low; they respect consumers' choices; and they promise to make those choices better informed and more rational (although much behavioral psychology suggests that such disclosure may not actually affect the deeper sources of consumer irrationality).[75] Recent research, and the examples that follow, demonstrate that regulating through information disclosure is far more complicated and problematic than policy makers think.

Review of the empirical studies shows that policies aimed at improving information often fail on a variety of grounds.[76] First, in

*The Department of Justice's own inspector general excoriated the agency for recklessly mismanaging this operation. See Charlie Savage, "Justice Inquiry Faults Its Own in Guns Fiasco," *New York Times*, September 20, 2012.

formation imperfections in product markets and workplaces do not seem to cause significant welfare losses. Product- and workplace-related illness and injuries and adverse drug reactions have declined or remained stable, but the declines are due to market forces, not government regulation. Federal Trade Commission advertising regulation "raise[s] doubts about whether [it] has enabled consumers to make more informed choices." And studies of disclosure programs seeking to protect investors, air travelers, and motorists find that the costs sometimes exceed the benefits. Some reasons for this ineffectiveness include consumer inattention to the mandated information, inaccuracies in that information,* consumer loyalties to particular vendors, regulatory limits on disclosing some potentially useful information, and higher direct or indirect regulatory costs. The many federal regulators of financial institutions—the Fed, the Comptroller of the Currency, the FDIC, the Commodity Futures Trading Commission, the Consumer Financial Protection Bureau, and others—impose varying disclosure rules that can actually obscure consumers' and investors' understanding.[77] (I ignore *state* regulators here.) Labeling requirements can produce benefits, Winston finds, but some of them may well have occurred anyway through market-driven disclosure or through media attention to the hazards.[78] He also finds that state-level programs regulating advertising, occupational licensing, and "lemon laws" do no better.[79] A recent study of New York and San Diego programs mandating that restaurants post government sanitation ratings finds grade inflation, inconsistency, misallocated inspection resources, and no discernible reduction in foodborne illness.[80]

Christine Jolls, an expert on behavioral law and economics, has studied the Family Smoking Prevention and Tobacco Control Act of 2009, which mandates large graphic health warnings, similar to those already required in many other countries, on cigarette advertisements

---

*Even automobile fuel economy disclosures, mandated by the EPA and highly salient to auto shoppers, are quite misleading, especially with newer technologies. See Joseph B. White, "Why Your Car's Mileage May Not Always Measure Up," *Wall Street Journal*, January 30, 2013.

and packaging. (These mandates have been judicially enjoined for now on the ground that they unconstitutionally compel speech by tobacco companies) Knowing precisely what risk information to require and in what format is tricky; if it is wrong it can mislead consumers who rely on it. The very information on which regulators must rely for determining these facts and deciding these disclosure-relevant questions is *itself* prone to confounding ambiguities, provider tactics, and systematic errors. Experts hotly contest the precise facts about the risks in question (e.g., smoking, salt consumption, fatty foods, breast cancer screening, prostate surgery, and countless other practices). Regulators must draw their policy inferences—about what risks to disclose, and how—from consumer surveys, laboratory experiments, and other sources whose results reflect consumers' existing ignorance, irrational cross-cutting biases (psychologists have identified over forty of them in laboratory contexts!), and understandable confusion about the meaning of the questions they are asked. Jolls finds that the act's mandated warnings are somewhat effective in reducing factual misperceptions of smoking risks, but that even gripping, highly salient warnings cannot easily reduce these misperceptions.[81]

Only three years after the Dodd-Frank financial and corporate reform law was enacted, some of its disclosure provisions are already backfiring. According to a *New York Times* analysis, the law's ostensibly simple requirement that each public company disclose the ratio between the chief executive's compensation and the median salary of its employees is encountering all sorts of complications that should have been obvious at the outset. Even more perverse, the SEC estimates that the provision requiring firms to disclose the "conflict minerals" used in their products will cost them $3–4 billion just for initial compliance; industry estimates are as high as $16 billion. Yet this immense cost is evidently producing few benefits and is actually making some situations worse. For example, disclosure of the median salaries of "all" employees can mislead the public by including relatively low-paid workers in less-developed countries, while disclosing executives' compensation by revealing what their counterparts in other firms are paid has encouraged them to demand even higher salaries.[82]

SUBSIDIZING MARKETS

Government often seeks to alter market outcomes by subsidizing private actors in hopes of influencing their decisions—to save, invest, consume, or engage in other kinds of transactions—in ways that policy makers consider socially desirable. Some of these, such as social net programs, are redistributive by explicit design, but all of them are redistributive in effect (that is, they move resources from one group to another).

These subsidies can take a number of different forms using a variety of techniques: direct cash or near-cash subventions (e.g., food stamps, Social Security); loan or other guarantees that reduce the cost of capital (e.g., student loans, Federal Housing Administration mortgages) or the risk of loss (e.g., the Pension Benefit Guaranty Corporation); exemptions or deductions from otherwise applicable taxes (often called "tax expenditures"); regulatory exemptions (e.g., for small businesses); public investment in private companies (bailouts of failing companies like American International Group); provision of free or below-cost benefits (Veterans Administration hospitals); special competitive advantages (e.g., lower borrowing costs for megabanks); and many others. Taken together, these subsidies comprise a substantial portion of federal domestic spending (assuming that one treats tax expenditures, say, as equivalent to government spending for this purpose).

Such subsidies often suffer from systematic inefficiencies and inequities. Many of them are target inefficient (discussed in chapter 2) in the following senses: recipients would have engaged in the desired conduct anyway (without the subsidy), they do not need the subsidy, or both. For example, the government has given immense tax advantages (relative to a tax baseline) to various retirement vehicles such as individual retirement accounts (IRAs) even though they are used disproportionately by relatively affluent people who would likely have set up retirement accounts anyway and thus have little marginal effect on household savings.[83] The favorable tax treatment of health insurance premiums disproportionately benefits "Cadillac" insurance plans enjoyed mostly by corporate executives and members of strong labor unions.

Some government subsidies are, predictably, bad bets (defined in chapter 2) and, relatedly, create moral hazard (discussed in chapter 5). Consider some of our largest, most prominent programs.

Housing loans. The most arrant example is the large number of recipients of subprime housing loans that Fannie Mae and Freddie Mac subsidized and pressed lenders both to give and not to foreclose against delinquency. Such government-promoted moral hazard was an important cause of the Great Recession and its protracted aftermath.

Indeed, more than five years later—*and even with all the benefits of hindsight*—the Federal Housing Administration (FHA) is following those agencies' catastrophic examples. The FHA, which is legally required to be self-supporting, has created so much moral hazard in housing and housing finance markets and administered its loans so irresponsibly that it will almost inevitably require a huge Treasury bailout;[84] only the amount is uncertain. Indeed, the FHA was $13.5 billion in the red at the end of 2012, even using an accounting method that includes assumed future earnings in current capital, which vastly understates the true deficit and which no private financial lender could get away with using.[85] A study based entirely on foreclosure estimates made by the FHA's own auditor and detailed individual loan data found that 40 percent of the loans made in 2010—several years *after* the housing bubble had burst and *after* the bailouts of the insolvent Fannie Mae and Freddie Mac had occurred—were made to borrowers who failed to meet the FHA's own credit score and debt-to-income standards for viable loans. The study also found that the agency fails to adequately monitor the risks on its loans, fails to charge guarantee fees adequately reflecting the risk of nonpayment, and concentrates its loans in areas likely to generate very high foreclosure rates.[86] Indeed, the FHA, which had been in better financial shape than Fannie and Freddie when the housing crash occurred, adopted the same disastrous game plan that they had used, relentlessly expanding its portfolio and pumping money into the plunging housing market in order to prop up home prices with high-risk loans. Tragically, this pattern of high-risk loans continues: in the first quarter of 2012, the same share of the FHA's outstanding loans, 40 percent, had subprime attributes.[87] More than three years after an independent auditor found significant deficiencies in the FHA's systems for monitoring loans, the agency still has not installed a more modern one.[88]

Low-income housing. The federal government operates other housing subsidy programs. Although I cannot review them here in any detail, independent analysts generally find that those which subsidize housing developers, financial institutions, and municipalities are far more inefficient than Section 8 of the Housing Act of 1937 (as amended) and other programs that directly subsidize low-income consumers of housing. Section 8 has its own problems, chiefly in its implementation—for example, many landlords refuse to accept Section 8 tenants, the vouchers are not worth enough in low-vacancy, high-rent communities, and the program's habitability conditions often go unenforced—but its target efficiency makes it a better policy instrument for meeting low-income housing needs than supply-side subsidies.

Student financial aid. The provision of financial aid to college students is among the largest domestic programs. (Although I refer to it as a "program," it is actually a suite of programs including direct loans, loan guarantees, grants, tax preferences, and institutional support.) Its general goals are desirable: to increase educational opportunity and thus assure individuals wider access to the American dream; to benefit the rest of society by expanding its human capital; and to overcome a supposed market failure in which only subsidies can induce private banks to finance education for young people given the uncertain prospects of their ability to repay.

The program has expanded to immense proportions since its start with the National Defense Education Act of 1958 and later extension through the Higher Education Act of 1965. An August 2013 government report shows that 57 percent of college students now receive federal aid, up from 47 percent only four years earlier.[89] In July 2013, the Consumer Financial Protection Bureau (CFPB) estimated that the total of outstanding student loans, almost all of them guaranteed by the federal government, reached $1.2 trillion—a 20 percent increase since the end of 2011[90]—and almost doubled since the end of 2008. With the bill paid by taxpayers, the program is a classic example of "distributive" politics—broad coalitions that concentrate benefits and disperse costs. This form of politics spawns policies with ever-expanding benefits, vast inefficiencies, policy entrenchment, and political resistance to change.

Like many such distributive policies, it is poorly targeted. Relatively few of the subsidies go to low-income families; instead, they tend to transfer resources "from the less well off to the more well off."[91] And the Congressional Budget Office has found that these loans do not alter some students' educational attainment.[92] For them, they are simply a taxpayer-provided subsidy. A study that evaluated another program, Hope and Lifetime Learning tax credits, found that it did not have *any* effect on college attendance.[93] One reason is that those who receive these credits would likely have attended college without them. And a new income-based repayment feature will actually most benefit high-income, high-debt people.[94] This skewing of benefits to the middle and upper class is unsurprising; politicians across the political spectrum use the program in their appeals to better-off voters.[95] In 2013, the Education Department's own inspector general reported large and growing fraud, much of it facilitated by community colleges, committed by both student borrowers and Pell grantees, including over 34,000 participants in crime rings.[96] As the *Wall Street Journal* editorialized, the new income-based repayment scheme further incentivizes delinquency: "Take out a big loan, work 10 years for the government repaying as little as possible, and then have your debt entirely forgiven. . . . Borrowers who enroll in [such] plans owe on average three times more than those who opt for the standard 10-year amortization schedule. They thus present the greatest risk to taxpayers. . . ."[97]

But even more disturbing than poor targeting and widespread fraud is the vast level of student debt and loan delinquency. According to the New York Federal Reserve Bank, 35 percent of student loan recipients under age thirty who were required to make payments were at least 90 days late on them, up from 26 percent in 2008 and 21 percent in 2004.[98] For every borrower who defaulted, at least two more were delinquent in their payments.[99] The *New York Times* noted that the total of $76 billion in default was "greater than the yearly tuition bill for all students at public two- and four-year colleges and universities."[100] The program, in short, is an engine of moral hazard. After all, the borrowers have few assets and the government demands no collateral, has no underwriting requirements, and asks little or nothing about students' ability to repay or about what sort of education they intend to pursue. Students take on greater debt with evidently little concern about future default. Student debt *rose* by more than 56 percent, adjusted for inflation, from 2007 to 2012—a much faster growth rate than credit card debt.[101] This, in a period when the mortgage crisis should have caused the government to focus on moral hazard problems and in which overall private household debt *fell* by 18 percent.[102] Students who borrow average about $40,000 in debt by graduation, almost twice what it was a decade ago; professional and graduate students' debt is about $56,000.[103]

Student loans have the highest delinquency rates of *any* federal credit program (reaching 11 percent in 2012) and even higher delinquency rates than for private auto, home equity, and mortgage loans; indeed, they approximate the credit card delinquency rate. And the delinquency steadily worsens. In March 2012, subprime borrowers held an estimated 33 percent of outstanding student loans, up from 31 percent in 2007. Also, the gap between college costs and borrowing limits continues to widen, prefiguring more defaults and dropouts.[104] As of 2012, nearly one in every six borrowers with a loan balance was in default (which occurs when a loan is delinquent for 270 days), and they were defaulting more quickly; the two-year rate was 9.1 percent, the highest in more than a decade. Moreover, according to the New York Fed, these rates actually *understate* the delinquency problem because many borrowers were not yet required to make payments for one reason or another. And in a grim augury of future defaults, the government's new direct loan program, instituted in 2010 when it stopped guaranteeing private loans and then rapidly expanded during the weak job market, seems to have made matters worse. In August 2013, the CFPB found that 22 percent of the 27.8 million borrowers under the new program were *already* in default or in predefault forbearance.[105]

Even as the economy improves, the situation grows more dire. Indeed, this student debt overhang threatens to retard the recovery. The outspoken proborrower director of the CFPB likens the situation to the subprime mortgage disaster.[106] And to make matters worse, Congress has misled the public by imposing an accounting method on the federal lending agencies that systematically underestimates the risk of default and thus its ultimate costs to taxpayers.[107]

To its credit, the government recently stepped up collection efforts. It estimates recovery of 80 percent of the defaulted debt, or $12 billion—although a 2007 academic study found a recovery rate closer to 50 percent.[108] But even these efforts are flawed. The private collection agencies, which cost the government $1.4 billion a year, may actually increase defaults by skewing incentives. Colleges with very high debt levels and default rates (mostly for-profits[109]) continue to participate, while any sanctions will only come in the future. In April 2013, Sallie Mae had to withdraw its bond offering from the market because investors in the secondary market that securitizes these loans showed so little confidence in its ability to collect on these delinquent loans,[110] which forced the agency to hive off the huge losses that it anticipates from these delinquencies in order to protect its other, profitable operations.[111]

Quite apart from moral hazard, the program has produced some seriously perverse and unforeseen consequences. First, it seems to have contributed to tuition increases, which directly contradicts the program's goal of increasing student access. Tuition and fees have nearly tripled over the last twenty years, rising much faster than wages, presumably in part because federal aid has increased what students can pay. Another explanation is that federal aid may increase the demand for higher education, and with no offsetting factors, this pushes up the price of tuition.[112] Second, the program may have encouraged institutions to substitute federal money for their own financial assistance, thus reducing the program's net effect.[113] It may also have contributed to the doubling of the administrative staff-student ratio since 1975, while the faculty-student ratio has changed very little.[114] Third, it may have encouraged many marginal students to over-invest in higher education by foregoing options—cheaper on-the-job training or earlier entry into the labor force, for example—that may be better for them on balance but that are undervalued if they underestimate their risk of future default.[115] They may also be underestimating the large risk—47 percent, if community colleges are included—that they will not complete college, a risk that is even larger for students from poor families.[116] Federal data published in February 2013 indicate that many of these loans go to art, music, and design students who carry a disproportionate debt load while facing limited future income prospects.[117] These debts are not dischargeable in bank-ruptcy—a rare concession to the moral hazard problem (but one that many in Congress want to change).[118] The CFPB rightly fears that however the bankruptcy discharge issue is resolved, these debts may limit students' future ability to obtain loans, which will limit their adult opportunities and hobble the economy.[119]

Given the program's sheer size, visibility, and cost, one would expect the government to have conducted comprehensive assessments of its effectiveness, but it has seldom done so—in contrast to, say, the frequent assessments of Head Start. (Recall, however, that Congress continues to lavish funds on Head Start despite many findings of ineffectiveness; see chapter 6.) GAO reports in 2002 and 2005 called for more assessments of the effectiveness of student grant and loan programs and tax preferences in promoting students' attendance, choice, persistence, and completion.[120] The few studies that have been done reveal mixed results. Some show small increases for some of these parameters, while others show no effects; no studies show large positive effects.[121]

The GAO found that many of these programs and tax preferences had never been studied, and even among those that had, vital aspects of effectiveness remained unexamined. Studies on the tax credits show them to be significantly under-utilized by those who would qualify, probably because of their complexity.[122] No research existed on how the program's tax credits affected students' persistence in their studies or the type of schools they decided to attend.[123] According to a 2012 GAO report, no research exists on any aspect of effectiveness for tax-exempt savings programs, the student loan interest deduction, or the parental personal exemption.[124] This lack of data on the effectiveness of such popular, long-standing, and costly programs is deplorable and symptomatic of the more general problem of official disinterest in assessment data. Researchers have examined the effects of Title IV aid and federal tax expenditures only "on a limited basis—in particular, only for certain states, types of schools, and groups of students."[125] This leaves extensive gaps in policy makers' knowledge about the programs' effectiveness. In 2002, the GAO recommended that the Department of Education study their impact on student attendance, choice, completion, and college costs. Three years later, the GAO found little progress. Its 2012 report concluded that the Department's most recent assessment efforts were "fairly narrow in scope" and "unlikely to yield broadly applicable lessons about the effects of Title IV aid on student attendance, choice, persistence, or completion."[126] Even more dismaying, Nobel Prize–winning economist James Heckman recently found that college-age people from disadvantaged backgrounds may not be able to benefit from them, absent pre-school interventions.[127]

In sum, this very costly program reaches a large number of people and enables many students to attend college who could not otherwise afford it. This is no small thing. But on the other side of the ledger, it disproportionately benefits those who need it least, and harms the many students who are encouraged to borrow sums that they cannot repay because they drop out of school, end up in jobs that pay too little, or default for other reasons. Remarkably little rigorous assessment has been done of the program's effectiveness concerning any of its key policy parameters, and what research there is suggests that it is not only ineffective but causes some serious harm. Not surprisingly, reform proposals abound. Congressman Tim Petri, for example, proposes a plan modeled on those used in the United Kingdom, Australia, and New Zealand, in which employers deduct student loan payments automatically from paychecks in order to reduce the number of graduates who default on their loans and accumulate large fees owed to collection agencies. His bill proposes shifting all repayment to an income-contingent plan that would cap payments at fifteen percent of discretionary income and would eliminate loan forgiveness. To protect borrowers, interest would accrue instead of compounding, and would stop accruing once it reached 50 percent of the initial balance.[128]

Green energy. Federal incentives for domestic energy production go back to the nation's very founding. In 1789, the first Congress imposed a tariff on the sale of British coal brought here as ship ballast. Throughout the twentieth century, the government promoted energy production and technology through a variety of direct and indirect subsidies including tax preferences, price controls, trade restrictions, provision of subsidized public services, regulation, conservation subsidies, and refusals to tax negative externalities. The great bulk of these subsidies went to oil and gas and, to a lesser extent, nuclear production.[129] Coal, which policy has subsidized in a number of ways, creates a large climate change externality.

Today the distribution of energy subsidies is altogether different. In 2011, the Institute for Energy Research, using Department of Energy data, calculated that the subsidies per unit of electricity actually produced was 64¢ for oil, gas, and coal; 82¢ for hydropower; $3.14 for nuclear energy; $56 for wind energy; and $775 for solar energy; In 2009, fossil fuels accounted for 78 percent of energy production but received only 12.6 percent of tax incentives. Renewable energy sources (most of which were hydropower) accounted for 11 percent of production but received 77 percent of the tax subsidies, not including direct subsidies. (On the revenue side, fossil fuel industries paid more than $10 billion in taxes; renewables were a net drain.[130]) The subsidy imbalance is even greater on a per-energy-unit basis: renewables receive three times as much as fossil fuels per kilowatt hour.[131]

Since the 1970s, federal policy has increasingly focused on promoting renewable ("clean") energy alternatives in order to reduce pollution, greenhouse gases, and dependence on foreign suppliers, as well as foster economic growth.[132] If this policy were achievable in a cost-effective manner, no sensible person could possibly object. Success, however, is extraordinarily elusive. First, some regulations—those seeking to redirect product choices to improve green energy efficiency, for example—arbitrarily assume consumer irrationality and market failures.[133] Second, energy is produced today in more globalized markets shaped in part by opaque political decisions. This makes predicting future market conditions—the unattainable holy grail of all investors and other economic actors throughout history—more difficult than ever.

Unless one views clean energy as a moral imperative that trumps all other considerations, it is far from being cost-effective relative to conventional sources—a fact that as of June 2013 showed little sign of change. The costs of conventionals, particularly relatively clean natural gas, are far lower today despite smaller subsidies, and are declining even more due to new discoveries and technologies. Renewables, moreover, face a host of challenges. Much of the new infrastructure necessary to produce, gather, and distribute renewables to users in sufficient quantities is not in place and will be costly, and some EPA rules are perverse—for example, requiring refiners rather than producers to comply with biofuel mandates.[134] Moreover, conventionals benefit from a deeply entrenched political status quo that renewable advocates cannot readily overcome.

Perhaps most important, Americans are profoundly skeptical that the government is competent to direct subsidies in the right forms to the right technologies at the right times. As chapter 4 discusses, this skepticism is firmly embedded in our political culture; it has only deepened over time. But it has been magnified by some recent incidents in which the government promoted unsuccessful "green" technologies, wasting large subsidies that were poorly targeted and managed; in some cases, politicization of these subsidies is alleged. The most notorious case was Solyndra, which received $535 million in federal loan guarantees for low-cost solar cell production before closing its doors, partly due to unexpected Chinese competition.[135] (It is cold comfort to American taxpayers that Solyndra's main competitor in

China also went bankrupt due to unforeseen market shifts.[136]) Large subsidies to electric carmakers like Fisker and Coda Holdings have also failed, as they have in other countries.[137] Even Tesla Motors, sometimes touted as the exception to this pattern of failure, has survived only through a combination of large subsidies primarily benefitting its extraordinarily wealthy investors. As the *Wall Street Journal* put it, "even if Tesla's cars do sell, the policy question is why billionaires in California couldn't have financed the business themselves. Why should middle-class taxpayers whose incomes are falling still pay to subsidize the purchase of cars that only the affluent can afford?"[138]

The ethanol fiasco is a far more important, costly, and even tragic example of government failure in promoting particular technologies that advantage specific political interests. Far from merely being pure technocratic choices, these efforts are almost always politicized both at their inception and after vested interests become entrenched. Under pressure from some environmentalists, the Bush administration decided that ethanol would soon become plentiful and cheap and could be pivotal in reducing fossil fuel consumption. Congress agreed, and mandated a year-by-year gallon quota for biofuels, predicting that the United States would produce about 240 million gallons a year by 2011; even with lavish subsidies, the actual figure was about seven million.[139] But at the same time, it also required automakers to improve fuel efficiency in their cars, which reduces gasoline demand.

What has ensued (if one is charitable) is a classic case of unforeseen and perverse consequences. Under the statutory biofuel formula—which ignores supply, demand, or price conditions—lower-than-expected fuel demand means that gasoline blends must contain higher-than-expected amounts of ethanol. To produce the ethanol, huge quantities of corn must be processed and burned as fuel rather than being used for human food or livestock feed. (Brazil uses sugarcane as its ethanol feedstock rather than corn, which is less fuel-efficient but has stronger support from Midwestern corn, wheat, and soybean producers and the ethanol industry—together known as the ethanol lobby.) This ethanol-driven demand for corn consumed almost half of the drought-depleted crop in 2012—a vastly higher percentage than predicted in 2005—and the formula demands much more by 2015. Indeed, it diverts as many calories from the world market *every year* as some of the worst famines experienced in the last fifty years.[140] Because the United States supplies 60 percent of global exports, this diversion—exacerbated both by the shortage of refined gasoline because of an export exemption from the ethanol requirement and by a severe drought—has raised corn and food prices significantly throughout the world. This has increased world hunger, especially in poor countries with corn-based diets, alarming world food programs.[141]

Ethanol policy has also had other perverse effects. It has raised domestic gasoline prices, which especially hurts lower-income drivers, increased the price difference between premium and regular gasoline, which in turn affects new car models that require or recommend the use of premium, and encouraged refiners to export their gasoline to foreign markets where the quotas don't apply, further tightening the domestic market and raising prices. Desperate for ethanol to meet the mandated quotas, gasoline refiners must buy up "ethanol credits" in what was a thinly traded market, ratcheting up the prices even further.[142] Nor does the program even produce significant environmental benefits, for ethanol is neither "clean" nor energy-efficient in its cycle of manufacturing, transportation, and consumption; it actually lowers fuel economy.[143]

To the consternation of the food, livestock, and poultry industries and environmental advocates, but to the delight of the ethanol lobby, which has profited greatly from the policy and exerted powerful influence in the 2012 election year, the EPA refused to relax the ethanol requirement, finding that the requirement did not "severely harm" the economy.[144] With ethanol policy, apparently, nothing succeeds like failure.

REDIRECTING MARKETS

Policy makers sometimes want to channel existing market activity into areas that they believe have been neglected. An important example is the Community Reinvestment Act of 1977 (CRA), designed to increase bank lending to low- and moderate-income (LMI) neighborhoods thought to be victims of stereotype-driven "redlining." The law states that all banks insured by FDIC have an obligation to meet the credit needs of the LMI areas in which they are chartered to do business, consistent with safe and sound banking practices, and requires the bank regulators to examine banks to assure compliance with this obligation and to take this information into account when considering banks' applications for regulatory approvals. (Beginning in the 1960s, Congress had already prohibited discrimination in credit and housing markets on the basis of race, sex, or other personal characteristics.) Starting in 1989, the CRA and its implementing regulations were amended to provide for public disclosure of the nonconfidential results of the regulatory compliance assessments and ratings of each bank; to require use of this information in considering merger applications; to address complaints that the regulatory process was too burdensome, process-oriented, and politicized; to require studies and reports on the CRA's effect on credit in LMI areas, including default rates; and to increase uniformity among the various regulatory agencies.

Assessments of the CRA's effectiveness vary considerably. Some studies have concluded that the LMI credit market suffers from certain market failures that the CRA remedies, and that it has increased loans in LMI areas without higher default rates or harm to banks' profitability,[145] although a recent study finds that loans made just before CRA examiners are scheduled to appear are 15 percent more likely to be delinquent.[146] Others have questioned the need for the CRA, arguing that banking is a competitive industry with strong incentives to make profitable loans wherever they can (the law does not require them to make unprofitable loans), that discrimination was illegal long before the CRA, that the financial services industry has been transformed in ways that invalidate the CRA's orientation to local markets, and that the law's ambiguity and lack of clear criteria invite regulatory overreach and manipulation and politicization by advocacy groups.[147] Despite some critics' claims to the contrary, however, there is little or no evidence that the CRA contributed significantly to the 2008 subprime mortgage crisis.

REINTRODUCING MARKETS

Sometimes the level of inefficiency and unfairness created by a regulatory system becomes so great that political entrepreneurs are able to create reform coalitions consisting of policy experts, government regulators, politicians whose constituents would benefit from more competition, and firms eager to exploit open market opportunities—coalitions committed to allowing greater, or even complete, sway to market forces.* During the 1970s and early 1980s, driven partly by that era's stagflation and the market distortions created by price controls, Congress (pushed by some reform-minded regulators) enacted landmark laws deregulating airlines, surface transportation, natural gas prices, and oil prices. These reforms largely succeeded; the airline example is discussed in chapter 11.

More controversial today is the dismantling of many federal banking controls that started in 1980, which shows how just how toxic for taxpayers (and investors) a policy of mixing regulation and markets can be. Congress, responding to powerful market forces driving change in the industry, enacted seven partial deregulation statutes that have helped to guide its transformation while attempting to catch up with those market forces. The statutes deregulated deposit insurance rates; dismantled geographic restrictions on branch and interstate banking; repealed the Glass-Steagall Act's separation between commercial and investment banking; blurred distinctions among different types of financial institutions; and altered deposit insurance. These policy changes contributed—in ways too complex to disentangle here (or perhaps *anywhere*)—to enormous losses as large numbers of thrift institutions and banks failed during the next

*Airlines, fully deregulated at the federal level, still face market restrictions locally where monopolistic airport authorities control terminal and other operating rights. See Michael E. Levine, "Airport Congestion: When Theory Meets Reality," *Yale Journal on Regulation* 26 (2009): 37–88.

decade (costing taxpayers some $125 billion) and to the grave financial crisis that began in 2007, whose cost to taxpayers will likely be even greater once the tally is complete.[148] Indeed, many critics place much of the blame for this crisis on banks' vast proprietary trading with depositors' funds after Glass-Steagall's repeal in 1999.[149] Moreover, as chapter 5 explained, the Dodd-Frank law has arguably paved the way for even larger bailouts of megabanks in the future.

MIDWIFING INFANT MARKETS

Innovative activity by firms may generate positive spillovers that benefit potential competitors and the public at large. Economist Joseph Stiglitz points out that knowledge about new products often has the attributes of a public good. The demonstrated feasibility of a new technology lets other companies enter the burgeoning market and create even more technologies.[150] Yet because firms cannot capture these knowledge benefits as profits and will therefore underinvest relative to the socially desirable level, government subsidies can try to help fill this gap. Economic research, however, casts doubt on whether federal innovation policies have generally done so.[151]

Indeed, many scholars argue that the patent system is not only complex, costly, slow, and ineffective at protecting truly innovative products decreases innovation by tactical use of litigation to block entry, patent "trolls" who buy up patents to intimidate inventors and extract rents, and other anticompetitive techniques.[152] Some reforms seem to have worked; the 1984 Drug Price Competition and Patent Term Restoration Act (the Hatch-Waxman Act) encouraged innovation competition in the pharmaceutical industry while also expediting the FDA approval process.[153] Bureaucratic red tape inhibits some entrepreneurs from entering new markets. Thus, efforts to commercialize space exploration have been stymied by licensing and certification hurdles that have increased delay and costs without obvious justification.[154]

RECRUITING MARKETS FOR REGULATORY PURPOSES

With the rise of the environmental movement and regulatory programs in the 1960s, many economists argued that any desired level of environmental protection could be achieved at lower cost by utilizing economic incentives rather than, or in conjunction with, the dominant form of regulation known as command-and-control. (In practice, market-based regulation almost always operates in tandem with more conventional command-and-control techniques.[155]) Indeed, in the last decade, the superiority of market-based regulatory techniques has become "a virtual orthodoxy."[156]

These incentive-based policy instruments can take a variety of forms: taxes, subsidies, disclosure requirements, tort liability, and tradable permit (cap-and-trade) schemes, with the last of these being most popular. For climate change and air quality policy, most economists favor taxes on carbon, sulfur, and other major pollutants, but their pleas have fallen on deaf ears.[157] With cap and trade, the regulatory agency specifies an acceptable overall level of pollution (the cap) and then distributes initial pollution permits to existing or potential polluters—preferably by auction—which the permit holders can trade with others, remaining under the cap. The permits' price will vary according to supply and demand. Those able to control their pollution at a lower cost than the prevailing permit price will do so and sell their permits to those polluters whose control costs are higher than the permit price, which will induce firms to develop lower-cost ways to reduce their pollution. The list of market-based schemes of environmental regulation is growing[158]—a tribute to their potential superiority to traditional command-and-control systems.

I say "potential" because when one moves from economic theory to the empirical evidence comparing the effectiveness of command-and-control and market incentive schemes, the picture becomes considerably murkier—and not just because of the methodological difficulties in making such comparisons, which are considerable. A broad review of the research on incentive approaches finds that most programs are hybrids; that the two approaches suffer from some of the same weaknesses; that there are important differences within each of these categories—for example, command-and-control may use performance standards or input (technology) standards; that the political and legal dynamics surrounding each variant matter a lot; and that the design details are crucial to a scheme's effectiveness.

At a general level, some of the distortions that plague command-and-control regulation also afflict market-based systems, although the specifics will vary. First, political factors may undermine the effectiveness of market schemes. Indeed, the initial allocation of entitlements to pollute, and the exceptions that are allowed, reflect political factors both because the economic and competitive stakes are high and because political support is needed if the scheme is to be adopted in the first place. Inevitably, these initial allocations favor some polluters over others and the status quo over newer firms that try to enter or secure a niche in the market. Another political difficulty with market-based schemes is that liberal politicians and environmental advocates often denounce them as "licenses to pollute," which indeed they are—as are traditional tort liability rules. To an economically oriented policy maker, of course, this criticism misses the crucial point—that we should price a polluting activity at its full social cost, thus creating incentives to conduct it more efficiently—but this technocratic explanation only inflames those who find such an approach immoral.[159]

Third, market-recruitment schemes' effectiveness depends on manipulating the incentives of market actors to achieve programmatic goals, so the schemes must be based on accurate information and carefully designed to prevent distortions, abuses, evasions, and perverse consequences.[160] This danger is exemplified by the federal program creating a market in renewable energy credits that has already experienced more than $100 million in fraudulent, counterfeit credits,[161] and a United Nations scheme that has encouraged firms to actually increase pollutants so that they will be paid to reduce them.[162] Unless the program gets the prices right—which is even more difficult when managing natural resources whose ecosystems perform hard-to-value functions (e.g., wetlands) than when controlling pollution[163]—they will send the wrong market signals. For example, the European Union's leading cap-and-trade program for greenhouse gases allocated so many allowances that demand for the credits, especially given reduced economic activity, has sagged so low that the program faces collapse.[164] After all, the market did not fully price the externality before the program was established, so no reliable price standard exists until there is active trading in a thick market. Moreover, the price equivalents of nonmarket costs like the added insult of being exposed to a pollutant involuntarily, or fairness concerns about trading-induced "hot spots," are hard to resolve.[165]

Fourth, market schemes are difficult to enforce because the main administrative sanction—reducing or withholding an allocation in the future—may be too powerful to be credible. Indeed, this sanction could be the death knell for a firm that cannot operate without polluting. Fifth, just as pollution does not respect politiojurisdictional boundaries, a pollution market must be transjurisdictional to be fully effective, as pollution sources that are outside the scheme will have even more incentive to pollute to gain competitive advantage over those subject to the scheme's controls. This prisoner's dilemma dynamic may actually increase total pollution. Yet it may be impossible to get every jurisdiction to participate and comply. The goal of the Clean Development Mechanism (CDM) established under the Kyoto Protocol is to reduce carbon emissions in those countries where it is cheapest and most efficient to do so. Yet the United Nations panel assessing the CDM found, in the words of the usually understated *Economist* magazine, a "complete disaster in the making," with an oversupply of pollution permits (along with the economic recession) driving their price down so low that the scheme is a shambles.[166] In April 2013, the *New York Times* confirmed this prediction, reporting that the European Union's Emissions Trading System under the CDM was "dealt a potential death blow" when it refused, despite very low market prices for permits due to economic stagnation and other factors, to raise the price to reduce pollution,[167] and this failure may doom other emissions trading plans, especially global schemes.[168]

Again, my point here is not that market-recruiting regulation is ineffective. Quite the contrary; it may be superior to command-and-control alternatives in particular cases. For example, the 1990 Clean Air Act amendments, which established an emissions trading scheme for sulfur dioxide, have been overwhelmingly successful.[169] Rather, the point is that recruiting markets for regulatory purposes sometimes fails. Here as elsewhere, God (and the devil) is in the details.

CHAPTER 9

The Limits of Law

L aw is everywhere. Like the metaphorical fog in Charles Dickens's *Bleak House*, it seeps silently into each nook and cranny of our lives, affecting virtually all behavior and relationships. This is simply a fact of life. We may want more or less of it, and we may wish that it took different forms, contained different principles, and prescribed different rules. But like the air we breathe, we cannot do without it.

Law is the dominant instrument of public policy, and the American polity entertains growing ambitions for it. Modern public law— the body of statutes, agency rules, and court decisions that aims to shape primary behavior by authorizing officials to allocate resources or impose sanctions—assigns redistributive and regulatory roles that are more expansive than ever before. Neither conservative nor neoliberal resistance to its advance has stemmed this tide, which has reached into domains of choice and intimate relations previously unregulated by law. Sexual harassment law now regulates much workplace speech and conduct. Disability law now shapes job and building designs, management practices, and educational policies. Environmental law affects activities ranging from indoor smoking to outdoor barbecues. The list of law's imperial conquests in recent decades is very long indeed. "Never before," Jonathan Rauch writes, "has the government concerned itself so minutely with the detailed interactions of daily life."[1]

Law's contemporary reach was not inevitable, at least in retrospect. Policy makers did not extend law to new activities inadvertently; they did so only after receiving grim warnings of slippery slopes, unforeseen consequences, and the tendency of law to beget more law. Despite having been advised "don't go there," they did, often eagerly. Significantly, this pressure for more law has come both from liberals advocating more state regulation and redistribution, and from conservatives eager to criminalize or curtail private conduct of which they disapprove.

Law's strengths are formidable and essential. In principle and often in practice, it secures order and justice; resolves disputes; facilitates transactions; guides and restrains official power; expresses public values; shapes our incentives to advance our goals; and assures a degree of fairness to, and formal equality among, fellow citizens. Every state that values these goals (alas, many do not) has sought to achieve them through some system of formal rules and sanctions. As legal scholar Neil Komesar has shown, cultural norms, formal education, markets, and all other social institutions for shaping behavior exhibit their own characteristic features and drawbacks.[2] To say that law fails, then, is only to say that it fails to be perfect. As noted in chapter 2, the pivotal question is always, failure compared to what?

Precisely because of law's powerful allure, policy makers must attend carefully to its limits—by which I mean constraints or incapacities that are inherent in the use of *any* law; so long as we use law to make public policy, they are essentially inescapable. (It is hard to think of a public policy that does not take the form of law. Jawboning or efforts at moral suasion, valuable as they may be, do not count as "public policies" in my usage). In thinking about how to design policies, policy makers need to distinguish these inevitable entailments of law *qua* law, on the one hand, from the limits that are contingent on law's use to form a given substantive policy, on the other hand. This distinction, of course, is clearer analytically than in practice: we cannot always be sure whether the causes of a particular policy failure are the inherent, inescapable limits of law, or are instead causes that might be remedied by improving a particular law's substantive content.

I focus here on law's inherent limits because these limits seriously diminish law's performance and reputation, whereas those limits that are "merely" contingent to particular policies are far too numerous and policy- and content-specific to be cataloged in the way that the inherent ones can. Advocates beguiled by laws' promises should be curious about why so many of them disappoint us, why our disappointment is itself a problem, and how this problem might best be addressed. I presume that a public that better understands the sources of law's failures will entertain more realistic expectations about its possibilities. Laws that first arouse and then dash people's hopes also discredit the reformist impulse, leaving in its wake the kind of mistrust evidenced in chapter 1. Only by realistically assessing law's capacities can we preserve and extend its immense contributions to social progress, while at the same time minimizing the effects of its entailments on future policy failures. A more critical, refined appreciation of these limits might, perhaps paradoxically, *increase* public support for those reforms that law *can* successfully implement.

Finally, I emphasize law's limits for an important ideological reason as well. The "old system" described in chapter 1 placed a thumb on the scales to restrict ambitious social policy, creating a kind of rebuttable presumption against more public law. It demanded affirmative justification for more public law—not because it opposed change but because its deepest commitment was to individual freedom and autonomy. It preferred to risk too little public law than to risk too much. This system, of course, was transformed by the progressive, New Deal, and Great Society eras, and by the rights revolution that began to flourish in the 1960s. Today, our far greater experience of law's limits in a more activist state may help to guide us toward a more nuanced use of it.

In this chapter, I consider seven limits on law's policy effectiveness. Again, these limits apply *inevitably, whenever we use law*— which in the policy realm essentially means all the time. These inherent, policy-impairing properties of law are (1) its ubiquity; (2) the simplicity-complexity trade-off; (3) its ambiguity; (4) its discretion;

(5) its procedural apparatus; (6) its inertia; and (7) its crowding-out effects on spontaneous, low-cost cooperation. To be clear, these limits have many desirable aspects. Indeed, some of the procedural apparatus is constitutionally required. But as I propose in chapter 12, some of the costs that they entail might be reduced.

UBIQUITY

Our culture exhibits plenty of lawlessness, but it is never "lawless." No state of nature devoid of law exists. Indeed, even when law claims to be merely observing or regulating human or physical nature as a distinct, objective thing, law is actually constructing it, altering it. The law designating parts of the Grand Canyon as a national park transformed it from an awesome natural panorama into an object of administration, albeit one that retains its physical grandeur and veneration. Even the most intimate, spontaneous action is governed by at least one enforceable rule, although that rule is often one that protects privacy or autonomy by creating a zone in which other rules are not allowed to intrude.

Several important policy implications follow from this inescapability of law. First, law's distinctive limitations—the focus of this chapter—prevent it from doing certain things well. It can police domestic violence but it cannot mandate affection or equitable sharing of household responsibilities. It can reward character but it cannot create character. (Indeed, in a dynamic that Immanuel Kant explained, a law that seeks to reward character—for example, by awarding a prize for exemplary behavior—may actually reduce the motive and value of the autonomous will that is character's ultimate source.[3]) It can subsidize innovation but it cannot innovate itself. When policy makers' choices are law or nothing, they may opt for law even if it risks a failed policy, and we may deem this choice reasonable. This dilemma helps to explain, for example, why foster care policies are always so troubled. We understandably refuse to leave the welfare of at-risk children up to parental authority, informal social norms, or the market. Nevertheless, the gravitational force of law's limits increase the likelihood of failure.

A second policy implication is that any effort by law to transcend its inherent limits still depends on a new law that inescapably possesses many if not all of those same limits. This is what I mean by "inherent" limits. Because there is no metalaw that is not law, policy reform must itself take the form of law. Reform may improve the policy's substantive content, of course, and this may produce a desirable change in direction or execution, but law's limits will still haunt the reformed policy. Again, there is no escaping them so long as law is the policy's vehicle. This is one reason (there are usually others) why policy reforms often replicate some (hopefully not all) of the deficiencies of the original—why, for example, tax and campaign finance reforms that were designed to close undesirable loopholes always seem to create new ones. (One person's loophole, of course, is another person's targeted policy.) The reform law, like its predecessor, will exhibit (among other inherent limits) ambiguity and discretion, which are the progenitors of many loopholes.

THE SIMPLICITY-COMPLEXITY TRADE-OFF

Ordinarily, we assess people and things according to the numerous dimensions along which they vary—for example, size, strength, beauty, speed, intelligence, morality, humor, culpability, and value. In contrast, law often attempts to govern this complex reality through simple binary, yes-or-no, in-or-out categories (e.g., guilt or innocence, eligible or ineligible). Even when law opts for more complex rules, however, the ones that it uses tend to be far simpler than the reality that they mean to govern; they seldom use the continuous more-or-less categories that refine our perceptions and discourse and render our understanding of everyday life nuanced, apt, and intelligible. The citizen beholding law's artificial, reductionist classifications often protests in the name of common sense: "The real world isn't black or white; it is all a matter of degree."[4]

This limitation accounts for a major complaint about legal rules, often expressed with "one size fits all" and "cookie cutter" metaphors. Among countless examples is the Small Business Administration's essentially uniform treatment of all small businesses, defined as entities with fewer than five hundred employees. Small businesses are indeed the main engines of jobs, innovation, and economic growth, but this is true of only a small percentage of them, as economist Aaron Chatterji notes: "Less than a quarter of America's 27 million small businesses have employees. An even smaller portion grow beyond 20 employees. And many of them don't want to. . . . 75 percent of small-business owners aren't aimed for growth at all. They're basically just looking for a steady job as their own boss. . . . Yet the government has traditionally placed the neighborhood store and the high-potential startup in the same catchall category. It offers them the same loan programs, counseling services and other assistance. And that means lots of small companies, not to mention the economy as a whole, get short-changed." Despite some recent legislation seeking to focus more attention on the innovators and job creators, the lack of differentiation still dominates small business policy.[5] Regulations under the Dodd-Frank Act similarly lump banks of very different sizes together despite the very different kinds of markets they serve and their different capacities for regulatory cost-spreading.[6]

Let me first define *simplicity* and *complexity* before going on to consider the trade-offs between them. A legal system is complex to the extent that its rules, processes, institutions, and supporting culture possess four features, which I define immediately below: density, technicality, differentiation, and indeterminacy or uncertainty. The Volcker Rule, discussed in chapter 8, is a paradigmatic example of complexity. To the extent that the law does not possess those features, it is simple. Density and technicality are features of the system's rules. *Dense* rules are numerous and encompassing. They occupy a large portion of the relevant policy space and seek to control a broad range of conduct, which causes them to collide and conflict with their animating policies with some frequency. An example of a dense legal regime is pension law, which cuts across and seeks to integrate a wide variety of practices in a large number of disparate industries calling for many different legal specialties such as tax, labor and employment, investment, fiduciary, and social entitlement law.

Technical rules require special sophistication of expertise on the part of those who wish to understand and apply them. Technicality is a function of the fineness of the distinctions that a rule makes, the specialized terminology it employs, and the refined substantive judgments it requires. The Internal Revenue Code is probably the leading example of a set of technical rules.

A legal system is *institutionally differentiated* insofar as it contains a number of decision structures that draw upon different sources of legitimacy, possess different kinds of organizational intelligence, and employ different decision processes for creating, elaborating, and applying the rules. Product safety, for example, is governed by statutory provisions, regulatory standards promulgated by several different agencies and private technical organizations, tort litigation, and common law contract principles.

Complexity's final feature—*indeterminacy*—is a quality both of rules and of legal processes and institutions. Indeterminate rules, processes, and institutions are usually open-textured, flexible, multifactored, and fluid. Turning on diverse mixtures of fact and policy, indeterminate rules tend to be costly to apply and their outcomes are often hard to predict. The familiar reasonableness standard in tort and many other areas of law is such a rule. Indeterminacy's relation to legal complexity is itself complex. Ironically, rules and institutions that are designed to reduce the law's indeterminacy may actually increase it, due to the cumulative effect of their density, technicality, and differentiation. Indeterminacy, then, may be a consequence, as well as a defining feature, of complexity.

Some of the fundamental trade-offs between simple and complex legal rules are obvious, and sophisticated policy makers surely appreciate them. Still, it is difficult for them to know in any given context what the different trade-offs presented by all the rules under consideration actually are, and it is also difficult to go on to the next steps, comparing and then evaluating the choices that these competing trade-offs present. Yet getting these trade-offs "right" is essential to effective policy making. (I put "right" in scare quotes to call attention to the difficult normative issues that these trade-offs will raise).

There are some good arguments for using simple classifications and rules in particular policy contexts. Legal scholar Richard Epstein, cleverly making a virtue of an apparent paradox, has called for "simple rules for a complex world."[7] By strategically suppressing complexity, simple rules allow us to make, apply, and comprehend law more cheaply and apply it with more predictability than if the rules sought to track the profuse variety and complexity of social life.[8] We can more readily and cheaply bargain around bright-line legal rules that we find inefficient or otherwise undesirable[9]—assuming that the law permits us to do so, which it often doesn't.[10]

Policy makers also know about certain familiar legal techniques that can temper and counteract this simplicity of categories and rules. Lawmakers can include more categories, replace bright-line tests with more flexible, contextual standards (this technique is discussed below), and permit exceptions to rules. Unfortunately, each of these three complexifying techniques carries its own disadvantages. Multiplying categories makes law more costly to understand and to apply, and makes its outcomes less predictable. Moving from rules to more open-ended standards delegates more discretion to those who apply and enforce them, such as citizens, juries, or bureaucrats, which makes them more difficult to control and thus invites arbitrariness while reducing their predictability. Allowing exceptions to a rule may swallow, weaken, delegitimate, or transform it.[11]

In the remainder of this section, I first explain why public law has become more complex over time in almost all areas of public policy,* and then consider how this increased complexity affects government performance.

---

*Strenuous attempts to codify private law (contracts, torts, property, family law, and the like) and to make it more uniform across the states have met with some success. But simplification efforts in public law are few and far between; it is hard to think of a major example of success in codifying it.

Increasing complexity seems to be a feature of almost all other systems, physical and social; it perhaps reflects a secular, even universal, process of entropy.[12] In law, this dynamic is certainly not inexorable, as the replacement of writ pleading with much simpler code pleading and the replacement of tort law for industrial accidents with workers' compensation systems demonstrates. Nor does the complexity grow at the same rate and at the same time in all areas of the law. Yet for all these qualifications, the strength and generality of this trend are striking. One can discern it throughout the legal system—in the form, subject matter, goals, interpretation, and remedial infrastructure of legal norms. The term *legal norms* is used here rather than *legal rules* to avoid confusion from the distinction, made immediately below, between rules and standards, both of which are legal norms. I discuss these four features in turn.

The form of legal norms. Many legal norms have evolved from relatively precise, acontextual, determinate, and hard-edged forms to relatively ambiguous, contextual, indeterminate, and open-ended ones. These two forms are often referred to as *rules and standards.* (My colleague Carol Rose calls them "crystals and mud.")[13] Rules are not always simple, and standards are not invariably complex, but these two formal categories do describe paradigmatic, antipodal types. They express distinctive ways in which the law views, values, argues about, and influences the nature of social relationships. Further, these formal types affect substance, shaping both particular legal outcomes and the balance among competing social ideals and practices.

A movement from rules to more complex standards has been evident for some time. At the "metalaw" level, the evolution of legal norms from common law principles to statutes to administrative regulation, although animated in part by a quest for greater certainty, has only produced more open-ended complexity and indeterminacy. Efforts to achieve greater certainty have generally failed, as the history of administrative law demonstrates. A generation of scholars, officials, and reformers urged that agencies make policy through rule making rather than through the traditional case-by-case adjudication, in large part because of the greater certainty that rules were thought to afford. Nevertheless, there has been a retreat from rule making back to adjudication in several important policy sectors, largely because of the higher political and judicial review costs of the former.[14]

Agency discretion has also increased, which in turn generates more legal complexity. Although the legal system employs many techniques to constrain and guide discretion—statutory language, judicial review, legislative oversight, public participation, and procedural requirements are examples—the pervasive delegation of discretion to agencies (and to courts) means that the resulting legal regime is almost certain to become more dense, technical, institutionally differentiated, and indeterminate than if the legislature had simply promulgated a rule itself. There are often compelling public interest reasons to confer discretion, even given the risk that it will sometimes be abused. Greater legal complexity, however, should be seen as one more consequence of doing so.

One much-touted move toward legal simplicity and certainty is telling in this respect. The congressionally mandated federal sentencing guidelines established a generally binding grid for judges' criminal sentencing decisions. Many legal scholars and prominent judges have severely criticized this reform as a misguided attempt to achieve some of the virtues of clear, simple rules—especially horizontal equity—by reducing the largely standardless discretion that sentencing judges previously enjoyed. To these critics, the guidelines represent a more general style of contemporary legal thought in which numerous cases are aggregated and treated uniformly despite their real differences. This critique gained widespread support, and the Supreme Court seemed to agree, restoring judicial discretion in sentencing by ruling that the guidelines are not mandatory but merely advisory.[15] This is not to say that all simplifying grids have been rejected; the Social Security disability insurance grid system was challenged and upheld by the Court,[16] and there are other examples, as with more categorical payment systems under Medicare. But moves from legal complexity toward greater simplicity tend to be challenged politically and in the courts.

The subject matter of legal norms. The administrative state emerged from the effort to regulate areas of activity previously governed primarily by informal or contractual norms, and other areas previously regulated at lower levels of intensity or lower levels of government. It elaborated new bodies of law bearing all of complexity's hallmarks. Dense norms occupied much of the field of activity. Regulatory law also brought more technicality; specialized lawyering became so essential that the profession had to reorganize along new lines. New institutions—highly differentiated agencies and the diverse structures to which they give rise—proliferated. Although meant to increase certainty, regulation actually reduced it on balance because of its greater ambition and its preservation of much of the common law regime.

Two examples will illustrate the point. Before the reapportionment cases and the Voting Rights Act of 1965, the federal law for voting rights was relatively simple, concerned largely with reapportionment, fraud, and egregious forms of intentional racial discrimination. Today, however, this body of law also involves the detailed federal regulation and review of thousands of state and local election laws involving structures of representation, voting rules, annexations, municipal finance, voter identification, the allocation of legislative business, and much more.[17] Bewilderingly complex public law has penetrated even fields that were formerly matters of private law. Employment and benefits law, for example, is now a dense mixture of private contracting, state common law and federal court adjudication, federal and state statutes, detailed agency regulations, and other sources of law.[18]

The goals of legal norms. Before the age of statutes, the administrative state, and an avowedly policy-making judiciary, the policy ends invoked by American lawmakers were generally modest. Legislatures' principal goals were to facilitate private ordering and to establish public policies to buttress that system, while common law courts usually hewed to a formalistic conception of judging that emphasized (at least at the level of judicial rhetoric) a fidelity to *stare decisis* and legislative intent, rather than an articulated instrumentalism.

The New Deal changed all that, and the change it wrought accelerated in the decades that followed, particularly in the Great Society programs, ushering in the "new system" discussed in chapter 1. New legislative goals, largely implemented by administrative agencies, included health and safety, equal opportunity, income redistribution, financial security for the elderly, stabilization of markets, development of infrastructure, governmental reform, and many more. This transformation of public and private law invited judges to abandon even the pretense of formalism. Spurred on by many legal scholars, they openly embraced a conception of role, a style of thought, and a decisional rhetoric that legitimated judicial policy making in various areas.

Once judges adopted an explicitly policy-oriented style, the more complex character of their new course quickly became clear. Leaving the familiar, secure terrain of formalism for the more exhilarating but perilous realm of policy making, a larger number of decision-relevant goals came into view. This multiplicity of goals necessitated new legal doctrines capable of encompassing and harmonizing them. In tort law, for example, the courts pursued cost-internalization and loss-spreading goals, "inventing" the doctrine of enterprise liability in the process. The same imperatives led courts in both private and public law to adopt certain common decision methodologies that vastly complexify the system: for example, interest-balancing, sequential burden shifting, and spasmodic and tactical deference to other institutions. By requiring judges to balance numerous diverse, and inevitably conflicting, policy goals, these doctrines are bound to be both technical and indeterminate. Institutional differentiation only magnifies this complexity, for the doctrines must be applied by agencies to whom the courts accord notoriously ill-defined deference and with whom they share adjudicatory power.

The interpretation of legal norms. The interpretation of legal texts is an ancient problem, as the Talmud vividly demonstrates. Still, today's Babel-like cacophony of legal hermeneutics is unprecedented.

For whatever reason—the influence of postmodernist literature theories on legal thought, the related emphasis on interpreting norms contextually, the triumph of realism and instrumentalism over formalism in law, and more general delegitimation of traditional sources of authority—a plethora of competing approaches has thrown the field wide open. No clear winner is likely to emerge anytime soon, as the warring interpretative methodologies of Supreme Court justices Stephen Breyer and Antonin Scalia, not to mention the law professoriate, suggest.[19] Meanwhile, the technicality and indeterminacy of statutory norms grow apace.

Remedial infrastructure. I have primarily discussed the markedly increased complexity of the substantive legal rules that comprise the vast field of public policy. Much the same is true of the quite separate body of law that prescribes the remedies that one can invoke to enforce those rules. Indeed, recent decades have witnessed a remedial revolution, with the elaboration of many new or renovated enforcement techniques: novel injunctive remedies; statutorily created causes of action (i.e., rights to sue); judicially implied causes of action; judicially expanded remedies against government; and other categories. This enlarged remedial infrastructure increases the formal accountability of law to aggrieved parties, but it also expands judicial influence over policy making by multiplying courts' opportunities to interpret and apply the law.

Is legal complexity a problem?[20] If we suppose that legal rules are largely epiphenomenal, merely reflecting the underlying social conditions to which they relate, then a denser, more intricate legal system may be both inevitable and desirable. After all, social interdependencies have increased. Cultures and markets have fragmented and diversified. Transformative technologies have emerged in every corner of life. Public and private bureaucracies have proliferated. Mustn't law keep pace with this social complexity? Perhaps, but the whole point of exploring law's inherent limits, as this chapter does, is to understand the inescapable trade-offs between a simpler or more complex law. In the analysis that follows, I focus on complexity's effects; simplicity's effects, of course, are precisely the opposite. I distinguish three of these effects: transaction costs, governance costs, and delegitimation costs.

Transaction costs. Like friction in mechanics, these costs are ubiquitous and limit the system's performance. Complex law tends to be more cumbersome to administer, more difficult for lawmakers to formulate and agree upon, and more difficult to reform once established. Administrators and subjects of such law must invest more in order to learn what it means, when, and how it applies, and whether the costs of complying with it are worth incurring. Other costs of administering a complex legal system include those related to bargaining about and around the system's rules and litigating over them. Thus, legal complexity magnifies transaction costs by generating more uncertainty. Although complexity does not alone generate all of the costs—some would exist even in a simple legal system with simple rules—it is clearly an important source of them. Just how costly legal complexity is depends in part upon our incentives and our capacities to comply, which in turn are shaped by our values, intelligence, technology, and social control mechanisms.

Complexity-induced costs can be both inefficient and unfair. They can impose dead-weight losses, create frustrating delays, consume the energies of talented individuals, breed new and intractable disputes, and discourage compliance. Promoting passivity and entrenching the status quo, legal complexity can stultify a society that often depends of vigorous action to solve problems. Complexity's costs, moreover, impose disproportionate burdens on the poor by raising prices and necessitating the services of lawyers and other professionals trained in the management of complexity. Complexity alters ours incentives and tests our capacities, straining their limits. Even as complexity increases, the constraints on those capacities—especially social values and intelligence—are relatively fixed, at least in the short run. At some point, complexity's demands are bound to outstrip our capacities to manage them; and unless the forces that propel complexity can somehow be reversed, this gap will widen.

Even government policies targeted at sophisticated, well-counseled businesses can be defeated by their complexity. A recent *Wall Street Journal* article reports that Congress's efforts to use targeted tax breaks such as the Work Opportunity Tax Credit to induce companies to hire more workers, boost energy efficiency, buy more equipment, and so forth have utterly failed. They are so confusing, cumbersome, and costly—requiring, among other things, an army of expensive "tax-credit consultants"—that most of the companies forego the subsidies, pay more tax than is legally required, and lose the international competitive advantages that Congress meant to confer.[21]

Governance costs. When a rule must be agreed upon by a number of rule makers, its formulation entails costs; the more numerous those whose assents are necessary, the more costly the agreement will be. A complex law multiplies these costs.

The familiar image of a legal landscape constituted by the existing rules and practices helps to show why. As the body of rules grows more dense, the legal landscape becomes more thickly populated and harder to traverse. Concealed declivities, sudden detours, arterial congestions, unexpected cul-de-sacs, puzzling signs, and jarring encounters abound. Because integrating new rules with existing ones is tricky and dangerous, the system must develop another layer of meaning: rules about rules. In this locale, it is no longer enough to know one's location and destination; one cannot survive without a great deal of local knowledge about when the buses run, whether cabs will venture into certain neighborhoods, which vendors are trustworthy, and where it is safe to walk. People with a choice do not venture out unattended. Experienced guides equipped with maps and special know-how are essential, for only the initiated can lead a newcomer through the honeycomb of enclaves, each with its local patois, exotic cuisine, peculiar customs, and belligerent pride.

A legal landscape this complex engenders several kinds of governance costs that have generally been overlooked. First, those who make legal rules become more risk-averse. Even fervent reformers hesitate to alter a landscape that is so hard to read; they know that in a more polycentric legal world, any change will have ripple effects, ramifying widely, swiftly, and unpredictably throughout the system's web. When the risks of error are magnified, rule makers are more likely to adhere to even an unsatisfactory status quo. This increased risk aversion surely contributes to the bleak policy-making deadlock, the sense of drift, that exists today in so many policy fields.

Institutional differentiation spawns legal indeterminacy, another governance cost. The proliferation of policy-making institutions multiplies the sources of innovation, information, and legitimacy—precious resources in any social system. On the other hand, this diversity also encourages conflict and raises decision costs. The only way to reach agreement among institutions may be to adopt open-ended, multifactored, or otherwise indeterminate legal standards. These standards do not really reduce conflict but simply use delegated authority to move the policy conflict from one rule-making locus to others, usually agencies and courts. Patricia Wald, formerly a judge on the U.S. Court of Appeals for the District of Columbia circuit, underscored this point when she defended the ostensibly simple "Chevron test" (for allocating interpretive power between courts and agencies) against those who would prefer a more refined, complex standard:

> Judges of radically different political and social viewpoints can only reason together on the basis of a few relatively simple propositions that they can all agree govern, so that disputes can be narrowly focused on their application. The *Chevron* decision, warts and all, has accomplished this. . . . Were we to switch to a broader framework of what is good regulatory policy or which of thirty canons apply, our debates would be less focused, our work would be more complex, and our differences would more frequently prove irreconcilable. A simple decisional framework may be essential to collegial decisionmaking in a court of widely differing views.[22]

Delegitimation costs. If the complex legal landscape contains many pitfalls for the governors, it is terra incognita for the governed. In a society that values negative liberty and "personal space," the density of the legal system—the penetration of law into every corner of human life, or what has been called "hyperlexis"[23]—is bound to be a source of deep resentment. When rules are indeterminate, their precise meanings cannot be easily grasped, nor can their applications be readily predicted. Confusion and uncertainty follow. If the rules are technical, they will often be opaque to the common mind and to common sense, common experience, and even common morality. Intelligible only to experts, the law is likely to mystify and alienate lay citizens whose intelligence it often seem designed to mock. When this Delphic law also emerges from an institutional black box that is itself dense and difficult to comprehend, its legitimacy—the sense of "oughtness" that the lawmakers hope will attach to it—is diminished.

Complexity is not neutral in its effects; it advantages some groups and disadvantages others, a fact well understood by those who seek to influence the shape of the law. Once citizens begin to suspect that these advantages and disadvantages are distributed by design rather than randomly, they will come to view complexity in an altogether different, less tolerant light. Profound cynicism about and alienation from the legal system are likely to follow. Although public disgust may occasionally prompt what my colleague John Langbein calls a "legal implosion," this is surely exceptional. More commonly, I suspect, the public suffers excessive complexity in silence, responds with informal simplifications, or simply fails to comply.

Tax law is the great example of this problem, especially because its complexity is widely (though not universally) believed to be unavoidable.[24] Although tax law includes many simple bright-line rules and sharp, quantitative thresholds, the policy context of tax administration requires exceptionally dense, detailed, and technical rules elaborated through a differentiated system of agencies and tribunals. The government's stakes in revenue collection are the highest; it is a matter of political and programmatic survival. Many taxpayers, especially the wealthiest ones who generate the most tax revenue, seek advice from highly trained, well-paid accountants, financial planners, and tax lawyers all intent upon one thing: minimizing their tax liability by interpreting the provisions as opportunistically as possible without going over the legal line. The only way the government can prevent them from gaming the system is to knit a fabric of rules that is so tight and seamless as to leave no opening for strategic exploitation by tax-payers and their loophole-seeking minions. (Most taxpayers, of course, cannot afford such minions. The time-value cost of complying with federal tax laws in this mind-numbingly complex system has been estimated at $194 billion a year).[25]

Courts are aware of this special context and usually defer to the government's interpretation of these legal materials except where it is clearly erroneous. In a number of other policy areas—immigration and international trade, for example—the government girds for battle by adopting a purposefully complex set of rules designed to defeat every argument or stratagem that a wily, determined, sophisticated, and probably better-paid antagonist might try to deploy.

Taxpayers bewildered by tax law's complexity and uncertainty appear more likely to violate it. In turn, voluntary compliance, which is so critical to the tax law's integrity, depends upon its intelligibility. "Erosion of taxpayer morale," tax scholar James Eustice observed, "is not an unimportant side effect of all this confusion—if taxpayers think the whole system is unknowable, the temptation to use self-help to fashion their own private tax shelters becomes well-nigh irresistible."[26] According to Nina Olson, the longtime taxpayer advocate at the Internal Revenue Service, complexity is the system's greatest problem.[27]

All of these weighty objections to legal complexity would not necessarily be decisive in any particular policy context. A simpler regime might be even worse. The trade-off, however, is inescapable.

AMBIGUITY

All language is ambiguous to some degree—that is, capable of multiple meanings, owing to the limits of any language, including one like English with its immense vocabulary. Legal language thrives on ambiguity. And therein lies a pervasive limit on law's effectiveness in policy making.

First, the language of law is often abstract; the more abstract the idea being conveyed, the more the language conveying it will contain ambiguities. The most important example of this in law is "reasonable" or "reasonableness," which are used to define the requisite standard of behavior not only in negligence law but in countless other legal contexts. Similar ambiguities pervade law: fairness (as in "fair representation" in labor law), justice (as in "just compensation" in eminent domain), dueness (as in "due process of law"), equality (as in "equal pay for equal work"), good faith (as in fiduciary law), comparability and appropriateness (as in disability law), and countless vague standards. Ambiguous formulations like these are ordinarily left to juries, judges, or agencies to define more specifically and authoritatively, with little to guide them but intuition, common experience, or (in the case of agencies) familiarity with the problem. Absent such authoritative guidance, members of the public who wish to invoke or comply with the law are left to guess at its meaning.

Moreover, the politics that surrounds lawmaking (and contract writing, which is a form of private lawmaking) makes ambiguity an all-too-valuable tool for policy makers. With intense disputes over so many issues, and with the need for some prompt resolution of them, compromise is needed. Ambiguity is the trusted handmaiden of compromise, whether the disagreement occurs among legislators, administrators, judges, contract negotiators, parents, or other decision makers. Papering over differences is perhaps the most common and serviceable way to reach a decision on a principle *now* while deferring—to other times and perhaps to other decision makers or modalities—the question of how that principle will be reified in its more specific applications. Incompletely specified constitutions, statutes, contracts, and other legal instruments are ubiquitous because their advantages (agreement now, while minimizing negotiation and prediction costs) exceed their disadvantages (parties are left hostage to future events).[28] No general rule can prescribe an optimal level of ambiguity; it all depends on context, and determining that level is a skill that grows with experience.

But this compromise through ambiguity carries its own risks. First, democratic accountability suffers when Congress leaves the hard pol-

icy trade-offs to unelected agency officials (and to judges who ultimately review the officials' actions). Congress is all too eager to pass
the buck while reserving the right to castigate the bureaucrats who fill
in the policy blanks that it left open. The Supreme Court's "nondelegation doctrine," discussed in the next section, has not reduced Congress's strong incentives to enact vague, open-ended, buck-passing
laws. To be sure, these incentives do not always carry the day. Congress sometimes passes very detailed statutes, arguably too detailed
to allow for flexible policy implementation at the agency level. The
Dodd-Frank law on financial regulation is a recent example.

Second, compromise through ambiguity does not solve the problem of legal uncertainty so much as perpetuate it—and the political
conflict that surrounds it. The Affordable Care Act, for example, nowhere defined "affordable," yet much of the law's impact depends on
what it means. Predictably, this pivotal ambiguity has stirred up a
political hornet's nest, stalling and perhaps crippling implementation
of the act's main provisions.[29]

Legal ambiguity also reduces law's effectiveness by increasing the
power of the final interpreter. This is usually the court system. In part,
the highly controversial method of constitutional interpretation known
as originalism reflects uneasiness with the amount of discretion that
such ambiguities confer on the courts. (As Justice Robert H. Jackson
wryly noted in a concurring opinion, "We are not final because we are
infallible, but we are infallible only because we are final."[30] On non-
constitutional interpretations, however, Congress often gets the last
word.[31]) With the Supreme Court deeply divided on interpretive approaches, this judicial finality adds a kind of "meta-ambiguity" to the
system—that is, ambiguity about the terms on which ambiguities will
be (1) identified (judges often disagree about whether a text is indeed
ambiguous), and (2) resolved (judges' opinions often create new ambiguities, sometimes more than they dispel).

A related consequence of legal ambiguity is to breed litigation.
Some plaintiffs hope that a lawsuit will resolve the ambiguity and
thus establish their legal right. Others claim ambiguity in an oppor-

tunistic effort to use litigation to delay compliance, bludgeon opponents into settlement, secure better terms through negotiation, or otherwise improve their bargaining power. But even litigation that might reduce legal ambiguity remains problematic, for reasons discussed below.

DISCRETION

The existence of legal ambiguity is only one reason why officials who apply the law in specific cases—that is, judges and agency personnel—claim discretion, here the discretion to interpret law and, to that extent, to make it. But even if legal texts were crystal clear, discretion would abound. Indeed, policy makers usually design it into the system—and for good reason.[32] To paraphrase Samuel Johnson on a very different subject, discretion is the tribute that law pays to complexity. But even if discretion were not designed into a legal system—indeed, even if lawmakers sought to eliminate it entirely—a residuum would persist. This residual discretion is where law ultimately ends; it is law's most implacable limit.

The most clairvoyant policy makers cannot anticipate all the kinds of cases that inevitably arise under any complex scheme. Even if they could anticipate the general, categorical character of such cases, they could not assess in advance how the contingent facts and features of the disputes that arise under these general categories should be applied to determine the outcome of a specific conflict.[33] Moreover, discretion serves a straightforward functional purpose by enabling policy makers to allocate different tasks to subordinate institutions possessing disparate competencies, analytic processes, and sources of legitimacy. It is a kind of trust by policy makers in the common sense, as well as legal fidelity, of those who will exercise it.[34]

When a law precludes officials from exercising discretion in the administration of a complex adjudicative scheme, it practically guarantees failure: the outcomes of many specific cases dictated by such a law will be unjust and perverse. Public dissatisfaction with the discretion-denying scheme will grow. And the needed discretion—like a strong stream blocked in one direction—will find its way back into the system in indirect, opaque, and policy-distorting ways.

A telling example is the Illegal Immigration Reform and Immigrant Responsibility Act of 1996, whose approach to discretion has in some ways aggravated the knotty policy problem of illegal immigration. There, Congress severely restricted the immigration agency's traditional authority to grant humanitarian relief to the undocumented on a case-by-case basis under generally defined discretionary standards, substituting mandatory detention and removal in almost all cases. This policy has had truly perverse results. More detentions than necessary impose huge human and fiscal costs. Long-resident aliens with no criminal records and strong family and community ties here that would have resulted in discretionary relief before 1996 are being deported to countries they hardly know. The agency is constantly attacked for its reflexive bureaucratic cruelty, often by the Congress that mandated its rigidity. Nor has the discretion vanished; it simply has flowed into more opaque, less accountable channels (e.g., decisions not to arrest in the first place).[35]

In the far more common policy situation where Congress does allow discretion, much of the political debate centers on the delegation's precise terms: who will exercise it, its type and breadth, the procedures that must be followed, and the influence Congress may retain over the delegate's decision, among other issues. Some commentators denounce such delegations as abdications of Congress's constitutional lawmaking responsibilities.[36] They seek to invalidate them by invoking the nondelegation doctrine, according to which the Supreme Court struck down the New Deal's centerpiece, the National Industrial Recovery Act, on the ground that Congress had failed to specify a limiting principle on the president's discretionary authority to implement the law as he saw fit.[37] Although this doctrine has been largely moribund since it was announced in 1935, the Court sometimes uses it to interpret broad grants of authority more narrowly.

This nondelegation doctrine, however, is generally misguided.[38] In fact, Congress's choices about a delegation—about how it distributes implementation power among the other branches, the locus of expertise, the importance of context-specificity to problem-solving, and competing modes of public participation and lawmaking process—constitutes a fundamental policy decision that will in turn strongly influence the agency's particular policy choices. Arguably (depending on its terms), Congress's delegation to an agency represents the most consequential set of policy choices of all. Whether or not Congress gets this choice "right" in any particular delegation, the choice is replete with difficult political, institutional, and functional trade-offs that courts are poorly equipped to second-guess.

My defense of congressional delegations to agencies, however, does not deny the risk of excessively broad delegations. For all discretion's policy-making virtues, it can threaten the most precious rule-of-law values—legitimacy, accuracy, dignity, consistency, predictability, transparency, and democratic accountability—if it is too broad or uncontrolled. An example is prosecutorial discretion to decide whether or not to initiate a criminal proceeding against a person or entity, and if so how to conduct it and what sanctions to seek. This discretion is probably the greatest power than an official can exercise against an individual, and it is often abused by overzealous, politically ambitious officials. This danger is only magnified by the vast expansion of federal criminal law in recent decades,[39] and also by Supreme Court decisions giving prosecutors very broad immunity from civil liability.[40] Analogous forms of prosecutorial discretion exist outside the criminal justice area, although the sanctions for violations are usually less severe. In the myriad federal programs, agency officials are expected, as a practical and sound policy matter, to act against some but not all rule violations. Indeed, they must make choices about whether and how to act in many policy actions other than rule compliance. Agencies' passivity and inaction partly reflects the relative difficulty of legally challenging their nonactions.

The vast field of administrative law prescribes how almost all of this agency discretion is to be controlled without sacrificing the considerable virtues of delegation. (Under the Administrative Procedure Act and other laws, some agency discretion is protected from judicial review). Even the purest, most "lawless" grant of discretion—the president's constitutional power to pardon criminals[41]—is limited by some procedural rules.[42] Although administrative law contains a number of discretion-controlling techniques, each of them is seriously flawed. Thus, judicial review of agency decisions entails the many disadvantages of litigation described earlier and in the next section, while also requiring reviewing courts to make policy judgments (in the guise of legal ones) on technical issues for which they usually are ill-equipped. Agencies can usually control their own discretion by issuing clarifying or narrowing regulations, but seldom want to limit their future freedom of action—which, after all, is a central aspect (and usually a virtue) of their power. Congress can restrict agencies' discretion, but this will deprive them of the flexibility and authority they need to identify and resolve the difficult policy issues that it delegated to them. Congress's oversight, appropriations, and confirmation powers can be potent forms of control over agency policy choices, but also crude, intermittent ones. This pervasive discretion helps to explain why the government responded to the 2008–9 financial crisis through deal making of a kind normally practiced in the private sector, which was conducted by the two federal agencies least constrained by law, the Federal Reserve and Treasury.[43] In the end, the risk that agencies will abuse their discretion and arbitrarily harm members of the public remains formidable and resistant to legal remedies.

PROCEDURAL APPARATUS

It is impossible to think coherently about law without also thinking of the procedures through which law must be created, identified as law, interpreted, elaborated, applied to specific cases, enforced, and revised. This is particularly true of the procedures that surround the decisions of administrative agencies. One cannot begin to assess law's effectiveness as our predominant policy instrument without appreciating the nature and consequences, both positive and negative, of these procedures.

First, some essential background. In some cases, these procedures are constitutionally required by the Due Process Clauses of the Fifth and (for state governments) Fourteenth Amendments. Briefly, a constitutionally defined process is due whenever the government acts in ways that "deprive" one of a "protected interest" in "life, liberty, or property." Each of the quoted phrases is a term of legal art with its own dense history and highly complex jurisprudence. The specific procedures that are constitutionally required in a particular situation—for example, the type and timing of a hearing, the kind of evidence that may or must be used, the nature of the official decision maker, the explanation of reasons for the decision, the scope of judicial review, and so forth—depend on what is known as the *Mathews v. Eldridge* test, named for the Supreme Court decision that defined it.[44] This judicially applied test balances three factors: (1) the importance of the interest at stake; (2) the risk of an erroneous deprivation of that interest because of the procedures used and the probable value of additional procedural safeguards; and (3) the government's interest.[45] In the vast majority of administrative decisions, however, the decision procedures used by the agency are fairly standard, well-established ones that raise no constitutional issues. In designing these procedures, the agency must balance a number of competing values, in much the same spirit as *Mathews v. Eldridge*. These values focus on the various dignitary and accuracy benefits of particular procedures, and on their corresponding costs, especially to the government.

For present purposes, the important point is that the legal procedures that surround public programs constrain their effectiveness in some important ways. Like the other limits of law discussed in this chapter, procedural forms are inherent in public policy making; they go with the substantive content of law and are inseparable from it. Different procedures may be more or less effective in promoting legality, fairness, accuracy, regularity, transparency, accountability, honesty, and other procedural values that vitally affect the design and implementation of public policies. Civil litigation includes a variety of procedural techniques that private lawyers have cultivated to both challenge and shape important public policies.

Private class actions, which are largely unknown outside the United States, illustrate the point. They affect governmental power and policies in fundamental ways. Sometimes functioning alongside conventional administrative regulation, sometimes as an alternative to it, they are driven and shaped by the private incentives of entrepreneurial lawyers and their clients, not by the public values and priorities of politically accountable policy makers.[46] Private class actions may reinforce those public values, as in some securities and antitrust enforcement litigation, or they may undermine them, as in some mass tort cases.[47] Thus, legal scholar Samuel Issacharoff refers to class actions as a form of "regulatory pluralism," showing that they may relate to state power in three distinctive ways: as challenges, as complements, and as rivals.[48]

In the discussion that follows, I shall assume that legal procedures used do in fact promote these rule-of-law values. My purpose, however, is to explain how at the same time these procedures powerfully and inevitably limit policy effectiveness. I briefly consider five of these limits: (1) budgetary costs; (2) delay; (3) opportunistic behavior; (4) lawyers and courts; and (5) effects on program substance.

Budgetary costs. Procedures are invariably costly in terms of the lawyers needed to design and assess their legality, and the personnel needed to staff them. Also, procedural manuals must be written and employees trained in how to use the procedures. These are costs to the government only. The private costs imposed by government programs are massive—many examples are discussed in other chapters—but as we saw in chapter 4, they do not appear on any public budget and thus may be given less attention than is warranted.

Delay. Depending on the procedures, they can entail significant delay—not just from the time required for the procedures themselves but also because of the protracted agency and court litigation that may result. Sometimes the delay is caused by the agency itself, as when the immigration enforcement agency (ICE) misplaces files, requests continuances, and must retrace its steps. In other cases, the delay may be caused by the program beneficiary or target, but although the agency may be able to penalize delay, it may be reluctant to do so if the person lacks resources or is one whom the agency has some duty to help. In any event, delays may compromise the program's integrity, credibility, and effectiveness; they may also produce harmful regulatory inaction.[49] This is certainly the case with the ICE, but it is also true of the courts and many other government programs whose procedures contribute to large case backlogs.

Opportunistic behavior. All costs and delays benefit someone, and those created by law are no exception. Many actors and interests—criminal defendants out on bail, debtors pressed by their private or governmental creditors, undocumented immigrants hoping to stay as long as possible, those benefitting from policies that may be repealed—welcome the sluggishness that legal procedures induce. But this inertia is just the beginning of procedural opportunism. Procedures present endless possibilities for gaming. Parties' abuse of the discovery process in litigation is notorious and itself exceedingly costly. Indeed, the ability of parties to impose such costs on their adversaries—including the government—is a crucial consideration in decisions about whether to initiate, continue, or settle lawsuits and on what terms. Thus, opportunism of this kind can be outcome-determinative quite apart from the substantive merits of parties' claims.

The *New York Times* recently reported a classic example, the much-heralded California Environmental Quality Act of 1970, which environmentalists consider a model for the nation. According to the *Times*, the program has "open[ed] the door to lawsuits—sometimes brought by business competitors or for reasons unrelated to the environment—that regardless of their merit, can delay even green development projects for years or sometimes kill them completely." San Francisco's plan to paint bicycle lanes was delayed for four years by a lawsuit claiming that the lanes could cause pollution.[50] Federal environmental laws provoke similar "greenmail" litigation.

Lawyers and courts. If the substance of public policy is the province of politicians, economists, policy analysts, and interest groups, *process* is the playground of lawyers. Formally trained in the law of due process, and of civil, criminal, and administrative procedure, they specialize in the analysis, both legal and functional, of different procedural systems.[51] For present purposes, the important point is that the procedures that the law invariably attaches to government programs—either because they are constitutionally required or because no orderly program can function without them—are a focus of interest to lawyers whose zealous representation of private clients involves holding agencies to procedural standards that will serve their clients' interests.

Significantly, a lawyer ordinarily can challenge the adequacy of an agency's procedures or its compliance with those procedures more easily and successfully than she can attack its policies and decisions on substantive grounds. This incentivizes lawyers to demand from agencies more process, or more punctilious compliance with existing process, largely without regard either to the cost of increased process or to its effect on overall program performance. This is also true—but much less so—of private law rules that operate under the precedent-respecting principle of *stare decisis*. Implicit or explicit in these demands is the threat of litigation. This is the client-protecting lawyers' job, and they perform it well. But the process does produce excesses, distortions, rigidities, and other social costs.[52]

Effects on program substance. Policy makers and program officials fear litigation. With some reason, they anticipate that the intrusion of courts into their domain will attract adverse publicity, alter officials' incentives, consume scarce bureaucratic and beneficiary resources, require additional procedures or other programmatic changes, and reduce the officials' policy and operational autonomy. Indeed, federal judges in certain notorious cases—especially those involving prisons, school and housing integration, and other programs whose operation can raise constitutional issues—may even issue "structural injunctions," empowering the plaintiffs' lawyers and courts to monitor and supervise the programs, sometimes to a remarkably detailed extent.[53] Officials facing these threats to their autonomy are tempted to head them off by making programmatic changes along the way. In some cases, they may even welcome the litigation, hoping that the court will order the program to do what might otherwise be politically infeasible, such as spending more money to raise program standards. Officials may institute these judicially prodded programmatic changes, moreover, even if the lawsuit ultimately fails.

Officials wishing to minimize litigation risk will operate their programs accordingly. They are more likely to reject innovations that might be challenged,[54] substitute broad discretion for clear rules, make concessions to "squeaky wheels," add more elaborate processes, alter internal information flows in order to stymie whistleblowers, increase the ratio of lawyers to program staff, and restrain the disciplining of disgruntled or incompetent employees. Such responses to litigation risk, whatever their bureaucratic or political advantages, are bound to affect programs' effectiveness. There is much to the claim that many complex projects that drove our progress in the not-so-distant past, such as the Hoover Dam and other infrastructure, could not be undertaken today due to the costs and delays created by strategic litigation—or the threat of it.

INERTIA

I explained in chapter 6 (in the section titled "Inflexibility") that once public law is on the books, it is very difficult to amend or repeal. (This is less true of common law rules where a more flexible principle of *stare decisis* operates.) Obviously, this inertia can be overcome—after all, statutes are sometimes repealed and policies changed—but a law's staying power, absent some sunset provision, is striking. This inertial force reflects at least two factors. First, it is built into the constitutional system discussed in chapter 3, with its numerous veto points, separation of powers, and other obstacles to assembling an effective majority coalition. Second, legal inertia reflects the value accorded to vested interests and to the settled expectations that develop around them. Entitlement reform is said to be the "third rail" of American politics, making it extremely difficult to modify pensions, health care benefits, and other features of the status quo. For present purposes, the striking point is that this inertia persists pretty much regardless of the law's substantive content, and like the other limits of law discussed in this chapter, it applies to all public policies.

CROWDING-OUT EFFECTS

Law's relationship to social norms is a complex and little-understood one. Law may sponsor an existing or new norm and may manage to transfer to the norm some of the law's own prestige and power. This "halo effect," of course, can cut both ways; advocates for same-sex marriage want law's legitimating sanction, whereas it is precisely this legitimation that opponents fear.

But there are darker, more paradoxical possibilities than halos. Law's embrace may cast a shadow over norms; indeed, it may kill them with its kindnesses. Its adoption or encouragement of a norm can actually discourage the desired act by altering the social meanings that people convey when they comply with or violate it.[55] When law compels an act—charity or patriotism, for example—observers cannot readily distinguish spontaneous, voluntary behavior from an obligatory performance of the act, thus blurring what the act signals to others. Even when law merely rewards an act—subsidizing organ donations, for example—it may change the values that people ascribe to the act and thus alter their behavioral responses to it. Law may in effect cut off the norm's oxygen supply, smothering the authenticity and autonomy of will that vitalized the norm, thereby endangering precisely what the law hoped to promote. The late William Stuntz, a criminal law professor, noted a similar paradox: when a community perceives enforcement as unfair or overzealous, criminals suffer less social stigma, in effect lowering the price of their crimes.[56] The fact that the state has adopted a norm may actually encourage some people to defy and violate it, especially if it is only weakly enforced, as with laws against teenage smoking or drinking.[57] Finally, law—however well-intended—can weaken or divide local communities in which "bonding" and "bridging" social capital are crucial to their effective functioning.[58]

CHAPTER 10

The Bureaucracy

Every public policy is run through a bureaucracy. In America, bureaucracy is often used as an epithet, evoking ubiquitous red tape, rigidity, soullessness, waste, unreasonableness, impenetrability, and Kafkaesque cruelty and arbitrariness. Other than systematic scholars of the subject like Max Weber,[1] James Q. Wilson,[2] and Donald Kettl,[3] few have a kind word to say about it. Nevertheless, bureaucracy—the exercise of legal authority by a large, complex, more or less permanent body of officials required to act according to rules, procedures, precedents, institutional and documented memory, hierarchical accountability, and a culture of legality—is a necessary (though insufficient) feature of a contemporary liberal democracy and the rule of law.*

Chapters 1 and 2 explained my reasons for focusing on policy failures,† but there is an additional reason to do so here. The federal bureaucracy is not simply a neutral organizational instrument for carrying out public policies whose effectiveness is determined elsewhere. Far from being epiphenomenal, it independently shapes those policies by virtue of its own structural, endemic features. Some of these features (limited technical competence and mediocre education) may contribute to policy failures, while others (procedural regu-

---

*Even the least rule-bound, most discretionary decisions made by a federal official—presidential pardons—are processed by a bureaucracy (here, the Office of the Pardon Attorney in the Department of Justice). See, generally, Rachel E. Barkow, "Prosecutorial Administration: Prosecutor Bias and the Department of Justice," *University of Virginia Law Review* 99 (2013): 271–342.

†The exceptions are the successes to be discussed in chapter 11.

larity and public spiritedness) can promote success. Before proceeding, some description of the bureaucracy is in order.

THE BUREAUCRACY: BASIC FACTS

Federal civilian employment—approximately two million workers—has remained fairly constant in size for more than fifty years,* and constitutes an ever-smaller share of the population.[4] (At the same time, federal contractors and consultants have mushroomed, along with state and local government employment.) From 1970 to 2010, almost all civilian executive branch agencies reduced their workforces. The major exception was the Department of Justice, which is largely explained by the Bureau of Prisons, whose staff grew by 90 percent between 1990 and 2009 (even as its prisoner population increased by 355 percent). About 85 percent of federal employees work outside the Washington, D.C., metropolitan area.[5]

The bureaucracy's power, however, is best measured not by the number of employees but by its discretionary authority—that is, the ability to choose courses of action and to make policies not spelled out in advance by laws. By this test, the power of the federal bureaucracy has grown enormously, particularly through congressional delegations of authority in three areas: (1) subsidies to particular groups and organizations; (2) conditional fiscal transfers to state and local governments; and (3) regulation of various sectors of society and the economy. As political scientists James Q. Wilson and John DiIulio put it, "appointed officials can decide, within rather broad limits, who shall own a television station, what safety features automobiles shall have, what kinds of scientific research shall be specially encouraged, what drugs shall appear on the market, which dissident groups shall be investigated, what fumes an industrial smokestack may emit, which

---

*This total does not include the U.S. Postal Service, an independent agency within the executive branch, with 546,000 employees in 2012, the third largest civilian employer in the nation after the federal government and Walmart. Nor does it include the roughly thirteen million people who work indirectly for the federal government as employees of private firms and state or local agencies that are largely, if not entirely, supported by federal funds. Nearly three persons earn their living indirectly from the federal government for every one earning it directly.

corporate mergers shall be allowed, what use shall be made of national forests, and what prices crop and dairy farmers shall receive for their products."[6]

The federal bureaucracy consists of three groups of federal employees—the competitive service, the Senior Executive Service (SES), and the excepted service—and a fourth group consisting of federal contractors, which are private for-profit or nonprofit organizations that federal agencies pay to perform specified tasks.

The competitive service. Many officials are appointed only after they have passed a written examination administered by the Office of Personnel Management (OPM) or met certain selection criteria (such as training, education, or experience) devised by the hiring agency and approved by the OPM. When competitive candidates can be ranked, the agency must usually appoint one of the three top-ranking candidates. In recent years, the competitive service has become decentralized so that each agency now hires its own people without an OPM referral, and examinations have become less common for three reasons: dissatisfaction with the cumbersome OPM system; agencies' need for more professionals who could not be ranked on the basis of a standard exam; and affirmative action. Agencies can also hire on a "name-request" basis in which they inform OPM that they want to hire a particular person.

The Senior Executive Service. In 1978, Congress created the SES, about eight thousand top federal managers who would perform an integrating function between short-term political appointees and the career service. They could (in theory) be hired, fired, and transferred more easily than ordinary civil servants—although anyone removed from the SES was guaranteed a job elsewhere in the government. SES members would be paid more and be eligible for substantial cash bonuses if they performed their duties well. The disappointing experience with the SES reform is discussed later in this chapter.

The excepted service. Almost half of federal employees are not hired by OPM but instead by agencies that have their own selection procedures. About 3 percent of the excepted employees are appointed on grounds other than, or in addition to, merit in order to allow the president to select people for policy making and politically sensitive posts who agree with his policy views. These include (1) presidential appointments authorized by statute, many of which require Senate confirmation; (2) "Schedule C" appointments to jobs having a "confidential or policy-determining character" below the level of cabinet or subcabinet posts; and (3) "noncareer executive assignments" given to high-ranking members of the regular competitive service or to persons brought into the civil service at these high levels, who are deeply involved in the advocacy of presidential programs or participate in policy making. These three groups of excepted appointees constitute the patronage available to the president and his administration. The number of political appointees in the executive branch has increased dramatically over time, reaching more than three thousand, of which one thousand are agency heads (and ambassadors). They enable a new president to reach deep inside every corner of the government and put loyalists in charge. His campaign uses these positions to reward key supporters and to dump others.[7]

When president John F. Kennedy took office in 1961, he had 451 political jobs to fill. When president Barack Obama took office in 2009, he had more than four times that number, including nearly four times the number of top cabinet posts. (In the nineteenth century, practically every federal job was a patronage job. For example, when Grover Cleveland, a Democrat, became president in 1885, he replaced some 40,000 Republican postal employees with Democrats.) A president can often "blanket in" patronage appointees already holding office, making it difficult or impossible for the next administration to fire them.

THE DISTINCTIVELY PROBLEMATIC NATURE OF THE FEDERAL BUREAUCRACY

In titling this section, I describe the federal bureaucracy not merely as problematic, but as *distinctively* so. By this, I mean to make a comparative claim that the rest of the chapter will support: although all bureaucracies in liberal democratic states raise fundamental questions of public support and functional effectiveness, these questions are raised more acutely in the United States. Here our federal bureaucracy arouses not ambivalence but actual hostility and anxiety that are deeply rooted in American individualism and in other elements of our political institutions and culture (see chapters 3 and 4) and have no real counterpart in other modern democratic states. Private-sector bureaucracies, especially in large corporations, may exhibit some of these same problems,[8] but there the opportunities for reform, and the penalties for failure to do so, are far greater than in the public sector.

Paul Light's recent book, *A Government Ill-Executed*,* warns that even optimally designed policies would be undermined or distorted by a poorly functioning bureaucracy. His message is crystal clear and profoundly dismaying: the federal career service is in serious crisis, experiencing a long-term decline in quality, accountability, vision, energy, and professional commitment.[9] Drawing on Light's data and other sources, this chapter will analyze the main causes of these conditions. I organize the analysis around the following ten themes: (1) congressional influence over administration; (2) legalism; (3) leadership; (4) layering; (5) compensation, status, performance, and morale; (6) discipline; (7) senior executive service; (8) lower-level compliance; (9) contracting out; and (10) isolation.

Congressional influence over administration. Virtually all advanced liberal democracies in the world are organized as Westminster-type systems in which the executive and legislative branches are under the unified control of the party that has won a majority of seats in the legislature (parliament). Among other things, this means that little if any separation of powers exists between the legislative and executive branches; together, they constitute the "government" under the leadership of the prime minister, who is also the leader of the controlling party (or coalition) in parliament.

The American system could hardly be more different, and the consequences of this difference are far-reaching. Here, there is a radi-

---

*The phrase is from Alexander Hamilton, perhaps our most fervent strong-government advocate.

cal separation—constitutionally, politically, and practically—between the powers of the president and the administrative agencies under his authority, on the one hand, and those of Congress on the other. This separation is true, albeit to a lesser extent, even when the president's party also controls both houses of Congress.

For present purposes, this radical separation is of foundational importance. As the late Nelson Polsby observed, "the American Congress has no close counterpart anywhere in the world in the autonomous power that it exercises as a collective entity."[10] Most important, Congress has the constitutional power, numerous levers of policy influence, and political incentives to compete fiercely and incessantly with the president to shape the administration and its policies, and Congress often wins this struggle.[11] A leading scholar of bureaucracy, Donald Kettl, explains,

> Through the legislative process, Congress controls the structure of federal agencies. It sets the budgets under which they operate, as well as the size of their staffs . . . despite the president's common title of "chief executive," the bureaucracy is far more the creature of Congress. . . . Congress and, especially, congressional committees, frame much of the political reality of bureaucracy. . . . Not only does the fragmented nature of Congress create administrative fragmentation, but so, too, does the array of interest groups . . . these issue networks tend to fragment bureaucratic power. There is really no such thing as "the bureaucracy." . . . For political forces seeking to influence administrative action, however, the fragmentation [among congressional subcommittees] is a blessing. It creates multiple points of access to the administrative system. . . .[12]

The importance of this pervasive congressional influence can scarcely be exaggerated, as it affects each and every federal policy. Indeed, the vast growth in recent decades of congressional staff, along with its technical and professional credentials and policy-specific institutions, has increasingly shifted the balance of power in the competition with the White House for control of the bureaucracy in favor of Congress. Bureaucrats, recognizing the extent of congressional power over almost every aspect of their work and careers, often are at least as responsive to congressional pressures as they are to their agency and White House superiors.[13]

This analysis has so far treated the president and "his" bureaucracy as a monolith, albeit one subject to pervasive congressional penetration. But this interbranch competition is affected by a second struggle for policy influence—one among (1) the president, represented by the White House staff; (2) the agencies that comprise the executive office of the president (especially the Office of Management and Budget (OMB), the Council of Economic Advisors, and the director of national intelligence); and (3) the rest of the executive branch, including those departments and agencies that are legally under the president's direct control. (The president's influence over the "independent" regulatory agencies, located within the executive branch for some but not other purposes, is more limited and indirect.) These executive branch agencies, strongly influenced by Congress and by outside groups with access both to key congressional committees and to the White House, often pursue their own interests, resisting and sometimes even subverting the president's policy agenda.[14] The free-for-all, then, is both between the two branches and within them. This scrum contributes significantly to the incoherence of policy design and implementation and thus to its ineffectiveness.

Legalism. One consequence of the competition for influence is greater use of formal legal rules—both procedural and substantive—to govern decisions by administrative officials that would otherwise be discretionary. As the sociologist Max Weber discussed, this tendency toward legal formalism is characteristic of all bureaucracies, public or private, and is often viewed as vindicating, if not constitutive of, the rule of law. I and most other students of the modern administrative state find this view extreme. Law can and in most cases should guide, structure, and constrain discretion, but in complex legal and policy systems like ours, discretion is both inevitable—an observation emphasized by legal realists for more than a century—and generally desirable if exercised within legal parameters. This point was discussed in chapter 8.

The crucial questions, then, are: What is the optimal type and extent of discretion that lawmakers should delegate to the bureaucracy? And how is that discretion best controlled in the interests of rule-of-law values? There are no simple answers to these questions, of course; the answers depend on the particular circumstances, which is why the Supreme Court long ago essentially abandoned the nondelegation doctrine in favor of other techniques for regulating discretion (see chapter 3).

The uncertain, back-and-forth struggle between and within the Congress and the executive branch over control of agency decisions often takes the form of detailed rules and procedures, sometimes referred to as "hyperlexis" (discussed in chapter 8). Another competitor for control of administration, albeit more intermittently, is the federal court system; since the late 1960s, the courts have exercised ever more demanding review of agency decisions, both procedural and substantive (discussed in chapter 3). These inter- and intrabranch struggles seem to have much more to do with competing institutions' efforts to infuse agency decisions with their distinct values than with any systematic efforts to improve agency effectiveness. Depending on one's perspective, the outcomes of these struggles either render agencies more accountable to elected officials or hamstring them in ways that undermine effective policy making and implementation. The resulting forms of bureaucratic legalism engender much of the "red tape" that so often turns citizens against the government. Although citizens tend to direct their fury at the bureaucracy, it is the legislative and judicial lawmakers who ultimately are most responsible for the red tape.[15]

Some legalistic rules and procedures are imposed by the agencies themselves for a variety of reasons: protecting officials against criticism ("it's not me, it's the rule"); making their work easier by using a rule-driven checklist approach ("I have no choice; this requirement is on the mandated list"); or implementing perceived legislative policy ("Congress wanted it this way"). But as political scientists Eugene Bardach and Robert Kagan show in their study of federal health and safety inspectors, "going by the book" has many disadvantages both for program effectiveness and for the inspectors themselves.[16]

Leadership. The quality of leadership of the federal bureaucracy—the political appointees—is compromised in two important ways: selection and tenure. Light's data indicts the very process by which presidential appointees to executive branch agencies are vetted. This process applies even to officials who are many layers below the top and do not require Senate confirmation. It is not merely sluggish,* centralized, and bureaucratic; it is also a minefield for aspirants to public service, one that treats candidates as "innocent until nominated." President Barack Obama's remarkably quick start in nominating his cabinet and key subcabinet subordinates made the subsequent withdrawals of several of them in the first month after his inauguration all the more humbling. As Light noted at the time, "They were really fast in the first 100 meters . . . but this is a 10,000-meter process, and they've slowed down quite dramatically. I would have bet you the farm they'd break the recent record, but now they're on pace to become the slowest."[17] This delay might be acceptable if the process produced higher-quality officials, but Light, after considering various indices of quality, finds that the opposite is true.[18] The state of the federal service, he concludes, has been declining since the years of president Jimmy Carter, when presidents and other top officials began to attack the bureaucracies that they led. Agency effectiveness is also undermined by leadership vacuums caused by protracted vacancies at the top. In the crucial Department of Homeland Security, for example, over 40 percent of its senior leadership positions were either vacant or had an "acting" placeholder when the president finally nominated a new secretary in October 2013. The notorious underenforcement of the federal gun laws by the Bureau of Alcohol, Tobacco, Firearms, and Explosives (see chapter 5) is partly due to the absence of a Senate-confirmed director for *six years*, reflecting the success of the National Rifle Association's agency-weakening efforts;[19] and when

---

*The process took about two months to get president John F. Kennedy's appointees confirmed by the Senate, and more than nine months for president George W. Bush's. See Paul C. Light, *A Government Ill-Executed: The Decline of the Federal Service and How to Reverse It* (2008), 87–88.

confirmation finally did occur, it only managed to sneak by through extraordinary proceedings and a last-minute changed vote.[20] The director of the Consumer Finance Protection Board was not confirmed for two years, creating enormous uncertainty about its policies.[21] In the more than five years since the Federal Home Finance Agency was created to oversee Fannie Mae, Freddie Mac, and the Federal Home Loan Banks, the Senate has failed to confirm a director despite the pivotal role that these agencies had in the housing and banking crises. Much the same is true of the president's controversial recess appointments. Indeed, their legal validity is now in question and may not be resolved for years.[22] And given the massive fraud, waste, abuse, and ineffectiveness in federal programs (see chapter 6), the president's failure, despite senators' urging, to fill inspector general (IG) vacancies for as many as five years in some of the largest cabinet departments, agencies accounting for almost a quarter of the federal budget, is crippling their vital watchdog functions. (Because many *acting* IGs will return to their old positions in the agency when an IG is named, their statutory independence may be compromised.[23])

Hugh Heclo, a leading scholar of the federal bureaucracy, noted in his aptly titled book *A Government of Strangers* that political appointees cannot guide their career subordinates effectively if they are too transient. To lead effectively, they must remain on the job long enough "not only to learn about the substance of programs and how to operate in the Washington networks but also to use what has been learned. Policy priorities are not immune to change, but they are most likely to respond to leaders who are around long enough to build support, to institutionalize changes in the bureaucracy, and to string together the narrow margins available at any one time to a strand of policy development."[24] Other political scientists agree, noting that appointees' competence and credibility as leaders necessitates enough continuity in office.[25]

The data on appointees' tenure is not reassuring on this point. A study of presidential appointees from 1989 to 2009—including full-time civilian, Senate-confirmed appointees to all departments, single-headed independent agencies, and organizations within the Executive

Office of the President—found an overall median tenure of only 2.5 years; one quarter of them served more than 3.6 years while another quarter served for less than eighteen months. Cabinet-level officials had a median tenure of 3.3 years, a year longer than lower-level appointees (2.3 years).[26] Another study of these appointees, but including multiheaded agencies and going back to 1977, finds slightly longer tenures.[27]

Layering. Comparatively speaking, the federal bureaucracy is notable for the sheer number of political appointees who penetrate deeper into the bureaucracy. This contrasts sharply with many parliamentary governments in which only the very top officials' positions change hands with a new government. In Denmark, for example, there is only a single political appointee—the minister—above the career service. In the United Kingdom, career civil servants operate just below the ministers.[28]

Heclo's 1977 book noted the problematic "thickening" of the leadership cadre in federal agencies due to new layers of political appointees on top of the core of civil servants. Writing three decades later, Light shows that this layering has only increased. He finds "more layers of leaders and more leaders per layer" among both political appointees and the senior career service. Between 1961 and 2009, the number of layers or ranks by title in the average cabinet-level agency jumped from seven to eighteen.[29] This development, Light says, largely reflects two factors that together increase pressures for promotion: the rapid aging of the federal workforce as baby boomer employees unleash what one study calls a "retirement tsunami,"* and the desire to circumvent frequent congressional pay freezes. Even the supposedly management-oriented George W. Bush administration presided over "a significant expansion in both the height and width of the federal hierarchy well beyond best practices anywhere else, most notably in the business sector." This growth and widening has occurred despite the new orthodoxy of hierarchical flattening and decentralized authority in the corporate and nonprofit sectors, and

*Reflecting the exceptional growth in federal employment in the 1960s and 1970s, an estimated 60 percent of its white-collar workforce and 90 percent of the Senior Executive Service will be eligible to retire by 2016. Light, *A Government Ill-Executed*, 135.

the lip service given to this orthodoxy in the "reinventing govern-ment" movement that swept the public sector in the 1990s.[30]

The extent of this layering is suggested by the titles that are open for occupancy by senior (and not so senior) officials, titles that Gilbert and Sullivan would have parodied. Dear reader, I'll bet that you did not know that there are now many federal officials who are denomi-nated "deputy deputy assistant secretary," "associate deputy assistant secretary," "deputy associate deputy administrator," and "chief of staff to the associate deputy assistant secretary," and that this thickening has occurred in almost every department. As Light notes, "Once estab-lished somewhere in government, titles spread like kudzu as depart-ments and agencies copy each other at will"—what Senator Daniel Patrick Moynihan called "the iron law of emulation."[31] "Bluntly put," Light writes, "you are nobody in Washington, D.C., if you do not have a chief of staff."[32]

This layering would merely be amusing fodder for Jon Stewart, talk radio hosts, and other bureaucracy bashers were its public policy consequences not so grave. Citing the examples of NASA's *Challenger* and *Columbia* tragedies and the FBI's failure to heed its low-level agents' warnings about specific terrorist threats before 9/11, Light at-tributes these calamities to bureaucratic thickening and implies that these are only the failures that come to public attention, surely just the tip of the iceberg.[33] He finds that in those categories of frontline fed-eral positions providing the most important public services (e.g., air traffic controllers and IRS agents), employees in 1996—almost twenty years ago—reported upward through *sixteen* layers; on policy and budget questions, "the average federal employee received guidance through nearly *sixty* layers of decision makers."[34] One expert on politi-cal leadership notes considerable tension between top civil servants and political appointees, as they seek to convince each other to adopt their different perspectives on policy making. Leaders' openness to technical expertise, he finds, declines as the layering between them and their career subordinates increases, citing the inability of C. Ever-ett Koop, the Surgeon General under President Reagan, to get through to him on smoking and public health policy issues.[35] Layering may explain why the chief digital architect of the Obamacare website was unaware of a subordinate's report on serious security risks.[36]

Reorganization can actually magnify this thickening. Light finds that splitting an existing department "can produce a hierarchy greater than the sum of its former parts."[37] Even in the administration of president Bill Clinton, which reduced overall federal employment significantly (largely through the post–Cold War peace dividend), the middle levels of government grew relative to the lower levels, which impedes a fair allocation of accountability for failure and credit for success.[38] It also increases the career service's sense of isolation from the important developments in their agencies.

Compensation, status, performance, and morale. A lively debate rages over how well federal bureaucrats are compensated compared with their private-sector counterparts, with much disagreement over which private counterparts are appropriate for comparison, which levels of the bureaucracy are being compared, which aspects of employment should be included, and what effect unmeasured variables—say, motivation and creativity—have on the comparison.

The evidence sheds some light on these questions. Federal employees have greater job security and more valuable benefits than comparable private-sector workers—guaranteed defined-benefit pensions (very rare in the private sector today), retiree health coverage, and other fringes.[39] Except at the top levels, they are paid more than they would earn in private-sector jobs requiring comparable skills. Census data on workers who switch between federal and private-sector jobs indicate that those moving from federal to private incur an average salary reduction of 3 percent, while those who move the other way receive a salary increase averaging 9 percent.[40] Moreover, an analysis of annual time use data compiled by the Bureau of Labor Statistics indicates that full-time federal workers work 2.7 fewer hours in a typical workweek than their private-sector counterparts do—the equivalent of 3.8 fewer forty-hour workweeks per year.[41] The analysis, however, produces a different result when high-level public and private employees are compared. With a far more compressed pay scale in the public sector, top federal managers are paid significantly less than their private-sector counterparts can earn, particularly in today's talent-seeking market.[42] In large part, this compression at the high end results from constraints imposed by Congress, which fears political blowback if it raises its own members' salaries; as Kennedy School of Government professor Jack Donahue notes, "Just as no building in Washington, D.C. can be taller than the Capitol dome, so too (by law or by custom) a congressperson's salary sets the ceiling for all but a handful of federal jobs."[43] Finally, a recent comparison of compensation (including benefits) of federal employees with their central government counterparts in other OECD countries finds that U.S. officials are paid significantly more both in absolute terms and as a share of average compensation in the respective countries. (As with comparisons to private sector counterparts, this pattern does not hold at the very top levels due to compression.[44])

Light assesses the status of the civil service by asking, "Do the *right* young Americans want a federal job?" His answer—based on his surveys of college seniors, alumni of the nation's top public-service graduate schools, and presidential management fellows who entered the federal government through its most prestigious recruitment program—is no: "The federal service comes in last in almost every indicator, from the motivation to make a difference to organizational resources."[45] College seniors preferred nonprofit organizations as an instrument for their public service career goals. Public-service graduates who took jobs in the federal government were harshly critical of the sector, appeared far less willing to stay, and were least likely to say that they wanted their children to pursue a career in public service. Kennedy School masters of public policy students preferred nonprofit and business careers; in 2005, only a quarter started in the federal government. The presidential management fellows—in Light's words, "the very best and brightest the federal government can recruit"—were deeply dissatisfied with their experience: "Although some indicators improved over time, almost every indicator of job satisfaction—quality of work, access to resources, respect for their peers, and trust in their own organization—fell over the two years of their fellowships."[46]

How well do civil servants perform their jobs? The short answer is that we don't know and are unlikely to find out. The government and others have periodically attempted to establish performance measurement regimes, but these regimes have failed, usually for reasons specific to the government's structure. Given the diverse bureaucratic tasks within the government, standard performance metrics are difficult to devise and apply. Moreover, the assessments that these regimes produce generally have no bite—not because of the agencies' recalcitrance but because political factors obscure the measurements and dilute their usefulness. Political scientist Beryl Radin, for example, notes that the budget process is driven by political factors whose force would utterly dominate efforts to use employee performance assessments as incentives. These factors are far less significant in the private sector, where conducting and using such assessments is easier because of the profitability criterion, which has no real counterpart in government. Indeed, such assessments are also easier in parliamentary democracies where only the executive wields effective power over the bureaucracy and where some sanctions for poor performance—"name and shame," for example—are more effective because government agencies have better reputations in the first place. In contrast, the public and politicians constantly disparage the federal bureaucracy; a bad report card from the OMB is less likely to count for much.[47]

As the earlier discussion of federal workers' attitudes toward their jobs suggests, morale in civil service is very low. Light's survey data on civil servants' attitudes toward their work indicates that although they were satisfied with most objective aspects of their jobs, including benefits and job security (but not pay), they were far less satisfied than their business and nonprofit counterparts with their opportunities to develop new skills and to accomplish something worthwhile, and with public respect for their work. Their morale is lower than that of their private nonprofit counterparts. None of the resources needed to perform their jobs well are sufficiently available. Especially at the middle and lower levels, where most of the work of government gets done, they criticize the competence of their own colleagues and rate their organizations unfavorably in terms of spending money wisely, helping people, acting fairly, and being worthy of trust. No wonder, then, that they say they work for the government for the pay, benefits, and security rather than out of a sense of public spirit; that for Americans entering the job market, federal services "come in last in almost every indicator, from the motivation to make a difference to organization resources" well behind private nonprofit organizations; and that this chorus of criticism by these most knowledgeable people has increased over the years.[48]

Disciplining incompetent workers. No organization can function effectively unless it can terminate incompetent or misbehaving employees. Yet it is almost impossible to fire, demote, or suspend civil service employees. It occurs only when a superior is prepared to invest a great deal of time and effort in the attempt to persuade the Merit Systems Protection Board to terminate the employee. It can take one to two years to fire a federal employee,[49] which helps to explain why the federal government fired only 0.55 percent of its workers in 2010—11,668 of its 2.1 million employees; in comparison, the private sector fires about 3 percent of workers annually for poor performance.[50] Civil servants, as a practical matter, have lifetime tenure. As noted above, this problem of indiscipline has applied to the SES as well.

Light reports that when he surveyed federal employees on how good their organizations are at disciplining poor performers, only 9 percent answered "very good," while 67 percent answered "not too good" or "not good at all." This is one reason for low morale in civil service.[51] The ineffectiveness of employee disciplinary procedures may grow even more frustrating under the Whistle Blower Protection Act of 1989, which will make managers even more reluctant to discipline their workers for fear that this will trigger lawsuits claiming retaliation against workers for reporting their superiors' misconduct.

Senior Executive Service. As noted earlier, the SES was established to create an elite corps of bureaucratic leaders—roughly comparable to the highly trained graduates of special schools of public administration traditionally staffing the top levels of the French government—whose expertise, compensation, accountability, and performance would be equivalent to comparable executives in the private sector and well above their civil service subordinates.

Unfortunately, the SES has not worked out nearly as well as expected. A 2002 National Academy of Public Administration report found that while private-sector compensation increased substantially, that of the SES did not keep pace; the vast majority of workers were bunched at or near the statutory pay ceiling. Indeed, SES officials at one agency earned less than junior analysts employed by the agency's private contractor; the disparity, of course, has only increased since then. Virtually no SES officials lost their positions due to poor performance, job dissatisfaction was widespread, and 75 percent of them believed that the experiment had not achieved its goals.[52] To Donahue (writing in 2008), "[t]here would be more grounds for optimism here if the SES experiment had fallen short because of obvious errors in design or implementation. But the initiative has probably turned out about as well as could have been expected, given a maelstrom of political, economic, and managerial forces that can frustrate even well-intentioned and carefully crafted campaigns."[53]

Securing bureaucratic compliance. James Q. Wilson emphasized that the effectiveness of policy design and implementation depends critically on an agency's ability to secure policy compliance by its lower-level officials. It is especially difficult, Wilson noted, for agencies to cultivate a sense of purpose, status, or solidarity that could induce them to carry out the agency's mission. Management's ability to accomplish this most basic of bureaucratic tasks, he explained, depends on whether the agency is, in his terms, a production, procedural, craft, or coping organization. In production organizations (his examples are the IRS* and Social Security), managers can observe both the work and its results and thus evaluate workers on the basis of their effectiveness. In procedural organizations (examples: inspectors in the Occupational Safety and Health Administration and in the military), processes can be observed but outcomes cannot, so higher-level officials must manage on the basis of process rather than out-

---

*This example now seems quaint in light of the revelations in 2013 about a rogue IRS unit's targeting of conservative nonprofit groups for discriminatory treatment.

come. In craft organizations (examples: the Forest Service, Army Corps of Engineers, and Justice Department, where workers adhere to professional norms), managers can evaluate and reward operators on the basis of the results they achieve even if the former do not know how the latter are achieving them. In coping organizations (examples: academic and police agencies), neither outputs nor results are observable. There managers and operators will be in constant conflict; the former will focus their efforts on the latter's most easily measured activities, and effective management is almost impossible.[54] These four categories are not airtight, of course, but they can help us predict how particular agencies are likely to perform.

Contracting out. One of the most distinctive aspects of the federal bureaucracy is its extensive but opaque relationship with the private sector. Light points out that the government uses contracts, grants, and unfunded mandates to state and local governments not simply to deliver needed goods and services more effectively but also to make itself seem smaller than it actually is. A longstanding freeze on the number of federal employees (dating to 1951) has driven the growth of the "hidden government"; from 1990 to 2005 alone, Light estimates that as many as 2.5 million contracting jobs were created, while the civil service *shrank* by approximately 400,000. This has resulted in a prodigious number of such jobs: contract and grant-based employment by 2005 was, according to Light's calculations, approximately 7,634,000 and 2,892,000, respectively, out of an estimated 13,165,000 people "employed" by the government (excluding military personnel). Such a workforce allows government to present itself as much smaller than it really is. Indeed, the above numerical estimates rest solely on Light's speculation because the government does not keep—nor, it has been argued, would it even be able to keep—an exact count of the number of contractors and grantees it employs. This happens for two reasons: first, contractors themselves do not keep employee counts, Light argues, "in part because doing so would allow the federal government . . . to estimate actual labor costs and profit"; second, state and local agencies "make no effort whatsoever to quantify the number of hours their employees spend administering federal mandates."[55]

Whether the tactical use of "hidden government," "government by proxy," and legal limits on agency staffing fools congressional and other critics of "bloated bureaucracy" is doubtful. Yet many profess to be shocked—*shocked!*—at the revelation in 2013 that core spying and data-mining functions of the National Security Agency are performed by private contractors. *Half a million of them have top-secret security clearances*, yet NSA control of them appears to be dangerously loose.[56] Government-wide, no one seems to know how much of this outsourcing occurs, how much of it would be optimal in different agencies, how much discretion should be permitted given the risk of political favoritism in contracting, or many other aspects of how these practices work.[57] As we have seen, the federal bureaucracy is highly differentiated and serves many political masters—Congress, the president, the public, its own workers, and powerful outside interest groups that lobby for contracts, as in the aerospace industry—each with different incentives to support outsourcing, and at different levels.

What seems clear, however, is that the vast amount of contracting reduces accountability and transparency, and raises serious questions about agencies' ability to manage these contracts effectively and measure contractors' performance.[58] As contracting has become the fastest growing component of federal discretionary spending, these questions have taken on ever-greater urgency. In his 2008 book, Light noted that agency procurement offices are often too small to effectively oversee megacontracts that can involve thousands of subcontractors. "Contract management," he observed, "has been a recurring item on the GAO 'high risk' list of roughly two dozen troubled federal programs and systems for the better part of two decades. GAO put Defense, Energy, and NASA contract management on its very first high-risk list in 1990, and has yet to remove them. . . . With contracts now running more than $500 billion a year and grants approaching the $100 billion mark, lack of accountability for results is particularly troubling."[59] By all accounts, Obamacare's website contractors were egregiously mismanaged.

Isolation. Writing of the public sector generally, but in terms that certainly apply to the federal service, Donahue describes the "segregation" that has occurred between the ethos and environment of public- and private-sector work in the last few decades. (He might have added that federal employees' defined-benefit pensions afford them a measure of retirement security that most private sector workers can only envy.) In the private economy, "[p]eople endowed with native wit, education, ambition, and luck discovered ever-wider opportunities and ever-richer rewards." But "by the early years of the twenty-first century the economic distances separating Americans were wider than they had been in living memory. Employment became a game with higher and higher stakes, and Americans learned to play the game hard. . . ."

> This didn't happen in government. Today's public sector mostly missed the transformation that swept over the rest of the working world. Government jobs, for good and for ill, tend to operate under the rules that defined the middle-class economy in the decades following World War II. Risk is dampened. So is opportunity. Rewards at the top are not all that different from those below. Nearly all workers, from janitors to governors, earn middle-class salaries. Unions thrive.* Change is gradual. Layoffs are rare. Promotions come slow. The role of money—as a motive and as a symbol—is circumscribed.[60]

Despite generations of blue-ribbon commissions and other reports urgently calling for much the same kinds of fundamental reforms of our civil service, it is increasingly a backwater.[61] The consequences of this increasingly demoralized, poorly equipped, marginalized, publicly scorned, and (literally) undisciplined workforce for government performance are deeply dismaying. These employees are, after all, the shock troops, the implementers, the ultimate instruments of our public policies. If they are not up to the job, then neither is our government. Alexander Hamilton, who ardently desired a strong, effective government, had no doubt on this score: "A feeble execution is but another phrase for a bad execution; and a government ill-executed, whatever it may be in theory, must be, in practice, a bad government."[62]

---

*The federal government, the least unionized part of the public sector, is still more unionized than the most-unionized private industry (utilities). John Donahue, *The Warping of American Government Work* (2008), 77.

CHAPTER 11

Policy Successes

The preceding chapters have focused on policy failures, for three main reasons. First, there are so many significant failures. Taken individually, and especially in the aggregate, they exact a heavy toll on social welfare—under any plausible definition of that concept. Although some readers may view my criteria of success (see chapter 2) as too demanding, the criteria are really quite minimal. The very least that citizens can reasonably demand of a program is that it be socially beneficial on net, be cost-effective, meet its stated performance and cost goals, serve those who need it most, and use the most appropriate policy tools available. Second, and most obvious, failed policies are the ones that most need to be reformed or abandoned and that can therefore benefit most from the book's diagnoses (part 2) and remedies (chapter 12). Third, triumphalist accounts of our system, sometimes referred to as American exceptionalism,[1] are always in need of tempering. We do well to remember that our history is replete with failures.*

But successes there have been, and they are worth revisiting here so that we might learn from them about why and to what extent they improved American society, and what light they can shed on today's policy making. Although these programs are almost universally seen

---

*For example, a leading proponent of American exceptionalism, the historian Bernard Bailyn, notes that the early colonists' experiences "were not mainly of triumph but of confusion, failure, violence, and the loss of civility. . . ." Bernard Bailyn, *The Barbarous Years: The Peopling of British North America: The Conflict of Civilizations, 1600–1675* (2012), xv.

as successes in retrospect, we shall see that the historical evidence tends to be more mixed, revealing some significant flaws that were criticized at the time or are apparent in retrospect.[2] For example, as noted below, while the Second Morrill Act wisely extended the land-grant system to more states, it also institutionalized segregated and inferior institutions for blacks, and the immense success of the Voting Rights Act is marred by its facilitation of perverse racial gerrymandering. More relevant to the book's larger inquiry, some of these flaws roughly correspond to reasons for the endemic policy failures analyzed in earlier chapters.

After reviewing some historical successes, I shall devote the bulk of this chapter to contemporary ones, focusing on nine of them: (1) Title II of the Social Security Act (old age and survivors insurance); (2) the interstate highway system; (3) the food stamp program (now known as the Supplemental Nutrition Assistance Program); (4) the Voting Rights Act of 1965; (5) the Immigration Act of 1965; (6) the Earned Income Tax Credit of 1975; (7) the Airline Deregulation Act of 1978; (8) the Welfare Reform Act of 1996; and (9) the National Institutes of Health. Like earlier successes, these programs exhibit some important flaws, which are easier to identify (and in some cases, to quantify and perhaps rectify) than in the historical cases because we now have far better data, analytic techniques, and monitoring for policy assessment purposes. Some of these flaws are more readily rectified than others, but they serve to remind us of a fundamental point stressed in chapter 2: the term *policy success* is always a qualified, relative one; it is a matter of degree. The same is true for many *policy failures*, of course, although some of them—the War on Drugs, the ethanol program, and many policies directed at Native Americans, for example—appear to be unmitigated disasters (except to the narrow interests that benefit from them).

Finally, I am by no means suggesting that the policy successes discussed in this chapter are the only ones out there. Far from it. The National Institute of Standards and Technology facilitates commerce. Our national park system is peerless. Federal support for AIDS research has led to great advances in curative techniques.* Despite occasional public health fiascos like the swine flu inoculation program,[3] the government can claim many important public health successes—for example, campaigns against lead poisoning, auto accidents, smoking,† and, most recently, the human papillomavirus.[4] The Centers for Disease Control and Prevention have gained great scientific credibility.[5]

Some other policies are widely thought to have been successful, yet their governmental provenance is disputed—for example, the Internet.[6] Also, the government's actual causal contributions to the improved social conditions may be questionable. The Civil Rights Act of 1964 is perhaps the most important example. The decline of discrimination on the basis of race, religion, gender, and sexual orientation in almost all areas of American life is stunning, albeit still incomplete.[7] Yet the complexity of social forces and the limits of law generally (see chapter 8) make it hard to know just how much the 1964 act produced this progress. Economist Thomas Sowell notes that the trajectory of black progress was the same before and after the act.[8] Some of the conditions that prompted its enactment were pushing independently in the same direction.[9] The act (against the expressed intent of its main sponsor, Hubert Humphrey) has spawned affirmative action, whose net benefits to equal opportunity are doubtful.[10] Economists June and Dave O'Neill recently reached a similar conclusion: that the civil rights laws—except for racial minorities in the South directly following the 1964 act—had little to do with the vastly improved job opportunities, wages, and working conditions for women and minorities, which overwhelmingly reflected other factors such as their greater education and skills.[11] The same is true of the large presence

---

Prevention of AIDS, as distinguished from cure or delay, presents a different problem. Success depends on changing individual behaviors in the face of moral hazard created by the availability of a cure. See Tomas J. Philipson & Richard A. Posner, *Private Choices and Public Health: The AIDS Epidemic in an Economic Perspective* (1993).

†Actually, it was a *private-sector* initiative—a series of widely read *Readers Digest* articles starting in 1952—that first highlighted smoking risks. And *private* litigation forced the industry to run health warnings three years before Congress banned tobacco ads on regulated media. Robert L. Rabin, "Reexamining the Pathways to Reduction in Tobacco-Related Disease," *Theoretical Inquiries in Law* 15 (forthcoming, 2014).

of women in the pharmacy industry.[12] While antidiscrimination laws surely played *some* positive role, they seem to have been but one factor among many. In contrast, the causal efficacy of the Voting Rights Act of 1965, discussed below, is incontrovertible.

I do not count Medicare as a policy success despite its immense popularity and the universal access to vital health care for seniors that it affords. First, many national commissions have found for decades that because it reflects the large inefficiencies of the underlying health care system that it finances, Medicare is very cost-ineffective compared with plausible alternatives. Second, the most important policy implementers are three quarters of a million private providers whose strong professional commitments conflict with governmental priorities,[13] and who need not accept Medicare patients at all and are increasingly refusing to do so.[14] Third, and related, it made almost $48 billion in improper payments in 2010,[15] far more than any other public program (and even more since then; see chapter 6). Fourth, based on current projections and current law on benefits and revenues, it is fiscally unsustainable due to implacable demographic trends and health care cost increases that are on track to render the Medicare Trust Fund for hospital care (Part A) insolvent by 2026.[16] Fixing the health care system that Medicare finances will be much harder than fixing Social Security (a successful program discussed below); the necessary reforms will be far more painful, which of course is why our politicians assiduously avoid promoting them. Some compromise must eventually be reached, but one can only guess at what its contours might be.

Dramatic crime reduction is an indubitable government success,[17] but I do not include it here because it is localities, not the federal government, that are mainly responsible for criminal law enforcement—as they are for community college systems, land use policies, and many public health gains. And because the book does not cover defense, national security, and foreign policy, I do not discuss successful policies instituted by the military,* including the all-volunteer force and the integration of racial minorities and women.[18]

---

*Consider James Q. Wilson's observation, "One can stand of the deck of an aircraft carrier during night flight operations and watch two thousand nineteen-year-old boys faultlessly

THE HOMESTEAD ACT OF 1862

The history of American land policy is a rich and complex one that goes back to the terms of the original colonial settlements and continues today in constant struggles between economic and environmental interests, and among all levels of government. One of the most important decisions at the Philadelphia Convention was to give Congress the responsibility for owning, managing, and disposing of public lands, as well as relations with the Indian tribes that occupied much of the territory that Americans were eager to settle. One reason for this decision was that land claims were at the heart of many international disputes and diplomatic relations. This momentous allocation of power simply shifted to the halls of Congress an unending series of legal, political, and policy disputes between the federal government and the states, especially the newly formed "public lands" states which, unlike the original thirteen, were denied title to the lands within their borders that Congress had not granted to them. These disputes ranged, among other things, over how best to encourage settlement and exploitation of the western and southern reaches of the continent, on what terms, for which purposes, and for whose benefit. The stakes in these political struggles were especially high because the federal government looked to the proceeds from the sale of public lands, along with tariff revenues and postal fees, to pay for the burgeoning country's national debt and growing infrastructure (canals, railroads, post roads, and other "internal improvements"), as well as to reward military veterans and promote schools and other social institutions. At the same time, the states exerted immense pressures to release the lands under easy terms.

According to Paul W. Gates, the leading historian of our public land policy, fundamental disagreements about its purposes and methods have divided American political leaders throughout our history. That said, "the most fateful and basic decision was the one made at the outset and allowed to stand until the end of the nineteenth cen-

---

operate one of the most complex organizational systems ever created." James Q. Wilson, *Bureaucracy: What Government Agencies Do and How They Do It* (1989), 371.

tury: that the lands should be disposed of rather than retained in public ownership. . . . [A]lmost at once, the new government began to give away significant quantities of land and thus undercut its own sales. . . . [T]hrough the year 1828, one finds that almost half the conveyances represented donations."[19] In addition to emphasizing the transfer of lands into private hands for private development, early policies instituted a title system tied to actual surveys and verification ("a victory of order over anarchy") and sales through auctions in order to minimize sweetheart contracts and avoid the need for the government to set prices itself. The government put so much land on the market, however, that prices seldom rose much above the legislated minimum price and much of the land remained unsold, or if sold was neither settled nor developed; instead, it was occupied by squatters, exploited by trespassers, and held by large and small speculators. Lax enforcement and widespread use of false affidavits emasculated reforms authorizing squatters to obtain preemptive title through cash purchases at low prices if they could prove that they had occupied and improved the land through their efforts. Despite (or perhaps because of) several economic crises in more settled areas, Congress adopted new policies in order to accelerate the privatization of public lands. These policies included sliding scale pricing, large-scale donations to veterans and others if they would occupy the land, donations to new and future states for a variety of purposes, and grants to railroads. Nevertheless, underdevelopment continued, partly because the government-suppressed prices attracted so many speculators and partly because of endemic corruption, mismanagement, fraud, and nonenforcement in these programs.[20]

In the 1840s, reformers dissatisfied with this state of affairs began to mobilize in favor of free land for homesteaders. This movement, abetted by reformers like Horace Greeley, mustered a number of arguments for free land, including the safety valve that it would create for poor farmers and impoverished workers in the east, antipathy to land speculators and monopolists, the insignificance of federal land revenues, and opposition to slavery. The new Republican Party endorsed the idea, and Congress in 1860 enacted a watered-down version of a free land program that protected speculators, state land sale revenues, and Southern interests. Even so, president James Buchanan vetoed it, exacerbating the sectional divide and contributing to Abraham Lincoln's election later that year. The Republican victory assured enactment, and the Homestead Act of 1862 went into effect at the beginning of 1863.

The act looms large in the public imagination about how America's continental "manifest destiny" was achieved. Our national identity and popular culture build upon stirring memories and images of courageous, entrepreneurial pioneers striking out with their families for the wilderness with little but their horse-drawn Conestoga wagons, hunting and farming implements, homespun clothes, and dreams of a better life. Frontier homesteading on free land, the stuff of Hollywood Westerns and family lore, was the quintessential exercise of, and metaphor for, freedom—a critical "safety valve" for American democracy, according to the influential Western historian Frederick Jackson Turner.[21] Interestingly, policy makers were so eager to draw new settlers into their expansionist vision that the act promoted homesteading by noncitizen European immigrants as well. In this respect, Aziz Rana argues, the lawmakers' key distinction was between residents they considered settlers (Americans and Europeans) and nonsettlers (e.g., blacks, Chinese, Mexicans), not between citizens and aliens.[22] This distinction also rationalized the brutal campaigns against Native Americans.

The act, according to Gates, culminated "a series of moves intended to end the policy of using the public lands as a source of revenue for the government."[23] It entitled any person who was the head of a family or twenty-one years of age, and who was a citizen or who had filed a declaration to become one, to homestead by entering 160 acres of land held at $1.25 per acre or eighty acres held at $2.50 per acre. The act also allowed for "preemption"—the right of squatters who had worked the land to acquire title free or at a very low price. Gates's exhaustive analysis of the twists and turns of land policy during the rest of the century defies summary, and it is probably impossible to separate the act's significance from the effects of the large number of other laws that together constituted the nation's land policy in the nineteenth century.

Gates found that the act succeeded in some important respects and failed in others, contrasting his view with that of other historians who stress its failures.[24] First, "many blunders were made in legislating for the administration and disposal of the public lands, [including] poorly drafted legislation, the mediocre and sometimes corrupt land officials, the constant effort of settlers, moneyed speculators and great land companies to engross land for the unearned increment that might extract from it." Second, Congress was aware of the history of abuse of the public land laws by speculators and others, and sought to prevent their repetition by requiring that the land be settled and cultivated and that title go only to actual residents, but the law's safeguards were relatively weak, allowing such abuses to continue. Third, the effort to promote homesteading was constrained by other policy goals. Indeed,

> Anxious landseekers moving westward after 1862 may well have wondered whether the Homestead Act was the boon it was supposed to be. The 125 million acres of railroad lands, the 140 million acres of state lands, and the 175 million acres of Indian lands were all closed to homesteading. So also were the millions of acres held at high prices by speculators who had bought in the fifties. In every public place advertisements called attention to privately owned land whose advantages were said to surpass those of lands open to homestead.[25]

Despite these shortcomings, and maladministration of the act, Gates found the federal land system

> to have worked surprisingly well, if we may judge by the results. Outside the cotton-growing South where the plantation system prevailed before 1860 and tenancy and sharecropping subsequently, suitable public land was being acquired by small owner operators and tenancy was less common. Disregarding the southern states, a total of 1,738,176 farms had been created in the public land states by 1880 and only in four states . . . did the farms average over 160 acres. Of these farms, [80 percent of the total] were owner operated. This is good evidence that the railroad grants, the land given to endow the states, and even the speculative purchases were being divided into single family farms.[26]

What can this brief account of the Homestead Act—which Gates called "one of the most important laws which have been enacted in the history of this country"[27]—teach us about policy effectiveness, either in that particular case or more generally? One answer is, not very much. More than 150 years after enactment, over a century after open land homesteading ended, and lacking the kind of program-specific data and policy assessment tools that are often available to today's analysts, no clear judgments about effectiveness are possible. The rapid settlement of the West, moreover, was "overdetermined"; many factors besides the act caused it.

Still, two points about the act's putative success can illuminate contemporary policy-making challenges, the first by analogy and the second by comparison. First, the act's implementation was by all accounts (including Gates's) seriously flawed. Some of those flaws may have been peculiar to a time when the bureaucratic apparatus was relatively limited, immature, and highly corrupt.[28] But other flaws continue to apply to today's policy making: skewed official incentives, poorly informed predictions, legal ambiguity, market dynamics, ease of evasion, and weak enforcement. Second, the act's purpose was highly attractive: to give a resource (land) to a sympathetic target group (homesteaders) for a socially desirable purpose (cultivating empty land), on an administratively objective basis (essentially first come, first served), and with no opportunity cost (at that time, unoccupied land had no better use). No contemporary policy can boast anything remotely like these remarkable, success-promoting features.*

THE MORRILL ACT OF 1862

In a largely agricultural, decentralized society that also esteemed education highly, the notion of establishing institutions of advanced education and research in agricultural science was attractive. In the 1850s,

---

*A contemporary analogue might be the Federal Communications Commission's power to free up the valuable airwave spectrum that it controls and allocates, although the spectrum is limited for technical reasons and competition for it is intense. Se Edward Wyatt, "U.S. Pushes Agencies to Free Up Spectrum," *New York Times*, June 15, 2013.

proposals were advanced in Congress to make federal land grants to states for the purpose of creating such institutions. Members were divided over the amount of these land grants and how they should be distributed among the states, with Senator Justin Morrill of Vermont proposing that the land be allocated to states according to the size of their congressional delegations. When Congress enacted his proposal in 1859, President James Buchanan vetoed it on federalist grounds. In 1861, with a new president waging a new war against secessionist states, Morrill sponsored a new bill—this time requiring that the land-grant colleges teach military tactics in addition to agricultural science and engineering—which was enacted the next year. It was among the earliest federal programs using grants to encourage states to implement federal policies.[29] Each of the remaining states received a land grant of thirty thousand acres for each of its members of Congress. The land, or the proceeds from its sale, must be used for a college "without excluding other scientific and classical studies, and including military tactics, to teach such branches of learning as are related to agriculture and the mechanic arts . . . in order to promote the liberal and practical education of the industrial classes in the several pursuits and professions in life." The act excluded states in rebellion but later extended the grants to them as well as to states that subsequently entered the Union and to territories. Where the federal government did not own enough land in a particular state to fulfill the grant terms, it gave that state scrip with which it could acquire and then sell federal land in other states, using the proceeds to purchase land for the college within its own borders. (Cornell University, my alma mater, cleverly used scrip to acquire valuable timberland in Wisconsin, which when sold generated disproportionate proceeds [relative to the statutory formula] for its beautiful campus in upstate New York.) In the end, 17,400,000 acres were granted under the act.

In 1890, Congress enacted the Second Morrill Act, which extended the grants (now in the form of cash, not land) to the former Confederate states but required that they either adopt race-blind admissions or establish a "separate but equal" institution for persons of color. These states did the latter, creating what came to be called "black land-grant colleges." These colleges were never treated equally; under the dual systems established by the states, they suffered deplorable discrimination for many decades. Only after a quarter century of civil rights litigation did the Supreme Court finally order them to dismantle the dual systems and establish a unitary one.[30] Tragically, the states often complied in ways that ostensibly conferred formal equality on the black colleges but in fact jeopardized their ability to continue their remarkable successes in educating minority students under very unequal conditions and in helping to build a black middle class.

SOCIAL SECURITY

Popular, well-intentioned programs may be ineffective (e.g., Head Start), and unpopular programs may be effective (e.g., certain taxes). Social Security Old Age, Survivors, and Disability Insurance has been both popular *and* effective since its inception in 1935. (The disability insurance portion of Social Security, in which states play an adjudicatory role, is much more troubled, as discussed in chapter 5.) Indeed, it is the single most popular federal program. Paying cash benefits to those who have reached retirement age or suffered the death of a spouse, Social Security provides an essential financial safety net beneath private savings. It has largely eliminated poverty among the elderly.[31] While it has grown steadily since its inception, both its administrative costs and its error rate are very low.[32]

From the administrative and political points of view, the program enjoys immense advantages that few other programs possess. The program sends checks each month to a vast number of people, most of whom depend on them to pay for life's necessities. Henry Aaron, a Brookings Institution economist and a leading expert on the program, notes, "Of families 65 or over, 64 percent received half or more of their income, and 22 percent received all of it, from Social Security in 2008."[33] Because these payments are calculated under a long-standing statutory formula, the agency need not exercise much discretion, case-by-case adjudication, or law enforcement, so its administrative costs are low. Most important, the payments are financed by dedicated, automatically deducted payroll taxes and a substantial transfer of wealth from current workers to retirees, who are (collectively speaking) their own parents.

Until now, these transfers have been a very good deal for retirees, who received significantly more money than they paid in as workers, and have received it over a longer life expectancy than they likely anticipated. The use of a "trust fund" label, which is factually and psychologically misleading, imbues present and future beneficiaries with an illusory sense of immunity from claims by politicians wishing to use the funds for other purposes—an illusion that these same politicians take pains to maintain. The transfers have not been too onerous to workers in the past because of workforce, wage, and productivity growth, coupled with a healthy dependency ratio (i.e., of workers, including young immigrants, to retirees). Accordingly, political support for the program has been extraordinarily strong, particularly among present and future beneficiaries, who vote at much higher rates than the relatively young workers who pay into the system. Social Security's special advantages have driven its singular policy and political success in the past.

Whether policy makers have squandered some of those advantages—and thus reduced the prospects for its continued success—is a question of the greatest urgency and importance. Consider what has changed in recent years. Rightly or wrongly, younger Americans, unlike their parents, no longer have confidence that the program will be there for them at the same benefit levels when they reach retirement age—or that it will continue to be a good deal for them. The economic and demographic conditions that have up until now sustained generous Social Security benefits, and hence the program's popularity, no longer exist and are unlikely to return. Unless politicians can agree on the steps needed to shore up its financing given these new realities, past success will become future failure. Fortunately, the variables that policy makers can tweak—tax rate, taxable wage base, retirement age, inflation index, means testing of benefits, the phasing in of changes, and others—are fairly straightforward and (if adopted soon) need not be too onerous or threaten the universality that was instrumental in the program's original enactment and contributes to its popularity today. (The flip side of this universality, of course, is its target inefficiency.) For example, Aaron finds, "Gradually raising the fraction of earnings subject to tax from the current 84 percent of earnings to the historical target of 90 percent of earnings, boosting the payroll-tax rate from 6.2 to 7 percent, and taxing currently exempt cash compensation would fully close Social Security's projected long-term financing gap."[34]

THE GI BILL

Even seven decades after its enactment, perhaps no federal program is praised more, and more extravagantly, than the GI Bill. One historian of the Bill wrote, "I cannot overstate the value and meaning of the GI Bill. Its sweep was so vast, its impact so particular, that only one conclusion seems self-evident: The bill made a reality of Jefferson's concept of creating independent yeomen."[35] Be that as it may, the GI Bill's path to enactment—unanimous votes in the House, Senate, and conference committee—reflected an exotic combination of political forces led by the American Legion, the Hearst newspapers, and some very conservative Southern congressmen in opposition to the administration of president Franklin D. Roosevelt, which proposed a much more modest package. The legislative process was also complicated by the Bill's omnibus form, which was most unusual at that time and crossed the jurisdictional lines of so many different committees.[36]

To returning veterans without a dishonorable discharge who had served for at least ninety days, it extended many different types of social benefits: approximately 80 percent of the age cohort in question; low-interest guaranteed loans for homes, farms, or businesses; financial assistance to pursue more education or training; and weekly unemployment benefits for up to one year. World War II veterans constituted 80 percent of the generation in question. Just over half of them, far more than expected, used the education and training benefits, which continued for a maximum of four years, depending on the length of service, and covered all tuition and fees as well as subsistence payments to the veteran and dependents. By 1947, they accounted for 49 percent of students enrolled in American colleges. More than twice as many, a total of 5.6 million, used the benefits for vocational or business schools, apprenticeships, on-the-job training, and on-the-farm training.[37] It is noteworthy that benefits for veterans of subsequent wars have not been as generous as the Bill.[38]

Suzanne Mettler, the leading scholar on the GI Bill's social effects, makes a point about it that applies, mutatis mutandis, to so many other programs assumed to be effective. She notes that

> despite the G.I. Bill's popular reputation as a highly effective program, we know surprisingly little about even its first-order effects, meaning the scope of its coverage and the depth of its socioeconomic impact. To be sure, the bill's higher education provisions in particular have been lauded, cited as the source of vast social change on the presumption that they expanded access to advanced education for over two million Americans. But evidence for such claims has been surprisingly rare. [Studies of its effects on educational attainment] are limited in their ability to explain the determinants of program usage, leaving it unclear whether the provisions were genuinely accessible only to the average veteran. They also tend to overlook entirely the effectiveness of the subcollege programs. . . . And inquiry into the G.I. Bill's impact on subsequent participation in civil and political life . . . has been practically nonexistent. . . . [W]e know little about the actual effects of this program on the individuals who benefited from it.[39]

Several scholars have disparaged the program's fairness and effect on inequality. Ira Katznelson, for example, characterizes the GI Bill as an affirmative action program for white males, while Lizabeth Cohen emphasizes its ratification of the discriminatory and inegalitarian status quo.[40] In contrast, Mettler's review of the empirical data (her own and others) considers the GI Bill as a creature of its time, asks whether it improved these unjust conditions, and concludes that it did. She and other students of the program acknowledge that it did not dislodge the entrenched racial and gender inequalities of the day—including racially segregated and gender-discriminating educational institutions, housing markets, and mortgage loan practices[41]—but they argue that the Bill helped to pave the way for future progress in these areas, especially with respect to the education and training benefits. Thus, Mettler finds that 20 percent of the veterans who attended college under the Bill reported that they would probably or definitely not have done so without its benefits, that 77 percent who used its vocational training benefits would not have done so absent the program, and that it reduced class and religious minority barriers to higher education. Although nonwhites were much less likely to be veterans, higher proportions of them than whites took advantage of the Bill's education and training benefits.[42] Women used them less not only because a relatively small number were veterans, but also because social mores made them less likely to work outside the home. Mettler also finds social benefits in terms of civil participation. Even controlling for veterans' socioeconomic backgrounds and education levels, those who used the Bill belonged to 50 percent more civic organizations and participated in 30 percent more political activities and organizations than the nonrecipients.[43]

The GI Bill's success, then, reflects a number of factors: its unanimous support in Congress, the feelings of admiration and indebtedness that Americans felt toward veterans of "the greatest generation," the popular conviction that World War II was, at least by its final victory, the "good war," and its focus on enhancing human capital. Finally, the program's substructure was an example of Wilson's "majoritarian politics" (chapter 5)—large, broad, diffuse groups of both beneficiaries (veterans) and cost-bearers (taxpayers)—that is a recipe for political support and sustainability.

THE INTERSTATE HIGHWAY SYSTEM

The Interstate Highway System occupies a special place in the American consciousness. In the words of Earl Swift, the interstate highways "are intrinsic to our everyday life, to the modern American experience, to what defines the physical United States. They form the nation's commercial and cultural grid, binding its regions, bridging its dialects, snaking into every state and major city in the Lower Forty-eight. They've insinuated themselves into our slang, our perception of time and space, our mental maps."[44]

Such grandiose language matches the system's physical scale, which runs for more than 46,000 miles, making it one of largest public works projects in world history. In 2011, vehicles traveled 2.9 million miles on it. This engineering feat was costly: between 1958 and 1991, federal and state governments spent almost $129 billion to construct the system; 89 percent of this came from the federal government.[45]

This enormous expenditure of federal funds was the culmination of a long political sequence, stretching back, by some accounts, to Thomas Jefferson's 1806 plans for a National Road through the Cumberland Gap. While popular, the National Road remained the only substantial federal highway throughout the nineteenth century. However, the appearance of first the bicycle in the late 1860s and then the automobile in the late 1890s led to a demand for better roads, known as the Good Roads Movement.[46] This, combined with New Deal fervor for federal expansion, resulted in the Federal Highway Act of 1938, which created a Bureau of Public Roads to test the feasibility of a toll-financed national network of highways. In 1956, the administration of president Dwight D. Eisenhower pushed through the Federal-Aid Highway Act of 1956, which provided for an interstate system of 41,000 miles and a Highway Trust Fund to finance it through gasoline and other automobile taxes on a pay-as-you-go basis, without technically adding to the national debt.[47]

Studies suggest that the system's economic benefits have far outweighed its costs, by a factor of six to one. It has made long-distance travel faster, easier, and safer for millions of drivers, saved an estimated 187,000 lives, and prevented twelve million injuries.[48] It helped to underwrite our rapid economic growth, expanding markets for businesses, giving consumers access to previously unavailable products, facilitating national supply chains, and otherwise enabling companies to reduce costs and improve productive efficiency.[49]

Still, its costs cannot be ignored—and appear to be growing. Obtrusive highways now crisscross the nation, marring once beautiful and untouched sceneries. Small roadside towns and businesses disappeared as expressways passed them by. The automobile contributed to urban sprawl and helped to undermine many urban centers. Urban expressway construction displaced many low-income residents, contributing to the socioeconomic segregation of many late-twentieth-century cities.[50] The system, moreover, has fallen into disrepair; as much as $92 billion in annual spending is needed to maintain the highways, yet the vast increase in registered vehicles—from 74 million in 1960 to almost 250 million today—necessitates modernization and expansion.[51] At the same time, the Highway Trust Fund is approaching insolvency.[52]

Much has changed, and the system must change with it. Funding construction through gasoline taxes, an example of a "majoritarian politics" paradigm (chapter 5), created a large, diffuse group of beneficiaries (drivers) who internalized the costs of constructing and maintaining the system. But as cars have grown more fuel efficient, drivers no longer internalize the full cost of supporting the highways, so other revenues will be needed. Contemporary environmental concerns, alternative means of transportation, and the information technology revolution raise the issue of whether our transportation and economic needs can be met in other, less costly ways. Even the defense justifications for the system have lost some force over time, with less need to truck masses of troops and machinery across the continent. The system may also have led to underinvestment in alternative forms of transport, especially rail, whose efficiency may be greater for some services.[53] Still, the immense fixed investment already in the system, increasing population and drivership, and the political support for physical infrastructure spending probably assure its continued success.

THE FOOD STAMP PROGRAM

After a number of small, temporary pilot programs dating back to the 1930s, Congress adopted the food stamp program on a permanent basis in 1964, and vastly expanded it ever since. Now known as the

Supplemental Nutrition Assistance Program (SNAP), it is the federal government's most important income supplement for most low-income Americans, while also helping them to gain a nutritionally adequate diet. (Politically, it has been the quid pro quo for urban liberals' support for farm subsidies—what Charles Lane calls a Faustian bargain;[54] in 2013, the House's version of the farm bill broke that link for the first time in forty years by excluding food stamps.[55]) The monthly benefits averaged $133 per person in 2012, with the federal government paying all benefit costs while splitting the program's administrative costs with the states, which operate it. Along with unemployment insurance, SNAP is our leading countercyclical entitlement program. Americans will not countenance children and poor people going hungry, especially during economic downturns. SNAP has been a robust response to these concerns. In addition, SNAP is well targeted by some measures. Of the almost forty-eight million participants at the end of 2012, roughly 45 percent are children, nearly 75 percent are in families with children, and more than 25 percent are in households with seniors or people with disabilities. The Center for Budget and Policy Priorities, a leading advocate for the program, notes that 92 percent of the expenditures go to the eligible households, with the rest going to defray the federal share of administrative costs. Benefits can be quickly distributed to sudden disaster victims, and the benefit formula includes a substantial work incentive.[56] In these important senses, food stamps are a policy success.

SNAP's cost, however, has exploded, reaching almost $75 billion in 2012 and putting 15 percent of Americans on the program, a far greater share than in 2009. In the process, its targeting seems to have grown more diffuse. Thus, even though the Great Recession officially ended in 2009 and unemployment dropped substantially from its 10 percent peak in October 2009 to 7.7 percent in February 2013, SNAP continued to expand. It exploded from 28.2 million users in 2008 to almost 48 million at the end of 2012, the same period in which other major entitlement programs either leveled off or declined—and the Congressional Budget Office predicts that further drops in unemployment will only slightly reduce SNAP enrollment. Increases in poverty—from 37.3 million people in 2007 to 48.5 million in 2011—explain only about half of SNAP's growth. The rest seems to reflect eased federal standards, and more aggressive enrollment campaigns and laxer enforcement by the states, which bear none of the costs—an institutional form of the moral hazard discussed in chapter 5, in addition to whatever individual moral hazard is created by the easier eligibility policies at a time when job opportunities are once again expanding.[57] Congress will have to consider these issues along with reforms to other entitlement programs.

THE VOTING RIGHTS ACT OF 1965

Richard Pildes, a leading public law and voting rights scholar, has rightly called the Voting Rights Act of 1965 (VRA) "a sacred symbol of American democracy [and] the most effective civil rights statute enacted in the United States."[58] In the name of political equality and fundamental justice, the VRA succeeded in vastly expanding black and other minority registration and voting. It did so primarily by prohibiting literacy tests and numerous other devices that had been used to reduce minority voting, and by sending federal observers and registrars into Southern states to aid in enforcing the new law. The express purpose of the VRA—to equalize access to the ballot box—was achieved almost immediately. By 1972, the white and black registration and voting rates had converged in all of the states covered by the act. Georgia's registration gap, for example, had almost completely closed by 1972, going from 35.2 percent to 2.8 percent. Today, Mississippi has the third highest ratio of black-to-white voter turnout; Massachusetts has the lowest.[59]

This change, which likely exceeded even the most optimistic expectations in the tumultuous civil rights era when it was enacted, has had sweeping structural effects on American politics, even going beyond the two-term presidency of Barack Obama. Electoral politics in the South became competitive for the first time since Reconstruction, with two-party competition and minority voters increasingly constituting a swing-voting bloc. The system of congressional leadership also changed, with the South losing its previous dominance. The federal courts, spurred by litigation under the VRA, became much bolder in intervening in and regulating electoral structures and thus outcomes. The two-party system became more ideologically coherent, as the Democrats moved to the left with the Republicans, gaining a large number of conservative, previously Democratic voters in the Southern states, moving to the right.[60] In all of these ways, the VRA stands as one of the most consequential laws in American history, with most of its consequences being unquestionably desirable.

A second remarkable achievement of the VRA is a dramatic increase in minority office holding at all levels of government—not just in the White House. The number of black elected officials has grown from 500 in 1965 to 1,469 in 1970 to more than 10,500 in 2011.[61] At the city and county levels, these numbers increased from 715 in 1970 to close to 5,000 in 2000. Latinos, Asian Americans, and other minorities have similarly experienced large increases in elected officials at all levels.[62]

Unlike the unalloyed success of the VRA in increasing minority voting, however, the techniques used to swell minority office holding have in the process distorted or violated other cherished political and social values. Congress had assumed that once the VRA secured minorities' right to vote and have their vote counted, and increased the number of minorities actually voting, many minorities would run for office and many of those would be elected. But many state and local electoral structures—particularly at-large elections—made it hard for them to gain election because the white majority still constituted a majority in those at-large units. Litigation quickly challenged these at-large arrangements as "minority vote dilution," arguing that the VRA protected not only minorities' right to cast a vote and have it counted but also to have it be *effective* in the sense that the vote would have an equal chance to elect representatives of the voter's choosing—who were defined, under a theory of "descriptive representation," as candidates of the same race and ethnicity as the voter. This conception of effectiveness could only be satisfied through a system of single-member districts representing groups of voters who were racially/

ethnically defined and geographically concentrated enough to assure election. The Supreme Court upheld this vote dilution theory in 1969,[63] leading to decades of such federal court challenges to state and local laws that designed electoral maps for elections to state and local legislatures and to the U.S. House of Representatives.

These challenges largely succeeded in convincing the federal courts to require three elements: (1) single-member districts; (2) single-member districts drawn in ways that would assure election of a minority candidate; and (3) a statewide districting map that maximized the number of minorities elected to the legislature as a whole. In effect, elements 2 and 3 encouraged and sometimes required legislatures (and the lower courts) to racially gerrymander the entire statewide districting plan to assure the desired result. Given the opportunity, and perhaps obligation, to gerrymander the plan, and given blacks' overwhelmingly and predictably liberal Democratic voting, legislators used both racial and partisan criteria to design the districting map, usually in the interests of incumbents.

The methodology just discussed has heightened rather than dispelled the significance of race in the minds and actions of officials and ordinary citizens. The Supreme Court, like the general public in its attitudes toward other forms of affirmative action, is sharply divided about whether or not this legitimation of racial consciousness is socially desirable—about whether (stated oversimply) we should view it as merely a serviceable but temporary tactic needed to transcend the tragic legacy of slavery and racism, or whether it is instead aggravating racial divisions, thus making that halcyon day ever more distant.[64] This racially inflected regulation of districting and electoral practices is magnifying zero-sum conflicts *among* black, Hispanic, and Asian groups (although Asians are still too few to claim many districts under the VRA's group-oriented criteria). These conflicts are almost certain to intensify in the future, as their relative populations and political aspirations change.[65]

This race-conscious districting has lent itself to narrow partisan opportunism and manipulation, only thinly concealed by legislators under the banners of VRA compliance and racial justice. Indeed, the

Department of Justice's own inspector general recently criticized its voting rights unit for partisan conduct in VRA enforcement, with conservative career lawyers harassed by their colleagues.[66] And in a perverse twist that in politics is no irony, scholars find that partisan legislatures often use VRA-constrained redistricting to *reduce* minority influence overall. This happens because the district mappers, aided by easy computer manipulation, typically distribute minority voters among districts through techniques that "pack, crack, and stack" them in districts for maximum partisan and incumbent advantage, consistent with VRA constraints.[67]

Another problem with the VRA today is the rigid and anachronistic application of its Section 5, which requires the Department of Justice (DOJ) to preclear even trivial election law changes in those states that the fifty-year-old statutory formula designated for supervision. Today, those states generally have robust intra- and interparty competition, and their minorities now have significant political power to protect their interests.[68] Clearly, times have changed dramatically for the better. As noted above, Mississippi now has the highest ratio of black to white voter turnout in the nation, and Massachusetts the lowest. Politicians are unlikely to rectify this anachronism, but the Supreme Court did so in June 2013 in the *Shelby County* case when it struck down the original coverage formula as unconstitutionally out of date.[69] Even before this decision, a small but growing number of jurisdictions were availing themselves of Section 5's "bailout" provision, which freed them from the onerous preclearance regime. Pildes argues persuasively that even apart from the formula, the VRA's voting rights protection model is ill-suited to today's challenges. The contemporary problem, he argues, has less to do with discrimination than with "a substantive right-to-vote" model that would focus on issues such as early, absentee, and same-day voting, accurate and secure voter databases, uniform administration, voter identification, and the like.[70]

Putting these "second generation" problems of VRA implementation to one side, we should ask two questions about the VRA's striking policy success: Which conditions accounted for it? And how common or replicable are they in today's policy world? In its "first generation," the VRA sought to secure what is perhaps the most fundamental right in a democracy: the right to vote and to have that vote counted. Where this right is denied for racial or ethnic reasons, the injustice is simply indefensible and society's obligation to enforce enforce the right is simply unarguable. In this case, the moral imperative was magnified by the courage and human appeal of the Selma, Alabama, marchers in 1965 and the palpable brutality of those who opposed them, the nearly universal revulsion and indignation that this behavior aroused throughout the nation, and the determination and moral fervor of a preternaturally forceful president who came from the South, controlled both houses of Congress, and utterly dominated the politics of the day.[71] Indeed, the VRA soon became something of a sacred cow, as evidenced by its renewals in 1970, 1974, 1982, and 2006 despite strong arguments (especially in 2006) for repealing or revising certain provisions (especially the formula in Section 5).

But if these conditions largely explain the VRA's enactment and durability, more is needed to account for its policy effectiveness in meeting its first-generation challenge.[72] One reason is the nature of the right being protected. Voting is a simple, physical, unambiguous act—in contrast, say, to being "disabled" or "seeking work" for welfare program eligibility. The law clearly specifies the most common legal impediments to voting and categorically prohibits them, as well as other devices with vote-suppressing effects. Although some politicians and officials opposed it, the many who stood to gain from black votes, usually liberals and moderates, were intent upon enforcing the law, as was the DOJ under Democratic and moderate Republican administrations. (As noted earlier, many Republicans, having learned to use VRA-driven districting to their personal or partisan advantage, are among the law's most ardent supporters.)

Another reason for the VRA's success is that it became self-enforcing and then self-reinforcing over time. Efforts to intimidate would-be black voters did not vanish, and some analysts maintain that they persist today, albeit in different forms.[73] But once the VRA enabled blacks to vote in large numbers, self-interested politicians (especially but not only Democrats) had to take notice or risk retaliation at the polls by blacks and their political allies. As blacks became a significant voting bloc that could influence the outcome of close elections in many Southern states, the retrogression danger receded. Finally, the federal courts played a pivotal role in aggressively enforcing the VRA—for example, by interpreting the VRA to prohibit such retrogression. As we have seen, they intervened in many redistricting disputes to preserve and indeed maximize black voting power, interventions that the Supreme Court has begun to limit only in the last decade—partly out of concerns about heightened race consciousness in districting, and partly out of frustration with its inability to find neutral principles for reviewing such districting.[74]

A third reason for the VRA's success is that it regulates government institutions, not private markets. State and local governments are constitutionally subordinate to Congress in this particular realm (voting rights) and are subject to direct controls and coercion, if necessary. This leverage is imperfect, to be sure, but it can be quite effective in combination with a clearly defined and morally compelling right and a self-reinforcing dynamic like the situation just discussed. In contrast, market actors have numerous ways (described in chapter 7) to neuter or circumvent government policies, usually without even breaking the law.

Probably no other law combines the VRA's moral, implementational, and political advantages. These advantages have only increased over time, notwithstanding the law's growing anachronisms. Certainly the landmark 1965 immigration law, to which I now turn, had none of the VRA's advantages. In that sense, it may be more typical of policy making's limitations.

THE IMMIGRATION AND NATIONALITY ACT OF 1965

No law has had a greater impact on the long-term character of American society than 1965's immigration reform (sometimes referred to as the Hart-Celler Act). Interestingly, its importance was not heralded at the time, especially compared with the civil rights law enacted only a year earlier. Although some scholars have depicted this demographic transformation as a classic case of unintended consequences, many of the law's supporters did anticipate these changes in general if not in detail—particularly the increase in immigration from Asia and Latin America that would occur soon after its effective date in 1968.[75] By far the most important of the new law's enduring achievements was its repeal of the system of racially and ethnically biased national origins quotas, which had essentially been in place since 1921 and which had been reaffirmed (over President Harry Truman's veto) in the comprehensive immigration legislation enacted in 1952. Inspired by the civil rights law enacted the year before (which received much more public attention), the 1965 act eliminated discrimination on the basis of race or national origins in granting permanent admission to the United States. At the same time, it substituted a per-country limit of twenty thousand admissions for every country outside the Western Hemisphere, and ended the traditional exemption of Western Hemisphere nationals from the quotas, instead subjecting them to a regional numerical quota but without the per country limit applicable to the rest of the world. It also allocated the overall visa quota according to a preference system of seven categories based on family ties, labor skills, and Cold War refugee claims. Many elements of this visa system have been revised since 1965. For example, the Western Hemisphere no longer enjoys a special status, the allotment of permanent visas is much larger, and temporary ("nonimmigrant") visa categories have proliferated. But the basic regulatory structure for legal immigration—an overall quota, per-country limits, preference categories based on family ties, labor skills, and humanitarian claims—remains in place and is likely to continue. (Reforms, should they occur, may well increase the number of permanent and temporary visas for highly skilled workers and perhaps for seasonal farm workers.)

Like the immigration waves that preceded it, the 1965 law's expansion of both the numbers and the diversity of the immigration flow has transformed our society in countless ways, almost all of them beneficial. Americans support *legal* immigration—the 1965 law's focus—not just because so many identify as the descendants of immigrants but also because of the immense social gains that it has produced: economic expansion and competitiveness, population growth, cultural diversity and enrichment, invigoration of religious communities, promotion of tolerance, a solidarity that is civic rather than primordial, and much more.[76] Americans tend to admire legal immigrants both as a group and as individuals, and believe that they have been good for the country.[77] They are generally assimilating well.[78] Our openness to ethnically diverse immigration positions us well to meet the challenges of a mobile, diverse, globally competitive twenty-first century. All of this is the bountiful legacy of the 1965 law.*

It is large-scale *illegal* immigration—a problem that the 1965 law did not anticipate but may have inadvertently encouraged†—that has had Americans up in arms (literally, in the case of the Border Patrol and some private militias) for the last thirty years. Indeed, one of the few things that President Obama and the 113th Congress seem able to agree upon is that policy reforms are needed to reduce illegal immigration—although disagreement about the precise nature of the reforms could well derail reform, as it did in 2007. The policy choices in this area are very difficult indeed. Although the political stars seem aligned to an unusual degree in the 113th Congress, enactment remained uncertain at the time of this writing (September 2013).[79] Effective implementation in this chronically troubled area would be even more doubtful.[80]

Legal immigration policy in the mold of the 1965 law has been a much easier row to hoe.‡ What explains the policy's success? Here, as with the Homestead and Morrill Acts, it reflects three factors: (1) fed-

---

*The 1965 law does have its flaws. Relative to our population, the number of new admissions is now much lower than it is in many other countries in the Organisation for Economic Co-operation and Development. I have proposed larger quotas, giving more weight to skills, and auctioning off at least some visas. See Shuck, *Diversity in America*, 123–31.
†The 1965 law subjected Mexican and other Western Hemispheric workers to quotas for the first time, and shortly after Congress had terminated the long-standing Bracero Program that had brought many Mexican laborers here to work in recurring seasonal cycles.
‡In practice, legal and illegal immigration are not wholly separate categories, but are linked in several ways. The tighter the legal immigration controls, the greater migrants' incentive to enter illegally; many legal immigrants were once out-of-status immigrants; large illegal populations create pressure to accord them legal status; and so forth.

eral distribution of a resource that is essentially free to the government (there, abundant federally owned land; here, visas); (2) a mission deeply consonant with American ideology (there, manifest destiny and settler freedom;[81] here, the melting pot and national renewal through self-reliant immigrants); and (3) strong evidence that legal immigration, particularly of highly skilled workers, increases innovation, entrepreneurship, and economic growth.[82] These three factors came together fruitfully in the 1965 law and in subsequent legal immigration expansions, but this combination is rare—and unlikely to be replicable in an era when government has no more essentially free resources (except perhaps for more green cards) to bestow to manifestly worthy claimants.

THE EARNED INCOME TAX CREDIT OF 1975

The Earned Income Tax Credit (EITC) is generally regarded among the most successful social policy innovations for low-income families of the past fifty years.[83] It was passed in the wake of Congress's failure to enact president Richard Nixon's family income maintenance plan, and began as what Yale University tax scholar Anne Alstott calls "a small, obscure provision of the federal tax code" that evolved into "one of the largest programs in the U.S. social-welfare system [and] the largest cash-transfer program for low-income working families."[84] Congress expanded eligibility and benefits in 2009, 2010, and again in 2013. In 2010, when some twenty-seven million working families and individuals received EITC benefits, the average for a family with children was $2805, and for a childless family, $262. In 2011, the program lifted about six million people out of poverty, including three million children—more than any other program.[85]

The EITC garners praise from every quarter, including both political parties and most policy analysts, which helps to explain why it has grown faster than other cash transfer programs for the poor and unemployed. A principal reason for its popularity is that it encourages work. The amount of the tax credit rises for each dollar of wage earnings, up to the statutory limit. It includes an additional child tax credit tied to work. And because the credit is refundable, eligible families can benefit even if they do not pay federal income tax. In another sign of its widespread popular support, twenty-five states provide EITC supplements.

Even so, the EITC is criticized on a number of grounds. The first is its inadequacy. Alstott, for example, contests the common claim that the program "makes work pay." She stresses that the labor market in which low-income people work is characterized by such low pay, job instability, and harsh working conditions that the EITC, even when coupled with a minimal social safety net, fails to adequately meet their needs. She also criticizes the definition of the baseline measure used to support claims about the program's antipoverty effects. Second, the Internal Revenue Service estimates that roughly one in four EITC claims are paid in error due to some combination of governmental errors, honest taxpayer errors, and fraud.[86] The Government Accountability Office found that the program made almost $17 billion in improper payments in 2010, the fourth highest level in federal programs, after Medicare, Medicaid, and unemployment insurance.[87] This problem has increased as the program has grown and become more complex for taxpayers to use. Related to this complexity is the reverse problem: many eligible families do not apply for the tax credit. Third, the form of the benefit—a lump-sum payment once a year—does not help beneficiaries as a monthly wage supplement would.[88] Fourth, its benefit for noncustodial working men is very low.[89] Finally, the effective marginal tax rate at the benefit phase-out level is high, reducing work incentives at that point.

THE AIRLINE DEREGULATION ACT OF 1978

Airlines were regulated by the federal government since the advent of commercial aviation, largely under postal and military authorities. In 1938, however, Congress established a comprehensive regulatory scheme for commercial airlines under the authority of the Civil Aeronautics Board (CAB), which controlled their fares, entry, exit, and terms of service. The abolition of this system in 1978 reflected a number of unusual factors carefully elaborated on by political scientists Martha Derthick and Paul Quirk.[90] The analytical and political paths to deregulation had been cleared in 1975, a time of economic distress, when Supreme Court justice Stephen Breyer, then a renowned Harvard Law School professor and scholar of regulation, worked as special counsel to the powerful and mediagenic senator Ted Kennedy. They organized a set of hearings that presented evidence, including the fare and service patterns from airline competition within California, that systematically refuted the arguments for continued regulation.

Two reform-minded CAB chairmen, John Robson and Alfred Kahn, used this record to begin dismantling the regulatory system. Kahn, who was appointed by president Jimmy Carter in 1977, was an eminent economist and expert on regulation who was determined to complete the job. As noted by economist Elizabeth Bailey, who was then a CAB member, Kahn was an effective advocate before Congress and had access to the White House. He brought together an unusually effective team of academics and committed reformers that adopted "sunshine" rules for agency meetings and pursued deregulation administratively in ways designed to make Congress more comfortable with the deregulatory agenda. The rapid success of air cargo deregulation, which had been proposed by Robson in 1976 and enacted in 1977, also helped to push passenger fare deregulation over the goal line the next year.[91] Deregulation of the railroads earlier in the 1970s also helped, as did substantial reform of trucking regulation by the Carter administration.[92]

In the thirty-five years since airline deregulation, the results have been very favorable. In a recent review of the evidence, Bailey finds that consumer welfare increased by about $28 billion a year as of 2005, partly due to increased load factors. Rates have fallen more on long routes than on short ones, and airlines increasingly differentiate business fares from more price-conscious leisure travelers. Frequent-flyer programs and computer reservation systems have flourished. Unexpectedly, airline networks moved from linear point-to-point systems created by the CAB into hub-and-spoke systems, enabling better scheduling of flights to facilitate one-day round trips. New nonstop service to many cities was added. Low-cost new-entrant carriers gained a market share of nearly 30 percent by 2007, with Southwest and US Airways becoming major players in the industry. The lower fares and increased efficiency by American carriers in turn have spurred privatization of many foreign carriers and kept international fares lower than otherwise.[93] Investment in the industry has increased.[94]

Notwithstanding these immense gains for consumers from deregulation, problems remain. Airport delays and congestion have increased, carrier consolidations have raised concentration in some markets, volatility in fuel prices and thus fares has continued, and air traffic control technology has not kept pace. Some of these conditions reflect the failure to institute congestion pricing, which also reflects monopolistic practices by airport authorities governed by local law and politics, not federal policy.[95]

THE WELFARE REFORM ACT OF 1996

The politics and policy of cash assistance to America's poor—which is what most commentators mean by the term *welfare program*—have always been extraordinarily vexed, far more so than in European liberal democracies. Brookings Institution researchers Gary Burtless and Ron Haskins note,

> While almost two-thirds of Americans agree with the statement that "income differences in the United States are too large," policies aimed at reducing income differences command relatively little popular support. On the whole, Americans are not particulary concerned about the income distribution and are less persuaded than citizens in other rich countries of the need for public policies to temper inequality. . . . A large majority of Americans believes that individuals should bear primary responsibility for supporting themselves, whereas voters in other rich countries are more inclined to believe that governments have an obligation to assure that everyone is provided for. Large majorities of Americans also believe their society offers an equal opportunity for people to get ahead and think that hard work will ordinarily translate

into a better life. . . . Residents of other rich countries are less likely to think their societies provide equal opportunity and are more inclined to believe that differences in individual success are due to luck or personal connections rather than individual effort.[96]

Since the defeat of President Nixon's guaranteed family income plan in 1971, no European-style family allowance or other such universal welfare program has come close to passing either house of Congress. Instead, Congress has preferred to expand two large programs: the Earned Income Tax Credit, and the Supplemental Nutrition Assistance Program, both discussed above. The United States spends a much smaller fraction of its budget on poor families than do other countries in the Organisation for Economic Co-operation and Development.[97] The budgetary going to the elderly rather than to children is vastly disproportionate, in my view.

Burtless and Haskins continue,

When major reform in social assistance finally came in 1996 . . . the main focus . . . was AFDC [Aid to Families with Dependent Children], the principal cash assistance program providing aid to working-age parents and their children. The reform passed in 1996 was designed to reduce dependency on cash assistance by ending the automatic entitlement to benefits. AFDC was abolished and replaced with Temporary Assistance for Needy Families (TANF). The new law placed pressure on all states to adopt aggressive policies to restrict or eliminate cash benefits to poor parents who were capable of working but now did not work. Work requirements were stringent, and the new law imposed financial penalties on states that failed to require parents to meet them but also gave states flexibility to create their own sanctions within the federal law framework. The law also imposed time limits on the assistance payments families could receive. Most families could receive federally financed benefits for no longer than five years. The law permitted states to impose even shorter time limits, and more than half of them did so.[98]

Many liberals bitterly opposed TANF—some prominent ones even resigned from the Clinton administration in protest—but it passed with overwhelming bipartisan support. Going into effect at a time when the economy was growing strongly and the unemployment rate was low, the results were far more dramatic than even the optimists predicted: the welfare rolls experienced a large and sustained decline, the first in more than six decades of the welfare program, and the employment rate of low-income single mothers reached its highest level ever, leaving them with a real net income gain of 25 percent. The child poverty rate saw its first sustained decline since the 1960s, and for black children and children in single-parent families reached its lowest levels ever. Almost every index of child well-being except obesity improved. Since then, two recessions—a mild one in 2001, and a very deep one since 2008—have eroded some of these gains: the employment rate of never-married mothers, the group that is hardest to find jobs for, is down, and the poverty rate is up. Nevertheless, more are employed, and they are less poor than they were before the 1996 law (even without counting benefits not included in the poverty measure).[99]

The gains from the 1996 welfare reform and other work-related subsidies are certainly no cause for smugness. Seventeen years later, the law's incentives have not yet lifted all mothers and their children out of poverty—not by a long shot. Many who have benefited from the program are stuck in low-wage jobs, and others still do not work full-time or at all. Some of these women are so dysfunctional that no program or personal desire to work will enable them to hold any jobs, much less decently paying ones. As a group, however, never-married mothers, and single mothers more generally, have clearly improved their and their children's living standards and prospects. Interview studies show that they express pride in these gains and in their status as workers. Over time, they may be able to progress further as they accumulate job skills, experience, and work habits, and as the economy improves.[100] None of this progress is preordained, of course, but there is now more reason for hope than there was before the reform.

The decline in welfare dependency after 1996 reflected a number of interacting factors: welfare reform, a robust economy, expanded EITC and child care benefits, and others.[101] The reasons for the 1996 law's contribution are fairly clear. It created strong incentives, both positive and negative, for the most uneducated, untrained, and un-promising welfare recipients to join the workforce. As shown by their high employment rates, poor mothers responded to these incentives even more resourcefully than most policy makers had expected despite their often chaotic domestic circumstances. The federal law meshed well with many experimental state and local welfare-to-work programs, helping states pay for job search and readiness, health insurance, child care, and other vital work support services. Most politicians did not cave in to the intentionally inflammatory "dying in the streets" rhetoric; instead, they figured that the program could hardly be worse than the status quo of welfare dependency and that many of the poorest of the poor would end up better off. Both Congress and the states resisted the temptation to cut and run once the recipients' situations improved; the governments largely maintained their efforts over time, mindful of how fragile these gains could be. Knowing the mixed record of earlier welfare-to-work programs on reducing welfare dependency, government tried something new and stuck with it. Even today, virtually every state still runs a strong welfare-to-work program, in part because the programs are relatively inexpensive. (Even so, critics argue that some of the state programs have manipulated the federal requirements and use the flexible TANF block grant funds for purposes other than paying cash welfare or moving mothers to work.[102]) This approach has also found favor in Europe, where governments have also adopted strong work requirements in many of their welfare programs, unemployment insurance, and even disability programs.[103]

THE NATIONAL INSTITUTES OF HEALTH

One domain in which even small-government advocates generally concede an important role to the federal government is basic research—the creation of knowledge—in areas where private actors lack strong incentives to invest. This may be because the research involves enormous uncertainty, private investors cannot gain intellectual property rights enabling them to extract full economic value from an investment in it,* or other strategic considerations discourage private investment. The federal government has played an important, perhaps essential, role in seeding some of our most transformative technological advances, including many components of the digital revolution.[104]

The National Institutes of Health (NIH) consist of a variety of domain-specific organizations funded by the federal government. The NIH's 2012 budget was $30.9 billion, which works out to just under $100 per capita in the population, and it constitutes only 0.8 percent of the federal budget and only 3.5 percent of the Department of Health and Human Services budget.[105] The social value generated by NIH research is difficult to determine because its downstream effects are affected by a number of factors (including investments by private companies); a long lag time exists between basic research and social impact; and objective data is hard to gather and analyze. Nevertheless, those analyses that have been conducted, mostly on pharmaceutical innovation, suggest that this research has been highly cost-effective.[106]

A 2011 article in the *New England Journal of Medicine* usefully summarizes the published studies on the relationship between pure biomedical research financed and conducted by public-sector research institutions (PSRIs), and applied research done by the private pharmaceutical industry. (The authors broadly define PSRIs to include all universities, research hospitals, nonprofit research institutes, and federal laboratories in the United States.) I can do no better than quote at length from this summary:

> Historically, there has been a clear distinction between the roles of public-sector research and corporate research in the discovery of new drugs and vaccines to solve unmet medical needs. PSRIs have performed the upstream, basic research to elucidate the underlying mechanisms and pathways of disease and identify promising points of intervention, whereas corporate researchers have performed the downstream,

---

*For example, the share price of Celera, J. Craig Venter's private venture to sequence the human genome, collapsed in March 2000 when President Clinton announced that the genome sequence could not be patented.

applied research to discover drugs that can be used to treat diseases and have then carried out the development activities to bring the drugs to market. The intellectual property that protects the investment in developing these drugs is created in the applied-research phase. An excellent example of this traditional approach was Julius Axelrod's research at the National Institutes of Health (NIH) regarding the basic mechanisms of neurotransmitters, for which he received the Nobel Prize in 1970. This research provided the foundation for the pharmaceutical industry's discovery of an entirely new class of drugs, the selective serotonin-reuptake inhibitors (SSRIs), which have been important in the treatment of depression. All the major SSRIs were discovered by pharmaceutical companies with the use of Axelrod's basic discoveries and are therefore not included in our study (e.g., Eli Lilly's discovery of fluoxetine [Prozac], which received approval from the Food and Drug Administration [FDA] in 1987). However, Richard and Judith Wurtman at MIT discovered the role of these drugs in the treatment of premenstrual dysphoric disorder and obtained a method-of-treatment patent for this new use. MIT licensed their work to Interneuron Pharmaceuticals, which later licensed it to Eli Lilly. Eli Lilly then received FDA approval for a new use of fluoxetine and created a separate product, Sarafem, for this new use. Thus, we have included Sarafem in our study.

There is little dispute about the importance to drug discovery of basic research at PSRIs under the traditional approach. Studies by Cockburn and Henderson showed the complex relationships between public and private research in the pharmaceutical industry. Zycher et al. found that at least 80 percent of 35 major drugs that they studied were based on scientific discoveries made by PSRIs, whereas Toole found a quantifiable correlation between investment in publicly funded basic research and corporately funded applied research: an increase of 1 percent in the funding of public basic research led to an increase of 1.8 percent in the number of successful applications for new molecular entities (compounds that have not been approved for marketing in the United States) after a lag of about 17 years. He found that a $1 investment in public-sector basic research yielded $0.43 in annual benefits in the development of new molecular entities in perpetuity.

Historically, PSRIs did not play a major role in the downstream, applied phase of drug discovery, in which the actual products are discovered and patented. However, in the mid-1970s, the newly emerging tools of biotechnology—recombinant DNA and monoclonal antibodies—allowed PSRIs to create and patent biologic drug candidates and discover and patent small-molecule drugs. At that time, all products created in academic institutions were owned by the government, which granted only nonexclusive licenses. This system resulted in the ineffective transfer of academic technologies. For instance, by 1978, the government had licensed less than 5 percent of the 25,000 to 30,000 patents it owned.

In 1980, Congress passed two pieces of legislation that transformed the ownership, management, and transfer of intellectual property that is created by PSRIs. First, the Bayh–Dole Act (Public Law 96–517) allowed universities, nonprofit research institutes, and teaching hospitals to own the intellectual property resulting from federally funded research and to license it according to terms of their choosing. Second, the Stevenson-Wydler Technology Innovation Act (Public Law 96–480), as amended by the Federal Technology Transfer Act of 1986 (Public Law 99–502), provided a corresponding authority to federal laboratories. Under this new approach, inventions that arose from PSRIs, in addition to being freely published in the scientific literature, could also be converted into intellectual property and transferred through license agreements to the private sector for commercialization and public use. The new approach is thought to be considerably more effective than government ownership of academic inventions and was introduced just as the fruits of the biotechnology revolution started to emerge.[107]

The study concluded that PSRIs have contributed to the discovery of 9.3 to 21.2 percent of all drugs involved in new drug applications approved from 1990 to 2007, and that PSRIs tend to discover drugs expected to have disproportionately important clinical effects.

The Human Genome Project (HGP), which took the NIH and its associated researchers thirteen years to complete, is generally recognized as the federal government's most important long-term investment in biomedical science. A study conducted by the Battelle Technology Partnership Practice sought to estimate the social benefits from HGP, and while such estimates are inevitably speculative to some degree, their general parameters are suggestive. The study found that the government's investment of $5.6 billion by 2010 generated, directly and indirectly, $796 billion in economic output, personal income exceeding $244 billion, and 3.8 million job-years of employment. In the single year 2010, according to the study, the genomics-enabled industry paid back in taxes to all levels of government the entire federal investment in the HGP. This, despite the fact that the bulk of the HGP's likely medical, agricultural, energy, and environmental benefits still lie in the future.[108]

The success of NIH research seems overdetermined. It is a rarefied hothouse of scientific talent, a jewel in the federal government's crown that attracts some of the best scientists in the world for short or long-term stints. From a purely economic point of view, powerful arguments favor public funding of basic research. Politically, powerful industries like pharmaceutical manufacturing and bioengineering support much of this research, which is an essentially free (to them), valuable input into their own businesses. Quite apart from its social benefits, NIH research funding supports prestigious institutions, creates high-end jobs, and interfaces with dynamic technology industries.

REPRISE: WHAT DO THESE SUCCESSFUL POLICIES HAVE IN COMMON?

In the end, it is hard to know for sure just why these (and other) policies succeeded where so many others have failed. No two policies are exactly alike, of course; many variables are in play. And judgments about success and failure are often contestable, as I noted in chapters 1 and 2. Even so, this chapter's examples suggest some convergent reasons for their success:

Some were redistributive policies in which benefits were distributed very broadly and essentially for free. (The resources used by these programs were not actually free. All entailed opportunity costs, but these costs seemed very low at the time and were viewed as both fulfilling a moral obligation and making a sound investment for the future.) The beneficiaries of the Homestead Act and the Morrill Act received valuable land grants, education, and research services at essentially no cost to themselves. The government owned an immense patrimony of empty land (save for the relatively small, isolated number of Native Americans) that would be essentially worthless until it could be settled, cultivated, and used in ways that would enrich the nation as a whole. The GI Bill was a reward for patriotic service.

Some of these redistributive programs involve relatively simple centralized administration and correspondingly few implementation obstacles. The most important example is Social Security retirement and survivor's benefits, which is essentially a data-management and check-writing operation. While private retirement programs are widespread, cognitive, psychological, and financial factors prevent many people from saving enough to avoid penury in old age, a condition that Social Security has forestalled.[109]

Some successful redistribution programs are administratively more challenging because they involve some role for the states and because of concerns about fraud and moral hazard (work incentives). SNAP and EITC are examples. For both political and program integrity reasons, these concerns are especially salient in programs that distribute valuable resources to poor people of working age. But because nourishment of dependent children, the disabled, and others is the most basic, morally compelling human need, the program's success at guaranteeing this (as the market does not) has subordinated these concerns even as the program struggles to meet them. The outcome of the political imbroglio in 2013 in which the farm and food stamp programs are being held hostage to one another will reveal whether and on what terms the legislative bargain so essential to food stamps can be sustained.

Programs that provide public goods such as communications networks, basic research, and transportation infrastructure are the natural province of government—particularly the federal government. The NIH supports biomedical research that private firms will not adequately provide even with robust intellectual property rights.[110] Some national infrastructure, as with the interstate highway system and the Defense Advanced Research Projects Agency's research, was justified as an essential national defense asset but has had far broader effects on the public. The national park system and the Smithsonian Institution are precious patrimonies (even though some of their functions are managed privately).

Some successful policies replaced earlier ones that were morally objectionable, hugely wasteful, and unpopular. The EITC and welfare reform supplanted much-vilified New Deal and state systems of income support for the poor that voters were convinced weakened work incentives and enabled immoral conduct. The VRA ousted an oppressive, unconstitutional political regime. The Immigration Act of 1965 replaced a national origins quota system that mocked our inclusive principles, foreign policy, and economic interests. The deregulation of airlines, railroads and trucking, and energy industries displaced controls that Congress came to be persuaded were grossly inefficient.

The beneficiaries and administrators of most of the successful programs were, in an important sense, pushing against an open door. The dominant culture had already endorsed and praised the programs' implementing actions: homesteading; establishing educational institutions; building human capital through college education; interstate mobility; the feeding of low-income children, the elderly, and the disabled; more competitive airlines; diverse immigration; and voting rights. (The NIH's success simply required researchers to engage in more of the same old activity, and to do it better.) *To succeed, then, the programs largely needed to engage the actors' self-interest; they did not need to create new values or transform deeply rooted behaviors.* Sometimes more forceful intervention was needed, as with the VRA, where opposition was fierce and sometimes violent. But in the other cases, the government only had to establish the entitlement or incentive, get out of the way, and let beneficiaries' self-interests do the rest. Derek Bok makes a similar point, noting, "It is no accident that the United States enjoys its greatest successes in fields—such as the private economy, scientific research, and technological innovation—where the government need only encourage individualism and creativity by limiting restrictions on competition or by subsidizing creative people, while we lag other major democracies whenever the government undertakes more complicated tasks such as devising a healthcare system or an effective urban policy."[111]

Some programs can only succeed by altering behavior, but some behaviors are more tractable than others. I venture that the ones that government might take on in the future are more intractable than those it has tried to change in the past. They are the high-hanging fruit, if only because the incentives of politicians and social reforms dictated harvesting the low-hanging ones earlier. For example, it was hard enough for the 1996 welfare-to-work law to increase work effort on the part of uneducated, low-income mothers by using wage subsidies, job referrals, and child care vouchers, and for the EITC to use wage supplements to reward low-income workers. But it is much harder to alter the parenting and work practices of low-income families through programs like Family Rewards in New York City. The city's cash payments—to induce families to visit doctors and dentists, work thirty hours per week, attend school, and improve academic performance—have had decidedly meager results.[112] Welfare-to-work and wage supplements deploy more familiar, salient, and powerful incentives. Simpler behaviors tend to be more tractable. Thus, smokers' choices are relatively straightforward (smoke, smoke less, or quit) compared with the complex series of countless small decisions faced by the obese (what to eat, in what quantities, at what times, with what exercise, etc.). The strength of signals to people from their salient subcultures—religious communities, for example—also seems to affect their motivation and ability to alter their conduct. Peter Rossi's Brass Law of Evaluation (see chapter 1) reminds us how pivotal such behavioral variables are to program success.

Policy success, then, ultimately depends on precisely what a program's participants must do and how they must do it in order for it to work. In *Uncontrolled*, Jim Manzi reviews the experience with randomized field trials (RFTs) of proposed or adopted innovations in public policy, business, political strategy, and social science. In arguing that promising results must be replicated before being instituted as policy, Manzi elaborates on the kinds of effectiveness factors that I have just mentioned:

> First, we should be very skeptical of claims of the effectiveness of new programs. Empirically, the vast majority of criminal justice, social welfare, and education programs fail replicated, independent, well-designed RFTs. Though almost any reasonable-sounding program will probably

work under some conditions, most fail most of the time. The burden of proof should always be on those who claim that some new program is worth investment.

Second, within this universe of programs that are far more likely to fail than succeed, programs that attempt to improve human behavior by raising skills or consciousness are even more likely to fail than those that change incentives and environment. [Of the many ideas for pushing welfare recipients into the workforce tried in the late 1980s and early 1990s,] only adding mandatory work requirements succeeded in moving people from welfare to work humanely. And within mandatory-work programs, those that emphasized just getting a job were more effective than those that emphasized building skills. The list of both "hard" and "soft" attempts to change people to make them less likely to commit crime that do not work is also almost endless—prisoner counseling, transitional aid to prisoners, multisystemic therapy, intensive probation, juvenile boot camps, Job Corps, etc.—but the only program demonstrated to reduce crime rates in replicated RFTs across 103 documented trials is broken-windows policing, which concentrates enforcement on targeted areas and changes the environment in which criminals operate. Similarly, it is extremely difficult to find any curricular, training, or related programs that drive sustained gain in academic performance in replicated RFTs, but creating choice for students in an environment in which schools are released from collective bargaining and other constraints appears to create improvement. Therefore, we should generally seek to change incentives and environments, rather than try to change people. This is not to say that direct behavior improvement programs can never work—a program of nurse visitations to expectant and new mothers is a well-known example of a discrete program that has apparently succeeded in replicated independent RFTs—though, as with this example, those that succeed are often extensions of traditional public health measures.[113]

These findings are essential to sound policy making where what is being targeted is individual behavior. It is easier to alter people's incentives than to change their values or character. Policy environments are more tractable than the people who inhabit them. What seems to work in a pilot project run by true believers often fails when it is routinized and bureaucratized in the less rarified real world. Only field testing—as rigorous as social science can muster—can provide a reliable basis for optimism about government-promoted behavioral change. (See chapter 12.)

Sometimes, external forces are simply too potent for any government program to master. For example, sixty years after *Brown v. Board of Education* was decided and fifty years after Title VI was enacted, the percentage of black children who still attend majority nonwhite schools remains roughly the same (about 75 percent).[114] It largely reflects old housing patterns, new locational choices, and changing demographic conditions (e.g., higher birthrates for minorities than for whites) over which the federal government has little or no control. (Indeed, its own housing programs exacerbated the original residential segregation.) We may well discover that the public's eating habits are also largely beyond the government's control. Sociopaths' access to firearms,[115] and large-scale prevention of criminal recidivism,[116] seem to be other tragic examples. The persistence of these conditions is not for lack of government efforts and commitment. Instead, it is due to limits on the behavioral variables that the government can legitimately control and effectively alter.

PART 3

Remedies and Reprise

CHAPTER 12

Remedies: Lowering Government's Failure Rate

The pages of this book are littered with scores of federal policy failures—programs that create fewer benefits than costs, are cost-ineffective, or are perversely targeted—and only a relative handful of major successes (see chapter 11). Even allowing for some disagreement about definitions and some of the assessments I have reported and presented, this is a deeply dismaying record. Moreover, as I noted in chapter 1, there are strong reasons to believe that these failures are but the tip of the iceberg—a longer book could have easily multiplied examples—and that the public increasingly senses this.

Unfortunately, this dismal record is not confined to a limited policy space or only a few policy instruments. To the contrary, the failed programs discussed in this book cover a vast range of domestic policies, as well as all of the specific policy tools discussed in chapter 3: grants, contracts, insurance, subsidies, regulation, and the rest. Nor are these failures marginal or insignificant. In fact, they include some of our largest, most durable, most visible, and most fiercely defended programs. Together, they account for a substantial share of total non-defense discretionary spending.

We saw in chapter 11 that some major entitlement programs like food stamps and Social Security pensions can be counted as among government's great achievements despite some significant fiscal, administrative, and policy design problems. We also saw that these programs tend to possess certain distinctive attributes that largely explain

their achievements, but that relatively few programs have these features or can realistically hope to adopt them. Indeed, as was noted
there, demographic and fiscal trends have placed some of the successful ones at grave risk of losing the long-term solvency that underwrites their popularity and viability.

In light of this endemic failure of important federal programs in
so many areas and forms, an urgent question naturally arises: *What
can be done?* This is an exceedingly difficult question to answer. Indeed, even posing, much less answering, this remedial question begs
many others. Two of the most basic are: What normative assumptions
drive judgments about what "better" policy means? How incremental
or comprehensive should the remedies be? I addressed the first question in chapter 2—defining the essential criteria for policy success and
failure as efficiency, equity, and manageability—but the second question requires a bit more discussion. This book has shown that many,
perhaps most, governmental failures are *structural*. That is, they grow
out of a deeply entrenched policy process, a political culture, a perverse official incentive system, individual or collective irrationality,
inadequate information, rigidity and inertia, lack of credibility, mismanagement, market dynamics, the inherent limits of law, implementation problems, and a weak bureaucratic system. But if the reasons
for failure are structural, the reader then may well ask, why are the
reforms that I propose in this chapter largely incremental rather than
attacking these structures head-on? Are they not like bandages placed
on a purulent infection?

Near the end of chapter 1, I defended a cautious incremental
approach to reforming complex systems. Not only does political
reality preclude radical change; the remorseless law of unintended
consequences applies most strongly to attempts—especially when
the reformers are politicians in the grip of the very failure-inducing
forces detailed in this book—to alter sociopolitical structures in the
face of immense complexity, opacity, uncertainty, and value trade-
offs.* As political scientist Nelson Polsby warned, "The complexity

---

*A classic example is the moratorium on special interest earmarks adopted with much
fanfare after the 2010 congressional elections. Urged by President Barack Obama in his

of the American political system may as well be directly acknowledged. . . . [It] stymies proposed reforms based on false analogies with simpler systems."[1] Also cautious is Derek Bok's magisterial, admirably balanced 2001 book, which analyzes why our government has fallen into such disrepute and how it might be fixed. Bok, a "melioristic realist" (like me; see chapter 1), canvasses many possible structural reforms but ends up being equivocal about almost all of them[2]—for reasons that help to explain why most durable public policies evolved gradually through a series of smaller steps rather than through comprehensive, radical lurches.* This is how my granddaughter is learning to walk and how our political system learns to improve policy. I shall elaborate on these points below in the "Policy Process" section.

There is another reason for caution: any serious reform proposal must be subjected to an analysis far more extensive and probing than is possible here. The analysis must clarify the proposal's conflicting goals; adduce and scrutinize the relevant facts; predict the proposal's downstream political and policy effects; and compare its benefits and costs to the status quo and other alternatives, all with special attention to the easily ignored costs borne by "invisible victims" (discussed in chapter 2); and consider any other trade-offs that it entails. This requires a deep immersion in a program's operational details and political context by analysts with no ax to grind. Any responsible reformer, whether incrementalist or radical, should demand this.

I organize this chapter around three approaches, in declining order of generality. The first two—cultural changes conducive to better policy, and structural reforms of a constitutional nature—are each unlikely to appear on the policy horizon, albeit for somewhat differ-

---

State of the Union message and celebrated by good government advocates everywhere, it seems to have impeded the political bargaining and compromise necessary to resolve the 2012–13 "fiscal cliff" and other standoffs. Indeed, the fiscal cliff legislation *itself* contained earmarks—probably for this reason. See Alicia Mundy, "Room for Favors in 'Cliff' Deal," *Wall Street Journal*, January 29, 2013.

*The post–Civil War amendments and the New Deal are the great exceptions. The Great Society is a more arguable case; most of its programs (other than civil rights) were built on earlier reforms.

ent reasons that I shall explain. The third approach, which constitutes the bulk of the chapter, is much more achievable. It proposes an array of reform ideas that could improve performance across a wide variety of policy domains, ideas whose details can of course be designed only after careful analyses of the kind just described. For fixes specific to particular programs, the reader must look elsewhere, including the endnotes attached to my discussions of those programs in earlier chapters.

CULTURAL CHANGES

In chapter 4, I explored ten features of American political culture (while treating an eleventh, its broad deference to market forces, separately in chapter 7). These features are more or less distinctive among liberal democracies, although just *how* distinctive is unimportant for present purposes. I also observed there that "our political culture is one important reason, along with others analyzed in this book, why the United States is a difficult nation to govern effectively." Given the impediment to sound policy making posed by these cultural features, it is tempting to think that they can be changed. But as I noted there, the nature of our political culture makes this hope as unrealistic as it is understandable.

I do not believe that these features of our political culture represent past choices that are readily reversible. Quite the contrary: some of these cultural values are constitutionally inscribed and all are so deeply embedded in our national psyche that they are alterable, if at all, only slowly and at the margins, particularly since there is no evidence of any widespread popular wish to repudiate them. Nor do I contend here that these values *should* be abandoned, even on the doubtful assumption that they *could* be. To responsibly support such a change, one would first have to clarify and then assess the intricate normative and empirical trade-offs. Such an analysis far exceeds this book's scope.

Nor are these the only obstacles to changing our political culture. A culture, after all, is not a discrete thing that can be isolated, manipulated, and then reformed. It comes as a package, a *gestalt*, a composite of many interpenetrating beliefs, modes of thinking and feeling, patterned behaviors, and multifarious, often fluid, identities. Much of a culture is ineffable and opaque even (perhaps especially) to those who practice it. And because we only dimly understand what it "is" and how it "works" (and even that, only at a fairly high level of abstraction), we know little about how it changes, much less how *to* change it. Even attitudes about specific policy issues—abortion, gun control, and campaign finance regulation, for example—tend to evolve slowly (or not at all[3]) and in ways and for reasons that are difficult to disentangle. (Attitudes toward gay people and same-sex marriage are a striking exception to this attitudinal stability.[4]) Finally, even if we can imagine culture changing within a reasonable time frame, two questions remain that are highly relevant to our inquiry here: first, how *public policy*—as distinct from other, less instrumental, less manipulable social forces—can bring it about; and second, how certain we can be that changing a particular cultural feature (supposing that it is tractable to policy) will be good *on balance*, given that the change may sacrifice its more desirable aspects.

Of the particular cultural features identified in chapter 4, only four—decentralization, protection of individual rights, acceptance of social and economic inequality, and suspicion of technical expertise and official discretion—seem remotely tractable to policy-driven change. Although our political system has institutionalized decentralization in many different ways (discussed in chapter 4), the policy system as a whole has grown more centralized over time. (Recall the "new system" described by James Q. Wilson and John DiIulio in chapter 1.) Still, the advantages of decentralization and the sources of resistance to centralization are both very great, and I see no evidence that Americans are willing to forego either the advantages or the resistance. As for Americans' obsession with individual rights, many respected commentators—beginning with Alexis de Tocqueville—have criticized it, calling for more emphasis on communal responsibilities.[5] Little has come of this critique; the rights revolution continues its way, most recently with the protection of gay people and the disabled, albeit individualism here is often couched in communal terms, as with same-sex marriage. Social and economic inequalities have been the subject of bitter contention from our earliest days. Today, the debate over the causes, effects, and remedies for the stalled mobility experienced in recent decades is a prominent feature of our politics, with no clear resolution in sight. There are many plausible proposals to reduce these inequalities, but the logically prior question is what policies, if any, might alter public attitudes about inequalities in the first place. The answer to *this* question is not at all clear. Finally, widespread suspicion of experts and discretion shows no signs of waning, despite eloquent pleas for greater public trust.[6] And as with decentralization, a healthy skepticism in these matters is advantageous in a democracy like ours, so only a modest increase in earned deference would be desirable.

CONSTITUTION-LEVEL REFORMS

Americans may view the Constitution as a sacred document, specifying our most fundamental political principles, but it is not wholly sacrosanct—nor is it much emulated abroad today.[7] Two and a quarter centuries after its adoption, it occasions constant, countless controversies among lawyers and citizens over not just what it has been understood to mean but what it *ought to provide*. I have just explained why in a political and social system as intricate and interrelated as ours is, we should view proposals to reform our political system in its most fundamental respects with a skepticism and caution that are every bit as profound as the deep structures that would be transformed. Unforeseen consequences in such situations are not just probable; they are a certainty. And some of those consequences are likely to be as unwelcome as they are unexpected. The following discussion should be read with this caveat very much in mind.

Several constitution-level changes might be designed to mute the strong parochial bias of our national politics. Lawyer and political scientist Sanford Levinson, for example, takes particular aim at the Electoral College and the equal representation of all states in the Senate, regardless of their population.[8] Were we writing on a blank slate today, he argues, we would not tolerate a Senate in which Wyoming has the same representation as California despite their seventyfold difference in populations, much less an Electoral College that extends this gross distortion to a process that precludes direct popular election of the president. I accept Levinson's "blank slate" argument. It does not follow, however, that any deviation from the one person, one vote (OPOV) model of representation is undemocratic. For many reasons—beginning with the need to hold the Union together, and the desire to give greater weight to certain interests that otherwise would always be outvoted—a democratic polity might choose to make certain concessions to some minority groups, such as agricultural interests, that are valuable parts of our national community. We certainly cherish equal representation in the OPOV sense, but it is not our only political value and it may properly be made to yield a bit to others.

The important question here is how much it must yield. This a matter of degree about which reasonable people will differ, and it is constrained by the great advantages of decentralization. With Levinson, I believe that the Senate, and indirectly the Electoral College, now magnify a constitutional, institutional, and cultural bias that favors local over regional and especially national interests.* This pronounced parochialism shapes, and to a degree deforms, many of our federal programs by allocating resources and authority away from the areas (including localities) where most people live and where their needs arise. Given urban and regional voting patterns, changes that modestly reduced this bias—by affecting representation in the Senate but also by rule changes that facilitated cloture, for example—would likely move public policy, and national politics more generally, in a liberal direction. But the justification (for me) lies in securing more political accountability and equality. If so, let the votes fall where they may.

Another reform that would mute the existing localistic bias would be to give the president line-item veto power. Depending on the form

*Chapter 4 discussed this bias. Thirty years ago, I suggested electing some representatives in Congress under OPOV but by *regional or national at-large* constituencies. Peter H. Schuck, "Industrial Policy's Obstacles," *New York Times*, September 6, 1983.

that such a change takes, it may or may not require a constitutional amendment. It would tend to counteract the strong propensity of members of Congress to logroll for wasteful pork barrel projects for their constituents at the expense of the national interest in efficient priorities in government spending.* It would also affect budgetary politics more generally. More generally, it would significantly increase the president's power to protect what he views as national interests (as well as other political concerns) in his interactions with Congress. But the political and policy effects of this shift would extend well beyond appropriations legislation to political tactics more generally, which makes its effects very difficult to predict. Still, the fact that the vast majority of states already give their governors this authority in one form or another is somewhat reassuring.[9] Although states' political systems do differ from the federal system in many ways, their experiences would make this change at the federal level less of a leap in the dark than would, say, reforming the Senate's essential structure, which has no such precedent.

Strong arguments also exist for a congressional districting process, now conducted largely by state legislatures, that reduces the present wholly politicized partisan and racial gerrymandering of House constituencies, one in which legislators in effect decide who will vote for them. Close students of the districting process, which is now limited only by a few weak constraints imposed by Supreme Court decisions, believe that it produces members who are less accountable to the median voters in their districts, whose only real challengers are in party primaries dominated by a relatively small number of voters at the ideological extremes, and whose seats are otherwise quite safe. Several states have sought to remedy this abuse by enacting *relatively* nonpartisan districting commissions—"relatively" because some person or body with political authority must select commission members—that political scientists are now assessing. In the

---

*Such projects do have their political uses; as noted in chapter 5, they can lubricate an otherwise stalled legislative process, which may or may not serve the public well. A famous example was the "bridge to nowhere" in Ketchikan, Alaska (population 8,900). Ultimately, however, national protests and ridicule ended the project.

most recent assessment of this experience, districting expert Bruce Cain finds that although they have reduced line-drawers' conflicts of interest, they have not eliminated the partisan wrangling and commission deadlocks.[10] Whether instituting such a reform at the federal level would require a constitutional amendment would depend on its precise form.

Campaign finance regulation is a perennial favorite among structural reformers, but it is so replete with political, consequential, and constitutional difficulties—many discussed in chapter 7—that I conclude that the only reforms that merit unequivocal support are those that would give challengers access to free television and mail privileges that would increase their access to voters in ways that incumbents already exploit, magnifying their already considerable advantages.

CROSS-CUTTING REFORMS

Chapters 3 through 10 identified many deeply embedded defects that contribute to government ineffectiveness and failure. For analytical purposes, I analyzed these defects under a number of different headings: policy process; incentives; irrationality; information; rigidity; lack of credibility; mismanagement; misunderstanding of markets; implementation; and bureaucracy. In the rest of this chapter, I shall use these same headings to organize my presentation of reform ideas that could improve policy outcomes across the board. (These headings overlap somewhat; some reforms could fit under several of them.)

POLICY PROCESS

Any first-year law student quickly learns that the relationship between procedure and substance is a very close one. Indeed, they are so tightly coupled that separation is possible only at the conceptual or definitional level. Nowhere is this fact clearer than in federal policy making. Earlier chapters have demonstrated that substantive policy coherence and effectiveness are almost always hostage to decision processes in which Congress plays a highly interventionist set of roles. These congressional roles are firmly embedded in our political culture, constitutional framework, and commitment to electoral responsiveness and accountability. They could only be altered significantly if we moved to an altogether different kind of government structure— say, a Westminster-type parliamentary system in which parties were stronger, members were far more politically dependent on the chief executive than they are now, and policies were more coherent (but not necessarily more effective).* Even if such a transformation were possible, which I strongly doubt, it is impossible to show that it would actually improve policy outcomes without sacrificing some deeply cherished features of our current system.

That said, the preceding chapters have shown that Congress is the single greatest *institutional* source of government failure. Its poorly designed policies, tendency to subordinate broad but diffuse interests to narrow but well-organized ones, rigidity and inertia in the face of new challenges, lack of credibility in maintaining earlier policy commitments, insouciance about implementation problems, gerrymandered representation system, and other defects give it much to answer for. Unsurprisingly, astute critics have advanced plausible, thoughtful proposals for its fundamental reform, and I cite some of them in an endnote.[11] However, I do not present them here for two reasons (other than space). First, they are political nonstarters. Congress is well aware of its poor reputation with the public, but shows no interest in reforming itself. Nor can outsiders do it without a well-organized rebellion by voters that is nowhere in prospect. Second, the earlier point about the risks of tinkering with complex, poorly understood human systems applies in spades to our Congress-centered politics whose countless moving parts will adjust opportunistically and in unforeseen ways to any reform.

---

*For a comparative anaylsis, see R. Kent Weaver & Bert A. Rockman, *Do Institutions Matter? Government Capabilities in the United States and Abroad* (1993), 11–41. A more incremental alternative—requiring voters to choose between each party's slates of candidates, instead of allowing them to split their votes for president and members of Congress—is thoughtfully discussed in Derek Bok, *The Trouble with Government* (2001), 287–91.

Instead, I prefer to focus this section on reforms to the policy-making process that might gain Congress's assent (or not require it) and that one can more confidently predict will improve substantive policy outcomes. I present them in no particular order.

The General Accountability Office is one of Congress's most valuable institutions, providing auditing, investigation, advice, and assessments on a vast array of programs that often highlight problems in policy design or implementation that enrich public policy debates and often arouse Congress to action. Resources for its core functions should be expanded, and its findings given greater publicity. The same is true of the offices of inspectors general in the departments, whose independence and investigation capacity can alert the public to needed policy and administrative changes.

Congress's own procedures might better facilitate collegiality, which should in turn foster compromise. Norman Ornstein, a leading expert on Congress, has long urged that the legislative schedule be changed in ways that would improve the members' ability to engage in committee work, legislative debate, and lubricating informal interactions, as well as their time working at home with constituents.[12] With his colleague Thomas Mann, Ornstein has also proposed many other, more formal changes designed to overcome partisan gridlock and encourage political moderation: alternative voting rules, including instant runoff reallocations; easier registration and voting systems; open primaries; campaign finance reforms; filibuster reform; and others.[13] Other political scientists have their own proposals, including some designed to encourage compromise.[14] Although all deserve serious attention, there are good grounds for skepticism about their political viability—and even about their efficacy if just grafted onto the existing system.[15]

Drawing on analogous efforts by health care institutions to reduce avoidable in-hospital problems, I have proposed a legislative checklist that congressional committees should use to ensure that their statutes address issues—many procedural or not particularly controversial—that will almost certainly generate costly, time-consuming, and unnecessary litigation if not addressed by Congress in advance.

Congress should have to comply with the same rules that it imposes on the public, yet as noted in chapter 3 it has in effect exempted itself from doing so in many cases. If members are obliged to feel the burdens of the laws that Congress enacts rather than being freeloaders on their own creations, they may become wiser legislators.

Transparency throughout the domestic policy process should be encouraged. Fortunately, new technologies are opening up new opportunities to improve not only transparency but innovation, collaboration, citizen participation, feedback, and decision making.[16] Law professor and former Obama administration official Beth Noveck has advanced many proposals for such reforms.[17]

INCENTIVES

In chapter 5, I explained that policy makers up and down the line face incentives that produce policies that are often myopic; favor small well-organized groups over vastly larger but more diffuse ones; encourage logrolling coalitions at the expense of the general public; ignore government "internalities"; and create perverse incentives for private actors that end up imposing costly inefficiencies on the taxpayers. Moral hazard, a type of incentives defect analyzed in chapter 5, is particularly important because it afflicts so many large programs, imposes immense costs on taxpayers, and threatens to impose even more in the future. Fortunately for policy reformers, it is also a familiar problem that private insurers have been managing for centuries[18]—and for which at least partial remedies exist.

The most obvious remedy for moral hazard, of course, is to avoid creating it in the first place.* Some of the programs criticized in chapter 5 for their moral hazard are candidates for outright repeal or substantial change, depending on a more detailed analysis. Fannie Mae and Freddie Mac, discussed below, are the most important current examples. Other programs, even if retained, should be required to reduce their moral hazard through the various techniques discussed

---

*Insurers, for example, will not issue a life insurance policy to one who lacks an "insurable interest" in the insured event, which of course is why one may not insure a stranger's life.

in chapter 5,* such as more data-based screening, monitoring, risk-adjusted cost sharing, and tougher enforcement. The student loan programs, for example, are ripe for screening criteria that would avoid committing scarce public funds to particularly bad bets when better bets can use them more effectively and with fewer defaults. It is folly to imagine that all high school graduates should go on to college at public expense, when in truth good vocational training would serve many of them far better and screening criteria can make successful outcomes reasonably predictable. Where student loan programs do cover vocational training, the government's costs are far lower, even taking into account the high default rates.

More generally, all programs vulnerable to significant moral hazard should require cost-sharing adequate to assure that beneficiaries have enough skin in the game to act responsibly, with the amounts scaled to what they can afford. Formulas for determining financial need and risk of default are already in wide use in various private and public programs. This approach might borrow a technique in the Coastal Barrier Resources Act of 1982, which provides that on sensitive coastlines that were then undeveloped, any future development would not receive federal subsidies, such as flood insurance and post-storm relief. In this spirit, the government might declare, for example, that once Hurricane Sandy victims receive their current bailout funds, the federal responsibility for reconstruction subsidies is over.[19] (A 2013 report by the Department of Housing and Urban Development's inspector general, finding that as much as $700 million in federal post-Katrina reconstruction aid to Louisiana homeowners may have been misspent, makes this approach even more urgent.[20])

Another moral hazard reform, here directed at the Federal Deposit Insurance Corporation, might use the stress testing process mandated by the Dodd-Frank law to provide a more reliable, refined basis for differentiating premiums according to risk. Indeed, targeted publication of that risk information could enable private insurers to bid for the deposit insurance business.

*Recall that *some* moral hazard may be inevitable, given certain legitimate program goals. See chapter 6.

Reforming the system of mortgage guarantees dominated by Fannie Mae and Freddie Mac to reduce moral hazard is imperative, as Congress recognized in putting it into conservatorship. This system, discussed in chapters 5 and 8, encouraged a housing bubble and overleveraging by homeowners and financial institutions that produced a financial catastrophe in 2008 whose immense effects will continue to be felt for years to come. Experts disagree about precisely how to allocate responsibility for this calamity and therefore about the best remedies. No one doubts, however, that a primary cause was the agencies' promotion of subprime lending and overleveraging in the secondary mortgage market and by homeowners, and that these behaviors were spurred and abetted by the implicit government guarantee, private securities rating agencies, and supervising congressional committees.[21] At a minimum, we should drop the pretense that these agencies are private entities and should include their operations on the government's balance sheet.

Plausible proposals have been advanced to eliminate the government's exposure to losses in this important market. As the study by Dwight Jaffee and John Quigley discussed in chapter 5 shows, the policy rationales for Fannie and Freddie's housing programs are not convincing, and the western European experience, especially in Denmark, confirms this.[22] If the government must continue to play a role, these economists argue, the appropriate model is not the government-sponsored enterprise but the Federal Housing Administration (FHA), which for almost eighty years underwrote loans to low-income home buyers on an actuarial basis without government subsidy.[23] Unfortunately, as chapter 8 explained, the FHA recently abandoned its successful traditional model in the wake of the Fannie/Freddie meltdowns, with costly results for taxpayers.

The Housing Commission of the Bipartisan Policy Center has offered a different proposal. Cofounded by former Senate majority leaders of both parties with members representing a broad range of interests and ideologies, the commission also represents the interests of Fannie Mae and Freddie Mac and of groups that received substantial funding from them.[24] It claims that its plan would sharply reduce the government's exposure to home mortgage losses by (1) phasing out Fannie and Freddie; (2) relying almost entirely on private capital to finance home purchases; (3) using the government only as a "public guarantor" exposed only after three layers of private capital subject to stricter capital requirements have paid; (4) requiring safer, more transparent servicing and securitization processes; and (5) returning the FHA to its traditional role: assisting first-time home buyers with down payment resources.[25] Critics of this proposal worry that the "public guarantor" will still have poor incentives, remain vulnerable to fraud, and improperly price risks.[26] After all, many of these same regulators, funders, and agencies utterly failed to foresee, much less prevent, the last crisis, despite some experts' dire warnings.[27] Other regulatory proposals are being developed, but all involve significant risk to taxpayers[28]—which makes Jaffee and Quigley's privatization approach for this market a promising way to avoid another huge bailout. Policy makers should resist the siren song of those who plump for new subsidies by assuming that they will be more successful than existing ones are.[29]

Reducing moral hazard on the part of government agencies and program beneficiaries is only one way to improve incentives. Another is to strengthen the long-standing efforts at "management by objective" (MBO), sometimes called "performance management." This technique has long been promoted by reform-minded officials and academics.[30] Reaching back at least to president Lyndon Johnson's Planning-Programming-Budgeting System, it requires each program to specify and quantify its goals in advance insofar as their nature permits.[31] Properly implemented, it encourages officials to "buy in" to the pursuit of certain outcomes whose attainment can be measured, and then holds them accountable for the results. It also tends to discipline their predictions by introducing sanctions against tactical overpromising. (Hopefully, incentives not to *under*promise already operate.) Some goals cannot be quantified, of course, but good managers can often devise imperfect but serviceable proxies for them. Once policy makers are confident that MBO is being properly implemented at the program level, they can fashion financial and other incentives to reward success. (Congressional authorization for such changes to the bureaucratic compensation system is probably required, as in the 1978 civil service reform law.) President Bill Clinton's much-touted National Performance Review, led by vice president Al Gore, included many interesting ideas and some significant improvements.[32]

In reality, however, such reforms have been long on promise and short on achievement. According to Jack Donahue, who advocates them, these efforts have had little effect: "The transformation of America's public sector to date is both limited and, perhaps more importantly, distorted. Some eminently sensible changes remain stubbornly stalled. Some second-order, silly, or questionable reforms have outpaced the fundamentals."[33]

Almost all government programs designed to provide services to the public do so by funding providers in the expectation that they will render the desired service to the program beneficiaries. Because providers tend to be far better organized than the consumer/beneficiaries, however, this arrangement disproportionately serves the former's interests. Once they have the funds, their incentive is to use them with only minimal oversight by the agency and with little or no accountability to the consumers whom they are supposed to be serving—other than whatever indirect effect consumer feedback may have on the politicians who authorize and fund these programs. Congress should instead direct that federally funded services be provided, insofar as possible, in the form of consumer vouchers subject to appropriate conditions to protect policy goals. Congress has done this with Section 8 housing and with food stamps, and many states have done so for private schooling. This form of program delivery, which Milton Friedman proposed more than fifty years ago,[34] is certainly no panacea for the problems facing the poor: for example, many landlords will not accept Section 8 vouchers, quality control of charter schools by parents is difficult, and food stamps may be used to buy unhealthy meals. But it does allow consumers to make their own trade-offs, increases providers' incentives to perform effectively and responsively, and informs policy makers about how well public funds are being used.[35] The logic of this approach extends to all publicly funded services, not just those for the poor. Many of the Affordable Care Act's problems might have been avoided by providing coverage in the form of income- and wealth-tested vouchers rather than through the act's highly complex, jerry-built system. Many private employers already use choice vouchers to fund health care for their employees, and will likely do so even more under the act.[36] Indeed, Congress should make vouchers, regulated to prevent fraud or consumer abuse, the default form of federally provided access to noncash benefits.

Policy makers should attend more to the architecture of individual incentives and choices—particularly their status quo and other cognitive biases—and then take this architecture into account in designing specific programs. I discuss below the difficulties of this approach, associated with scholars Richard Thaler and Cass Sunstein,[37] (under "Limits of Law") in connection with simplification strategies and "nudges."

Competitive incentives can improve government performance by rewarding effectiveness and punishing failure. In chapter 4, I discussed the Tiebout effect, under which communities vie with one another in providing different combinations of services and taxes in order to attract residents who "vote with their feet" and hence a greater tax base. States and localities, however, also compete for financial capital, talent, infrastructure, and successful programs, as in the public school systems. Although this competition already exists, federal policy makers might heighten and exploit it. An encouraging (but allegedly politicized) example is the Obama administration's Race to the Top program in public education; a counterexample is its stifling of voucher-based school choice in its own backyard testing ground, the District of Columbia. Another approach, of ancient lineage, is for the government to incentivize not only scientific discoveries (which is common) but also new, demonstrably effective techniques of policy design, assessment, performance, and enforcement. A recent instance is the Federal Trade Commission's prize for the best software to block illegal robocalls.[38]

A more radical move toward competition would be for Congress or an executive order to require each agency—before opting to provide a new service itself—to analyze and publish its findings as to whether that service can be provided as well or better and at the same or lower cost (all things/costs considered) by privatizing it, much as agencies have been required to reduce paperwork, conduct cost-benefit analyses (CBA; see chapter 2), and consider effects on small businesses. The agency should remain free to provide the service directly, but only after explaining publicly why it is doing so in light of this analysis. This implies, however, that the agency's capability to manage contracts with private providers must be strengthened so that the federal responsibility is preserved, not abdicated.

Congress, even more than the agencies, should also systematically reconsider whether and to what extent regulated activities should instead be subjected, under certain conditions, to competitive bidding (Medicare is especially ripe for this),[39] deregulated (e.g., sugar and other crop subsidies), or privatized (e.g., the US Postal Service and Amtrak). Whether Congress would heed this recommendation, of course, is an entirely separate question—and doubtful, judging from its shackling of the Postal Service. Most tariffs and other trade restrictions tax consumers for the benefit of inefficient industries; they too should be repealed. But again, designing each of these reforms requires detailed study beyond the scope of this book. And as with performance management, a reality check is warranted: after a strong outsourcing push by the administration of president George W. Bush, the movement of federal nondefense jobs to the private sector was relatively trivial, perhaps one in a thousand.[40]

Short of deregulation, privatization, and outsourcing, policy experts have advanced a host of recommendations for legal changes that would likely improve governmental effectiveness across a broad range of policy domains. For example, almost all economists favor using taxes to reduce a broad range of harmful activities rather than relying on other forms of centralized regulation. Such Pigouvian taxes would make almost everyone better off and could be designed to be revenue-neutral or revenue-raising, depending on concerns about their distributive impacts.[41]

Government-sponsored innovation is shadowed by the Solyndra fiasco and other bad bets on emerging technologies (discussed in chapter 8), but numerous important counterexamples exist. Mariana Mazzucato's 2013 book *The Entrepreneurial State* heralds a new appreciation for the role that the government has played and might (if carefully implemented) play in the future in spurring socially transformative technologies.[42] A recent Kauffman Foundation study proposes wider dissemination of scientific research; growth-oriented tax reforms; improved financial regulation and reporting; enhanced efficiency and fairness of public and private law rules and processes; and legal reforms to protect identity and privacy and refine intellectual property rights.[43] Another volume presents novel approaches to health and safety regulation;[44] yet another study analyzes various forms of "collaborative governance" between the government and private providers (both regulated and unregulated, both for-profit and nonprofit) in a variety of policy areas (not all federal) that can often exploit private advantages in information, legitimacy, productivity, and access to financial resources.[45] Careful studies of successful, marketable innovations are sure to yeild many other lessons for government policy.

IRRATIONALITY

Earlier chapters, especially chapter 5, identified many powerful forces that combine to produce policies that, while rational for the often concentrated, well-organized interests that stand to gain from them, tend to be irrational from the perspective of the diffuse public that must usually bear the costs of policy failure.

The single best way to resist this tendency is to counter it with systematic and well-publicized analyses of the consequences of existing and proposed policies, which can then become a factor in the ensuing policy debates. Chapter 2 described the methodologies of cost-benefit and cost-effectiveness analyses, defended them against the standard criticisms, and noted that they are required for major executive branch agency regulations under a succession of executive orders going back almost forty years. Congress should endorse this system, lodged in an important Office of Management and Budget (OMB) unit, and extend it to the independent regulatory agencies as well. (Legislation to this effect has been introduced in several past Congresses.) It should also expand the definition of "major" regulations subject to the CBA requirement, while tailoring the rigor of each CBA to the likely costs of the regulation in question. According to Cass Sunstein, the regulation expert who administered this analytical process for President Obama, his agency attempted to include consideration of how regulations affect dignity and income distribution. It also began to use CBA to assess the effectiveness of *existing* regulations ("look-backs"), not just proposed ones.[46] Unfortunately, his office has only about fifty staffers and its budget is only 0.0001 of those of the regulatory agencies it needs to review.[47]

Another source of irrational policies is Congress's growing use of omnibus appropriations legislation, a notoriously crude policy-making vehicle that combines in a long, often unreadable bill many unrelated provisions on highly diverse subjects, each complex in its own right. As noted in chapter 6, this impedes the kind of deliberate, problem-focused analysis and debate that sound policy making requires. In principle, this technique is limited by internal congressional rules, but in practice, congressional majorities override these limits and use omnibus legislation for political and tactical reasons. Congress should make it more difficult to breach these limits.[48]

Policies are likely to be more rational to the extent that those who receive the benefits also bear the costs, and that both are made visible rather than (in the case of costs) being obscured. This unity of cost bearing and benefit receiving enables them to focus on the true value of the benefit, use the resources most efficiently, and be better informed about whether to support the policy. It also helps policy makers to target assistance to those who want and need it most. Unfortunately, as discussed in chapter 2, skilled politicians tend to abhor this unity, preferring to exaggerate the size and distribution of the benefits and hide and diffuse the costs.[49]

This unity is less feasible in programs targeted to poor people who cannot bear the costs, but even here the same goal can be met by giving low-income consumers vouchers with which to purchase the service. Policy makers should more extensively employ user fees, such as those charged to national park visitors, which should also reflect the full cost of the service, albeit with appropriate means-tested reductions for the poor.

INFORMATION

In chapter 1, I noted that two top budget and policy officials in the Bush and Obama administrations agree that less than 1 percent of government spending is backed by even the most basic evidence of cost-effectiveness; that less than 0.1 percent of government *health care* spending goes to evaluating the effectiveness of the other 99.9 percent; and that the government has largely ignored the "moneyball" revolution in which private-sector decisions are increasingly based on hard data.[50] In chapter 6, I gave systemic reasons for this official ignorance, some of them tactical in nature.

The good news is that policy information can be improved in many ways, and relatively cheaply. (The bad news is that policy makers must be induced to *act* on the improved information.) One approach, discussed above in the "Incentives" section, is to empower consumers to allocate their program benefits among competing providers rather than vice versa. Here are some others.

In chapter 11, I noted that the largely successful 1996 welfare reform legislation was enacted only after years of state-level experiments with different types of welfare-to-work programs. The Department of Health and Human Services facilitated such experiments by exercising its legal authority under Section 1115 of the Social Security Act to waive certain restrictions in order to promote and then assess policy innovations. The information gleaned from those programs had at least two positive effects. First, it increased Congress's confidence that reforms could succeed in reducing the welfare rolls while improving the prospects for women and children through work readiness and job training programs and wage supplements. Then Congress and the department used this experience-based information in the actual design and implementation of the new law. Today, states are seeking similar waivers from the Affordable Care Act of 2010 in order to determine how best to implement the new law. Carefully designed, large-scale policy experiments of this kind should be designed and funded. Devoting even a tiny percentage of program funding to effectiveness assessment would likely repay itself—according to estimates by Kennedy School of Government economist Jeffrey Liebman—a hundred times over.[51]

Most proposals for program change are based on theoretical hunches about which policies will have which effects, and why. Unfortunately, even inspired, informed guesswork is problematic. As Michael Abramowicz, Ian Ayres, and Yair Listokin note,

> theory alone cannot resolve many policy issues because different theories point in different directions. Scholars attempt to inform these debates by parsing historical data, but regression analysis of policy is fraught with complications. There is little policy variation on many topics of national importance, and the variation that does exist is correlated with many other factors. Empirical policy evaluation often resembles a drug study in which the experimental population does not receive an assigned treatment and instead gets to choose whether to take the medicine or the placebo.[52]

They propose instead to "randomize" law by having agencies conduct randomized, controlled experiments of proposed policy innovations before adopting them in more permanent form.[53] Designing such experiments outside the laboratory can be difficult, but Jim Manzi, whose work on policy effectiveness was discussed in chapter 11, shows that they are now routine in business, especially online— Google claims to have run some twelve thousand experiments in 2009, with about 10 percent leading to business changes—and are also used by political strategists and political scientists to test possible reforms.[54] Experiments' validity, of course, depends on how rigorously they are designed, but since companies' profits will be affected by their accuracy they have strong incentives to design them well. The Office of Information and Regulatory Affairs (OIRA) should be tasked with these research designs.

Policy makers, in contrast, shy away from doing so. They may cite the costs and delays occasioned by such experiments, even though the costs of misguided policies are infinitely larger and delays in instituting them may therefore be salutary. They may also fear that experimental results may cast doubt on their proposals, as most do.[55] Yet precedents do exist. Starting in 1968, the Department of Health, Education, and Welfare contracted with RAND to conduct the income maintenance and national health insurance experiments. Forty-five years later, the findings from these experiments continue to influence a variety of social policy debates, especially the design of health insurance reforms and cash assistance to low-income families. Such experiments are highly cost-effective, and their use should be expanded.[56] Indeed, Manzi's proposal to create a federal experimental agency to design and run these experiments is worth serious consideration.

Policy makers should also experiment with the kind of "social impact bond" (SIB) that New York City's mayor Michael Bloomberg has developed, based on early efforts in Britain, to test new policy approaches to reducing the high recidivism rates among incarcerated teenagers. With SIBs, a government contracts with private investors (here, Goldman Sachs) to fund the new approach at no initial cost to taxpayers. Under New York City's SIB, if the approach causes recidivism to drop by 10 percent, Goldman Sachs gets its money back. If it falls more than 10 percent, the firm receives a profit. But if recidivism does not decline by the target amount specified in the bond, it will lose some or all of its investment. With skin in the game, the firm's incentive is to rigorously assess the proposed innovation in advance, and if it buys the SIB to try to make the program work, which would also save money for the taxpayers due to lower crime and incarceration costs.[57] In June 2013, the firm announced that it will use the SIB form to finance early education programs.[58] The experience with SIBs should itself be rigorously assessed with randomized experimentation.

In their recent book *Big Data*, Viktor Mayer-Schonberger & Kenneth Cukier present many examples of how our capacities to gather, analyze, and perceive otherwise obscure patterns in large but often highly decentralized data sources can improve both the identification of, and solution to, problems by private and governmental actors in areas like public health, consumer protection, law enforcement, and product design.[59] Cass Sunstein, the Obama administration's former regulatory policy chief and a leading scholar on regulation, emphasizes the importance of officials accessing and using policy information that is widely dispersed in the private sector.[60] Policy makers in all branches of government should exploit these opportunities at least as eagerly as private interests are doing, while protecting the legitimate privacy interests that this avalanche of information may threaten. Because information is power, however, the pursuit, analysis, and use of these new and more broadly based sources of information are less straightforward and more politically tactical in the policy realm than in the private sector. Indeed, "big data" is already enabling private firms to influence diet, smoking, high blood pressure, medication compliance, and other public health challenges often hobbled by bureaucratic failure. A promising example is scientists' effective use of internet data-mining techniques to detect prescription drug side effects more quickly and accurately than does the Food and Drug Administration, which relies on its relatively cumbersome and flawed Adverse Event Reporting System.[61]

Intellectual property law, expressly authorized in the Constitution, is a vital protection and spur for innovation and information sharing. Experts in this field are sharply divided over the normative, empirical, and policy issues that surround intellectual property rights and processes, with traditionalists emphasizing the legal protections that are needed to incentivize innovation, and other groups, such as Creative Commons and advocates for a new open-source economics, emphasizing the innovation-chilling and innovation-blocking risks of overprotection and the promise of more collaborative arrangements.[62]

With the pace of new "blockbuster" drugs slowing in recent years, the stakes in getting intellectual property rules right are soaring.

The federal government should make better use of private sources of credible information for consumers. In a number of policy areas, industries have established programs to independently assess and certify the safety and quality of important products in ways that are faster, cheaper, and more reliable than the government could manage itself.[63] Some of these private certification programs relate to risks that state law primarily regulates (e.g., fire hazards, kosher food, and construction materials), but others, such as the Joint Committee on Accreditation of Health Organizations and bond rating agencies, operate in conjunction with federal programs (Medicare and securities regulation, respectively). Both of these examples (especially bond ratings in the wake of the financial crisis) have been severely criticized for conflicts of interest, lack of competition, and flawed procedures, and the Federal Trade Commission is investigating claims that programs for certifying forest products as "green" are being used to stifle competition.[64] (Leadership in Energy and Environmental Design certification of buildings as green has also proved misleading; its highest mark was given to the Bank of America Tower, one of the greatest "energy hogs" among New York skyscrapers.[65]) Policy makers should search for other policy areas in which qualified private certification systems—for non-gene-altered food, say[66]—can supplant or supplement direct government regulation. At the same time, we need to recognize that private regulatory systems (the National Collegiate Athletic Association, for example) often exhibit many of the pathologies of public ones,[67] and must assure that these systems actually protect the public values they are supposed to serve.

Better information can be especially valuable to low-income people who are more likely to be isolated from the institutions and informal grapevines that serve others so well. For example, economists Caroline Hoxby and Sarah Turner show that many high-achieving but low-income students who would not otherwise apply to high-ranked colleges and universities that grant substantial financial aid and have high graduation rates can be induced to apply and often gain acceptance via a simple program that mails information packets and follow-up materials to them *at a cost of only six dollars per student.*[68]

Other information-based techniques, increasingly common in the private sector, might be used by government agencies to improve their efficiency. An all-too-rare example of this is a novel use of crowdsourcing by the Defense Advanced Research Projects Agency to improve the design of military equipment.[69]

In 1990, Congress enacted the Federal Credit Reform Act, which requires agencies to use a method for accounting for the costs of federal loan programs that systematically misrepresents those costs, invariably by *underestimating* them. This method misinforms the public and officials about the true cost of government loans by calculating their net future cash flows to the government from the loans and then discounting that amount to present value for the year in which the loan is disbursed. The discount rate assumes, however, that the risk of default by private borrowers is the same as the vanishingly small risk of default by the U.S. Treasury—an absurdity that the Congressional Budget Office (CBO), an arm of Congress, urges replacement with a "fair-value accounting" method that would reflect the true private default risks.[70] This absurdity enabled senator Elizabeth Warren and some colleagues to erroneously claim, with straight faces, that the student loan program is highly profitable—despite the huge default losses described in chapter 8.[71] More generally, it suggests, incorrectly, that government can extend credit more cheaply than private lenders can. Congress should implement the CBO's recommendation for all federal loan programs.

RIGIDITY

As discussed in chapters 3 and 4, our policy-making system and political culture create many veto points, cementing the status quo bias described in chapter 5 and elsewhere in this book. Indeed, these veto points make it even harder to change a policy once it is established than to institute it in the first place because the inertial political forces that normally resist change are now augmented by the interests that have come to benefit from the current policy and do not want it changed, regardless of the need for reform.

Nevertheless, this bias, while powerful, is neither wholly implacable nor irremediable. Writing in 1997, I called attention to "how many complex, controversial issues Congress has managed to address and resolve (usually for better, sometimes for worse) in the last two decades even as special interest groups—much to the consternation of most commentators—proliferated and became more politically engaged. The period since the early 1970s has been one of truly remarkable policy innovation at all levels of government," in contrast to the dire predictions of Mancur Olson and others about what Jonathan Rauch called *Demosclerosis* in a 1994 book by that title. I offered many examples of sound public policy changes in the past that, with a few exceptions (see just below), remain largely in place: "the substantial, if not total, economic deregulation of basic industries such as telecommunications, financial services, energy, trucking, railroads, buses, and airlines; renovation of the welfare and social security programs entrenched since the New Deal; reform of the federal budgeting and inter-governmental systems; a dramatic reduction in the military's share of the national economy and budget; a vast expansion of the national park and wilderness systems; and an overhaul of the major tax, immigration, housing, agricultural, transportation, campaign finance, environmental, intellectual property, and civil rights laws."[72] The main exceptions are agricultural subsidy reform (repealed), budgeting reform (mostly ignored in practice), and federal mandate reform (also ignored). Some, like tax reform, need much updating.

In that 1997 article, I proposed some partial remedies for the policy system's status quo bias; I repeat them here in abbreviated fashion.

Congress and the executive branch should require proponents of subsidies and other expenditures to propose offsetting reductions in other areas, and should insist that lobbyists do so as well. This helps to place special interests in a zero-sum game where any costs that they add must come at the expense of other special interests, and it contrasts with the logrolling incentives (discussed in chapter 5) that so often lead to inefficient and inequitable policies. Such a rule, called "pay as you go" or "paygo," was enacted in 1990 with bipartisan support, but it expired in 2002; it was widely considered a success until a budget surplus reduced its bite. Paygo was reinstated in 2002 by congressional rule, not statute; it was mostly ignored, and no sequester (the enforcement mechanism) was ever invoked. In 2010, a bitterly divided Congress agreed to a statutory paygo system,[73] but the enforcement sequester is still routinely waived—partly because budget legislation in recent years has been enacted in an omnibus form as part of a "grand bargain" rather than in more discrete pieces. Until this changes, the paygo principle can perhaps best be vindicated through a combination of more pointed CBO disclosure of paygo violations and efforts to mobilize public awareness of the violations.

If paygo rules increasingly constrain special interests, however, the pressures generated by these groups do not disappear. Instead, they are simply channeled into regulations, private-sector mandates, special trust funds, borrowing authorities, and other off-budget areas of governmental activity where these constraints do not now apply, or are weaker. By extending the paygo approach to these off-budget areas, policy makers can further reduce special-interest abuses while still exploiting the informational resources that those groups bring to the policy process.

Paygo only affects *new* subsidies, but the status quo bias is of course most strongly reflected in those already on the books. Policy makers should review and rationalize the current programs that subsidize the activities of private business interests in the name of such attractive goals as regional development, job creation, export promotion, price stabilization, and national defense. Many of these "corporate welfare" programs, which take multiple forms, are unfair to their competitors, costly to taxpayers, and ineffective. In 2011, for example, the Export-Import Bank gave almost half its loan guarantees and other subsidies to those unfortunates Boeing and General Electric.[74] Rigorous CBA would likely expose many of these as policy failures.

Government can seek to increase the accountability of interest groups both to their members and to the public by requiring the groups to disclose information about their transactions that the public has a right to know. Even where disclosure is already required, as with federal election campaign contributions, much improvement is possible, particularly through the Internet and other "open government" mechanisms discussed above. Disclosure is often (not always) a better way to protect public values than imposing substantive restrictions on the groups' activities.

Sunset provisions for federal programs cannot assure that policy makers will bring a fresh perspective to old programs and ask the right questions about their continuing effectiveness, but they can help. One item on the legislative checklist proposed above should be a sunset date. The prospect that a program will face a sunset review can be a spur to better performance and needed reforms, but it does entail several disadvantages. First, it is common for Congress to simply extend or reauthorize programs without conducting a genuine substantive review. At the time of this writing (September 2013), for example, the No Child Left Behind Act of 2001 remains in this posture. Second, sunset reconsideration of existing policies may magnify the problem of government credibility, to which I now turn.

CREDIBILITY

I noted in chapter 6 that the democratic accountability of government necessitates that it change its policies in response to elections, other strong expressions of public opinion, and perceptions of policy need—but that this very uncertainty deters those whose cooperation is essential for policy success. Private actors and lower levels of government will enter an opaque, labile policy environment only reluctantly and at a higher price (in some form) reflecting the risk that Washington will change signals in ways that harm their interests. This problem impedes many otherwise mutually desirable arrangements. Earlier chapters presented a number of examples, most vividly in the

Oakland Project (see chapter 8) and most currently in the refusal of many states to expand their Medicaid programs under the Affordable Care Act for fear that once the three-year guarantee of full federal funding ends, the states will be locked into much higher costs. (Wags liken this prospect to "the gift of a baby elephant.") This problem is both constitutional and tactical in nature: no Congress or president may bind a subsequent one, which is always free, within its constitutional authority, to change the rules, and even if the president could somehow bind himself, he cannot as a political matter bind Congress—and vice versa.

As explained in chapter 6, there are no good solutions to this endemic problem.[75] The government can enter into contracts, issue performance bonds, and take on other legally enforceable obligations, but this will not affect the important regulatory and tax policies that Congress often changes, thus engendering great uncertainty costs. Regulatory agencies, bound by Congress's policies, are even more constrained in changing direction abruptly, even when the courts uphold them.[76]

That said, Washington can encourage private actors and other levels of government to rely on and cooperate with it by reducing the risks of doing business with it even though it might later change its mind. Law-and-economics scholars Michael Abramowicz and Ian Ayres have explored how such credibility enhancements might be designed, most notably with "commitment bonds."[77]

IMPLEMENTATION

As explained in chapter 8, many obstacles impede federal policy implementation. In earlier work, I focused on the special, additional difficulties that federal judges face in attempting to implement their complex institutional reform decrees (sometimes called "structural injunctions") in prisons, schools, housing projects, police departments, and other agencies. I proposed that they should not issue such orders before conducting a "decree implementation analysis" through public hearings and other techniques to help them predict what different requirements might actually entail in the real bureaucratic world that they hope to reform, and to fashion their decree in light of that better understanding.[78] A similar practice for legislative and executive policy makers before they make difficult policy decisions would be salutary; any delay produced by such consultation and analysis would likely be compensated for by better-designed, more effective policies. Policy implementation planners should recruit skeptics to perform the challenging function that opposing counsel provides in structural injunction proceedings. Manufacturers deciding whether to invest in a costly new product line would surely do no less, yet the obstacles to successfully implementing complex public policies are just as predictable and opaque as those in markets; in fact, they are probably more so.

As chapter 7 explained, many federal laws are enforced weakly, or not at all, and improper payments and fraud (which are not the same thing) are rife. One straightforward remedy is to hire more inspectors, auditors, and other enforcement personnel in situations—tax collection and child support enforcement, for example—where the delinquencies are enormous and additional enforcement personnel pay for themselves many times over. (The Treasury's Financial Management Service estimates that a dollar spent in federal debt collection in 2011 produced $52.42 in recoveries.[79]) Politics, not cost-effectiveness reasons, account for Congress's penny-wise, pound-foolish refusal to expand enforcement personnel in such areas.[80] Even more basic, the long-vacant inspector general positions in many agencies (see chapter 10) should be filled and generously funded.

Whistle-blowers privy to illegal conduct may be a valuable adjunct to agency enforcement, especially for regulators that supervise large organizations whose compliance levels are opaque to their regulators. Law professor David Engstrom has systematically analyzed a variety of whistle-blower approaches: *qui tam* lawsuits under the False Claims Act, a recently revised tax bounty program, a bounty scheme under the Dodd-Frank financial regulation overhaul, and the cash-for-information programs of the Securities and Exchange Commission and the Drug Enforcement Administration, among others. Today, such efforts are largely limited to remedying procurement, tax, and securities fraud, but Engstrom notes the relevant trade-offs in possibly extending them to other policy areas.[81]

Many other regulatory agencies are notoriously understaffed in comparison with their vast responsibilities and the growing size of the markets that they regulate. The FDA is a particularly clear example of this, but it is also true of federal banking agencies. As discussed in chapter 10, the use of private contractors may or may not be more efficient than staffing functions in-house—this judgment can only be made after agencies conduct detailed function-by-function analyses— but if contractors are to be used, the agency must be far better equipped with staff sufficiently expert to manage the contractual relationship.

THE LIMITS OF LAW

As chapter 9 explained, the very nature of public law places some severe limits—both constitutional and functional—on the effectiveness of the policies that it communicates and governs. Although most of these limits cannot be avoided, some of them might be eased.

1. In a 1992 essay on which chapter 9 draws, I proposed four principles for improving the balance between law's complexity and simplicity.[82] The "cost distribution" principle calls attention to situations in which a law imposes unnecessary complexity costs on diffuse, poorly organized groups to the advantage of politically influential groups that benefit from that complexity, perhaps by burdening smaller competitors and would-be entrants into their industry with additional costs. Reformers can seek to redress the competitive distortions created by this political economy. Under the "audience principle," a law's complexity should be tailored to the sophistication and cost-bearing capacities of those who will have to interpret and implement it. The legal scholar Boris Bittker noted that complex tax rules are less problematic if they are addressed to experts who must apply

them to uncommon transactions than if they are addressed instead to numerous lay people who must understand and apply time to common transactions. As it stands, the tax code has almost tripled in size just over the past decade, and 90 percent of tax filers pay for help to complete their returns.[83] Many scholars and policy experts (including Bittker) have proposed tax simplification reforms which could herald vast gains in both efficiency and fairness.[84] With taxation as perhaps the most vexing site of citizen-federal interaction, simplification would likely enhance democratic morale and the government's legitimacy as well. It is clearly a popular theme with voters.[85]

In addition to knowing *where* to simplify, we need to know *how* to simplify. The "mimicking principle" posits that by studying the ways in which people contract around the formal law, perhaps by selecting simpler competitors, policy makers may obtain good information about its inefficiencies, including excessive complexity, which they can use to make the policy mimic people's informal simplification strategies. Where feasible, lawmakers should follow a "user fee principle" to tax those who benefit from legal complexity for the extra costs associated with those benefits. Although it is usually hard to isolate, allocate, and quantify complexity costs, and doing so may not always be cost-effective, marginal complexity costs can sometimes be calculated and redistributed. For example, courts may tax litigants that demand excessive, hard-to-provide document searches by their opponents. Some statutes, including the new Affordable Care Act, exempt small businesses from certain complex and costly regulatory requirements.

2. Other things being equal, simpler programs involving fewer levels through which funds and administrative communications must pass are easier to implement effectively.[86] Bureaucratically "flatter" programs can reduce the kinds of conflicting interests and incentives that block the long road from program design to implementation, which helped doom the Oakland Project and other failed programs detailed in chapter 8. The federal government can use broader grants, rather than detailed federal administrative specifications, to support

state implementation of federal policies. This conflict between detail and delegation is old and probably inevitable,[87] but in balancing them Congress should put its thumb on the side of broader delegation. First, states play an enormously important policy role for reasons explained in chapters 3 and 4. Second, they have many ways to thwart federal efforts to dictate policy details. Third, they are far more politically accountable and efficient than in the bad old days of Jim Crow and courthouse politics.[88] Finally, they are likely to know best how to coordinate and deliver federally funded services through their own administrative apparatus to their own citizenry. This does not tell federal officials precisely how much control is needed to maximize the effectiveness of federal dollars administered by states, but it suggests that less is sometimes more.

3. Like simpler programming, simpler regulation can be more effective—again, other things being equal. This, of course, is a traditional mantra of business firms and other entities subject to everexpanding governmental requirements in countless policy areas. Most recently, however, the cry for simplification has been taken up by Cass Sunstein, as mentioned earlier. In his book, *Simpler: The Future of Government,* he proposes many simplification measures designed to influence the "architecture" of individual choice. Sunstein proposes regulatory "nudges," an approach that he and Richard Thaler had advocated earlier and which they call "soft" or "libertarian" paternalism[89]—nonmandatory approaches to regulation that can shape better choices.[90] Two nudge strategies, for example, are *"smart" disclosure requirements*, which present salient data that people can use with minimal cognitive effort, and *default rules*, which take account of their cognitive patterns, such as the status quo bias, and reduce the likelihood of clearly irrational choices. Sunstein applies this approach to school meals, pensions, health insurance, savings plans, public health, and other policy areas.[91] New research on health insurance underscores why such simplification is so important: only 14 percent of the insured, it finds, understand the basic concepts they need to shop for policies.[92] Incorporating "nudging" strategies into regula-

tions, he contends, can make regulations simpler and more effective, while maintaining freedom of choice.[93] Some commentators doubt that he can have it both ways and that regulators can know when they are increasing, rather than reducing, consumer rationality.[94]

Sunstein also promotes regulatory "look-backs" to make things simpler. He laments that cost-benefit analysis is often only applied to regulations before they are promulgated—and therefore before agencies have much good, empirical evidence on how they function in practice.[95] By reevaluating existing regulations using more recent information, agencies can simplify their rules and ease unnecessary regulatory burdens. During Sunstein's time at the OIRA, agencies solicited suggestions from the public on which regulations to examine and then streamlined or eliminated many of them based on retrospective analysis.[96]

4. Another approach to simplification is to alter the mix between legal rules and discretion in favor of the latter for policy implementers. Philip K. Howard has made this case most strongly in his book *The Death of Common Sense*, which provides numerous examples of situations at all levels of government in which law needlessly "suffocates" initiative and expert judgment by public and private decision makers who know better than regulators what needs to be done in particular contexts.[97]

5. In some situations, policy makers should control risks by relying on existing systems of private law—especially tort, contracts, and insurance—rather than by setting up new, costly, and inevitably overbroad systems of administrative regulation. This is not because private law is invariably effective—indeed, many scholars have made fine careers out of dissecting the tort system's many flaws[98]—but instead because that system may on balance still be more effective than the regulatory alternative. Under certain conditions—the wrongdoer's identity is known, victims can readily prove causation of harm, their damages are straightforward, defenses to liability are well designed, and contingency fees assure access to lawyers—tort law's limits are less problematic than where these conditions are absent and thus

justice requires a combination of regulation and compensation. Airline accidents illustrate the first type, and mass asbestos exposures the second.

CIVIL SERVICE BUREAUCRACY

Chapter 10 emphasized that improving bureaucratic performance is essential to greater policy success. Not surprisingly, many carefully designed proposals for doing so have been advanced, including the 1989 report of the National Commission on the Public Service chaired by Paul Volcker. Paul Light, whose empirical work on the civil service was featured in chapter 10, has extended and updated the commission's work in a 2008 book that offered comprehensive proposals to "reverse the decline" in the public service.[99] Light noted that almost half the federal workforce would reach retirement age in the next decade, creating a rare opportunity to reshape the federal service.[100] Among his proposals were to sort government missions based on their importance, difficulty, and past success; thin out the bureaucracy by reducing the number of layers between top and bottom to no more than six; reduce the number of managers by half; accelerate the hiring and appointments processes;* improve the incentives to "make a difference"; experiment with an up-or-out promotion system for federal supervisors modeled on the military; streamline the disciplinary process; reserve a quarter of all middle- and senior-level job openings for outside candidates; improve performance measurement and incentives; and strengthen oversight of contracts, grants, and mandates to state and local governments.[101] Our disappointing thirty-five-year experience with the Senior Executive Service raises doubts that Congress will promote or even permit Light's approaches. I have nothing to add to such proposals.

As we saw in chapters 6 and 10, the vast army of private contractors now dwarfs the cadre of federal employees. The political and

---

*Judging from the long delays in filling vacant leadership positions that led to a political crisis in the Senate in July 2013 over such appointments, the much-heralded Presidential Appointment Efficiency and Streamlining Act of 2012 has had little effect.

other reasons that generated this army, including Congress's political fear of appearing to enlarge the federal workforce, are most unlikely to change. This makes contract administration by federal employees at least as important a feature of federal policy making and implementation as the services that federal employees render directly. Thus, the OMB and the officials of contracting agencies should promote better contract administration, including control of contractor fraud, waste, and abuse, through the kinds of reforms discussed at the end of chapter 6.

CHAPTER 13

Conclusion

W e have completed a long journey into the heart of domestic policy failure. Along the way, we have reviewed a plethora of evidence documenting this failure and analyses of the systemic, deeply embedded reasons why it occurs so often. All Americans—liberals, conservatives, in-betweens, and even the socialist and libertarian fringes—are well-advised to accept these facts and reasons, and to ponder their implications for our collective future. Liberals should worry that their ability to generate public support for governmental programs is increasingly hostage to low quality performance and vulnerable legitimacy. Conservatives should accept the fact, demonstrated in chapter 1, that big government is here to stay while continuing to insist that its policies be effective and conform to our political and cultural values. The rest of us—"militant moderates" like me, those who have only a limited interest in policy, and those for whom government seems distant and mysterious—should insistently demand that government's ends be tailored to its institutional means and capacities.

Here, then, are these facts, distilled in summary form.

1. Government policies often fail to satisfy even the most minimal, reasonable standards, elaborated in chapter 2, that Americans observe in their private choices. In some cases, programs cost more (often *much* more) than they are worth. In others, what they do may be worth doing but could be done either at a lower cost or with more bang for the same buck. Still other programs mainly benefit those

who gain much less from them than would others who need them more. And yet these failures persist, as if immortal.

2. These policy failures do not occur always or in every respect. The government has produced some striking successes, and we can discern some of the reasons (see chapter 11). Alas, such successes are hard to replicate, while the failures are frequent and large enough to explain Americans' growing doubts about whether their expanding government can be counted upon to do the right thing (see chapter 1). Their doubts on this score are hardly new—indeed, they reach back to colonial times—but they have now reached levels that threaten a democracy based on the consent and confidence of the governed.

3. If these failures occurred only in a few substantive policy areas, the remedy would be obvious and straightforward: simply institute better policies. If they occurred only when Democrats or Republicans controlled the levers of power, we could simply vote the incompetents out of office. This book, however, has shown that neither of these solutions is adequate to the nature of government's problems, whose roots are deep. The failures are not just random, occasional, or partisan; they are large, recurrent, and systemic. Few are *total* failures— after all, the government's money and authority almost always do *some* group *some* good. But if the relatively small group of winners are powerful enough, the policy failures are that much more firmly entrenched. This is why—to pick but one example out of the many presented here—the manifestly inefficient, egregiously mistargeted agricultural subsidies that Congress thought it had reduced and reformed in 1996 are vastly larger today even where crop prices are higher.

4. The previous chapters put us in a position to understand the most endemic reasons for these failures. Structurally, they include our *decision making system*, which is the complex, opaque machine that processes the public's choices into specific policies (see chapter 3), and our unique *political culture*, which frames and constrains those choices (see chapter 4). These structures are both desirable and undesirable. They are desirable because the elements of this culture reflect our deepest constitutional, political, and social commitments as a people, and because they tend (and are meant) to limit both the

scope of government power and the ill effects when it fails. They are undesirable because some of these same elements work to make such failures more likely. Each element of process and culture entails normative tradeoffs both internally and in tension with the other elements. So deeply embedded in our national DNA are they that we can neither isolate their effects empirically nor contrive to modify them very much. For example, localism remains a powerful force in our public philosophy more than eighty years after the New Deal began to nationalize our politics and policy agenda. For good *and* for ill, this localism shapes government performance.

5. We have seen (in chapters 5 and 6) that the essential ingredients of sound policy are seriously wanting in our system. Increasingly, this system lacks, indeed stifles, socially desirable incentives; rational selection of ends and means; accurate, unbiased, up-to-date information; the capacity to adapt promptly and flexibly to a changing policy environment; credibility to those actors whose expectations and responses will ultimately determine policy success or failure; and a bureaucracy that can manage and implement policies effectively in the real world. Without these ingredients, even the best-intentioned policy choices are unlikely to dislodge, much less improve, the embedded status quo, and can even make matters worse.

6. Even a relatively well-crafted policy is vulnerable to powerful market forces (see chapter 7). Policy makers cannot readily bend these forces to their will without introducing new distortions, which nimbler, more incentivized, better-resourced market actors can often exploit to their advantage. The pillow metaphor is apt here: when officials push against a particular area of market activity, that activity is displaced to other, harder-to-control areas. This effect is most evident with tax and financial regulation where the market actors are usually better trained, counseled, compensated, and motivated, and more experienced, than their official adversaries whose compliance tools are relatively crude, slow-moving, and behind the technological curve. But this market actor advantage also favors even the relatively unlawyered, uneducated, low-status actors on the street, like illegal drug traders. For all these reasons, the mass compliance necessary for

effective policy implementation depends far less upon episodic agency enforcement than upon a fragile condition: citizens' internal sense of the rectitude, competence, and legitimacy of the law and of the officials who administer it (see chapter 9). The public opinion evidence presented in chapter 1 strongly suggests that this condition is a steadily eroding asset. Increasingly, this civic bargain is experiencing defections by citizens who resent both paying taxes to what they see as a feckless, expanding government, and being snookered by laws that others exploit. Once lost, this legitimacy may be impossible to restore. We may assume that most people today obey the law most of the time. (Of course, we probably wouldn't know if they didn't!) But this legitimacy is a contingent social fact, not a foregone conclusion.

7. Even the most rationally designed policies may run aground when they confront political, institutional, economic, and other complicating factors in the field. Chapter 8 began with the showcase Oakland Project, which was launched with significant policy advantages yet like so many others foundered on the shoals of implementation. That chapter's detailed compendium of evidence of policy failure—all of it published in peer-reviewed social science, government's own reports, and the nation's most respected newspapers—demonstrates that the Oakland Project's failure was no outlier. The programs reviewed there span numerous and disparate policy domains and deploy a wide variety of policy instruments and approaches—yet they fail to satisfy even the minimal criteria of effectiveness presented in chapter 2. One may certainly quibble with this or that assessment, of course, but the overall verdict of pervasive policy failure is overwhelming. At a minimum, those who want to dispute these assessments and defend these programs as now configured bear a heavy burden of disproof.

8. The most striking feature of this failure—other than its sheer frequency and pervasiveness—is how deep and structural its causes are. They are grounded neither in Democrats' abiding commitment to an activist domestic policy agenda nor in Republicans' traditional opposition to it. (Although these partisan ideologies do play their part, they largely offset each other). Nor is failure due to insufficient re-

sources or lack of official commitment. As chapter 1 shows, vastly expanded federal domestic spending and programming—in real terms, as a share of gross domestic product, and even when compared to some European welfare states—has been a steady trend. Might government's greater ambition be a *cause* of the public's lower confidence in its performance, or are the two trends merely coincidental? Only a controlled experiment, which is impossible, could answer this question for sure. Instead, I have shown that this relationship between government's growing ambition and its endemic failure is rooted in an inescapable, structural condition: officials' meager tools and limited understanding of the opaque, complex social world that they aim to manipulate. Since the tools are relatively fixed and the social complexity is ever-increasing, this chasm between policy means and ends can only widen in the future. The remedies proposed in chapter 12, if implemented, promise to improve government performance at the margin. Such marginal gains are very much worth pursuing, but the lesson of this book is that the chasm will remain too wide for policy makers to bridge except under the most favorable conditions. As chapter 11 suggests, however, these conditions are less likely to materialize in the future than they did in the past.

James Q. Wilson nicely captured the spirit of melioristic realism that has informed this book: "If we are to make the best and sanest use of our laws and liberties, we must first adopt a sober view of man and his institutions that would permit reasonable things to be accomplished, foolish things abandoned, and utopian things forgotten."[1] Just as we teach the facts of private life to our children, we must teach these facts of public life to ourselves, to each other, and to our governing institutions.

Notes

CHAPTER 1: INTRODUCTION

1. "Beyond GDP: A New Global Comparison of Standards of Living," *Economist*, September 20, 2010, http://www.economist.com/node/17079148.
2. Bruce Meyer & James Sullivan, *Winning the War: Poverty from the Great Society to the Great Recession*, National Bureau of Economic Research Working Paper 18718 (2013).
3. Peter H. Schuck & James Q. Wilson, "Looking Back," in Schuck & Wilson, eds., *Understanding America: The Anatomy of an Exceptional Nation* (2008), 628–29; Karlyn Bowman, Jennifer Marsico, & Andrew Rugg, "Polls on Patriotism: What You May Have Missed in the Polls," http://www.aei-ideas.org/2013/06/polls-on-patriotism/?utm_source=Today&utm_medium=web&utm_campaign=062813.
4. See, generally, Dalton Russell, *Democratic Challenges, Democratic Choices* (2004), chaps. 1–2.
5. Pew Research Center for the People and the Press, "State Governments Viewed Favorably as Federal Rating Hits New Low," April 15, 2013, http://www.people-press.org/2013/04/15/state-govermnents-viewed-favorably-as-federal-rating-hits-new-low/.
6. Pew Research Center for the People and the Press, "Distrust, Discontent, Anger, and Partisan Rancor," April 18, 2010, http://www.people-press.org/files/legacy-pdf/606.pdf. Trust in the mass media has also declined sharply, particularly among conservatives and independents. See Josh Vorhees, "The Numbers Say You Probably Won't Believe the Numbers We're about to Show You," *Slate*, September 21, 2012, http://www.slate.com/blogs/the_slatest/2012/09/21/distrust_of_media_gallup_poll_shows_record_number_of_americans_don_t_trust_the_media_.html?wpisrc=newsletter_jcr:content.
7. Karlyn Bowman & Andrew Rugg, *Five Years after the Crash: What Americans Think about Wall Street, Banks, Business, and Free Enterprise* (2013), 10.
8. Neil King Jr. & Rebecca Ballhaus, "Rancor in Washington Fans Public Discontent," *Wall Street Journal*, July 24, 2013.
9. Sheryl Gay Stolberg, "For 'Millenials,' a Tide of Cynicism and a Partisan Gap," *New York Times*, April 30, 2013.
10. Janet Hook, "Tough Place to Fill Job Openings: U.S. Senate," *Wall Street Journal*, June 17, 2013.
11. Adam Liptak & Allison Kopicki, "Approval Rating for Justices Hits Just 44% in Poll," *New York Times*, June 8, 2012.
12. AEI Public Opinion Study, *Attitudes toward the Federal Government*, February 2011, 8–11, 17, 22–23.
13. Pew Research Center, "State Governments Viewed Favorably."
14. See, e.g., President Barack Obama, State of the Union Address, February 12, 2013 ("After all, why would we choose to make deeper cuts to education and Medicare just

to protect special interest tax breaks? . . . It's not a bigger government we need, but a smarter government that sets priorities and invests in broad-based growth."); Bill Clinton, *Back to Work: Why We Need Smart Government for a Smart Economy* (2011), chap. 4 (suggesting reforms to make it run more efficiently); Democratic National Committee, "Moving America Forward," 2012 party platform, http://assets.dstatic.org /dnc-platform/2012-National-Platform.pdf ("We know that transparent and effective government makes economic sense" and blaming special interests as corrupting government programs); and Nicolas Confessore, "Attacking Bush, Clinton Urges Government Overhaul," *New York Times*, April 14, 2007 (Hillary Rodham Clinton calling for "smart government").

15. John J. DiIulio Jr., "Facing Up to Big Government," *National Affairs*, Spring 2012, 18–19.

16. Robert P. Jones, Daniel Cox, Juhem Navarro-Rivera, E. J. Dionne Jr., & William A. Galston, *Do Americans Believe Capitalism and Government Are Working?* (2013), 9.

17. Franklin Foer, "Obamacare's Threat to Liberalism," *New Republic*, November 24, 2013.

18. E. J. Reedy & Robert E. Litan, *Starting Smaller; Staying Smaller: America's Slow Leak in Job Creation* (July 2011), http://www.kauffman.org/uploadedFiles/job_leaks_starting _smaller_study.pdf.

19. Floyd Norris, "In Actions, S.&P. Risked Andersen's Fate," *New York Times*, February 8, 2013, B1.

20. See, e.g., Floyd Norris, "Bad Grades Are Rising for Auditors," *New York Times*, August 24, 2012.

21. See, e.g., "The Other Vampires: Credit Rating Agencies," *Economist*, May 15, 2010, 83.

22. William Alden, "Nasdaq's Latest Breakdown," *New York Times*, August 23, 2013; Julia Werdigier, "Computer Breakdown Halts Trading at London Exchange," *New York Times*, September 8, 2008.

23. See, e.g., Neil Barofsky, *Bailout: An Inside Account of How Washington Abandoned Main Street While Rescuing Wall Street* (2012); Sheila Bair, *Bull by the Horns: Fighting to Save Main Street from Wall Street and Wall Street from Itself* (2012); and Jesse Eisinger, "Lesson Learned after Financial Crisis: Nothing Much Has Changed," *New York Times*, March 20, 2013.

24. Melissa Eddy, "Crisis-Struck Europeans Say They're Losing Faith in Governments," *New York Times*, July 10, 2013, A6.

25. Pippa Norris, ed., *Critical Citizens* (1999); Joseph S. Nye, Philip D. Zelikow, & David C. King, *Why People Don't Trust Government* (1997). For a Carter-era study, see Seymour Martin Lipset & William Schneider, *The Confidence Gap: Business, Labor, and Government in the Public Mind* (1983).

26. DiIulio, "Facing Up to Big Government," 10.

27. "In Congress, Gridlock and Harsh Consequences," *New York Times*, July 8, 2013.

28. Thomas Mann & Norman Ornstein, *It's Even Worse Than It Looks: How the American Constitutional System Collided with the New Politics of Extremism* (2012).

29. Nancy L. Rosenblum, "Good Neighbor Nation: The Democracy of Everyday Life in America" (unpublished manuscript, 2013).

30. See Ronald Inglehart, "Postmodernization Erodes Respect for Authority but Increases Support for Democracy," in Norris, ed., *Critical Citizens*, chap. 12.

31. "We Have Met the Enemy, and He Is Us," http://www.thisdayinquotes.com/2011/04 /we-have-met-enemy-and-he-is-us.html. For a similar view of the problem, see Derek Bok, *The Trouble with Government* (2001), 13, 95.

32. Robert Higgs, *Crisis and Leviathan: Critical Episodes in the Growth of American Government* (1987).

33. Paul C. Light, *A Government Ill-Executed: The Decline of the Federal Service and How to Reverse It* (2008), 24–36.

34. Niall Ferguson, "The Regulated States of America," *Wall Street Journal*, June 19, 2013.

35. DiIulio, "Facing Up to Big Government."

36. Nye et al., *Why People Don't Trust Government* 186.

37. "The Size of the State," *Economist*, July 28, 2012, 23.

38. *Statistical Abstract of the United States, 2012*, Table 471.

39. See U.S. Government Accountability Office, *2012 Annual Report: Opportunities to Reduce Duplication, Overlap and Fragmentation, Achieve Savings, and Enhance Revenue*, http://www.gao.gov/products/GAO-12-342SP.

40. See, generally, Peter H. Schuck & Richard J. Zeckhauser, *Targeting in Social Programs: Avoiding Bad Bets, Removing Bad Apples* (2006).

41. U.S. Department of Defense, "Debt Is Biggest Threat to National Security, Chairman Says," http://www.defense.gov/news/newsarticle.aspx?id=65432. Secretary of state John Kerry agrees that ineffective policy accounts for much of this debt. See Michael R. Gordon, "Kerry Links Economics to Foreign Policy," *New York Times*, January 25, 2013.

42. "Over-Regulated America," *Economist*, February 18, 2012, 9.

43. "This Time It's Serious," Schumpeter, *Economist*, February 18, 2012, 71.

44. Niall Ferguson, "How America Lost Its Way," *Wall Street Journal*, June 8, 2013.

45. See, e.g., Joanne B. Freeman, *Affairs of Honor: National Politics in the New Republic* (2001); Pietro S. Nivola, "How, Once Upon a Time, a Dogmatic Political Party Changed Its Tune," http://www.brookings.edu/research/opinions/2012/11/14-war-1812-nivola; and Mark Bowden, " 'Idiot,' 'Yahoo,' 'Original Gorilla': How Lincoln Was Dissed in His Day," *Atlantic*, June 2013.

46. See, e.g., Adam Goodheart & Peter Manseau, "American History Hits the Campaign Trail," *New York Times*, July 8, 2012.

47. "Assessing Peter Schuck's *Diversity in America: Keeping Government at a Safe Distance*" (symposium), *Yale Law & Policy Review* 23 (2005): 78–79; citations omitted.

48. "FEMA Operations Criticized in Report," *New York Times*, April 15, 2006.

49. AEI Public Opinion Study, *Attitudes toward the Federal Government*.

50. See, e.g., James V. DeLong, "America's Crisis of Political Legitimacy," *The American*, August 28, 2012, http://american.com/archive/2012/august/americas-crisis-of-political-legitimacy.

51. Light, *A Government Ill-Executed*, 159–60.

52. Ibid., 36, 126–28.

53. James A. Morone, *The Democratic Wish: Popular Participation and the Limits of American Government* (1990).

54. Abby Goodnough, "Governor of Tennessee Joins Peers Refusing Medicaid Plan," *New York Times*, March 28, 2013, A17.

55. Gallup, "Americans Wary of Health Law's Impact," June 27, 2013, http://www.gallup.com/poll/163253/americans-wary-health-law-impact.aspx.

56. David Brooks, "Midlife Crisis Economics," *New York Times*, December 26, 2011.

57. Bowman & Rugg, *Five Years after the Crash*, 10.

58. Kelman, *Making Public Policy: A Hopeful View of American Government* (1987), 208–9.

59. James Q. Wilson & John J. DiIulio Jr., *American Government: The Essentials: Institutions and Policies*, 12th ed. (2011), 467–68; emphasis in the original.

60. Nate Silver, "Health Care Drives Increase in Government Spending," *New York Times*, January 17, 2013.

61. Ezra Klein, "Our Corrupt Politics: It's Not All Money," *New York Review of Books*, March 22, 2012, 42, 44.

62. DiIulio, "Facing Up to Big Government," 3–5.

63. Ibid., 3.

64. Even here, some failures seem clear enough. See, for example, the scathing congressional report on a major counterterrorism program. James Risen, "Criticism of Centers in Fight on Terror," *New York Times*, October 3, 2012.

65. See, e.g., Erica Goode, "Some Chiefs Chafing as Justice Department Keeps Closer Eye on Policing," *New York Times*, July 28, 2013; and Rachel L. Swarns, "After Decades in Institutions, a Bumpy Journey to a New Life," *New York Times*, September 30, 2012.

66. Anthony King & Ivor Crewe, *The Blunders of Our Governments* (2013).

67. Peter H. Schuck & James Q. Wilson, eds., *Understanding America: The Anatomy of an Exceptional Nation* (2008).

68. See, e.g., R. Kent Weaver & Bert A. Rockman, eds., *Do Institutions Matter? Government Capabilities in the United States and Abroad* (1993). One imaginative study compared the efficiency of postal services in 159 countries by mailing letters with a return address to nonexistent addresses in each country and seeing whether they were returned and, if so, how long that took. About 60 percent of the letters were returned, and this took an average of over six months; the international postal convention to which all of the countries are signatories specifies return within one month. No country met that standard; the United States returned all the letters within ninety days. Alberto Chong, Rafael La Porta, Florencio Lopez-de-Silanes, & Andrei Shleifer, *Letter Grading Government Efficiency*, National Bureau of Economic Research Working Paper 18268 (2012).

69. The closest general analyses that I have found are Amihai Glazer & Lawrence S. Rothenberg, *Why Government Succeeds and Why It Fails* (2001), and Clifford Winston, *Government Failure versus Market Failure: Microeconomics Policy Research and Government Performance* (2006). Both are excellent analyses, rich with insights that I will harvest for my own purposes here, but they eschew legal-institutional factors and focus almost exclusively on economic incentives. Thus, Glazer & Rothenberg note, "[We assume] an idealized political state where forward-looking politicians in a democracy attempt to realize, rather than subvert, policy objectives. Though . . . we refer to core features of democracies (most notably, how political turnover affects policy success and how endogenous support for a policy can make it more effective), we integrate them with considerations of economic behavior. Similarly, we neglect institutional and constitutional differences; though, for example, we often discuss the United States, our study aims to be generic and rarely relies on special features of the American system . . ." (3). And Winston notes that "although I recognize that policy assessments must account for institutional complexities and government entities that shape policy implementation and affect performance, I limit my discussion to the theoretical motivation for each policy, its essential features, and its economic effects" (11). My study, in contrast, emphasizes the special features of the American system that systematically affect policy implementation.

70. Peter Orszag & John Bridgeland, "Can Government Play Moneyball?" *Atlantic*, July–August 2013, 63.

71. Alan S. Gerber & Eric M. Patashnik, "Government Performance: Missing Opportunities to Solve Problems," in Gerber & Patashnik, eds., *Promoting the General Welfare: New Perspectives on Government Performance* (2006), 6. For my review of this book, see Peter H. Schuck, "Is a Competent Federal Government Attainable or Oxymoronic?" *Geo. Wash. Law Review* 973 (2009).

72. Terry M. Moe, "Delegation, Control, and the Study of Public Bureaucracy," *The Forum* 10 (2012): 13.

73. James Q. Wilson, "Policy Intellectuals and Public Policy," in *American Politics, Then and Now: And Other Essays* (2010), 32.

74. Peter H. Rossi, "The Iron Law of Evaluation and Other Metallic Rules," *Research in Social Problems and Public Policy* 4 (1987): 3–20. I am unaware of any refutation of these "laws."

75. Gerber & Patashnik, eds., *Promoting the General Welfare*.

76. See Alan S. Gerber & Eric M. Patashnik, "Sham Surgery: The Problem of Inadequate Medical Evidence," in Gerber & Patashnik, eds., *Promoting the General Welfare*, chap.

3. This indifference to evidence of cost-effectiveness is in stark contrast to the comparatively rigorous requirement of efficacy (and safety) for drugs and (to a lesser extent) medical devices.

77. Clifford Winston, "Urban Transportation," in Gerber and Patashnik, eds., *Promoting the General Welfare*, 77.

78. Edgar O. Olsen, "Achieving Fundamental Housing Policy Reform," in Gerber and Patashnik, eds., *Promoting the General Welfare*, 105.

79. Jay P. Greene, "Fixing Special Education," in Gerber and Patashnik, eds., *Promoting the General Welfare*, 130–41.

80. Winston, *Government Failure versus Market Failure*, 3.

81. E. J. Dionne Jr., remark at Brookings Institution workshop for the present volume, May 30, 2013.

82. Steven Kelman, *Making Public Policy: A Hopeful View of American Government* (1987), 271–72.

83. See, e.g., "D.C.'s Davis-Bacon Revolt," *Wall Street Journal*, June 7, 2013.

84. Isaiah Berlin, *The Crooked Timber of Humanity* (1990). The phrase is taken from Kant.

85. Jones et al., *Do Americans Believe Capitalism and Government Are Working?*, 13.

86. See, e.g., Michael Sandel, *What Money Can't Buy: The Moral Limits of Markets* (2012).

87. See Charles de Secondat Montesquieu, *The Spirit of the Laws* (1748) ("Commerce cures destructive prejudices. . . . It polishes and softens barbarous mores. . . ."); and Adam Smith, *Lectures on Justice, Police, Revenue and Arms*, ed. Edwin Cannan (1896), 253 ("Whenever commerce is introduced into any country probity and punctuality always accompany it."). For modern defenses of the morality of the market, see Arthur C. Brooks, *The Battle: How the Fight between Free Enterprise and Big Government Will Shape America's Future* (2010); Michael Novak, *Toward a Theology of the Corporation* (1990). See also Daniel Markovits, "Market Solidarity," lecture presented at Yale Law School, April 9, 2012.

88. See, e.g., Robert Wuthnow, "Religion," in Schuck & Wilson, eds., *Understanding America*, chap. 10.

89. James Q. Wilson, "Conclusion: America versus the World," in *American Politics, Then and Now*, 194–95.

90. For the provenance of this quote, see http://en.wikiquote.org/wiki/Daniel_Patrick_Moynihan.

91. Robert K. Merton, "The Unanticipated Consequences of Purposive Social Action," *American Sociological Review* 1 (1936): 895.

92. This distinction was made by Charles E. Lindblom in his classic "The Science of 'Muddling Through,'" *Public Administration Review* 19 (1959): 79–88.

93. Peter H. Schuck, *Meditations of a Militant Moderate: Cool Views on Hot Topics* (2006).

CHAPTER 2: SUCCESS, FAILURE, AND IN BETWEEN

1. Peter H. Schuck & Richard J. Zeckhauser, *Targeting in Social Programs: Avoiding Bad Bets, Removing Bad Apples* (2006).

2. Ibid., 41.

3. Jeffrey L. Pressman & Aaron Wildavsky, *How Great Expectations in Washington Are Dashed in Oakland; Or, Why It's Amazing That Federal Programs Work at All, This Being a Saga of the Economic Development Administration as Told by Two Sympathetic Observers Who Seek to Build Morals on a Foundation of Ruined Hopes*, 3d ed. (1984), xxiii.

4. Herbert A. Simon, *Administrative Behavior*, 3rd ed. (1976), 38–41.

5. Pressman & Wildavsky, *How Great Expectations in Washington Are Dashed in Oakland*, 113–16.

6. Simon, *Administrative Behavior.*

7. Kenneth J. Arrow, *Social Choice and Individual Values,* 2nd ed. (1963).

8. Steven Kelman, *Making Public Policy: A Hopeful View of Government* (1987), 208.

9. See, e.g., Louis Kaplow & Steven Shavell, *Fairness versus Welfare* (2002).

10. See, e.g., Susan Rose-Ackerman & Thomas Perroud, "Policymaking and Public Law in France: Public Participation, Agency Independence, and Impact Assessment," 19 *Columbia Journal of European Law* 223 (2013), especially part 4.

11. Stuart Shapiro, "The Evolution of Cost-Benefit Analysis in U.S. Regulatory Decision-making," in David Levi-Faur, ed., *Handbook on Politics of Regulation* (2011), 385.

12. See, e.g., Matthew D. Adler & Eric A. Posner, *New Foundations of Cost-Benefit Analysis* (2006); Richard L. Revesz & Michael A. Livermore, *Retaking Rationality: How Cost-Benefit Analysis Can Better Protect the Environment and Our Health* (2011); Frank Ackerman & Lisa Heinzerling, *Priceless: On Knowing the Price of Everything and the Value of Nothing* (2004); and Cass R. Sunstein: *The Cost-Benefit State: The Future of Regulatory Protection* (2003).

13. This has been called the "cost of costing." Guido Calabresi & Philip Bobbitt, *Tragic Choices: The Conflicts That Society Confronts in the Allocation of Tragically Scarce Resources* (1978), 21.

14. Mark H. Moore, *Recognizing Public Value* (2013).

15. Jonathan S. Masur & Eric A. Posner, "Regulation, Unemployment, and Cost-Benefit Analysis," *Virginia Law Review* 98 (2012): 579–634.

16. See Cass R. Sunstein, "The Value of A Statistical Life: Some Clarifications and Puzzles" (unpublished manuscript, 2013).

17. I thank Henry Aaron for making this point, analogizing to partial and general equilibrium analysis.

18. Daniel H. Cole, "Reconciling Cost-Benefit Analysis with the Precautionary Principle" (unpublished manuscript, 2012).

19. See, e.g., Gregory C. Keating, "Beyond Efficient Precaution: The Asymmetry of Harm and Benefit" (unpublished manuscript, 2012).

20. For some examples, see "The Rule of More," *Economist*, February 18, 2012, 77.

21. "The 'Social Cost of Carbon' Gambit," *Wall Street Journal*, June 28, 2013.

22. http://www.cdc/gov/immigrantrefugeehealth/laws-regs/hiv-ban-removal/final-rule .html.

23. Bjorn Lomberg, "An Economic Approach to the Environment," *Wall Street Journal*, April 23, 2012, http://online.wsj.com/article/SB10001424052702303513404577356414271425218.html.

24. Clifford Winston, *Government Failure versus Market Failure: Microeconomics Policy Research and Government Performance* (2006), 3–4.

25. Christopher DeMuth, "The Regulatory Budget," *Regulation*, March–April 1980, 34.

26. Stephen Breyer, *Breaking the Vicious Circle: Toward Effective Risk Regulation* (1993).

27. See generally, Schuck & Zeckhauser, *Targeting in Social Programs.*

28. For a history of this distinction, see Michael B. Katz, *In the Shadow of the Poorhouse: A Social History of Welfare in America* (1996).

29. Philip E. Tetlock, *Expert Political Judgment: How Good Is It? How Can We Know?* (2005), 231–33. Similar points about the marketplace of ideas are made in Richard A. Posner, *Public Intellectuals: A Study of Decline* (2001). For a negative review of the latter, see David Brooks, "Notes from a Hanging Judge," *New York Times Book Review*, January 13, 2002, 9.

30. On the lack of voter incentives to gain this information, see, generally, Anthony Downs, *An Economic Theory of Democracy* (1957).

31. U.S. Office of Management & Budget, *2013 Draft Report to Congress on the Benefits and Costs of Federal Regulations and Agency Compliance with the Unfunded Mandates Reform Act*, http://www.whitehouse.gov/sites/default/files/omb/inforeg/2013_cb/draft

_2013_cost_benefit_report.pdf (discussing implementation of Executive Order No. 13563, January 18, 2011).

32. Tetlock, *Expert Political Judgment*, Methodological Appendix, 239ff.

33. David A. Hyman, "Why Did Law Professors Misunderestimate the Lawsuits against PPACA?" *University of Illinois Law Review* (forthcoming, 2014).

34. David L. Rosenhan, "Warning Third Parties: The Ripple Effects of *Tarasoff*," *Pacific Law Journal* 24 (1993): 1185–89.

35. William Goldman, *Adventures in the Screen Trade: A Personal View of Hollywood* (1983).

36. Ibid., 2, 268.

37. Ibid., 22, 23, 75. See also Richard A. Posner's assessment of the accuracy of an overlapping category, public intellectuals, in Posner, *Public Intellectuals*.

38. Nate Silver, *The Signal and the Noise: Why So Many Predictions Fail—But Some Don't* (2012); Nassim Nicholas Taleb, *The Black Swan: The Impact of the Highly Improbable*, expanded ed. (2010).

39. See, e.g., Tetlock, *Expert Political Judgment*; Zeljka Buturovik, "Putting Political Experts to the Test," *Critical Review: A Journal of Politics & Society* 22 (2011): 389–96; and Tamas Meszerics & Levente Littvay, "Pseudo-Wisdom and Intelligence Failures," *International Journal of Intelligence & CounterIntelligence* 23 (2009): 133–47. For a defense of climate change models, see William D. Nordhaus, "Why the Global Warming Skeptics Are Wrong," *New York Review of Books*, March 22, 2012, http://www.nybooks.com/articles/archives/2012/mar/22/why-global-warming-skeptics-are-wrong/?pagination=false.

40. Steven Morrison & Clifford Winston, *The Economic Effects of Airline Deregulation* (1986).

41. Elisabeth Bumiller, "One Year Later, Military Says Gay Policy Is Working," *New York Times*, September 19, 2012.

42. Ryan Grim & Zach Carter, "Bank of America Dropping Plan to Charge Monthly $5 Debit Card Fee," *Huffington Post*, November 1, 2011, http://www.huffingtonpost.com/2011/11/01/bank-of-america-debit-card-fee_n_1069425.html.

43. Jeffrey A. Jenkins & Eric M. Patashnik, "Living Legislation and American Politics," in Jenkins & Patashnik, eds., *Living Legislation: Durability, Change, and the Politics of American Lawmaking* (2012), 17. On the Tax Reform Act, see Eric M. Patashnik, "Why Some Reforms Last and Others Collapse: The Tax Reform Act of 1986 versus Airline Deregulation," in Jenkins & Patashnik, eds., *Living Legislation*, chap. 8.

44. Jeff Bennett & Sharon Terlep, "U.S. Balks at GM Plan," *Wall Street Journal*, September 17, 2012. On the Treasury's slippery accounting methods for assessing this and other bailouts, see Gretchen Morgenson, "Seeing Bailouts through Rose-Colored Glasses," *New York Times*, May 20, 2012 (economists' critiques of the Treasury's methodology).

45. Andrew Ross Sorkin, "Plot Twist in the A.I.G. Bailout: It Actually Worked," *New York Times*, September 10, 2012.

46. The most prominent dissenter is Neil Barofsky, a former special inspector general overseeing the bailout programs and the author of *Bailout: An Inside Account of How Washington Abandoned Main Street by Rescuing Wall Street* (2012), who claims that the government has fudged its numbers to make the rescue seem successful. See also Gretchen Morgenson, "Banks, at Least, Had a Friend in Geithner," *New York Times*, February 3, 2013 (quoting Dean Baker).

47. Vesla M. Weaver, "The Significance of Policy Failures in Political Development: The Law Enforcement Assistance Administration and the Growth of the Carceral State," in Jenkins & Patashnik, eds., *Living Legislation*, chap. 11.

48. Harold Demsetz, "Information and Efficiency: Another Viewpoint," *Journal of Law & Economics* 12 (1969): 3.

49. Ibid., 10–11.

50. Derek Bok, *The Trouble with Government* (2001), 120–21.

CHAPTER 3: POLICY-MAKING FUNCTIONS, PROCESSES, MISSIONS, INSTRUMENTS, AND INSTITUTIONS

1. See, e.g., James Q. Wilson, ed., *The Politics of Regulation* (1980); and Peter H. Schuck, "The Politics of Regulation," *Yale Law Journal* 90 (1981): 702–25 (review of Wilson book).
2. See, generally, Robert D. Putnam, *Bowling Alone: The Collapse and Revival of American Community* (2001). For my critique of Putnam, see Peter H. Schuck, "In Diversity We (Sorta) Trust," *American Lawyer*, December 2007, 83–84.
3. See, e.g., Eliot Cohen, "The Military," in Peter H. Schuck & James Q. Wilson, eds., *Understanding America: The Anatomy of an Exceptional Nation* (2008), chap. 9.
4. Julia Werdigier, "Britain Offers Its Proposal to Privatize Mail Service," *New York Times*, July 11, 2013.
5. See, e.g., Richard A. Posner, "Natural Monopoly and Its Regulation," *Stanford Law Review* 21 (1968): 548–643.
6. Amihai Glazer argues in private correspondence that under certain conditions an individual might have an incentive to contribute to a *private* purchase of a public good.
7. This distinction is highlighted in Charles Wolf Jr., "A Theory of Non-Market Failures," *Public Interest* 55 (1979): 114–33.
8. Paul E. Peterson, *The Price of Federalism* (1995). On races to the bottom, see Jan K. Brueckner, "Welfare Reform and the Race to the Bottom: Theory and Evidence," *Southern Economic Journal* 66 (2000): 505–25.
9. Saul Levmore, "Internality Regulation through Public Choice," *Theoretical Inquiries in Law* 15 (forthcoming, 2014).
10. Gerald D. Skoning, "How Congress Puts Itself above the Law," *Wall Street Journal*, April 16, 2013.
11. For evidence, see Kay L. Schlozman, Sidney Verba, & Henry E. Brady, *The Unheavenly Chorus: Unequal Political Voice and the Broken Promise of American Democracy* (2012). For theory, see Mancur Olson Jr., *The Logic of Collective Action: Public Goods and the Theory of Groups* (1965).
12. Jerry L. Mashaw, "Administrative Due Process: The Quest for a Dignitary Theory," *Boston University Law Review* 61 (1981): 885–931.
13. Anne Joseph O'Connell, "Bureaucracy at the Boundary," *University of Pennsylvania Law Review* 162 (forthcoming, 2013).
14. Kirti Datla & Richard L. Revesz, "Deconstructing Independent Agencies (and Executive Agencies)," *Cornell Law Review* 98 (2013): 769–843.
15. Adrian Vermeule, "Conventions of Agency Independence," *Columbia Law Review* 113 (2013): 1175–79.
16. *A.L.A. Schechter Poultry Corp. v. United States*, 295 U.S. 495 (1935).
17. *Whitman v. American Trucking Associations, Inc.*, 531 U.S. 457 (2001).
18. The leading academic proponent of this view is David Schoenbrod; see his *Power without Responsibility: How Congress Abuses the People through Delegation* (1993).
19. See, e.g., Jonathan H. Adler, "Placing 'Reins' on Regulations: Assessing the Proposed REINS Act," *New York University Journal of Legislation and Public Policy* 16 (2013): 1–37; Jonathan R. Siegel, "The REINS Act and the Struggle to Control Agency Rulemaking," *New York University Journal of Legislation and Public Policy* 16 (2013): 131–85.
20. Peter H. Schuck, "Delegation and Democracy: Comments on David Schoenbrod," *Cardozo Law Review* 20 (1999): 775–93.
21. See, generally, Lee Epstein, William M. Landes, & Richard A. Posner, *The Behavior of Federal Judges: A Theoretical and Empirical Study of Rational Choice* (2013).
22. *National Federation of Independent Business v. Sebelius*, 132 S. Ct. 2566 (2012).
23. See, e.g., R. Shep Melnick, *Between the Lines: Interpreting Welfare Rights* (1994); R. Shep Melnick, *Regulation and the Courts: The Case of the Clean Air Act* (1983); and

Sean Farhang, *The Litigation State: Public Regulation and Private Lawsuits in the United States* (2010).

24. See, e.g., *Motor Vehicle Manufacturers Association v. State Farm Mutual Automobile Insurance Company*, 463 U.S. 29 (1983).

25. The principle that courts should remand to the agency where it has incorrectly interpreted the statute grows out of the *Chenery* litigation. See, *Securities and Exchange Commission v. Chenery Corporation*, 332 U.S. 194 (1947).

26. The distinction between competence and capacity is analyzed in Andrew B. Coan, "Judicial Capacity and the Substance of Constitutional Law," *Yale Law Journal* 122 (2012): 422–58.

27. See, e.g., *Securities and Exchange Commission v. Chenery Corporation*, 332 U.S. 194 (1947) (multiple remands); Peter H. Schuck & E. Donald Elliott, "To the Chevron Station: An Empirical Study of Federal Administrative Law," *Duke Law Journal* 1990 (1990): 984–1077.

28. *United States v. Booker*, 543 U.S. 220 (2005).

29. Mosi Secret, "Big Sentencing Disparity Seen for Judges," *New York Times*, March 6, 2012, A23.

30. Philip K. Howard, *The Death of Common Sense: How Law Is Suffocating America* (1994).

31. Rachel E. Barkow, "Prosecutorial Administration: Prosecutor Bias and the Department of Justice," *University of Virginia Law Review* 99 (2013): part II.

32. Robert A. Katzmann, *Regulatory Bureaucracy: The Federal Trade Commission and Antitrust Policy* (1980).

33. Margo Schlanger, "Offices of Goodness: Influence without Authority in Federal Agencies," September 9, 2013, http://ssrn.com/abstract=2322797.

34. Lester M. Salamon, ed., *The Tools of Government: A Guide to the New Governance* (2002), 1–2; emphasis in the original.

35. Ibid., 9.

36. See, generally, Christopher K. Leman, "Direct Government," in Salamon, ed., *The Tools of Government*, chap. 2.

37. Salamon, *The Tools of Government*, 4–5.

38. See, generally, Thomas H. Stanton & Ronald C. Moe, "Government Corporations and Government-Sponsored Enterprises," in Salamon, ed., *The Tools of Government*, chap. 3.

39. See, generally, Lester M. Salamon, "Economic Regulation," in Salamon, ed., *The Tools of Government*, chap. 4.

40. See, generally, Peter J. May, "Social Regulation," in Salamon, ed., *The Tools of Government*, chap. 5.

41. See, generally, Ron J. Feldman, "Government Insurance," in Salamon, ed., *The Tools of Government*, chap. 6.

42. See, generally, Janet A. Weiss, "Public Information," in Salamon, ed., *The Tools of Government*, chap. 7.

43. See, generally, Joseph J. Cordes, "Corrective Taxes, Charges, and Tradable Permits," in Salamon, ed., *The Tools of Government*, chap. 8.

44. See, generally, Steven J. Kelman, "Contracting," in Salamon, ed., *The Tools of Government*, chap. 9; and Ruth Hoogland DeHoog and Lester M. Salamon, "Purchase-of-Service Contracting," in Salamon, ed., *The Tools of Government*, chap. 10.

45. Daniel P. Gitterman, "Presidency, the Power of the Purchaser and Public Policy," *The Forum* 10 (2012): article 1, 1–39.

46. See, generally, David R. Beam & Timothy J. Conlan, "Grants," in Salamon, ed., *The Tools of Government*, chap. 11.

47. See, generally, Thomas H. Stanton, "Loans and Loan Guarantees," in Salamon, ed., *The Tools of Government*, chap. 12.

48. See, generally, Christopher Howard, "Tax Expenditures," in Salamon, ed., *The Tools of Government*, chap. 13.

49. See, generally, C. Eugene Steuerle & Eric C. Twombly, "Vouchers," in Salamon, ed., *The Tools of Government*, chap. 14.

50. See, generally, Peter H. Schuck, "Tort Liability," in Salamon, ed., *The Tools of Government*, chap. 15.

51. This apt formulation comes from Richard E. Neustadt, *Presidential Power* (1960).

52. Isaiah Berlin, *Two Concepts of Liberty* (1958).

53. See Peter H. Schuck, "Professor Rabin and the Administrative State," *DePaul Law Review* 61 (2012): 595: "To expect the administrative state to be coherent in any meaningful sense is equivalent to expecting the proverbial pig to wear lipstick."

54. Pietro Nivola, "Two Cheers for Our Peculiar Politics: America's Political Process and the Economic Crisis," http://www.brookings.edu/research/papers/2012/05/21-economy-politics-nivola.

55. Colleen McCain Nelson, "Tough Slog for Obama's Gun Orders," *Wall Street Journal*, April 29, 2013.

56. Wesley J. Campbell, "Commandeering and Constitutional Change," *Yale Law Journal* 122 (2013): 1104–81.

57. Nelson W. Polsby, "The Political System," in Schuck & Wilson, eds., *Understanding America*, 20.

58. Martha Derthick, "Federalism," in Schuck & Wilson, eds., *Understanding America*, 145.

59. Polsby, "The Political System," 23.

60. Alan I. Abramowitz, *The Disappearing Center: Engaged Citizens, Polarization and American Democracy* (2010), 142–57; Thomas Mann, "Polarizing the House of Representatives: How Much Does Gerrymandering Matter?" in Pietro Nivola & David W. Brady, eds., *Red and Blue Nation? Characteristics and Causes of America's Polarized Politics* (2006).

61. See, generally, Richard Briffault, "Super PACs," *Minnesota Law Review* 96 (2012): 1644.

62. *Citizens United v. Federal Election Commission*, 558 U.S. 50 (2010); *SpeechNow.org v. Federal Election Commissionn*, 599 F.3d 686 (D.C. Cir. 2010).

63. On the "independent" voter phenomenon, see Nancy L. Rosenblum, *On the Side of the Angels: An Appreciation of Parties and Partisanship* (2010).

64. "Lonely at the Top," *Economist*, August 4, 2012, 55.

65. Russell J. Dalton, *The Good Citizen: How a Younger Generation Is Reshaping American Politics*, rev. ed. (2008).

66. On the wasted vote argument, see Peter H. Schuck, "The Thickest Thicket: Partisan Gerrymandering and Judicial Regulation of Politics," *Columbia Law Review* 87 (1987): 1356–61.

67. Torben Iversen & David Soskice, "Electoral Institutions and the Politics of Coalitions: Why Some Democracies Redistribute More Than Others," *American Political Science Review* 100 (2006): 165–81.

68. See S. Robert Lichter, "The Media," in Schuck & Wilson, eds., *Understanding America*, chap. 7.

69. Ibid., 204–7.

CHAPTER 4: THE POLITICAL CULTURE OF POLICY MAKING

1. See, e.g., Martha Bayles, "Popular Culture," in Peter H. Schuck & James Q. Wilson, eds., *Understanding America: The Anatomy of an Exceptional Nation* (2008), chap. 8.

2. For two very recent critiques of Congress, see Nolan McCarty, Keith T. Poole, & Howard Rosenthal, *Political Bubbles: Financial Crises and the Failure of American Democ-*

racy (2013); and Robert G. Kaiser, *Act of Congress: How America's Essential Institution Works, and How It Doesn't* (2013).

3. Bruce Katz & Jennifer Bradley, *The Metropolitan Revolution: How Cities and Metros Are Fixing Our Broken Politics and Fragile Economy* (2013).

4. See Nassim Nicholas Taleb, "Learning to Love Volatility," *Wall Street Journal*, September 16, 2012.

5. Pew Research Center for the People and the Press, "State Governments Viewed Favorably as Federal Rating Hits New Low," http://www.people-press.org/2013/04/15/state -govermnents-viewed-favorably-as-federal-rating-hits-new-low/.

6. I am grateful to Henry Aaron for pointing this out.

7. *Statistical Abstract of the United States, 2012*, tables 428 and 461.

8. Diane Cardwell, "Few Seize on a U.S. Bond Program Backing Green Energy," *New York Times*, May 8, 2012.

9. Martha Derthick, *New Town in Town: Why a Government Program Failed* (1972); Sam Dillon, "In School Aid Race, Many States Are Left Behind," *New York Times*, April 5, 2010.

10. See, e.g., Damian Paletta, "States Mine Federal Funds Long After Need Is Gone," *Wall Street Journal,* April 19, 2012 (states spend federal money even when the federal government wants them to stop because it is wasteful).

11. For examples and analysis, see Ronald J. Krotoszynski Jr., "Cooperative Federalism, the New Formalism, and the Separation of Powers Revisited: Free Enterprise Fund and the Problem of Presidential Oversight of State Government Officers Enforcing Federal Law," *Duke Law Journal* 61 (2012): 1629–59.

12. "Testing Times; No Child Left Behind," *Economist*, August 13, 2011, 28.

13. Motoko Rich, "'No Child Left Behind' Whittled Down by White House," *New York Times*, July 6, 2012 (twenty-six states exempted from proficiency goals, with ten more state and D.C. waiver applications pending).

14. U.S. Government Accountability Office, *Driver's License Security: Federal Leadership Needed to Address Remaining Vulnerabilities*, GAO-12–893 (September 2012).

15. Sarah Kliff, "It's Official: The Feds Will Run Most Obamacare Exchanges," http://www .washingtonpost.com/blogs/wonkblog/wp/2013/02/18/its-official-the-feds-will-run -most-obamacare-exchanges/.

16. Enrico Moretti, *The New Geography of Jobs* (2012). Our historically high worker mobility rate has resumed. "Americans Get Moving amid Torpid Recovery," *Wall Street Journal*, January 9, 2013. Canadians and New Zealanders are even more mobile. See Robert C. Ellickson, "Legal Sources of Residential Lock-ins: Why French Households Move Half as Often as U.S. Households," *University of Illinois Law Review* 2012 (2012): 376.

17. See, e.g., Nelson D. Schwartz, "As Rules Tighten, Gun Makers Lured Away," *New York Times*, August 5, 2013.

18. See John D. Donahue, "Tiebout? Or Not Tiebout? The Market Metaphor and America's Devolution Debate," *Journal of Economic Perspectives* 11 (1997): 78–80.

19. See, e.g., Christine Rossell & David Armor, "The Effectiveness of School Desegregation Plans, 1968–1991," *American Politics Quarterly* 24 (1996): 267–302; Katharine Q. Seelye, "4 Decades after Clashes, Boston Again Debates School Busing," *New York Times*, October 5, 2012.

20. Richard H. Thaler & Cass R. Sunstein, *Nudge: Improving Decisions about Health, Wealth, and Happiness* (2008).

21. Christine Jolls, "The New Behavioral Law and Economics" (unpublished manuscript, n.d.).

22. Ibid.

23. W. Mark Crain & Asghar Zardkoohi, "A Test of the Property-Rights Theory of the Firm: Water Utilities in the United States," *Journal of Law & Economics* 21 (1978): 395–408;

Jose A. Gomez-Ibanez, John R. Meyer, & David E. Luberoff, "The Prospects for Privatizing Infrastructure: Lessons from U.S. Roads and Solid Waste," *Journal of Transport Economcs & Policy* 25 (1991): 259–78; Walter J. Primeaux, "An Assessment of X-Efficiency Gained through Competition," *Review of Economics & Statistics* 59 (1977): 105–8.

24. Pew Global Attitudes Project, "Pervasive Gloom about the World Economy," July 12, 2012, http://www.pewglobal.org/2012/07/12/chapter-4-the-casualties-faith-in-hard-work-and-capitalism/.

25. See Peter H. Schuck, *Diversity in America: Keeping Government at a Safe Distance* (2003), chap. 5 (on affirmative action).

26. Lawrence M. Friedman, "The Legal System, in Schuck & Wilson, eds., *Understanding America*, 81–82.

27. James Q. Wilson, "American Exceptionalism," *American Spectator*, October 2, 2006, http://spectator.org/archives/2006/10/02/american-exceptionalism.

28. See, e.g., R. Shep Melnick, *Between the Lines: Interpreting Welfare Rights* (1994); R. Shep Melnick, *Regulation and the Courts: The Case of the Clean Air Act* (1983); Peter W. Huber & Robert E. Litan, *The Liability Maze: The Impact of Liability Law on Safety and Innovation* (1991); and Donald L. Horowitz, *The Courts and Social Policy* (1977).

29. Mary Ann Glendon, *Rights Talk: The Impoverishment of Political Discourse* (1991).

30. See, generally, David S. G. Goodman, *Groups and Politics in the People's Republic of China* (1984).

31. James Madison, "Federalist No. 10". I have dissected Madison's analysis with much admiration and some criticism in Peter H. Schuck, "Against (and for) Madison: An Essay in Praise of Factions," *Yale Law & Policy Review* 15 (1997): 553–97, reprinted in Peter H. Schuck, *The Limits of Law: Essays on Democratic Governance* (2000), chap. 7.

32. Theodore J. Lowi, *The End of Liberalism: The Second Republic of the United States*, 2d ed. (1979).

33. Ibid., 262–64.

34. Schuck, "Against (and for) Madison."

35. See, e.g., Lowi, *The End of Liberalism* (1969). Most recently, its contribution to social inequality has been emphasized. See Kay Lehman Scholzman, Sidney Verba, & Henry E. Brady, *The Unheavenly Chorus: Unequal Political Voice and the Broken Promise of American Democracy* (2012).

36. Eduardo Porter, "Unleashing Corporate Contributions," *New York Times*, August 29, 2012 (reviewing evidence).

37. Scholzman et al., *The Unheavenly Chorus*, 311.

38. Joseph A. McCartin, *Collision Course: Ronald Reagan, the Air Traffic Controllers, and the Strike That Changed America* (2011).

39. "Campaign Journal," *Wall Street Journal*, June 9, 2012.

40. See, e.g., Monica Davey & Steven Greenhouse, "Wisconsin May Take an Ax to State Workers' Benefits and Their Unions," *New York Times*, February 12, 2011; David M. Halbfinger, "Christie Declares 'New Normal' in Budget Proposal," *New York Times*, February 22, 2011. As an example of a more successful outcome, Rhode Island was able to garner strong bipartisan support for its pension reforms. See Girard Miller, "Rhode Island's Landmark Pension Reforms," *Governing*, December 8, 2011, http://www.governing.com/columns/public-money/rhode-island-landmark-pension-reforms.html.

41. Kate Taylor, "Health Care Law Raises Pressure on Public Unions," *New York Times*, August 5, 2013.

42. Schlozman et al., *The Unheavenly Chorus*.

43. Derek Bok, *The Trouble with Government* (2001), 180–81.

44. See John P. Heinz, *The Hollow Core: Private Interests in National Policy Making* (1993); "One Industry's Hold on the Senate," *New York Times*, April 2, 2013.

45. See, e.g., Keith Johnson, "Natural-Gas Export Fight Heats Up," *Wall Street Journal*, January 11, 2013.

46. See, generally, Jeffrey H. Birnbaum & Alan S. Murray, *Showdown at Gucci Gulch: Lawmakers, Lobbyists, and the Unlikely Triumph of Tax Reform* (1987).

47. Graham Bowley, "In Tax Overhaul Debate, Large vs. Small Companies," *New York Times*, May 24, 2013.

48. James Sherk & Todd Zywicki, "Obama's United Auto Workers Bailout," *Wall Street Journal*, June 14, 2012.

49. See, generally, David Freeman Engstrom, "Corralling Capture," 36 *Harvard Journal of Law & Public Policy* 31 (2013); Eric Helland & Jonathan Klick, "Why Aren't Regulation and Litigation Substitutes? An Examination of the Capture Hypothesis," in Cary Coglianese, ed., *Regulatory Breakdown: The Crisis of Confidence in U.S. Regulation* (2012), chap. 11.

50. "The Rich and the Rest," *Economist*, October 13, 2012, 12.

51. See Thomas B. Edsall, "What If We're Looking at Inequality the Wrong Way?" http://opinionator.blogs.nytimes.com/2013/06/26/what-if-were-looking-at-inequality-the-wrong-way/?emc=eta1&_r=0.

52. See, e.g., Jacob Hacker & Paul Pierson, *Winner-Take-All-Politics: How Washington Made the Rich Richer—And Turned Its Back on the Middle Class* (2010); and "The Rich and the Rest."

53. Scott Winship, "How Much Do Americans Care about Income Inequality?" April 30, 2013, http://www.brookings.edu/research/opinions/2013/04/30-income-inequality-winship; and Scott Winship, "How Much Do Americans Care about Income Inequality? Part II," May 15, 2013, http://www.brookings.edu/research/opinions/2013/05/15-do-americans-care-about-inequality-winship.

54. Alberto Alesina & Edward L. Glaeser, *Fighting Poverty in the US and Europe: A World of Difference* (2004), 184.

55. Peter H. Schuck, "Three Models of Citizenship," in Michael S. Greve & Michael Zoller, eds., *Citizenship in America and Europe: Beyond the Nation-State?* (2009), 170 (citing sources).

56. Ibid., 171–72.

57. Peter Westen, "The Empty Idea of Equality," *Harvard Law Review* 95 (1982): 537–96.

58. See Schuck, "Three Models of Citizenship."

59. Schlozman et al., *The Unheavenly Chorus*.

60. See, e.g., *Davis v. Federal Election Commission*, 554 U.S. 724 (2008) (invalidating "millionaire's amendment" of Bipartisan Campaign Reform Act).

61. Steven Greenhouse, "Union Membership Drops Despite Increase in Labor Force," *New York Times*, January 24, 2013.

62. See Schlozman et al., *The Unheavenly Chorus*, 426–28.

63. Winship, "How Much Do Americans Care about Income Inequality?" and Winship, "How Much Do Americans Care about Income Inequality? Part II."

64. Compare Jeffrey Bloomer, "Poll Shows Fivefold Increase in Ranks of U.S. Atheists," *Slate*, August 14, 2012, http://slatest.slate.com/posts/2012/08/14/american_atheists_1_in_20_americans_say_they_are_atheists_.html?from=rss/&wpisrc=newsletter_slatest, and Rodney Stark, "The Myth of Unreligious America," *Wall Street Journal*, July 5, 2013 (the proportion of self-described atheists has not increased even slightly since Gallup first asked in 1944; many who say "no religion" pray and believe in angels; nonrespondents are less likely to belong to a church).

65. See Robert Wuthnow, "Religion," in Schuck & Wilson, eds., *Understanding America*, chap. 10.

66. Much of the discussion in this section is taken from Schuck, *Diversity in America*, chap. 1.

67. The source for this quotation is cited in Schuck, *Diversity in America*, 342n29.

68. For a fuller development of this point, see Schuck, *Diversity in America*, 55–72, from which some of the discussion here is taken.

69. For a fuller development of this point, see Schuck, *Diversity in America*, 67–71, from which some of the discussion here is taken.

70. "State of Renewal," *Economist*, June 2, 2012, http://www.economist.com/node/2155 6247.

71. Richard H. Thaler, "Watching Behavior Before Writing the Rules," *New York Times*, July 8, 2012.

72. Lynn Eisenberg, "States as Laboratories for Federal Reform: Case Studies in Felon Disenfranchisement Law," *New York University Journal of Legislation & Public Policy* 15 (2012): 539.

73. See, e.g., Peter H. Schuck & Ron Haskins, "Welfare Reform Worked," *Los Angeles Times*, February 28, 2012.

74. Robert D. Putnam, "E Pluribus Unum: Diversity and Community in the Twenty-First Century: The 2006 Johan Skytte Prize Lecture," *Scandinavian Political Studies* 30 (2007): 137–74.

75. Matthew A. Baum, "Partisan Media and Attitude Polarization: The Case of Healthcare Reform," in Cary Coglianese, ed., *Regulatory Breakdown: The Crisis of Confidence in U.S. Regulation* (2012), chap. 6.

76. On the early republic, see Joanne B. Freeman, *Affairs of Honor: National Politics in the New Republic* (2001).

77. Peter H. Schuck & James Q. Wilson, "Looking Back," in Schuck & Wilson, *Understanding America*, 628–29.

78. Morris P. Fiorina, Samuel A. Abrams, & Jeremy C. Pope, *Culture War? The Myth of a Polarized America* (2d ed., 2006). They reply to their critics, Alan I. Abramowitz & Kyle L. Saunders, in Fiorina, Abrams, & Pope, "Polarization in the American Public: Misconceptions and Misreadings," http://sitemason.vanderbilt.edu/files/cARwUU/Fiorina.pdf.

79. Schlozman et al., *The Unheavenly Chorus*, 236–60.

80. Bill Bishop, *The Big Sort: Why the Clustering of Like-Minded Americans Is Tearing Us Apart* (2009)

81. Jed Handelsman Shugerman, "The Twist of Long Terms: Judicial Election, Role Fidelity, and American Tort Law," *Georgetown Law Journal* 98 (2010): 1351.

82. Stephen G. Breyer, *Breaking the Vicious Circle: Toward Effective Risk Regulation* (1993).

83. Paul M. Darden, David M. Thompson, James R. Roberts, Jessica J. Hale, Charlene Pope, Monique Naifeh, & Robert M. Jacobson, "Reasons for Not Vaccinating Adolescents: National Immunization Survey of Teens, 2008–2010," *Pediatrics* 131 (2013): 645–51; Dennis K. Flaherty, "The Vaccine-Autism Connection: A Public Health Crisis Caused by Unethical Medical Practices and Fraudulent Science," *Annals of Pharmacotherapy* 45 (2011): 1302–4. For the populist view on the vaccine-autism issue, see Louise Kuo Habacus & Mary Holland, eds., *Vaccine Epidemic: How Corporate Greed, Biased Science, and Coercive Government Threaten Our Human Rights, Our Health, and Our Children* (2011).

84. See, generally, Peter L. Strauss, Todd D. Rakoff, Cynthia R. Farina, & Gillian E. Metzger, eds., *Gellhorn and Byse's Administrative Law: Cases and Comments*, 11th ed. (2011).

85. Walter Lippman, *Public Opinion* (1922).

86. John J. DiIulio Jr., "Facing Up to Big Government," *National Affairs*, Spring 2012, 9.

87. Robert D. Putnam, *Bowling Alone: The Collapse and Revival of American Community* (2000).

88. Nancy L. Rosenblum, "Good Neighbor Nation: The Democracy of Everyday Life in America" (unpublished manuscript, 2013).

89. This passage is taken from Schuck & Wilson, "Looking Back," 630–31, which in turn draws on Wuthnow, "Religion."

90. See, generally, Arthur C. Brooks, "Philanthropy and the Non-Profit Sector," in Schuck & Wilson, *Understanding America*, chap. 18.

91. See, e.g., Robert Pear, "U.S. Clarifies Policy on Birth Control for Religious Groups," *New York Times*, March 16, 2012. The litigation is *University of Notre Dame v. Sibelius*, No. 312CV253RLM, 2012 WL 6756332 (N.D. Ind. December 31, 2012). See also, *Gilardi v. U.S. Dept. of Health and Human Services*, D.C. Cir., November 1, 2013.

92. Laurie Goodstein, "Illinois Bishops Drop Program over Bias Rule," *New York Times*, December 29, 2011.

93. James Piereson, "How Big Government Co-opted Charities," *Wall Street Journal*, July 18, 2013.

94. See, e.g., Marvin Olasky, *The Tragedy of American Compassion* (1992); and Theodore Dalrymple, *Life at the Bottom: The Worldview That Makes the Underclass* (2001).

CHAPTER 5: INCENTIVES AND COLLECTIVE IRRATIONALITY

1. For one synthesis of these studies, with bibliographical references, see James Q. Wilson & John J. Dilulio Jr., *The Essentials of American Government: Institutions & Policies*, 12th ed. (2011).

2. Nicholas R. Parrillo, *Against the Profit Motive: The Salary Revolution in American Government, 1780–1940* (2013).

3. Kelman, *Making Public Policy: A Hopeful View of American Government* (1987), 239–40.

4. Lee Epstein, William M. Landes, & Richard A. Posner, *The Behavior of Federal Judges: A Theoretical and Empirical Study of Rational Choice* (2013).

5. For a penetrating review of the public choice literature, see Terry M. Moe, "Delegation, Control, and the Study of Public Bureaucracy," *The Forum* 10 (2012): 1–45.

6. For a revealing discussion of the theory's strengths and weaknesses, see the review (by a proponent of the theory) of a book that alternately criticizes and uses it: Jonathan R. Macey, "Public Choice and the Legal Academy," *Georgetown Law Journal* 86 (1997–98): 1075–91 (reviewing Jerry L. Mashaw, *Greed, Chaos, and Governance: Using Public Choice to Improve Public Law* [1997]).

7. See, e.g., Donald P. Green & Ian Shapiro, *Pathologies of Rational Choice Theory: A Critique of Applications in Political Science* (1994); and Mashaw, *Greed, Chaos, and Governance*.

8. Steven A. Morrison & Clifford Winston, *The Economic Effects of Airline Deregulation* (1986).

9. The authoritative account is Martha Derthick & Paul J. Quirk, *The Politics of Deregulation* (1985). For a public choice theory explanation of the legislation, see Macey, "Public Choice and the Legal Academy," 1080.

10. Its budget in 2008 was an estimated $10 billion, with estimated annual operating costs of $1 billion. Barry Nield, "CERN's search for Higgs Boson God Particle Is among Most Expensive Science Ever," http://www.globalpost.com/dispatch/news/regions/europe/120704/cerns-search-higgs-boson-god-particle-among-most-expensive-scien. One might argue against this example on the ground that these costs were funded largely by other governments, not the United States, but public choice theory presumably would resist such a distinction. After all, vote-seeking politicians should behave pretty much the same in all democracies, mutatis mutandis.

11. William J. Broad, "So Far Unfruitful, Fusion Project Faces a Frugal Congress," *New York Times*, September 30, 2012.

12. James Madison, "Federalist No. 51."

13. See, generally, Elinor Ostrom, *Governing the Commons: The Evolution of Institutions for Collective Action* (1990).

14. On signaling theory and rational self-interest, see Eric Posner, *Law and Social Norms* (2000).

15. See, e.g., Tracey E. George, "Developing a Positive Theory of Decisionmaking on U.S. Courts of Appeals," *Ohio State Law Journal* 58 (1998): 1651.

16. See Jonathan Rauch, "Was Mancur Olson Wrong?" *The American*, February 15, 2013, http://www.american.com/archive/2013/february/was-mancur-olson-wrong (review of Gunnar Trumbull, *Strength in Numbers: The Political Power of Weak Interests* [2013]).

17. On the policy response to the financial crisis, see Roberta Romano, "Regulating in the Dark," in Cary Coglianese, ed., *Regulatory Breakdown: The Crisis of Confidence in U.S. Regulation* (2012), chap. 5.

18. See, generally, David Schoenbrod, "Government without Tricks" (manuscript in preparation), http://www.governmentwithouttricks.org.

19. Edward Wyatt, "Backer of an Open Internet Steps Down as F.C.C. Chief," *New York Times*, March 22, 2013.

20. Brian Galle, "The Tragedy of the Carrots: Economics and Politics in the Choice of Price Instruments," *Stanford Law Review* 64 (2012): 797–850.

21. Jonathan Rauch, *Government's End: Why Washington Stopped Working* (1999).

22. This dynamic has been elaborated upon in James M. Buchanan & Gordon Tullock, *The Calculus of Consent: The Logical Foundations of Constitutional Democracy* (1962).

23. John Ferejohn, "Logrolling in an Institutional Context: A Case Study of the Food Stamp Legislation," in Gerald C. Wright, Leroy N. Rieselbach, and Lawrence C. Dodd, eds., *Congress and Policy Change* (1986), chap. 9.

24. Jim Monke, *Budget Issues Shaping a Farm Bill in 2013,* Congressional Research Service Report R42484 (2013), 3; Marlin Stutzman & Michael Needham, "The 'Farm' Bill Is No Such Thing," *Wall Street Journal,* August 2, 2012.

25. Raymond Hernandez, "Congress Approves $51 Billion in Aid for Hurricane Victims," *New York Times*, January 28, 2013.

26. David A. Moss, *When All Else Fails: Government as the Ultimate Risk Manager* (2002), chap. 10.

27. Ibid., 327.

28. See, generally, Matthew Richardson, *Guaranteed to Fail: Fannie Mae, Freddie Mac, and the Debacle of Mortgage Finance* (2011).

29. Alex J. Pollock, "We Don't Need GSEs," testimony before the House Financial Services Committee, June 12, 2013, http://financialservices.house.gov/uploadedfiles/hhrg-113-ba00-wstate-apollock-20130612.pdf.

30. Dwight Jaffee & John M. Quigley, "The Future of the Government Sponsored Enterprises: The Role for Government in the U.S. Mortgage Market," in Edward L Glaeser & Todd M. Sinai, eds., *Housing and the Financial Crisis*, 361–417 (Chicago: University of Chicago Press, 2013).

31. Nick Timiraos, "Fannie's Windfall Blurs Debate over Its Fate," *Wall Street Journal*, April 3, 2013; Gretchen Morgenson, "Mortgages' Future Looks Too Much Like the Past," *New York Times*, March 24, 2013.

32. Edward Kane, quoted in Gretchen Morgenson, "Seeing Bailouts through Rose-Colored Glasses," *New York Times*, May 20, 2012.

33. Robert C. Posen, "The Future of Home Mortgages in the U.S.," Brookings Research, August 6, 2013.

34. Robert J. Shiller, "Owning a Home Isn't Always a Virtue," *New York Times*, July 13, 2013.

35. Benjamin M. Friedman, "How Americans Face Risk," *New Republic*, August 5, 2013, 55.

36. Jessica Silver-Greenberg & Nelson D. Schwartz, "Federal Regulators Make Public the 'Living Wills' of Nine Too-Big-to-Fail Banks," *New York Times*, July 4, 2012.

37. Michael R. Crittenden, "Challenges in Bid to Revamp Banks," *Wall Street Journal*, July 18, 2013.

38. "The Financial Instability Council," *Wall Street Journal*, July 16, 2013; Peter J. Wallison, "The FSOC Expands 'Too Big to Fail,'" *The American*, July 18, 2013, http://american .com/archive/2013/july/the-fsoc-expands-too-big-to-fail.

39. See Gretchen Morgenson, "One Safety Net That Needs to Shrink," *New York Times*, November 4, 2012; and Gretchen Morgenson, "Don't Blink, or You'll Miss Another Bailout," *New York Times*, February 17, 2012 (on the bailout in the form of releasing Bank of America from legal claims against it for mortgage-related fraud).

40. Floyd Norris, "Shades of 2007 Borrowing," *New York Times*, May 31, 2013.

41. Congressional Budget Office, *Fair-Value Accounting for Federal Credit Programs*, http://www.cbo.gov/sites/default/files/cbofiles/attachments/03-05-FairValue_Brief .pdf.

42. Committee on Education and the Workforce, U.S. House of Representatives, *Examining the Challenges Facing PBGC and Defined Benefit Pension Plans: Hearing before the Subcommittee on Health, Employment, Labor and Pensions*, 112th Cong. 3–4 (2012) (statement of Joshua Gotbaum, Director of the Pension Benefit Guaranty Corp); Ivan Osorio, "Benefit Guaranty Corporation's Real Crisis," *Forbes*, February 22, 2012, http:// www.forbes.com/sites/realspin/2012/02/22/the-pension-benefit-guaranty-corpora tions-real-crisis/.

43. Erwann Michel-Kerjan & Howard Kunreuther, "Paying for Future Catastrophes," *New York Times*, November 25.

44. Lizette Alvarez & Campbell Robertson, "Cost of Flood Insurance Rises, Along with Worries," *New York Times*, October 12, 2013.

45. See Bert Ely, "Savings and Loan Crisis," http://www.econlib.org/library/Enc/Savings andLoanCrisis.html.

46. Eric Lipton, Felicity Barringer, & Mary Williams Walsh, "Flood Insurance, Already Fragile, Faces New Stress," *New York Times*, November 13, 2012; Justin Gillis & Felicity Barringer, "As Coast Rebuilds and U.S. Pays, Repeatedly, Critics Ask Why," *New York Times*, November 19, 2012; Erwann Michel-Kerjan & Howard Kunreuther, "Paying for Future Catastrophes," *New York Times*, November 25, 2012.

47. Ron Nixon, "Income Guarantee Swells Crop Insurance," *New York Times*, May 2, 2013.

48. Henry Olsen, "Food (Stamps) for Thought," http://www.nationalreview.com/article /358914/food-stamps-thought-henry-olsen.

49. Another example is the Supplemental Agricultural Disaster Assistance program enacted in 2008.

50. See Peter H. Schuck & Richard J. Zeckhauser, *Targeting in Social Programs: Avoiding Bad Bets, Removing Bad Apples* (2006), especially chap. 4.

51. John D. Donahue, *The Warping of Government Work* (2008), 138.

52. Lawrence H. Summers, "Unemployment," http://www.econlib.org/library/Enc/Unem ployment.html; Kory Kroft, Fabian Lange, & Matthew J. Notowidigdo, *Duration Dependence and Labor Market Conditions: Theory and Evidence from a Field Experiment*, National Bureau of Economic Research Working Paper 18387 (2013); Henry Farber & Robert Valletta, "Do Extended Unemployment Benefits Lengthen Unemployment Spells? Evidence from Recent Cycles in the U.S. Labor Market," National Bureau of Economic Research Working Paper 19048, 2013.

53. R. Kent Weaver, *Ending Welfare as We Know It* (1998); Michael J. Graetz & Jerry L. Mashaw, *True Security: Rethinking American Social Insurance* (1999), 296–99.

54. George P. Shultz, Gary S. Becker, Michael J. Boskin, John Cogan, Allan Meltzer, & John Taylor, "A Better Strategy for Faster Growth," *Wall Street Journal*, March 25, 2013.

55. Moss, *When All Else Fails*, 124.

56. Daniel Gade, "Why the VA Is Buried in Disability Claims," *Wall Street Journal*, June 23, 2013.

57. Schuck & Zeckhauser, *Targeting in Social Programs*, 1–2.

58. Charles Murray, "The 3 Laws of Social Programs," http://www.aei-ideas.org/2012/12/the-3-laws-of-social-programs/.

59. Nicholas D. Kristof, "Profiting from a Child's Illiteracy," *New York Times*, December 9, 2012.

60. Alicia H. Munnell, "Lessons from the Income Maintenance Experiments," http://www.bostonfed.org/economic/conf/conf30/conf30a.pdf; Binyamin Appelbaum, "Study of Men's Falling Income Cites Single Parents," *New York Times*, March 20, 2013.

60. Felicity Barringer, "Homes Keep Rising in West Despite Growing Wildfire Threat," *New York Times*, July 6, 2013, A10.

62. Tyler Cowen, "The New Tug of War over Medicaid," *New York Times*, July 15, 2012.

63. Leslie Scism & Jon Hilsenrath, "Workers Stuck in Disability Stunt Economic Recovery," *Wall Street Journal*, April 6–7, 2012.

64. David Autor, Mark Duggan, & Jonathan Gruber, *Moral Hazard and Claims Deterrence in Private Disability Insurance*, National Bureau of Economic Research Working Paper 18172 (2012).

65. Joyce Manchester, Congressional Budget Office, *Testimony: The Social Security Disability Insurance Program*, March 14, 2013, http://www.cbo.gov/sites/default/files/cbofiles/attachments/43995_DI-Testimony.pdf.

66. See, e.g., Timothy Williams, "70 Indicted in Puerto Rico in Social Security Fraud Linked to an Agency Employee," *New York Times*, August 22, 2013.

67. Nicholas Eberstadt, *A Nation of Takers: America's Entitlement Epidemic* (2012), 52–58. On the alarming drop in the employment ratio, particularly for males, see Nicholas Eberstadt, "The Astonishing Collapse of Work in America," July 10, 2013, http://www.realclearmarkets.com/articles/2013/07/10/the_astonishing_collapse_of_work_in_america_100465.html.

68. Autor et al., *Moral Hazard and Claims Deterrence*, quoted in Scism & Hilsenrath, "Workers Stuck in Disability."

69. See, e.g., David H. Autor & Mark Duggan, *Supporting Work: A Proposal for Modernizing the U.S. Disability Insurance System*, http://www.brookings.edu/~/media/research/files/papers/2010/12/disability%20insurance%20autor/12_disability_insurance_autor.pdf.

70. William K. Rashbaum, "600 Long Island Rail Road Retirees to Lose Disability Pay in U.S. Inquiry," *New York Times*, July 2, 2013.

71. Richard Vedder, "The Wages of Unemployment," *Wall Street Journal*, January 16, 2013.

72. According to the *DSM-IV*, 46.4 percent of Americans will have a diagnosable mental illness in their lifetimes, and "the new manual will likely make it even easier to get a diagnosis." Robin S. Rosenberg, "Abnormal Is the New Normal," *Slate*, April 12, 2013, http://www.slate.com/articles/health_and_science/medical_examiner/2013/04/diagnostic_and_statistical_manual_fifth_edition_why_will_half_the_u_s_population.html.

73. Office of the Assistant Secretary for Planning and Evaluation, U.S. Department of Health and Human Services, "Affordable Care Act Expands Mental Health and Substance Use Disorder Benefits and Federal Parity Protections for 62 Million Americans," February 20, 2013, http://aspe.hhs.gov/health/reports/2013/mental/rb_mental.cfm.

74. The discussion that follows is taken from Charles Wolf, Jr., "A Theory of 'Non-Market' Failures," *The Public Interest*, Spring 1979, 114–33.

75. Alan S. Gerber & Eric M. Patashnik, "Government Performance: Missing Opportunities to Solve Problems," in Gerber & Patashnik, eds., *Promoting the General Welfare: New Perspectives on Government Performance* (2006), 11–13.

76. Michael Grunwald, *The New New Deal: The Hidden Story of Change in the Obama Era* (2012).

77. Philip Selznick, *TVA and the Grass Roots: A Study in the Sociology of Formal Organization* (1949).

78. Ted Gayer & W. Kip Viscusi, "Are Pollution Controls Worth Their Costs?" July 19, 2012, http://www.brookings.edu/research/opinions/2012/07/19-energy-regulations-gayer.

79. See, e.g., Rachel E. Barkow, "Prosecutorial Administration: Prosecutor Bias and the Department of Justice," *University of Virginia Law Review* 99 (2013): part II.A.

80. Carl Bialik, "Americans Stumble on Math in Big Issues," *Wall Street Journal*, January 7, 2012.

81. "Although 93% of their homes contain at least one Bible and a third claim to read it at least once a week, 54% cannot name the authors of the Gospels, 63% do not know what a Gospel is, 58% cannot name five of the Ten Commandments, and 10% think Joan of Arc was Noah's wife! Indeed, a recent survey found an astonishing number of born-again Christians whose views seem to flatly contradict the Bible." Peter H. Schuck, *Diversity in America: Keeping Government at a Safe Distance* (2003), 269–70, source cited in note 273.

82. Larry M. Bartels, "The Irrational Electorate," *Wilson Quarterly*, Autumn 2008, http://www.princeton.edu/~bartels/how_stupid.pdf. See also Christopher S. Elmendorf & David Schleicher, "Districting for a Low-Information Electorate," *Yale Law Journal* 121 (2012): 1846–86.

83. Daniel Kahneman, Paul Slovic, & Amos Tversky, *Judgment under Uncertainty: Heuristics and Biases* (1982).

84. Meghan Busse et al, "Projection Bias in the Car and Housing Markets," National Bureau of Economic Research Working Paper No. 18212.

85. Thomas Gilovich, *How We Know What Isn't So: The Fallibility of Human Reason in Everyday Life* (1991).

86. See Alan Schwartz, "Consumer Regulation and the Irrationality Assumption" (unpublished manuscript, 2012).

87. Cass R. Sunstein, Daniel Kahneman, David Schkade, & Ilana Ritov, "Predictably Incoherent Judgments," *Stanford Law Review* 54 (2002): 1153–1216.

88. Cass R. Sunstein, "The Law of Group Polarization," *Journal of Political Economy* 10 (2002): 175–95.

89. Richard H. Thaler & Cass R. Sunstein, *Nudge: Improving Decisions about Health, Welfare, and Happiness* (2008). See also Cass R. Sunstein, "Human Error and Paternalism," Storrs Lecture presented at Yale Law School, November 2012.

90. See Ryan Bubb & Richard H. Pildes, "How Behavioral Economics Trims Its Sails and Why" (unpublished manuscript, 2013).

91. Dan Kahan, "Fixing the Communications Failure," *Nature* 463 (2010): 296–297 (an overview of research findings).

92. Chris Mooney, *The Republican Brain: The Science of Why They Deny Science—and Reality* (2012). Economist-editorialist Paul Krugman endorses Mooney's position; see Krugman, "Grand Old Planet," *New York Times*, November 23, 2012.

93. Dan M. Kahan, Hank Jenkins-Smith, & Donald Braman, "Cultural Cognition of Scientific Consensus," *Journal of Risk Research* 14 (2011): 147–74; Dan M. Kahan, *Ideology, Motivated Reasoning, and Cognitive Reflection: An Experimental Study*, Cultural Cognition Lab Working Paper 107 (2012).

94. See, e.g., Louise Kuo Habacus, Mary Holland, & Kim Mack Rosenberg, eds., *Vaccine Epidemic: How Corporate Greed, Biased Science, and Coercive Government Threaten Our Human Rights, Our Health, and Our Children*, 2nd ed., 2012.

95. See, e.g., Jon Entine, "Anti-GM Corn Study Reconsidered: Seralini Finally Responds to Torrent of Criticism," http://www.aei.org/article/energy-and-the-environment/anti-gm-corn-study-reconsidered-seralini-finally-responds-to-torrent-of-criticism (on the genetically modified corn debate).

96. See chapter 10.

97. Jonathan Haidt, *The Righteous Mind: Why Good People Are Divided by Politics and Religion* (2012).

98. Bryan Caplan, *The Myth of the Rational Voter: Why Democracies Choose Bad Policies* (2007).

99. Ibid., 156–60.

CHAPTER 6: INFORMATION, INFLEXIBILITY, INCREDIBILITY, AND MISMANAGEMENT

1. Damien Cave, "Long Border, Endless Struggle," *New York Times*, March 3, 2013.

2. U.S. Government Accountability Office, "Goals and Measures Not in Place to Inform Border Security Status and Resource Needs," GAO 13–330T, February 26, 2013, http://www.gao.gov/assets/660/652331.pdf.

3. Compare, e.g., Sheila Bair, *Bull by the Horns: Fighting to Save Main Street from Wall Street and Wall Street from Itself* (2012); Peter Wallison, *Bad History, Worse Policy: How a False Narrative about the Financial Crisis Led to the Dodd-Frank Act* (2013); Neil Barofsky, *Bailout: How Washington Abandoned Main Street While Rescuing Wall Street* (2012); and Richard A. Posner, *A Failure of Capitalism: The Crisis of '08 and the Descent into Depression* (2008).

4. Steven Kelman, *Procurement and Public Management: The Fear of Discretion and the Quality of Government Performance* (1990). The review is Jerry L. Mashaw, "The Fear of Discretion in Government Procurement," *Yale Journal on Regulation* 8 (1991): 512–13.

5. See James Q. Wilson, *Thinking about Crime* (1975); and Peter H. Schuck, "Thinking about Crime," *New Republic*, December 20, 1975, 26–27 (review of Wilson book).

6. Peter H. Schuck, "Refugee Burden-Sharing: A Modest Proposal," *Yale Journal of International Law* 22 (1997): 243–97.

7. 78 Federal Register 42251–52, July 15, 2013.

8. Floyd Norris, "Clouds Seen in Regulators' Crystal Ball for Banks," *New York Times*, January 11, 2013 (on Office of Financial Research).

9. Gretchen Morgenson, "In an F.H.A. Checkup, a Startling Number," *New York Times*, December 2, 2012; Gretchen Morgenson, "Study Shows a Pattern of Risky Loans by F.H.A.," *New York Times*, December 13, 2012.

10. Michael S. Schmidt & Charlie Savage, "Gaps in F.B.I. Data Undercut Background Checks for Guns," *New York Times*, December 21, 2012.

11. Erica Goode & Sheryl Gay Stolberg, "Legal Curbs Said to Hamper A.T.F. in Gun Inquiries," *New York Times*, December 26, 2012.

12. Jennifer Steinhauer, "Congressional Committees Make Some Gun-Rights Provisions Permanent," *New York Times*, March 14, 2013.

13. Julia Preston, "Officials Concede Failure on Gauging Border Security," *New York Times*, March 21, 2013.

14. See, generally, Kelman, *Procurement and Public Management*.

15. James C. Scott, *Seeing Like a State: How Certain Schemes to Improve the Human Condition Have Failed* (1998).

16. See, generally, Stephen Breyer, *Breaking the Vicious Circle: Toward Effective Risk Regulation* (1993).

17. Beryl A. Radin, *Federal Management Reform in a World of Contradictions* (2012), 148–62.

18. See Peter H. Schuck & Richard J. Zeckhauser, *Targeting in Social Programs: Avoiding Bad Bets, Removing Bad Apples* (2006), 129–31.

19. Sephanie Banchero, "Head Start Programs Face a New Test," *Wall Street Journal*, April 27, 2012 (chart).

20. Grover J. "Russ" Whitehurst, "Is Head Start Working for American Students?" January 21, 2010, http://www.brookings.edu/blogs/up-front/posts/2010/01/21-head-start-white

hurst. The study is published at http://www.acf.hhs.gov/programs/opre/resource/head-start-impact-study-final-report-executive-summary.

21. Head Start Research, *Third Grade Follow-up to the Head Start Impact Study Executive Summary*, http://www.acf.hhs.gov/sites/default/files/opre/head_start_executive_summary.pdf.

22. Eduardo Porter, "Misdirected Investments in Education," *New York Times*, April 3, 2013.

23. "Little Steps," *Economist*, February 9, 2013.

24. Peter Orszag & John Bridgeland, "Can Government Play Moneyball?" *Atlantic*, July–August 2013, 64–65.

25. Grover J. Whitehurst & David J. Armor, "Obama's Preschool Proposal Is Not Based on Sound Research," July 24, 2013, http://www.brookings.edu/blogs/brown-center-chalkboard/posts/2013/07/24-preschool-proposal-whitehurst.

26. Carl Bialik, "Hurdles for New Line on Poverty," *Wall Street Journal*, September 21, 2013.

27. Nassim Nicholas Taleb, *Antifragile: Things That Gain from Disorder* (2012).

28. David Paul Kuhn, "Could Gas Prices Sink Obama's Reelection?" http://www.realclearpolitics.com/articles/2011/03/09/could_gas_prices_sink_obamas_reelection_2012_study_president_approval_gas_price_109157.html, cited in E. Donald Elliott, "Why the U.S. Does Not Have a Renewable Energy Policy," *Environmental Law Reporter* 43 (2013): 10098n31.

29. See, generally, Christopher Howard, *The Hidden Welfare State: Tax Expenditures and Social Policy in the United States* (1999).

30. See Robert Caro, *The Passage to Power: The Years of Lyndon Johnson* (2012).

31. See, however, Gerald N. Rosenberg, *The Hollow Hope: Can Courts Bring About Social Change?* (1991); and Michael J. Klarman, "How Brown Changed Race Relations: The Backlash Thesis," *Journal of American History* 81 (1994): 81–118.

32. See, e.g., Norman J. Ornstein & Thomas E. Mann, eds., *The Permanent Campaign and Its Future* (2000).

33. Anne Joseph O'Connell, "Qualifications: Law and Practice of Selecting Agency Leaders" (unpublished manuscript, 2012).

34. Paul C. Light, *A Government Ill-Executed: The Decline of the Federal Service and How to Reverse It* (2008), 82 (citing Hugh Heclo's 1987 study, "The In-and-Outer System").

35. U.S. Constitution, Art. I, Sec. 8, cl. 7.

36. See, generally, Richard R. John, *Spreading the News: The American Postal System from Franklin to Morse* (1998).

37. Gail Collins, "The Point of Lance," *New York Times*, January 16, 2013.

38. Joe Nocera, "It's D-Day for the Post Office," *New York Times*, July 30, 2012.

39. Ron Nixon, "Post Office Rebuffed Again on 5-Day Service," *New York Times*, March 22, 2013.

40. Stephen Greenhouse, "Postal Service Is Nearing Default as Losses Mount," *New York Times*, September 5, 2011.

41. "No Child Left Behind Act," *New York Times*, July 6, 2012.

42. See, generally, "Sponging Boomers," *Economist*, September 29, 2012, 75.

43. See, e.g., Daniel A. Sumner, " 'The World's Most Outdated Law': Why the Next Farm Bill Should Be the Last," *Atlantic*, April 25, 2003, http://www.aei.org/article/economics/the-worlds-most-outdated-law-why-the-next-farm-bill-should-be-the-last/?utm_source=today&utm_medium=web&utm_campaign=042913#mbl.

44. Robert J. Samuelson, "A Bumper Crop of Inertia," *Washington Post*, September 12, 2007.

45. Jonathan Gruber, "A Loophole Worth Closing," *New York Times*, July 12, 2009 (arguing for repeal of tax breaks for employer-provided health insurance); Yonah Freemark & Lawrence J. Vale, "Illogical Housing Aid," *New York Times*, October 31, 2012 (arguing for a cap on the mortgage interest deduction).

46. Theodore M. Hesburgh, "A Setback for Educational Civil Rights," *Wall Street Journal*, March 18, 2010.

47. "Fluoridation Debate, Redux," *New York Times*, March 18, 2012, SR 10; http://water. epa.gov/drink/contaminants/index.cfm.

48. "The Economic Impact of Significant U.S. Import Restraints," June 2002, 115–128, at http://www.usitc.gov/publications/332/pub3519.pdf.

49. John Bussey, "Oil and the Ghost of 1920," *Wall Street Journal*, September 14, 2012, B1.

50. "The Economic Impact of Significant U.S. Import Restraints," xviii.

51. Shaila Dewan, "Mortgage Aid Programs Were Halted, Papers Show", *New York Times*, May 2, 2012, B4.

52. Shaila Dewan, "New Defaults Trouble a Mortgage Program," *New York Times*, July 25, 2013, B2.

53. Annie Lowrey, "Treasury Faulted in Effort to Relieve Homeowners," *New York Times*, April 12, 2012, B3.

54. Edward Wyatt, "Obama Orders Regulators to Root Out 'Patent Trolls'," *New York Times*, June 4, 2013.

55. Carl Hulse, "Lesson Is Seen in Failure of Law on Medicare in 1989," *New York Times*, November 17, 2013.

56. Jonathan Weisman, "G.O.P. Claims Victory as Bill to Curb Flight Delays Passes," *New York Times*, April 26, 2013.

57. See, generally, Jerry L. Mashaw & David L Harfst, *The Struggle for Auto Safety* (1990).

58. Ross Levine, "The Governance of Financial Regulation: Reform Lessons from the Recent Crisis," *International Review of Finance* 12 (2012): 39–56.

59. See, e.g., Richard Rose & Phillip L. Davies, *Inheritance in Public Policy: Change without Choice in Britain* (1994).

60. Robert Pear, "In a Shift, Medicare Pushes Bids," *New York Times*, April 19, 2012.

61. Stuart H. Altman & David Shactman, *Power, Politics, and Universal Health Care: The Inside Story of a Century-Long Battle* (2011), 107–10.

62. Susan Martin, "Labor Migration to the United States: Challenges and Opportunities," paper presented at the Mortimer Caplin Conference, University of Virginia, December 7, 2012; Peter H. Schuck & John E. Tyler, "Making the Case for Changing U.S. Policy Regarding Highly Skilled Immigrants,"*Fordham Urban Law Journal* 38 (2010): 327–62.

63. James Madison, "Federalist No. 62."

64. Devjani Roy & Richard J. Zeckhauser, "Ignorance: Lessons from the Laboratory of Literature" (unpublished manuscript, 2013).

65. Scott R. Baker, Nicholas Bloom, & Steven J. Davis, "Measuring Economic Policy Uncertainty" (January 1, 2013), Chicago Booth Research paper no. 13-02, cited in Bill McNabb, "Uncertainty Is the Enemy of Recovery," *Wall Street Journal*, April 29, 2013.

66. William A. Galston, "Policy Uncertainty Paralyzes the Economy," *Wall Street Journal*, September 25, 2013.

67. Dani Rodrik & Richard Zeckhauser, "The Dilemma of Government Responsiveness," *Journal of Public Policy & Management* 7 (1988): 601–20. See also Amihai Glazer & Lawrence S. Rothenberg, *Why Government Succeeds and Why It Fails* (2001), 6.

68. On the banks, see Ryan Tracy & Michael R. Crittenden, "Small Banks Clutch Lifeline," *Wall Street Journal*, September 24, 2013.

69. Rick Lyman, "Tennesse Governor Hesitates on Medicaid Expansion, Frustrating Many," *New York Times*, November 16, 2013.

70. E. Donald Elliott, "Why the United States Does Not Have a Renewable Energy Policy," *Environmental Law Reporter* 43 (2013): 10097.

71. Stephanie Kirchgaessner, "Scientists Claim Funding Pinch is 'Demoralising a Generation,'" *Financial Times*, January 26, 2013.

72. *National Federation of Independent Business v. Sebelius*, 132 S. Ct. 2566, 2604 (2012)
73. Glazer & Rothenberg, *Why Government Succeeds and Why It Fails*, 80–81.
74. Kira R. Fabrizio, "The Effect of Regulatory Uncertainty on Investment: Evidence from Renewable Energy Generation," *Journal of Law, Economics, & Organization* 29 (2013): 765–98.
75. Glazer & Rothenberg, *Why Government Succeeds and Why It Fails*, 111. See also Schuck & Zeckhauser, *Targeting in Social Programs*.
76. Glazer & Rothenberg, *Why Government Succeeds and Why It Fails*, 144–45.
77. Eric M. Patashnik, *Putting Trust in the US Budget: Federal Trust Funds and the Politics of Commitment* (2000).
78. Nelson D. Schwartz, "Partisan Impasse Drives Industry to Cut Spending," *New York Times*, August 6, 2012; Rebecca Berg, "Fear of Year-End Fiscal Stalemate May Be Having Effect Now," *New York Times*, July 12, 2012.
79. Rob Portman, "The Regulatory Cliff Is Nearly as Steep as the Fiscal One," *Wall Street Journal*, August 17, 2012.
80. See, e.g., Reed Abelson & Katie Thomas, "Sense of Peril for Health Law Gives Insurers Pause," *New York Times*, March 30, 2012.
81. *National Federation of Independent Business v. Sebelius*, 132 S. Ct. 2566 (2012).
82. Abby Goodnough et al., "Opening Rush to Insurance Markets Hits Snags," *New York Times*, October 2, 2013.
83. See, e.g., Robert Pear, "Uncertainty over States and Medicaid Expansion," *New York Times*, June 28, 2102.
84. Steven Greenhouse & Jonathan Martin, "Unions' Misgivings on Health Law Burst into View," *New York Times*, September 12, 2013.
85. Laura Meckler, Jennifer Corbett Dooren, & Peter Nicholas, "U.S. Struggles to Meet Health-Law Deadline," *Wall Street Journal*, July 10, 2013.
86. Kim Dixon & Patrick Temple-West, "IRS Issues Final Rules on Obamacare's 'Individual Mandate,'" *Reuters*, August 27, 2013.
87. "Promises, Promises," *Economist*, April 20, 2013, 34; John Harwood, "Next Big Challenge for Health Law: Carrying It Out," *New York Times*, April 30, 2013.
88. Jackie Calmes & Robert Pear, "Crucial Rule Is Delayed a Year for Obama's Health Law," *New York Times*, July 3, 2013.
89. David Morgan, "'Obamacare' Mandate Delay Will Cost $12 Billion, Affect 1 Million Workers," http://www.reuters.com/article/2013/07/30/us-usa-healthcare-employers-idUSBRE96T1DI20130730.
90. "Employer Mandate? Never Mind," *Wall Street Journal*, July 5, 2013.
91. Robert Pear, "A Limit on Consumer Cost Is Delayed in Health Care Law," *New York Times*, August 13, 2013.
92. Ray Fisman & Tim Sullivan, "The Most Efficient Office in the World," *Slate*, July 31, 2013, http://www.slate.com/articles/business/the_dismal_science/2013/07/renewing_your_passport_visit_the_incredibly_efficient_new_york_city_passport.html?wpisrc=newsletter_jcr:content.
93. Kevin Sack, "In Discarding of Kidneys, System Reveals Its Flaws," *New York Times*, September 20, 2012.
94. Ian Lovett, "$4 Million Set for Man Left in D.E.A. Cell," *New York Times*, August 1, 2013.
95. Daniel Gade, "Why the VA Is Buried in Disability Claims," *Wall Street Journal*, June 23, 2013.
96. James Dao, "Veterans Wait for Benefits as Claims Pile Up," *New York Times*, September 28, 2012; James Dao, "Workers Point Finger at Their Own Agency amid a Backlog in Veterans' Benefits," *New York Times*, June 16, 2012; James Dao, "V.A. Aims to Reduce Its Backlog of Claims," *New York Times*, April 20, 2013.

97. Paul C. Light, "The Sequester Is an Overhaul Opportunity," *Wall Street Journal*, March 21, 2013.

98. U.S. Government Accountability Office, *Employment and Training Programs: Opportunities Exist for Improving Efficiency*, April 7, 2011, http://www.gao.gov/new.items/d11506t.pdf.

99. "The Job Training Mess," *Wall Street Journal*, May 9, 2012.

100. Ron Nixon, "Number of Catfish Inspectors Drives a Debate on Spending," *New York Times*, July 27, 2013.

101. Paul C. Light, *The Tides of Reform: Making Government Work 1945–1995* (1997), 2.

102. Erin Banco, "Cut Emissions? Congress Itself Keeps Burning a Dirtier Fuel," *New York Times*, August 9, 2013.

103. Helene Cooper, "Administration Torn on Response to Secret Service Scandal," *New York Times*, April 22, 2012.

104. *In re Aiken County*, No. 11–1271 (D.C. Cir., August 13, 2013).

105. Charlie Savage & Scott Shane, "Top-Secret Court Castigated N.S.A. on Surveillance," *New York Times*, August 22, 2013.

106. Office of Inspector General, U.S. Department of Defense, "Fraud, Waste, and Abuse Defined," http://www.dodig.mil/resources/fraud/fraud_defined.html.

107. U.S. Government Accountability Office, *Improper Payments: Moving Forward with Governmentwide Reduction Strategies*, February 7, 2012, http://www.gao.gov/assets/590/588228.pdf.

108. Ibid.

109. Danny Werfel, Office of Management and Budget, "Eliminating Billions in Payment Errors," http://www.whitehouse.gov/blog/2012/11/21/eliminating-billions-payment-errors.

110. U.S. Government Accountability Office, *High Risk Series: An Update*, February 2013, http://www.gao.gov/assets/660/652133.pdf; 268, table10.

111. U.S. Department of Health and Human Services and Department of Justice, *Health Care Fraud and Abuse Control Program Annual Report for Fiscal Year 2012*, February 2013, https://oig.hhs.gov/publications/docs/hcfac/hcfacreport2012.pdf, 1.

112. U.S. Government Accountability Office, *Program Integrity: Further Action Needed to Address Vulnerabilities in Medicaid and Medicare Programs*, June 7, 2012, http://www.gao.gov/products/GAO-12–803T.

113. David Wood, "Pentagon Reports Billions of Dollars in Contractor Fraud," February 3, 2011, http://www.politicsdaily.com/2011/02/03/pentagon-admits-to-billions-of-dollars-in-contractor-fraud/.

114. U.S. Citizenship and Immigration Services, *Annual Report for Fiscal Year 2008* (2008), 6.

115. Ron Nixon, "Millions in U.S. Subsidies Go to Dead Farmers," *New York Times*, July 31, 2013.

116. Ron Nixon, "Fraud Used to Frame Farm Bill Debate," *New York Times*, June 18, 2013.

117. James Dao, "Veterans Pension Program Is Being Abused, Report Says," *New York Times*, June 6, 2012; James Dao, "Duplicate Payments Bedevil Veterans' Pension System, Employees Say," *New York Times*, September 23, 2012; Robert M. Morgenthau, "The Death of Peter Wielunski," *Wall Street Journal*, September 24, 2012 (on mental health claims).

118. Treasury Inspector General for Tax Administration, *There Are Billions of Dollars in Undetected Tax Refund Fraud Resulting From Identity Theft*, http://www.treasury.gov/tigta/auditreports/2012reports/201242080fr.html.

119. For federal employees, see Light, "The Sequester Is an Overhaul Opportunity." For federal contractors, see Nicola M. White, "Senators Call for Crackdown on Tax-Delinquent Federal Contractors," *Tax Notes*, May 30, 2011, 928.

120. Eric Lipton, "Health Lobby Tries to Undo Dialysis Cuts," *New York Times*, August 29, 2013.
121. William K. Rashbaum, "600 Long Island Rail Road Retirees to Lose Disability Pay in U.S. Inquiry," *New York Times*, July 2, 2013.
122. See, e.g., Michele A. Fluornoy, "The Smart-Shopping Way to Cut the Defense Budget," *Wall Street Journal*, July 8, 2013.
123. Steven Kelman, "Remaking Federal Procurement," *Public Contract Law Journal* 31 (2002): 581–622; Flournoy, "The Smart-Shopping Way."

CHAPTER 7: MARKETS

1. Gretchen Morgenson & Robert Gebeloff, "Wall St. Exploits Ethanol Credits, and Prices Spike," *New York Times*, September 15, 2013.
2. This is recounted in John B. Taylor, "When Volcker Ruled," *Wall Street Journal*, September 8–9, 2012 (book review).
3. See, generally, Daniel Yergin, *The Prize: The Epic Quest for Oil, Money, and Power* (1991).
4. See, e.g., Eduardo Porter, "A Model for Reducing Emissions," *New York Times*, March 20, 2013.
5. See Laura Meckler, "Candidates Spar on Whether Government Fosters Success," *Wall Street Journal*, July 25, 2012.
6. See, generally, Peter H. Schuck, *Diversity in America: Keeping Government at a Safe Distance* (2003), chaps. 1–2.
7. See, generally, Albert O. Hirschman, *Shifting Involvements: Private Interest and Public Action* (1982).
8. See, e.g., Jeff Madrick, *The Case for Big Government* (2008).
9. The most recent example is Michael Sandel, *What Money Can't Buy: The Moral Limits of Markets* (2012).
10. For a general economic treatment of crowding out and crowding in in a variety of policy contexts, see Amihai Glazer & Lawrence S. Rothenberg, *Why Government Succeeds and Why It Fails* (2001).
11. Dwight Jaffee & John M. Quigley, *The Future of the Government Sponsored Enterprises: The Role for Government in the U.S. Mortgage Market*, National Bureau of Economic Research Working Paper 17685, December 2011.
12. Ibid., 64–65.
13. National Bureau of Economic Research, "Medicaid and the Long-Term Care Insurance Market," July 2005, http://www.nber.org/digest/jul05/w10989.html (summarizing study by Jeffrey Brown and Amy Finkelstein).
14. Robert Wood Johnson Foundation, *Public Program Crowd-Out of Private Coverage: What Are the Issues?* Research Synthesis Report 5 (June 2004), 11.
15. Ibid.
16. Robert Pear, "Online Health Law Sign-Up Is Delayed for Small Business," *New York Times*, November 28, 2013.
17. Arthur C. Brooks, "Philanthropy and the Non-Profit Sector," in Peter H. Schuck & James Q. Wilson, *Understanding America: The Anatomy of an Exceptional Nation* (2008), 547–48.
18. Ibid. (chap. 18).
19. For a historical exploration of these differences, see Marvin Olasky, *The Tragedy of American Compassion* (1992)
20. Jason Richwine & Andrew Biggs, *Assessing the Compensation of Public School Teach-*

ers, November 1, 2011, http://www.heritage.org/research/reports/2011/10/assessing-the-compensation-of-public-school-teachers.

21. Robert Pear, "Despite Democrats' Warnings, Private Medicare Plans Find Success," *New York Times*, August 26, 2012.

22. Benjamin Zycher, "Comparing Public and Private Health Insurance: Would a Single Payer System Save Enough to Cover the Uninsured?" http://www.manhattan-institute.org/html/mpr_05.htm.

23. James F. Blumstein, Mark Cohen, & Suman Seth, "Do Government Agencies Respond to Market Pressures? Evidence from Private Prisons," *Virginia Journal of Social Policy & Law* 15 (2008): 446–77.

24. See, generally, Jon D. Michaels, "Privatization's Pretensions," *University of Chicago Law Review* 77 (2010): 717–80.

25. Jonathan Macey, *The Death of Corporate Reputation: How Integrity Has Been Destroyed on Wall Street* (2013).

26. See, e.g., Robert C. Ellickson, *The Household: Informal Order around the Hearth* (2008); Lawrence Stone, *The Family, Sex, and Marriage in England, 1500–1800* (1977); and Michael Novak, *The Catholic Ethic and the Spirit of Capitalism* (1993).

27. See, e.g., Thomas E. Mann & Norman J. Ornstein, *It's Even Worse Than It Looks: How the American Constitutional System Collided with the New Politics of Extremism* (2012).

28. See, e.g., Jonathan K. Nelson & Richard J. Zeckhauser, *The Patron's Payoff: Conspicuous Commissions in Italian Renaissance Art* (2008).

29. See, e.g., Bill McKibben, *The End of Nature* (2006).

30. See, e.g., Michael Mandelbaum, *The Meaning of Sports: Why Americans Watch Baseball, Football, and Basketball, and What They See When They Do* (2005).

31. See, e.g., Philip E. Tetlock, *Expert Political Judgment: How Good Is It? How Can We Know?* (2005).

32. Floyd Norris, "Strong and Fast but No Time to Think," *New York Times*, August 3, 2012.

33. Such speed has its downsides. See, e.g., Nathaniel Popper, "Flood of Errant Trades is a Black Eye for Wall Street," *New York Times*, August 2, 2012. The "flash crash" of May 6, 2010, caused a drop of nearly $1 trillion. See Nelson D. Schwartz & Louise Story, "Surge of Computer Selling after Apparent Glitch Sends Stocks Tumbling," *New York Times*, May 6, 2010.

34. Glazer & Rothenberg, *Why Government Succeeds and Why It Fails*, chap. 1.

35. Peter H. Schuck, *Diversity in America: Keeping Government at a Safe Distance* (2003), 323.

36. Ibid., 324–31. For such critiques of antitrust enforcement, see, e.g., Robert H. Bork, *The Antitrust Paradox: A Policy at War with Itself* (1978). For critiques of civil rights enforcement, see, e.g., Richard D. Kahlenberg, *The Remedy: Class, Race, and Affirmative Action* (1996).

37. The classic account of this program is Jerry L. Mashaw, *Bureaucratic Justice: Managing Social Security Disability Claims* (1983).

38. Milt Freudenheim, "The Ups and Downs of Electronic Medical Records," *New York Times*, October 8, 2012.

39. Reed Abelson & Julie Creswell, "In 2nd Look, Few Savings from Digital Care Records," *New York Times*, January 11, 2013.

40. Ibid.; see also Reed Abelson, "Medicare Is Faulted on Shift to Electronic Records," *New York Times*, November 29, 2012.

41. Leora Horwitz, "A Shortcut to Wasted Time," *New York Times*, November 23, 2012.

42. For cautious optimism, see David Dranove, Chris Forman, Avi Goldfarb, & Shane Greenstein, *The Trillion Dollar Conundrum: Complementarities and Health Information Technology*, National Bureau of Economic Research Working Paper 18281 (2012).

43. W. Kip Viscusi, "The Lulling Effect: The Impact of Child-Resistant Packaging on Aspirin and Analgesic Ingestions," *American Economic Review* 74 (1984): 324–27.

44. See Kate Taylor, "Mayor Offers Ideas of Why Homeless Figures Are Up," *New York Times*, August 23, 2012.

45. Sam Peltzman, "The Effects of Automobile Safety Regulation," *Journal of Political Economy* 83 (1975): 677–726.

46. Robert W. Crandall & John D. Graham, "The Effect of Fuel Economy Standards on Automobile Safety," *Journal of Law & Economics* 32 (1989): 97–118.

47. Michael Heberling, "Government-Mandated Fuel-Efficiency Standards," *The Freeman: Ideas on Liberty* 56 (2006): 36–38.

48. See, e.g., Nicholas D. Kristof, "I Have a Nightmare," *New York Times*, March 12, 2005.

49. Ian Urbina, "As OSHA Emphasizes Safety, Long-Term Health Risks Fester," *New York Times*, March 30, 2013.

50. Casey B. Mulligan, *The Redistribution Recession: How Labor Market Distortions Contracted the Economy* (2012), 113–17.

51. http://www.aei.org/article/economics/dodd-franks-costs-will-be-paid-for-by-low-in come-bank-customers/?utm_source=today&utm_medium=paramount&utm_cam paign=092613.

52. Aaron Wildavsky, *Searching for Safety* (1988), 61–75.

53. Robert L. Rabin, "Reexamining the Pathways to Reduction in Tobacco-Related Disease," *Theoretical Inquiries in Law* 15 (2014): n16.

54. Clemens Bomsdorf, "Denmark Scraps 'Fat Tax' after a Year," *Wall Street Journal,* November 12, 2012.

55. Eric Lipton, "Banks Rally against Strict Controls of Foreign Bets," *New York Times*, May 1, 2013.

56. Mary Williams Walsh, "Experts Fear Life Insurers Are Courting Reserve Risk," *New York Times*, November 30, 2012.

57. "Over-Regulated America," *Economist*, February 18, 2012, 9.

58. Jason Zweig, "When Laws Twist Markets," *Wall Street Journal*, August 4, 2012.

59. Torstenn Persson, Gérard Roland, & Guido Tabellini, "Comparative Politics and Public Finance," *Journal of Political Economics* 108 (2000): 1121–61.

60. See James Q. Wilson, ed., *The Politics of Regulation* (1980). For a very recent review of the subject, see the Tobin Project, http://www.tobinproject.org/.

61. On OSHA, see, e.g., David Weil, "Enforcing OSHA: The Role of Labor Unions," *Industrial Relations* 30 (2008): 20–36. On the EPA, see, e.g., R. Shep Melnick, *Regulation and the Courts: The Case of the Clean Air Act* (1983). On the EEOC, see, e.g., Sean Farhang, *The Litigation State: Public Regulation and Private Lawsuits in the U.S.* (2010).

62. See, e.g., Peter Skerry, *Counting on the Census: Race, Group Identity, and the Evasion of Politics* (2000).

63. Marie Hojnacki & David C. Kimball, "Organized Interests and the Decision of Whom to Lobby in Congress," *American Political Science Review* 92 (1998): 776.

64. Mariano-Florentino Cuellar, "Coalitions, Autonomy, and Regulatory Bargains in Public Health Law," *Theoretical Inquiries in Law* 15 (forthcoming, 2014).

65. Joseph E. Stiglitz, *The Price of Inequality* (2012).

66. See, e.g., Jacob S. Hacker & Paul Pierson, *Winner-Take-All Politics: How Washington Made the Rich Richer—and Turned Its Back on the Middle Class* (2010); Lawrence Lessig, *Republic, Lost: How Money Corrupts Congress—and a Plan to Stop It* (2011); Timothy Noah, *The Great Divergence: America's Growing Inequality Crisis and What We Can Do About It* (2012).

67. Ezra Klein points out that cash is less important than gifts, favors, and relationships. See Klein, "Our Corrupt Politics: It's Not All Money," *New York Review of Books*, March 22, 2012, 42, 44 (reviewing Lawrence Lessig, *Republic, Lost*, and Jack Abramoff, *Capitol*

Punishment: The Hard Truth about Washington Corruption from America's Most Notorious Lobbyist [2012]).

68. Richard Hall & Alan Deardorff, "Lobbying as Legislative Subsidy," *American Political Science Review* 100 (2006): 69. See also Derek Bok, *The Problem with Government* (2001), 82–87.

69. See, generally, Eduardo Porter, "Unleashing Corporate Contributions," *New York Times*, August 29, 2012 (reviewing evidence).

70. The classic statement came in a prestigious American Political Science Association committee report. Austin Ranney, ed., "Toward a More Responsible Two-Party System," *American Political Science Review* 44, supplement (1950): 488–99.

71. John J. Pitney Jr., "Review of *Do Not Ask What Good We Do* and *It's Even Worse Than It Looks*," *The Forum* 10 (2012), 4.

72. Ben Protess, "On Wall Street, Suddenly Making Nice with Obama after Backing Romney," *New York Times*, November 8, 2012.

73. *Citizens United v. Federal Election Commission*, 558 U.S. 50 (2010).

74. See Michael W. McConnell, "A Defense of *Citizens United*" (unpublished manuscript, 2012).

75. "Carter: Unlimited Contributions 'Legal Bribery,'" *New York Times*, July 18, 2013.

76. Matt Bai, "How Did Political Money Get This Loud?" *New York Times Magazine*, July 22, 2012, 14, 16, 18.

77. Stephen Ansolabehere, John M. de Figueiredo, & James M. Snyder Jr., "Why Is There So Little Money in U.S. Politics?" *Journal of Economic Perspectives* 17 (2003): 105–30.

78. Porter, "Unleashing Corporate Contributions."

79. Klein, "Our Corrupt Politics," 44. See also the exchange on the politics of single-payer health care financing: Lawrence Lessig & Ezra Klein, "'It's Not All Money,'" *New York Review of Books*, May 10, 2012, 66.

80. Porter, "Unleashing Corporate Contributions" (on the Steven Levitt study).

81. See, e.g., Eduardo Porter, "Get What You Pay For? Not Always," *New York Times*, November 7, 2012; Brody Mullins, "Outside Groups Spent Big, but the Impact Isn't Clear-Cut," *Wall Street Journal*, November 7, 2012; Nicholas Confessore & Jess Bidgood, "Little to Show for Cash Flood by Big Donors," *New York Times*, November 8, 2012.

82. Frank O. Bowman III, "Are We Really Getting Tough on White Collar Crime?" *Federal Sentencing Reporter* 15 (2003): 237–241.

83. Russell G. Ryan, "Mum's the Word about SEC Defeats," *Wall Street Journal*, June 3, 2013.

84. Gary S. Becker, "Crime and Punishment: An Economic Approach," *Journal of Political Economy* 76 (1968): 169–217.

85. Floyd Norris, "Fraud Case Delayed by Two Months," *New York Times*, November 2, 2012 (Federal Energy Regulatory Commission may bring charges against the first "emerging growth" company under JOBS Act).

86. Jessica Silver-Greenberg & Ben Protess, "JP Morgan Faces Full-Court Press by U.S. Regulators," *New York Times*, March 27, 2013.

87. Anne Kates Smith, "Does the SEC Have Your Back?" May 2012, http://www.kiplinger.com/article/investing/T038-C000-S002-does-the-sec-have-your-back.html.

88. See, e.g., Rachel E. Barkow, "Prosecutorial Administration: Prosecutor Bias and the Department of Justice," *University of Virginia Law Review* 99 (2013): 271–342; and William J. Stuntz, "The Pathological Politics of Criminal Law," *Michigan Law Review* 100 (2001): 505–600.

89. See, generally, Donald L. Horowitz, *The Jurocracy: Government Lawyers, Agency Programs, and Judicial Decisions* (1977).

90. See Clifford Winston, *Government Failure versus Market Failure* (2006), 38n9.

91. *Oversight of the U.S. Department of Justice: Hearing before the Senate Commission on*

the Judiciary, 113th Cong. (2013) (statement of Eric. H. Holder Jr., attorney general of the United States).

92. *Canning v. NLRB*, 705 F.3d 490 (D.C. Cir. 2013). The Supreme Court will review the decision (Docket 12–1281).

93. See, e.g., James B. Stewart, "Another Fumble by the S.E.C. on Fraud," *New York Times*, November 17, 2012; Nathaniel Popper & Jessica Silver-Greenberg, "Mixed Verdict on Fraud at a Money Market Mutual Fund," *New York Times*, November 13, 2012 ("difficulty . . . in holding financiers accountable for precipitating the financial crisis").

94. See Arthur Levitt with Paula Dwyer, *Take on the Street: What Wall Street and Corporate America Don't Want You to Know* (2002), 132–33.

95. U.S. Securities and Exchange Commission, *In Brief: FY 2011 Congressional Justification*, February 2010, http://www.sec.gov/about/secfy11congbudgjust.pdf.

96. Stephen J. Choi, Karen K. Nelson, & A. C. Pritchard, "The Screening Effect of the Private Securities Litigation Reform Act," *Journal of Empirical Legal Studies* 6 (2009): 35–68.

97. Eric Lipton & Ben Protess, "Banks' Lobbyists Help in Drafting Financial Bills," *New York Times*, May 24, 2013.

98. See, e.g., Justin O'Brien, *Redesigning Financial Regulation: The Politics of Enforcement* (2007); Archie Parnell, "Political Interference in Agency Enforcement: The IRS Experience," *Yale Law Journal* 89 (1980): 1360–94.

99. Peter Eavis, "In Tighter Loan Rules, Wiggle Room for Banks," *New York Times*, January 10, 2012.

100. Jessica Silver-Greenberg, "Bank Deal Ends Flawed Review of Foreclosures," *New York Times*, January 11, 2013.

101. David S. Hilzenrath, "Judge Questions SEC Settlement with Citigroup," *Washington Post*, October 27, 2011.

102. U.S. Securities and Exchange Commission, Office of Investigations, *Investigation of Failure of the SEC to Uncover Bernard Madoff's Ponzi Scheme*, August 31, 2009, http://www.sec.gov/news/studies/2009/oig-509.pdf.

103. Ben Protess & Jessica Silver-Greenberg, "Blame Abounds over a Flawed Foreclosure Review," *New York Times*, April 4, 2013.

104. See, e.g., Walt Bogdanich, "2nd Official Dissented over Pequot Inquiry," *New York Times*, December 5, 2006; and National Resources Defense Counsel, "EPA Inspector General Finds Agency Undercut Ongoing Enforcement Suits against Polluting Power Plants," October 1, 2004, http://www.nrdc.org/media/pressreleases/041001.asp.

105. Internal Revenue Service, "IRS Releases New Tax Gap Estimates: Compliance Rates Remain Statistically Unchanged from Previous Study," IR-2012–4, http://www.irs.gov/uac/IRS-Releases-New-Tax-Gap-Estimates;-Compliance-Rates-Remain-Statistically-Unchanged-From-Previous-Study.

106. This is the title of Eric Redman's authoritative book on the subject; see Redman, *The Dance of Legislation,* 2nd ed. (2001).

107. Michael Cooper, "Gun Sales Surge as Nation Weighs Tougher Limits," *New York Times*, January 12, 2013.

108. See, e.g., Glazer & Rothenberg, *Why Government Succeeds and Why It Fails*, 27–33.

109. Lisa Bernstein has explored this relationship in a series of articles. See, e.g., "Opting Out of the Legal System: Extralegal Contractual Relations in the Diamond Industry," *Journal of Legal Studies* 21 (1992): 115–57; and "Private Commercial Law in the Cotton Industry: Creating Cooperation through Rules, Norms, and Institutions," *Michigan Law Review* 99 (2001): 1724–90.

110. See Peter H. Schuck, *The Limits of Law: Essays on Democratic Governance* (2000), chap. 13.

CHAPTER 8: IMPLEMENTATION

1. See, generally, Donald L. Horowitz, *The Courts and Social Policy* (1977); Peter H. Schuck, *Suing Government: Citizen Remedies for Official Wrongs* (1983), chaps. 1, 7; Ross Sandler & David Schoenbrod, *Democracy by Decree: What Happens When Courts Run Government* (2003).

2. Jeffrey L. Pressman & Aaron Wildavsky, *Implementation: How Great Expectations in Washington Are Dashed in Oakland; Or, Why It's Amazing That Federal Programs Work at All, This Being a Saga of the Economic Development Administration as Told by Two Sympathetic Observers Who Seek to Build Morals on a Foundation of Ruined Hopes*, 3rd ed., expanded (1984).

3. Derek Bok, *The Problem with Government* (2001), 136–42.

4. Pressman & Wildavsky, *Implementation*, 93.

5. Ibid., chap. 5.

6. Scott Patterson & Andrew Ackerman, " 'Volcker Rule' Faces New Hurdles," *Wall Street Journal*, November 20, 2013.

7. Alan S. Blinder, *After the Music Stopped: The Financial Crisis, the Response, and the Work Ahead* (2013), 296.

8. Julie Steinberg, "Volcker Rule Stirs Fresh Confusion among Big Banks," *Wall Street Journal,* July 8, 2013.

9. Michael D. Shear & Peter Eavis, "Obama Presses for Action on Bank Rules," *New York Times*, August 20, 2013.

10. Pressman & Wildavsky, *Implementation*, 147.

11. "Stuck to the Ground by Red Tape," *Economist Technology Quarterly*, June 1, 2013, 3.

12. Clifford Winston, *Government Failure versus Market Failure: Microeconomic Policy Research and Government Performance* (2006), 16–21.

13. Ibid., 22–25.

14. Ron Nixon, "Farm Subsidies Leading to More Water Use," *New York Times*, June 7, 2013.

15. Winston, *Government Failure versus Market Failure*, 82 (for the period 1996–2000).

16. Robert B. Semple Jr., "Where the Trough Is Overflowing," *New York Times*, June 3, 2012.

17. Sara Sciammacco, "The Downfall of Direct Payments," http://www.ewg.org/downfall -direct-payments.

18. See, e.g., Clifford Winston & Jia Yan, "Open Skies: Estimating Travelers' Benefits from Free Trade in Airline Services" (unpublished manuscript, March 2013; estimating annual gains of at least $5 billion to travelers from such agreements).

19. Winston, *Government Failure versus Market Failure*, 24–25.

20. See, e.g., Vivek Wadha, *The Immigrant Exodus: Why America Is Losing the Global Race to Capture Entrepreneurial Talent* (2012).

21. See George J. Borjas, *Heaven's Door: Immigration Policy and the American Economy* (1999). For a general review of immigration policy, see Peter H. Schuck, "Immigration," in Peter H. Schuck & James Q. Wilson, eds., *Understanding America: The Anatomy of an Exceptional Nation* (2008), chap. 12.

22. Winston, *Government Failure versus Market Failure*, 35–37.

23. David Olinger & Eric Gorski, "After 11 Years, U.S. Fire Program Analysis System Still Isn't Ready," *Denver Post*, July 1, 2012; U.S. Government Accountability Office, *Wildland Fire Management: Interagency Budget Tool Needs Further Development to Fully Meet Key Objectives*, GAO-09-68, November 24, 2008, http://www.gao.gov/new.items /d0968.pdf; U.S. Government Accountability Office, *Station Fire: Forest Service's Response Offers Potential Lessons for Future Wildland Fire Management*, GAO-12-155, December 16, 2011, http://www.gao.gov/assets/590/587075.pdf.

24. Sam Peltzman, "The Effects of Automobile Safety Regulation," *Journal of Political Economy* 83 (1975): 677–726.

25. W. Kip Viscusi, "The Lulling Effect: The Impact of Child-Resistant Packaging on Aspirin and Analgesic Ingestions," *American Economic Review* 74 (1984): 324–27.

26. W. Kip Viscusi, "Consumer Behavior and the Safety Effects of Product Safety Regulation," *Journal of Law & Economics* 28 (1985): 527–53.

27. Ian Urbina, "As OSHA Emphasizes Safety, Long-Term Health Risks Fester," *New York Times*, March 30, 2013.

28. John Mendeloff, "Enforcement Knowns and Unknowns" (unpublished manuscript, May 2012); John Mendeloff, e-mail to author, July 17, 2013.

29. Winston, *Government Failure versus Market Failure*, 42–43.

30. See, e.g., Gregg Easterbrook, *A Moment on the Earth: The Coming Age of Environmental Optimism* (1995).

31. See Winston Harrington, Richard D. Morgenstern, & Thomas Sterner, eds. *Choosing Environmental Policy* (2004).

32. Winston Harrington, Richard D. Morgenstern, & Peter Nelson, *On the Accuracy of Regulatory Cost Estimates*, Resources for the Future Discussion Paper (1999).

33. Winston Harrington, *Grading Estimates of the Benefits and Costs of Federal Regulation*," Resources for the Future Discussion Paper (2006), 21.

34. Environmental Protection Agency, *The Benefits and Costs of the Clean Air Act, 1970 to 1990* (1997).

35. For all three studies, see Environmental Protection Agency, "Benefits and Costs of the Clean Air Act," http://www.epa.gov/air/sect812/.

36. Indur Goklany, *Clearing the Air: The Real Story of the War on Air Pollution* (1999), chap. 6.

37. See, e.g., Peter W. Huber, "Safety and the Second Best: The Hazards of Public Risk Management in the Courts," *Columbia Law Review* 85 (1985): 298.

38. Richard L. Revesz & Allison L. Westfahl Kong, "Regulatory Change and Optimal Transition Relief," *Northwestern Law Review* 105 (2011): 1581–1633.

39. Mark Jacobson & Arthur van Benthem, *Vehicle Scrappage and Gasoline Policy*, National Bureau of Economic Research Working Paper 19055 (2013).

40. See, e.g., Joshua Linn & Virginia McConnell, "How Electric Cars Can Increase Greenhouse Gas Emissions," *Resources* 184 (2013): 33.

41. Kenneth A. Small & Clifford Winston, *Bounding the Welfare Effects of CAFE Standards*, Brookings Institution Working Paper, July 2013.

42. See David Popp, "Pollution Control Innovations and the Clean Air Act of 1990," *Journal of Policy Analysis and Management* 22 (2003): 641–60.

43. Richard Schmalensee & Robert N. Stavins, "The SO_2 Allowance Trading System: The Ironic History of a Grand Policy Experiment," *Journal of Economic Perspectives* 27 (2013): 111–12. However, see also Popp, "Pollution Control Innovations and the Clean Air Act of 1990," 658.

44. Winston, *Government Failure versus Market Failure*, 63.

45. Clifford Winston, "On the Performance of the U.S. Transportation System: Caution Ahead," *Journal of Economic Literature* (forthcoming, 2013).

46. Ibid.

47. Ibid.

48. Clifford Winston & Fred Mannering, *Implementing Technology to Improve Highway Performance: A Leapfrog Technology Is Going to Be Necessary*. Brookings Institution, May 2013.

49. Kenneth A. Small, Clifford Winston, & Carol A. Evans, *Road Work* (1989).

50. Winston, *Government Failure versus Market Failure*, 64–68.

51. Clifford Winston & Vikram Maheshri, "On the Social Desirability of Urban Rail Transit Systems," *Journal of Urban Economics* 62 (2007): 362–82.

52. Robert Puentes, Adie Tomer, & Joseph Kane, *A New Alignment: Strengthening America's Commitment to Passenger Rail*, http://www.brookings.edu/~/media/Research/Files/Reports/2013/03/01%20passenger%20rail%20puentes%20tomer/passenger%20rail%20puentes%20tomer.pdf.

53. Ron Nixon, "Amtrak Losing Millions Each Year on Food Sales," *New York Times*, August 2, 2012.

54. Daniel Hanson, "End the Amtrak Experiment," http://www.aei.org/article/economics/fiscal-policy/end-the-amtrak-experiment/.

55. Paul Vigna & Betsy Morris, "Boom Time on the Tracks: Rail Capacity, Spending Soar," *Wall Street Journal*, March 27, 2013.

56. James Sherk, "Repealing the Davis-Bacon Act Would Save Taxpayers $10.9 Billion," http://www.heritage.org/research/reports/2011/02/repealing-the-davis-bacon-act-would-save-taxpayers-$10–9-billion. See, generally, Armand Thieblot, *The Case against the Davis-Bacon Act: 54 Reasons for Repeal* (2013).

57. Winston, *Government Failure versus Market Failure*, 69, citing Joel Brinkley, "A U.S. Agency Is Accused of Collusion in Land Deals," *New York Times*, October 12, 2002.

58. Ron Nixon, "Amid Capitol Turmoil Postal Service Crisis Drags On," *New York Times*, November 6, 2013.

59. U.S. Government Accountability Office, *Multiple Employment and Training Programs: Providing Information on Colocating Services and Consolidating Administrative Structures Could Promote Efficiencies* (January 2011), http://www.gao.gov/assets/320/314551.pdf, 11.

60. Robert J. La Londe, professor of economics, University of Chicago Harris School of Public Policy, e-mail to author, September 12, 2013.

61. Elisabeth Rosenthal & Andrew W. Lehren, "Effort to Curb Coolant Falters, Sometimes at Home," *New York Times*, November 23, 2012; Elisabeth Rosenthal & Andrew W. Lehren, "As Coolant Is Phased Out, Smugglers Reap Big Profits," *New York Times*, September 8, 2012.

62. James Surowiecki, "The Underground Recovery," *New Yorker*, April 29, 2013, 22.

63. The classic treatment is Hernando De Soto, *The Other Path: The Invisible Revolution in the Third World* (1989). See also Peter H. Schuck & Robert E. Litan, "Regulatory Reform in the Third World: The Case of Peru," *Yale Journal on Regulation* 4 (1986): 51–78; and Friedrich Schneider, *The Shadow Economy in Europe, 2010*, http://media.hotnews.ro/media_server1/document-2011–05–8–8602544–0-shadow.pdf.

64. Robert Neuwirth, *The Stealth of Nations: The Global Rise of the Informal Economy* (2011), 18.

65. Friedrich Schneider, *Size and Measurement of the Informal Economy in 110 Countries around the World* (July 2002) http://rru.worldbank.org/Documents/PapersLinks/informal_economy.pdf.

66. "Bring On the Touts," *Economist*, August 4, 2012, 10.

67. Bruce Yandle, "Bootleggers and Baptists: The Education of a Regulatory Economist," *AEI Journal on Government and Society* 7 (1983): 12–16.

68. See Mark A. R. Kleiman, Nathan P. Caulkins, & Angela Hawken, *Drugs and Drug Policy: What Everyone Needs to Know* (2011), 2. Recent research suggests that marijuana is more toxic than previously believed. See Roni Caryn Rabin, "Legalizing of Marijuana Raises Health Concerns," *New York Times*, January 7, 2013.

69. James Q. Wilson, "Against the Legalization of Drugs," *Commentary* 89 (1990): 21–28.

70. Eduardo Porter, "Numbers Tell of Failure in Drug War," *New York Times*, July 4, 2012.

71. Randal C. Archibold, Damien Cave, & Ginger Thompson, "Mexico's Curbs on U.S. Role in Drug Fight Spark Friction," *New York Times*, May 1, 2013.

72. John Tierney, "For Lesser Crimes, Rethinking Life behind Bars," *New York Times*, December 12, 2012.

73. Kleiman et al., *Drugs and Drug Policy*, 198–206. See also Bill Keller, "How to Legalize Pot," *New York Times*, May 19, 2013.

74. Ana Campoy, "The Pot Business Suffers Growing Pains," *Wall Street Journal*, April 20, 2013.

75. Oren Bar-Gill, *Seduction by Contract: Law, Economics, and Psychology in Consumer Markets* (2013).

76. Omri Ben-Shahar & Carl E. Schneider, *More Than You Wanted to Know: The Failure of Mandated Disclosures* (2014); Clifford Winston, "The Efficacy of Information Policy: A Review of Archon Fung, Mary Graham, and David Weil's *Full Disclosure: The Perils and Promises of Transparency*," *Journal of Economic Literature* 46 (2008): 704–17.

77. Frank Partnoy & Jesse Eisinger, "What's inside America's Banks?" *Atlantic*, January–February 2013, 64–65.

78. Winston, *Government Failure versus Market Failure*, 27–59.

79. Ibid., 39–41.

80. Daniel Ho, "Regulatory Fudge: The Promise of Targeted Transparency and the Practice of Restaurant Grading," *Yale Law Journal* 122 (2012): 574–688.

81. Christine Jolls, "Product Warnings, Debiasing, and Free Speech: The Case of Tobacco Regulation," *Journal of Institutional & Theoretical Economics* 169 (2013): 53–78.

82. Steven M. Davidoff, "A Simple Solution That Made a Hard Problem More Difficult," *New York Times*, August 28, 2013.

83. Raj Chetty, John N. Friedman, Soren Leth-Petersen, Torben Heien Nielsen, & Tore Olsen, *Subsidies vs. Nudges: Which Policies Increase Saving the Most?*" Center for Retirement Research at Boston College 13–3, March 2013.

84. Annie Lowrey, "F.H.A. Hopes to Avoid a Bailout by Treasury," *New York Times*, November 17, 2012.

85. Gretchen Morgenson, "In an F.H.A. Checkup, a Startling Number," *New York Times*, December 2, 2012.

86. Gretchen Morgenson, "Study Shows a Pattern of Risky Loans by F.H.A.," *New York Times*, December 13, 2012.

87. Edward J. Pinto, "The Next Housing Bailout? Big Trouble Brewing at FHA," *Atlantic*, November 16, 2012, http://www.theatlantic.com/business/archive/2012/11/the-next-housing-bailout-big-trouble-brewing-at-the-fha/265359/.

88. Morgenson, "In an F.H.A. Checkup, a Startling Number."

89. National Center for Education Statistics, *2011–12 National Postsecondary Student Aid Study (NPSAS:12): Student Financial Aid Estimates for 2011–12* (August 2013), http://nces.ed.gov/pubsearch/pubsinfo.asp?pubid=2013165.

90. Rohit Chopra, "Student Debt Swells, Federal Loans Now Top a Trillion," http://www.consumerfinance.gov/speeches/student-debt-swells-federal-loans-now-top-a-trillion/.

91. Eduardo Porter, "Dropping Out of College, and Paying the Price," *New York Times*, June 26, 2013.

92. Deborah Lucas & Damien Moore, *Costs and Policy Options for Federal Student Loan Programs*, Congressional Budget Office publication 4101 (March 2010), http://www.cbo.gov/sites/default/files/cbofiles/ftpdocs/110xx/doc11043/03–25-studentloans.pdf, 13–14.

93. U.S. Government Accountability Office, *Student Aid and Postsecondary Tax Preferences: Limited Research Exists on Effectiveness of Tools to Assist Students and Families Through Title IV Student Aid and Tax Preferences*, GAO-05–684 (2005), http://www.gao.gov/assets/250/247314.pdf, 29, n40 (citing Bridget Terry Long, *The Impact of Federal Tax Credits for Higher Education Expenses*, National Bureau of Economic Research Working Paper 9553 (2003).

94. Andrew Martin, "Well-Off Will Benefit Most from Change to Student Debt Relief Plan, Study Says," *New York Times*, October 16, 2012 (in Jason Delisle & Alex Holt, *Safety Net or Windfall?: Examining Changes to Income-Based Repayment for Federal Student Loans*, [2012], http://edmoney.newamerica.net/sites/newamerica.net/files /policydocs/NAF_Income_Based_Repayment.pdf).

95. Adeshina Emmanuel, *Private Sector Role Is at Heart of Campaigns' Split on College Costs*, *New York Times*, September 8, 2012.

96. Josh Mitchell, "Student-Aid Scams Targeted by Schools, Government," *Wall Street Journal*, June 24, 2013.

97. "The Rolling Student Loan Bailout," *Wall Street Journal*, August 10, 2013.

98. "How Student Debt Tripled in 8 Years, and Why It's Becoming a Growing Economic Problem," http://www.businessinsider.com/ny-fed-student-loans-presentation-2013–2.

99. Tamar Lewin, "Education Department Report Shows More Borrowers Defaulting on Student Loans," *New York Times*, September 29, 2012.

100. Andrew Martin, "Debt Collectors Cashing In on Student Loan Roundup," *New York Times*, September 9, 2012.

101. Chopra, "Student Debt Swells."

102. Mitchell, "Student-Aid Scams" (chart but without more recent data cited by Martin).

103. Ruth Simon, "Student-Loan Load Kills Startup Dreams," *Wall Street Journal,* August 14, 2013.

104. Ruth Simon & Rachel Louise Ensign, "Risky Student Debt Is Starting to Sour," *Wall Street Journal,* January 31, 2013.

105. Josh Mitchell, "Many Can't Pay Student Loans," *Wall Street Journal,* August 6, 2013.

106. Jessica Silver-Greenberg & Catherine Rampell, "Sallie Mae Will Split Old Loans from New," *New York Times*, May 30, 2013.

107. Glenn Kessler, "Elizabeth Warren's Claim That the U.S Earns $51 Billion in Profits on Student Loans," *Washington Post*, July 11, 2013.

108. Ibid.

109. David Deming, Claudia Goldin, & Lawrence Katz, *The For-Profit Postsecondary School Sector: Nimble Critters or Agile Predators*, National Bureau of Economic Research Working Paper 17710 (2011).

110. Al Yoon, "Investors Say No to Sallie Mae Bond Deal," *Wall Street Journal*, April 26, 2013.

111. Silver-Greenberg & Rampell, "Sallie Mae Will Split Old Loans from New."

112. U.S. Government Accountability Office, *Student Aid and Postsecondary Tax Preference*, 31.

113. Andrew G. Biggs, "The Truth about College Aid: It's Corporate Welfare," May 21, 2012, http://www.aei.org/article/education/higher-education/costs/the-truth-about-college -aid-its-corporate-welfare/.

114. Benjamin Ginsberg, *The Fall of the Faculty: The Rise of the All-Administrative University and Why It Matters* (2011), 26.

115. Lucas & Moore, *Costs and Policy Options for Federal Student Loan Programs*, 13.

116. Porter, "Dropping Out of College, and Paying the Price."

117. Ruth Simon & Rob Barry, "A Degree Drawn in Red Ink," *Wall Street Journal*, February 19, 2013.

118. Consumer Financial Protection Bureau, *Private Student Loans* (2012), http://files .consumerfinance.gov/f/201207_cfpb_Reports_Private-Student-Loans.pdf.

119. Simon, "Student-Loan Load Kills Startup Dreams"; Mitchell, "Many Can't Pay Student Loans."

120. U.S. Government Accountability Office, *Student Aid and Tax Benefits: Better Research and Guidance Will Facilitate Comparison of Effectiveness and Student Use*, GAO-02–751 (2002), http://www.gao.gov/assets/240/235411.pdf, 5, 26–30; U.S. Govern-

ment Accountability Office, *Student Aid and Postsecondary Tax Preferences*, 27; U.S. Government Accountability Office, *Higher Education*, 33 (adding completion).

121. U.S. Government Accountability Office, *Student Aid and Postsecondary Tax Preferences*, 4.

122. U.S. Government Accountability Office, *Higher Education*, 29–31; U.S. Government Accountability Office, *Student Aid and Postsecondary Tax Preferences*, 20.

123. U.S. Government Accountability Office, *Student Aid and Postsecondary Tax Preferences*, 28.

124. U.S. Government Accountability Office, *Higher Education*, 33; see also U.S. Government Accountability Office, *Student Aid and Postsecondary Tax Preferences*, 28.

125. U.S. Government Accountability Office, GAO-12-560, *Higher Education*, 33.

126. Ibid., 39.

127. James J. Heckman & Flavio Cunha, "The Technology of Skill Formation," *American Economic Review* 97 (2007), 31–47.

128. Tom Petri, *Petri Introduces Student Loan Bill*, press release, December 17, 2012, http://petri.house.gov/press-release/petri-introduces-student-loan-bill; Andrew Kelly, "A Student Debt Cure Worse Than the Disease," *The American*, December 18, 2012, http://www.american.com/archive/2012/december/a-student-debt-cure-worse-than-the-disease.

129. "Long History of U.S. Energy Subsidies," *Chemical & Engineering News* 89 (2011): 30–31.

130. "The Energy Subsidy Tally," *Wall Street Journal,* August 18, 2012.

131. Bjorn Lomborg, "Green Energy Is the Real Subsidy Hog," *Wall Street Journal*, November 12, 2013.

132. See, generally, Daniel Yergin, *The Quest: Energy, Security, and the Remaking of the Modern World* (2011).

133. Ted Gayer & W. Kip Viscusi, "Overriding Consumer Preferences with Energy Regulations," *Journal of Regulatory Economics* 43 (2013): 248–64.

134. Matthew L. Wald, "Court Overturns E.P.A.'s Biofuels rule, Saying It Overestimated Production," *New York Times*, January 26, 2013.

135. Carol D. Leonnig, "Chu Takes Responsibility for a Loan Deal That Put More Taxpayer Money at Risk in Solyndra," *Washington Post*, September 29, 2011.

136. Keith Bradsher, "Chinese Solar Panel Giant Is Tainted by Bankruptcy," *New York Times*, March 21, 2013.

137. Bill Vlasic, "Breaking Down on the Road to Electric Cars," *New York Times*, April 24, 2013; Mike Ramsey, "Car Battery Start-Ups Fizzle," *Wall Street Journal*, May 31, 2012; Isabel Kershner, "Israeli Venture Meant to Serve Electric Cars Ending Its Run," *New York Times*, May 27, 2013.

138. "The Other Government Motors," *Wall Street Journal*, May 24, 2013.

139. "The Price of Green Virtue," *Wall Street Journal*, July 7, 2012.

140. Wolfram Schlenker, "The Effect of Climate Change and Biofuel Mandates on Agricultural Output and Food Prices," *NBER Reporter* 2013 (2013): 16.

141. Elizabeth Rosenthal, "As Biofuel Demand Grows, So Do Guatemala's Hunger Pangs," *New York Times*, January 6, 2012. Eurpean countries are also adopting such mandates. On the opposition of world food agencies to ethanol requirements, see "Ethanol vs. the World," *Wall Street Journal*, August 11, 2012.

142. Matthew L. Wald, "Ethanol Surplus May Lift Gas Prices," *New York Times*, March 16, 2013.

143. Colin A. Carter & Henry I. Miller, "Corn for Food, Not Fuel," *New York Times*, July 31, 2012.

144. Matthew L. Wald, "E.P.A. Upholds Federal Mandate for Ethanol in Gasoline," *New York Times*, November 17, 2012. The EPA also denied a waiver request by Texas governor Rick Perry during the 2008 drought emergency; see "Ethanol vs. the World."

145. See, e.g., Michael S. Barr, "Credit Where It Counts: The Community Reinvestment Act and Its Critics," *New York University Law Review* 80 (2005): 513–652.

146. Sumit Agarwal, Efraim Benmelech, Nittai Bergman, & Amit Seru, "Did the Community Reinvestment Act Lead to Risky Lending?" National Bureau of Economic Research Working Paper 18609 (2012).

147. See, e.g., Lawrence J. White, "The CRA: Good Goals, Flawed Concept," in Federal Reserve Banks of San Francisco & Boston, *Revisiting the CRA: Perspectives on the Community Reinvestment Act* (2009): 185–88.

148. Richard Scott Carnell, Jonathan R. Macey, & Geoffrey P. Miller, *The Law of Banking and Financial Institutions*, 4th ed. (2009), 24–32.

149. Peter Eavis, "Senators Introduce Bill to Separate Trading Activities from Big Banks," *New York Times*, July 12, 2013, B3.

150. Joseph E. Stiglitz, "Knowledge as a Global Public Good," in Inge Kaul, Isabelle Grunberg, & Mark A. Stern, eds., *Global Public Goods: International Cooperation in the 21st Century* (1999), 308, 310.

151. Winston, *Government Failure versus Market Failure*, 54.

152. See, e.g., Michael Heller, *The Gridlock Economy: How Too Much Ownership Wrecks Markets, Stops Innovation, and Costs Lives* (2010); Alex Tabarrok, *Launching the Innovation Renaissance: A New Path to Bring Smart Ideas to Market Fast* (2011); Matt Ridley, "A Welcome Turn Away from Patents," *Wall Street Journal,* June 22, 2013; and Charles Duhigg & Steve Lohr, "The Patent, Used as a Sword," *New York Times*, October 7, 2012.

153. Winston, *Government Failure versus Market Failure*, 59.

154. "Stuck to the Ground by Red Tape," *Economist*, June 1, 2012, Technology Section, 3.

155. For overviews, see Jody Freeman & Charles D. Kolstad, eds., *Moving to Markets in Environmental Regulation: Lessons from Twenty Years of Experience* (2007); Ted Gayer & John K. Horowitz, *Market-Based Approaches to Environmental Regulation* (2006), 110–11.

156. Jody Freeman & Charles D. Kolstad, "Prescriptive Environmental Regulations versus Market-Based Incentives," in Freeman & Kolstad, eds., *Moving to Markets in Environmental Regulation*, 4.

157. Dieter Helm, *The Carbon Crunch: How We're Getting Climate Change Wrong—and How to Fix It* (2012).

158. Robert Stavins, "Market-Based Environmental Policies: What Can We Learn from U.S. Experience (and Related Research)?" in Freeman & Kolstad, eds., *Moving to Markets in Environmental Regulation*, chap. 2; Gayer & Horowitz, *Market-Based Approaches to Environmental Regulation*, chap. 4.

159. See Jonathan Baron, William T. McEnroe, & Christopher Poliquin, "Citizens' Perceptions and the Disconnect between Economics and Regulatory Policy," in Cary Coglianese, ed., *Regulatory Breakdown: The Crisis of Confidence in U.S. Regulation* (2012), chap. 7.

160. See, e.g., Ryan Tracy & Ben Lefebvre, "Fraud Fears Put a Chill in Fuel Programs," *Wall Street Journal*, August 3, 2012.

161. Matthew L. Wald, "A Program for Green Fuels Has Drawn Counterfeiters," *New York Times*, October 12, 2012.

162. See, e.g., Elizabeth Rosenthal & Andrew W. Lehren, "Carbon Credits Gone Awry Raise Output of Harmful Gas," *New York Times*, August 9, 2012.

163. Freeman & Kolstad, "Prescriptive Environmental Regulations," 14.

164. "Extremely Troubled Scheme," *Economist*, February 16, 2013, 75; Felicity Barringer, "A Market in Emissions Is Set to Open in California," *New York Times*, November 14, 2012. On February 19, 2013, the EU's effort to rescue the Emissions Trading System seemed unable to prevent its collapse. Sean Carney, "Europe's Emissions Plan Hits Turbulence," *Wall Street Journal,* February 20, 2013.

165. Cass R. Sunstein, *The Arithmetic of Arsenic*, http://www.law.uchicago.edu/files/files/135.CRS_.arsenic.pdf.

166. "Complete Disaster in the Making," *Economist*, September 15, 2012, 72.

167. Stanley Reed, "Europe Vote Sets Back Carbon Plan," *New York Times*, April 17, 2013.

168. "ETS, RIP?" *Economist*, April 20, 2013, 75.

169. Nathaniel O. Keohane, "Cost Savings from Allowance Trading in the 1990 Clean Air Act: Estimates from a Choice-Based Model," in Freeman & Kolstad, eds., *Moving to Markets in Environmental Regulation*, 194.

CHAPTER 9: THE LIMITS OF LAW

1. Jonathan Rauch, "Tunnel Vision," *National Journal*, September 19, 1998, 2153.

2. Neil K. Komesar, *Imperfect Alternatives: Choosing Institutions in Law, Economics, and Public Policy* (1994), 103.

3. See Roland Benabou & Jean Tirole, "Incentives and Prosocial Behavior," *American Economic Review* 96 (2006): 1652–78.

4. For one such protest, see Philip K. Howard, *The Death of Common Sense: How Law Is Suffocating America* (1995).

5. Aaron Chatterji, "Why Washington Has It Wrong on Small Business," *Wall Street Journal*, November 12, 2012, http://online.wsj.com/article/SB10001424052702303768104577460040429463650.html.

6. "Unhappy Birthday to You," *Economist*, July 28, 2012, 64 (on a small bank's legal challenge to Dodd-Frank).

7. Richard A. Epstein, *Simple Rules for a Complex World* (1995).

8. See, generally, Peter H. Schuck, "Legal Complexity: Some Causes, Consequences, and Cures," *Duke Law Journal* 42 (1992): 1–52.

9. This is one of the implications of the famous Coase Theorem. Ronald J. Coase, "The Problem of Social Cost," *Journal of Law & Economics* 3 (1960): 1–44.

10. See, e.g., *Hanks v. Powder Ridge Restaurant Corp.*, 885 A.2d 734 (Ct. 2005).

11. See Peter H. Schuck, "When the Exception Becomes the Rule: Regulatory Equity and the Formulation of Energy Policy through an Exceptions Process," *Duke Law Journal* 1984 (1984): 163–300.

12. See, generally, Nicholas Georgescu-Roegen, *The Entropy Law and the Economic Process* (1971); and Talcott Parsons, *The Social System* (1951).

13. Carol M. Rose, "Crystals and Mud in Property Law," *Stanford Law Review* 40 (1988): 577–610.

14. See, e.g., Jerry L. Mashaw, "Regulation and Legal Culture: The Case of Motor Vehicle Safety," *Yale Journal on Regulation* 4 (1987): 257–316. But see also Jason Webb Yackee & Susan Webb Yackee, "Delay in Notice and Comment Rulemaking: Evidence of Systemic Regulatory Breakdown?" in Cary Coglianese, ed., *Regulatory Breakdown: The Crisis of Confidence in U.S. Regulation* (2012), chap. 8 (most agencies issue a good number of regulations relatively quickly).

15. *United States v. Booker*, 543 U.S. 220 (2005)

16. *Heckler v. Campbell*, 461 U.S. 458 (1983).

17. See, generally, Samuel Issacharoff, Pamela S. Karlan, & Richard H. Pildes, *The Law of Democracy*, 4th ed. (2012).

18. See, generally, John H. Langbein, David A. Pratt, & Susan J. Stabile, *Pension and Employee Benefit Law*, 5th ed. (2010).

19. See, e.g., Stephen G. Breyer, *Active Liberty: Interpreting Our Democratic Constitution* (2005); Antonin Scalia & Bryan A. Garner, *Reading Law: The Interpretation of Legal Texts* (2012); and Jack M. Balkin, *Living Originalism* (2011).

20. Most of this section is taken from Schuck, "Legal Complexity," part 2. Supporting references for the propositions in the text can be found there.

21. John D. McKinnon, "Firms Pass Up Tax Breaks, Citing Hassles, Complexity," *Wall Street Journal*, July 23, 2012.

22. Patricia M. Wald, "The 'New Administrative Law'—with the Same Old Judges in It?" *Duke Law Journal* 1991 (1991): 668–69.

23. For the provenance of this term, see Mila Sohoni, "The Idea of 'Too Much Law,'" *Fordham Law Review* 80 (2012): 1587n8. Sohoni is skeptical of the hyperlexis critique.

24. See, e.g., Michael J. Graetz, "100 Million Unnecessary Returns: A Fresh Start for the U.S. Tax System," *Yale Law Journal* 112 (2002): 261–310.

25. National Taxpayers Union, *A Taxing Trend: The Rise in Complexity, Forms, and Paperwork Burdens*, NTU Policy Paper #130 (April 17, 2012), http://www.ntu.org/news -and-issues/taxes/tax-reform/ntupp130.html.

26. James S. Eustice, "Tax Complexity and the Tax Practitioner," *Tax Law Review* 45 (1989): 19.

27. McKinnon, "Firms Pass Up Tax Breaks."

28. See Cass R. Sunstein, "Incompletely Theorized Agreements," *Harvard Law Review* 108 (1995): 1733–72.

29. Robert Pear, "Ambiguity in Health Law Could Make Family Coverage Too Costly for Many," *New York Times*, August 11, 2012.

30. *Brown v. Allen*, 344 U.S. 443, 540 (1953).

31. See Adam Liptak, "In Congress's Paralysis, A Mightier Supreme Court," *New York Times*, August 20, 2012.

32. The classic exploration of this subject is Kenneth Culp Davis, *Discretionary Justice: A Preliminary Inquiry* (1969).

33. For a recognition of the importance of agency discretion in immigration enforcement, see *Arizona v. United States*, 132 S. Ct. 292, 2499 (2012).

34. See Philip Howard, *The Death of Common Sense*.

35. Anthony Lewis, "Cases That Cry Out," *New York Times*, March 18, 2000.

36. The classic statement of this position is David Schoenbrod, *Power without Responsibility: How Congress Abuses the People through Delegation* (1993).

37. *A.L.A. Schechter Poultry Corp. v. United States*, 295 U.S. 495 (1935).

38. See Peter H. Schuck, "Delegation and Democracy: Comments on David Schoenbrod," *Cardozo Law Review* 20 (1999): 775–93.

39. See, e.g., Rachel Barkow, "The Prosecutor as Regulatory Agency," in Anthony S. Barkow & Rachel E. Barkow, eds., *Prosecutors in the Boardroom* (2011), chap. 8.

40. See, e.g., *Connick v. Thompson*, 131 S. Ct. 1350 (2011).

41. U.S. Constitution, Art. II, Sec. 2. This power has sometimes been abused, as in president Bill Clinton's January 20, 2001 pardon of Marc Rich.

42. U.S. Department of Justice, *Rules Governing Petitions for Executive Clemency*, http:// www.justice.gov/pardon/clemency.htm.

43. Steven M. Davidoff & David Zaring, "Regulation by Deal: The Government's Response to the Financial Crisis," *Administrative Law Review* 61 (2009): 466.

44. *Mathews v. Eldridge*, 424 U.S. 319 (1976).

45. For a critical assessment of the test, see Jerry L. Mashaw, "The Supreme Court's Due Process Calculus for Administrative Adjudication in Mathews v. Eldridge: Three Factors in Search of a Theory of Value," *University of Chicago Law Review* 44 (1976): 28–59.

46. Peter H. Schuck, "Mass Torts: An Institutional Evolutionist Perspective," *Cornell Law Review* 80 (1995): 941–989.

47. For some examples, see Peter W. Huber & Robert E. Litan, eds., *The Liability Maze* (1991); and Timothy D. Lytton, ed., *Suing the Gun Industry: A Battle at the Crossroads of Gun Control and Mass Torts* (2005).

48. Samuel Issacharoff, "Class Actions and State Authority," *Loyola University Chicago Law*

Review 44 (2013): 369–90. For a critique of antifraud security class actions, see William W. Bratton & Michael L. Wachter, "Reforming Securities Law Enforcement: Politics and Money at the Public/Private Divide," in Coglianese, *Regulatory Breakdown*, chap. 10.

49. Theodore W. Ruger, "Failure by Obsolescence: Regulatory Challenges for the FDA in the Twenty-First Century," in Coglianese, *Regulatory Breakdown*, chap. 12.

50. Ian Lovett, "Critics Say California Law Hurts Effort to Add Jobs," *New York Times*, September 4, 2012.

51. E. Allan Lind, Robert J. MacCoun, Patricia A. Ebener, William L. F. Felstiner, Deborah R. Hensler, Judith Rensnik, & Tom R. Tyler, *The Perception of Justice* (1989).

52. See, generally, Robert Kagan, *Adversarial Legalism: The American Way of Law* (2001).

53. Ross Sandler & David Schoenbrod, *Democracy by Decree: What Happens When Courts Run Government* (2002). If the lawyers do in fact take the program to court, officials can count on certain doctrinal and other litigation advantages. See, generally, Peter H. Schuck, *Suing Government: Citizen Remedies for Official Wrongs* (1983).

54. See, e.g., Jim Carlton & Max Taves, "For Now, Bullet Train May Go Nowhere," *Wall Street Journal*, July 9, 2012.

55. For examples and elaboration, see the sources cited in Peter H. Schuck, *The Limits of Law: Essays on Democratic Governance* (2000), 472n180.

56. William J. Stuntz, "Race, Class, and Drugs," *Columbia Law Review* 98 (1998): 1826.

57. Cass Sunstein, ""On the Expressive Function of Law," *University of Pennsylvania Law Review* 144 (1996): 2029–33.

58. Stephanie M. Stern, "The Dark Side of Town: The Social Capital Revolution in Residential Property" (unpublished manuscript, 2012).

CHAPTER 10: THE BUREAUCRACY

1. Max Weber, *The Theory of Social and Economic Organization*, trans. A. M. Henderson & Talcott Parsons (2012).

2. James Q. Wilson, *Bureaucracy: What Government Agencies Do and Why They Do It* (1989).

3. Donald F. Kettl, "Bureaucracy," in Peter H. Schuck and John Q. Wilson, eds., *Understanding America: The Anatomy of an Exceptional Nation* (2008), chap. 2.

4. This section borrows heavily, sometimes verbatim, from James Q. Wilson & John J. Dilulio Jr., *The Essentials of American Government: Institutions and Policies*, 12th ed. (2011), 406–11.

5. Kettl, "Bureaucracy," 39.

6. Wilson & Dilulio, *The Essentials of American Government*, 407.

7. Kettl, "Bureaucracy," 43–45.

8. Marshall W. Meyer, "The Growth of Public and Private Bureaucracies," *Theory & Society* 16 (1987): 215–35.

9. Paul C. Light, *A Government Ill-Executed: The Decline of the Federal Service and How to Reverse It* (2008).

10. Nelson W. Polsby, "The Political System," in Peter H. Schuck & James Q. Wilson, eds., *Understanding America: The Anatomy of an Exceptional Nation* (2008), 11.

11. Joseph Pratt Harris, *Congressional Control of Administration* (1980).

12. Kettl, "Bureaucracy,", 41–43.

13. Polsby, The Political System,", 7–11.

14. See, e.g., Curtis P. McLaughlin & Craig D. McLauglin, *Health Policy Analysis: An Interdisciplinary Approach* (2008), 245–46.

15. Herbert Kaufman, *Red Tape: Its Origins, Uses, and Abuses* (1977).

16. Eugene Bardach & Robert A. Kagan, *Going By the Book: The Problem of Regulatory Unreasonableness*, 2nd ed. (2007).

17. Paul C. Light, quoted in Peter Baker, "Obama Team Has Billions to Spend, but Few Ready to Do It," *New York Times*, February 18, 2009.
18. Light, *A Government Ill-Executed*, 96–99.
19. Peter Finn & Sari Horwitz, "Obama Move Signals a Bid to Bolster ATF," *Washington Post*, January 17, 2013.
20. Jeremy W. Peters, "In Senate, Arm-Twisting and Vote-Changing Lead to a Confirmation," *New York Times*, August 1, 2013.
21. Binyamin Appelbaum, "Senate Backs a Director for Financial Watchdog," *New York Times*, July 17, 2013.
22. *Canning v. NLRB*, 705 F.3d 490 (D.C. Cir. 2013).
23. Jared A. Favole, "Inspector General Vacancies Criticized," *Wall Street Journal*, June 20, 2013.
24. Hugh Heclo, *A Government of Strangers: Executive Politics in Washington* (1977), 237.
25. Matthew Dull & Patrick S. Roberts, "Continuity, Competence, and the Succession of Senate-Confirmed Agency Appointees, 1989–2009," *Presidential Studies Quarterly* 39 (2009): 432–53.
26. Ibid., 436–37.
27. Anne Joseph O'Connell, "Qualifications: Law and Practice of Selecting Agency Leaders" (unpublished manuscript, 2013).
28. Kettl, "Bureaucracy," 45.
29. Paul C. Light, "Perp Walks and the Broken Bureaucracy," *Wall Street Journal*, April 27, 2012.
30. Light, *A Government Ill-Executed*, 58, 73; Kettl, "Bureaucracy," 53.
31. Light, *A Government Ill-Executed*, 57, 72.
32. Ibid., 58–65.
33. Ibid., 56.
34. Ibid., 67; emphasis added.
35. Marty Linsky, private communication with the author, March 1, 2013. The Koop example is discussed in Holcomb B. Noble, "C. Everett Koop, Forceful U.S. Surgeon General, Dies at 96," *New York Times*, February 25, 2013.
36. Robert Pear, "Official at Health Site Says He Didn't Know of Potential Risk," *New York Times*, November 11, 2013.
37. Light, *A Government Ill-Executed*, 67, 70.
38. Ibid., 75–76, 197–99.
39. Andrew G. Biggs & Jason Richwine, "The Truth about Federal Salary Numbers," *Washington Post*, November 18, 2012.
40. Andrew G. Biggs & Jason Richwine, "For Federal Workers, the Grass Isn't Greener in the Private Sector," December 11, 2012, http://www.aei.org/article/economics/for-federal-workers-the-grass-isnt-greener-in-the-private-sector/#.UMfwPw50Y7s.email.
41. Andrew G. Biggs & Jason Richwine, "The Underworked Public Employee," December 6, 2012, http://www.aei.org/article/economics/the-underworked-public-employee/#.UMf1xHeyc3g.email.
42. John Donahue, *The Warping of American Government Work* (2008), 38–50.
43. Ibid., 81.
44. Andrew G. Biggs, "We're No. 1—in Public Employee Pay," http://www.aei.org/article/economics/were-no-1-in-public-employee-pay/?utm_source=today&utm_medium=paramount&utm_campaign=081313.
45. Light, *A Government Ill-Executed*, 139.
46. Ibid., 139–58.
47. Beryl A. Radin, *Federal Management Reform in a World of Contradictions* (2012), 148–64; Christopher Pollitt, "Performance Management in Practice: A Comparative

Study of Executive Agencies," *Journal of Public Administrative Research & Theory* 16 (2006): 25–44.

48. Light, *A Government Ill-Executed*, 110–20, 139, 143.
49. Ralph Smith, "Can a Fed Be Fired for Poor Performance?" http://www.fedsmith.com /2003/07/29/can-fed-be-fired-poor-performance/.
50. Dennis Cauchon, "Some Federal Workers More Likely to Die Than Lose Jobs," *USA Today*, July 19, 2011 (citing former research head of MSPB).
51. Light, *A Government Ill-Executed*, 115, 124. The former group perceived less poor employee performance.
52. Donahue, *The Warping of American Government Work*, 153 (citing study).
53. Ibid., 154–55.
54. Kettl, "Bureaucracy."
55. Ibid., 194–203.
56. Tim Shorrock, "Put the Spies Back under One Roof," *New York Times*, June 18, 2013.
57. Donahue, *The Warping of American Government Work*, 113; Kettl, "Bureaucracy," 54–56; Steven Kelman, *Procurement and Public Management: The Fear of Discretion and the Quality of Government Performance* (1990).
58. Radin, *Federal Management Reform*, 57–75; Shorrock, "Put the Spies Back under One Roof."
59. Light, *A Government Ill-Executed*, 210, 236. See also Jody Freeman & Martha Minow, eds., *Government by Contract: Outsourcing and American Democracy* (2009).
60. Donahue, *The Warping of American Government Work*, 5–6.
61. Ibid., chap. 4.
62. James Madison, "Federalist No. 70," quoted in Light, *A Government Ill-Executed*.

CHAPTER 11: POLICY SUCCESSES

1. See, e.g., Peter H. Schuck & James Q. Wilson, "Looking Back," in Schuck & Wilson, eds., *Understanding America: The Anatomy of an Exceptional Nation* (2008), chap. 21.
2. Adam Goodheart & Peter Manseau, "American History Hits the Campaign trail," *New York Times*, July 8, 2012.
3. Richard E. Neustadt & Harvey V. Fineberg, *The Swine Flu Affair: Decision-Making on a Slippery Disease* (1978).
4. Sabrina Tavernise, "Vaccine Is Credited in Fall of Teenagers' Infection Rate," *New York Times*, June 20, 2013.
5. Mariano-Florentino Cuellar, "Coalitions, Autonomy, and Regulatory Bargains in Public Health Law," *Theoretical Inquiries in Law* 15 (forthcoming, 2014).
6. L. Gordon Crovitz, "Who Really Invented the Internet?" *Wall Street Journal*, July 23, 2012 (reviewing Michael Hiltzik, *Dealers of Lightning: Xerox PARC and the Dawn of the Computer Age* [2000]).
7. See, e.g., Orlando Patterson, "Black Americans," in Schuck & Wilson, eds., *Understanding America*, 387–88.
8. Thomas Sowell, *Civil Rights: Rhetoric or Reality?* (1985).
9. Gerald N. Rosenberg, *The Hollow Hope: Can Courts Bring About Social Change?* (1991)
10. Peter H. Schuck, *Diversity in America: Keeping the Government at a Safe Distance* (2003), chap. 5; Peter H. Schuck, "Affirmative Action after *Fisher v. University of Texas*," unpublished ms., November 2013.
11. June E. O'Neill & Dave M. O'Neill, *The Declining Importance of Race and Gender in the Labor Market: The Role of Employment Discrimination Policies* (2012).
12. Claudia Goldin & Lawrence Katz, *The Most Egalitarian of All Professions: Pharmacy*

and the Evolution of a Family-Friendly Occupation, National Bureau of Economic Research Working Paper 18410 (2012).

13. Nicholas Bagley, "Bedside Bureaucrats: Why Medicare Reform Hasn't Worked," *Georgetown Law Journal* 101 (2013): 527–32.

14. Melinda Beck, "More Doctors Steer Clear of Medicare," *Wall Street Journal*, July 29, 2013.

15. "Medicare and Medicaid Fraud, Waste, and Abuse," General Accountability Office, GAO-11-409T, March 9, 2011.

16. Social Security Administration, "A Summary of the 2013 Annual Reports," http://www.ssa.gov/oact/trsum/.

17. See Franklin E. Zimring, *The City That Became Safe: New York's Lessons for Urban Crime and Its Control* (2012); and Matthew Yglesias, "We're on Track for the Lowest Murder Rate in 100 Years," *Slate*, May 17, 2013.

18. Eliot Cohen, "The Military," in Schuck & Wilson, eds., *Understanding America*, chap. 9; Charles Moskos, *All That We Can Be: Black Leadership and Racial Integration the Army Way* (1996). The integration of women and gay people are works in progress, with the former marred by pervasive sexual predation and the latter too recent to be assessed.

19. Thomas Le Duc, "History and Appraisal of U.S. Land Policy to 1862," in Howard W. Ottoson, ed., *Land Use Policy and Problems in the United States* (1963), 4–5.

20. Ibid., 5–27.

21. Frederick Jackson Turner, "The Significance of the Frontier in American History," in *The Frontier in American History* (1921).

22. Aziz Rana, *The Two Faces of American Freedom* (2010), 116.

23. Paul W. Gates, "The Homestead Act: Free Land Policy in Operation, 1862–1935," in Ottoson, ed., *Land Use Policy and Problems in the United States*, 28.

24. Ibid., 32n9.

25. Paul W. Gates, *History of Public Land Law Development* (1968), 393–97.

26. Ibid., 770–71.

27. Gates, "The Homestead Act," 33.

28. See, generally, Stephen Skowronek, *Building a New American State: The Expansion of National Administrative Capacities, 1877–1920* (1982). On the administration of land offices, see Jerry L. Mashaw, *Creating the Administrative Constitution: The Lost One Hundred Years of American Administrative Law* (2012).

29. Martha Derthick, "Federalism," in Schuck & Wilson, *Undertsanding America*, 129–30.

30. *United States v. Fordice*, 505 U.S. 717 (1992).

31. Gary V. Engelhardt & Jonathan Gruber, *Social Security and the Evolution of Elderly Poverty*, National Bureau of Economic Research Working Paper 10466 (May 2004).

32. U.S. Social Security Administration, "Social Security Administrative Expenses," http://www.ssa.gov/oact/STATS/admin.html (administrative cost); Matthew Yglesias, "The Social Security Administration Has a 99.996% Accuracy Rate for Paying Benefits to the Right People," http://mobile.slate.com/blogs/moneybox/2013/06/24/social_security_errors_they_re_incredibly_rare.html?wpisrc=newsletther_jcr:content.

33. Henry J. Aaron, "Social Security Reconsidered," *National Tax Journal* 64 (2011): 385–414.

34. "Progressives and the Safety Net," *Democracy Journal*, Winter 2013, 74.

35. Michael J. Bennett, *When Dreams Came True: The GI Bill and the Making of Modern America* (1996), x.

36. Ibid., chap. 4.

37. Suzanne Mettler, *Soldiers to Citizens: The G.I. Bill and the Making of the Greatest Generation* (2005), 6–7.

38. Glenn C. Altschuler & Stuart M. Blumin, *The GI Bill: A New Deal for Veterans* (2009), 210–12.

39. Mettler, *Soldiers to Citizens*, 8.

40. Ira Katznelson, *When Affirmative Action Was White: An Untold History of Racial Inequalities in Twentieth-Century America* (2005), 113–15; Lizabeth Cohen, *A Consumers' Republic: The Politics of Mass Consumption in Postwar America* (2003), 167–70.

41. See, e.g., Altschuler & Blumin, *The GI Bill*, chap. 7.

42. Mettler, *Soldiers to Citizens*, 55.

43. Ibid., 9–10.

44. Earl Swift, *The Big Roads: The Untold Story of the Engineers, Visionaries, and Trailblazers Who Created the American Superhighways* (2011), 6.

45. U.S. Department of Transportation, Federal Highway Administration, "Annual Vehicle-Miles of Travel, 1980–2011," January 2012, http://www.fhwa.dot.gov/policyinformation/statistics/2011/vm202.cfm.

46. Thomas L. Karnes, *Asphalt and Politics: A History of the American Highway System* (2009).

47. U.S. Department of Transportation, Federal Highway Administration, "Interstate FAQ," http://www.fhwa.dot.gov/interstate/faq.htm#question8 (updated May 2, 2013).

48. American Society of Civil Engineers, "U.S. Interstate Highway System: Monument of the Millennium," http://www.asce.org/People-and-Projects/Projects/Monuments-of-the-Millennium/U-S-Interstate-Highway-System/.

49. *Celebrating 50 Years: The Eisenhower Interstate Highway System, Hearing Before the House Subcomittee. on Highways, Transit & Pipelines of the House Commission on Transportation & Infrastructure*, 109th Cong. (2006) (testimony of Jonathan Gifford, Professor, School of Public Policy, George Mason University, et al.).

50. Mark H. Rose & Raymond A. Mohl, *Interstate: Highway Politics and Policy since 1939*, 3d ed. (2012), 111.

51. Center for American Progress, "Failing Infrastructure by the Numbers," August 17, 2007, http://www.americanprogress.org/issues/budget/news/2007/08/17/3372/failing-infrastructure-by-the-numbers/.

52. Carol Wolf, "U.S. Highway Trust Fund Faces Insolvency Next Year, CBO Says," January 31, 2012, http://www.bloomberg.com/news/2012–01–31/u-s-highway-trust-fund-faces-insolvency-next-year-cbo-says.html.

53. Paul Vigna & Betsy Morris, "Boom Time on the Tracks: Rail Capacity, Spending Soar," *Wall Street Journal,* March 27, 2013.

54. "End Food Stamps, with a Caveat," *Washington Post,* July 1, 2013.

55. Ron Nixon & Jonathan Weisman, "House Approves Farm Bill, without Food Stamp Program," *New York Times,* July 11, 2013.

56. Center for Budget and Policy Priorities, "Policy Basics: Introduction to the SNAP Program," November 20, 2012, http://www.cbpp.org/cms/index.cfm?fa=view&id=2226.

57. Damian Paletta & Caroline Porter, "Use of Food Stamps Swells Even as Economy Improves," *Wall Street Journal*, March 28, 2013. See Yonatan Ben-Shalom et al., "An Assessment of the Effectiveness of Anti-Poverty Programs in the United States," *Oxford Handbook on the Economics of Poverty* (2012), Sec. 4.1 (on labor market effects).

58. Richard H. Pildes, "The Future of Voting Rights Policy: From Anti-Discrimination to the Right to Vote," *Howard Law Journal* 49 (2006): 744; Richard H. Pildes, "The Politics of Race: Quiet Revolution in the South," *Harvard Law Review* 108 (1995): 1359–92.

59. U.S. Commission on Civil Rights, *The Voting Rights Act Ten Years After* (1975), table 3.

60. Adam Liptak, "Voting Rights Law Draws Skepticism from Justices," *New York Times*, February 28, 2013 (statement of Chief Justice John Roberts at oral argument).

61. Frank R. Parker, *Black Votes Count: Political Empowerment in Mississippi after 1965* (2011), 1; Joint Center for Political and Economic Studies, *National Roster of Black Elected Officials: Fact Sheet*, http://www.jointcenter.org/sites/default/files/upload/research/files/National%20Roster%20of%20Black%20Elected%20Officials%20Fact%20Sheet.pdf.

62. Carol Hardy-Fanta, Christine Marie Sierra, Pei-te Lien, Dianne M. Pinderhughes, & Wartyna L. Davis, "Race, Gender, and Descriptive Representation: An Exploratory View of Multicultural Elected Leadership in the United States" (2005), http://www.gmcl.org /pdf/APSA9–05–05.pdf, 3–4.

63. *Allen v. State Board of Elections*, 393 U.S. 544 (1969).

64. Compare, e.g., *Parents Involved in Community School v. Seattle School District No. 1*, 551 U.S. 701 (2007); and *Allen v. State Board of Elections* (Stevens, J., dissenting; Breyer, Stevens, Souter, & Ginsburg, J.J., dissenting).

65. See, generally, Schuck, *Diversity in America*, chap. 5.

66. Charlie Savage, "Report Finds Political Splits and Unprofessionalism in Voting Agency," *New York Times*, March 13, 2013.

67. J. Morgan Kousser, *Colorblind Injustice: Minority Voting Rights and the Undoing of the Second Reconstruction* (1999), 347–48.

68. "Voting Rights Watershed," *Wall Street Journal*, February 28, 2013.

69. *Shelby County, Alabama v. Holder*, 133 S. Ct. 2612 (2013).

70. Pildes, "The Future of Voting Rights Policy," 743.

71. Taylor Branch, *At Canaan's Edge: America in the King Years, 1965–68* (2006), 275–78.

72. It certainly helped that the Supreme Court quickly affirmed the law's constitutionality. *Katzenbach v. Morgan*, 384 U.S. 681 (1966).

73. Adam Liptak, "Voting Rights Act Is Challenged as Cure the South Has Outgrown," *New York Times*, February 17, 2013.

74. See, e.g., *Veith v. Jubilerer*, 541 U.S. 267 (2004); and *Georgia v. Ashcroft*, 539 U.S. 461 (2003).

75. See Peter H. Schuck, *Diversity in America*, 87–88.

76. See, e.g., Schuck, *Diversity in America*, chap. 4; and Peter H. Schuck, "Alien Rumination: What Immigrants Have Wrought in America,"105 *Yale Law Journal* 1963 (1996).

77. See, e.g., Peter H. Schuck, *Citizens, Strangers, and In-Betweens: Essays on Immigration and Citizenship* (1998), 4–11.

78. Jacob L. Vigdor, "Measuring Immigrant Assimilation in Post-Recession America," *Civic Report* 76 (2013), http://www.manhattan-institute.org/html/cr_76.htm#.UVXMCxyR98E.

79. Kristina Peterson, "Immigration's Tricky Politics," *Wall Street Journal*, September 7, 2013.

80. Peter H. Schuck, "Bordering on Folly," *American Lawyer*, October 2007, 83–86.

81. On the ideology of settler freedom, see Rana, *The Two Faces of American Freedom*.

82. See, e.g., Peter H. Schuck & John E. Tyler, "Making the Case for Changing U.S. Policy Regarding Highly Skilled Immigrants," *Fordham Urban Law Journal* 38 (2010): 327–62.

83. Robert A. Moffitt, "Economics and the Earned Income Tax Credit," in John J. Siegfried, ed., *Better Living through Economics* (2010), 88.

84. Anne L. Alstott, "Why the EITC Doesn't Make Work Pay," *Law & Contemporary Problems* 73 (2010): 285–314. Richard J. Zeckhauser and I proposed a wage supplement approach in Richard J. Zeckhauser & Peter Schuck, "An Alternative to the Nixon Income Maintenance Plan," *Public Interest* 19 (1970): 120–30.

85. Center on Budget and Policy Priorities, "Policy Basics: The Earned Income Tax Credit," http://www.cbpp.org/cms/index.cfm?fa=view&id=2505; Center on Budget and Policy Priorities, "Earned Income Tax Credit," http://www.cbpp.org/research/index.cfm ?fa=topic&id=27.

86. Internal Revenue Service, "Earned Income Tax Credit: Fraud," http://www.eitc.irs.gov /rptoolkit/faqs/fraud/.

87. U.S. Government Accountability Office, *Improper Payments: Recent Efforts to Address Improper Payments and Remaining Challenges*, http://www.gao.gov/new.items/d11 575t.pdf.

88. Moffitt, "Economics and the Earned Income Tax Credit," 102. See also Sara Sternberg

Greene, "The Broken Safety Net: A Study of Earned Income Tax Credit Recipients and a Proposal for Repair," *New York University Law Review* 88 (2013): 515–588; Sabrina Tavernise, "Antipoverty Tax Program Offers Relief, Though Often Temporary," *New York Times*, April 17, 2012.

89. Ron Haskins & John Podesta, "Making Work Pay Again—This Time for Men," July 3, 2013, http://www.brookings.edu/research/opinions/2013/07/03-men-working-wages -haskins.

90. See, generally, Martha Derthick & Paul J. Quirk, *The Politics of Deregulation* (1985).

91. Elizabeth E. Bailey, "Air-Transportation Deregulation," in Siegfried, ed., *Better Living through Economics*, chap. 8.

92. Lawrence S. Rothenberg, *Regulation, Organizations, and Politics: Motor Freight Policy at the Interstate Commerce Commission* (1994), 225n18.

93. Ibid.

94. Nancy L. Rose, "After Airline Deregulation and Alfred E. Kahn," *American Economic Review* 102 (2012): 379.

95. Michael E. Levine, "Airport Congestion: When Theory Meets Reality," *Yale Journal on Regulation* 26 (2009): 37–88.

96. Gary Burtless & Ron Haskins, "Inequality, Economic Mobility, and Social Policy," in Schuck & Wilson, eds., *Understanding America*, 531–32.

97. This statistic is somewhat misleading. See Peter H. Schuck, "Three Models of Citizenship," in Michael S. Greve & Michal Zoller, eds., *Citizenship in America and Europe: Beyond the Nation-State?* (2009), 169–72.

98. Burtless & Haskins, "Inequality, Economic Mobility, and Social Policy," 533–34, supplemented by e-mail from Haskins to the author, February 24, 2013.

99. Ibid., 535–36.

100. Ibid.

101. See Rebecca M. Blank, "The Role of Economics in the Welfare-to-Work Reforms of the 1990s," in Siegfried, ed., *Better Living through Economics*, 137.

102. Peter H. Schuck & Ron Haskins, "Welfare Reform Worked," *Los Angeles Times*, February 28, 2012, supplemented by e-mail from Haskins to the author, February 24, 2013.

103. Ivar Lodemel & Heather Trickey, *An Offer You Can't Refuse: Workfare Programs in International Perspective* (2001).

104. John B. Judis, "Steve Jobs's Angel," *New Republic*, September 2, 2013, 6; "The Entrepreneurial State," *Economist*, August 31, 2013, 59.

105. Gilbert Omenn, "Update of the SMRB Working Group on the Value of Biomedical Research," http://smrb.od.nih.gov/documents/presentations/2013/VOBR_01142013 .pdf.

106. Margaret E. Blume-Kohout, "Does Targeted, Disease-Specific Public Research Funding Influence Pharmaceutical Innovation?" *Journal of Policy Analysis and Management* 31 (2012): 641–60 (on the effect of NIH funding on discovery and testing of new drugs); Andrew A. Toole, "Does Public Scientific Research Complement Private Investment in Research and Development in the Pharmaceutical Industry?" *Journal of Law & Economics* 50 (2007): 81–104 (on how NIH funding is complementary to and stimulates private industry investment); Andrew A. Toole, "The Impact of Public Basic Research on Industrial Innovation: Evidence from the Pharmaceutical Industry," *Research Policy* 41 (2012): 1–12.

107. Ashley J. Stevens, Jonathan J. Jensen, Katrine Wyller, Patrick C. Kilgore, Sabarni Chatterjee, & Mark L. Rohrbaugh, "The Role of Public-Sector Research in the Discovery of Drugs and Vaccines," *New England Journal of Medicine* 364 (2011): 535–41.

108. Simon Tripp and Martin Greuber, *Economic Impact of the Human Genome Project*, May 2011, http://battelle.org/docs/default-document-library/economic_impact_of_the _human_genome_project.pdf.

109. Brian W. Cashell, "Social Security, Saving, and the Economy," in Paul O. Deaven & William H. Andrews, eds., *Social Security: New Issues and Developments* (2008), 103–6.

110. Paula Stephan, *How Economics Shapes Science* (2012), 6–7.

111. Derek Bok, *The Trouble with Government* (2001), 143–44.

112. Lisa Fleisher, "'Good Behavior' Still Pays Off," *Wall Street Journal*, September 25, 2013.

113. Jim Manzi, *Uncontrolled: The Surprising Payoff of Trial-and-Error for Business, Politics, and Society* (2012), 202–4.

114. Matthew Yglesias, "The Unforgiving Math of School Segregation," *Slate*, July 3, 2012, http://www.slate.com/blogs/moneybox/2013/07/03/unforgiving_math_of_school_segregation.html?wpisrc=newsletter_jcr:content.

115. See, e.g., James B. Jacobs, *Can Gun Control Work?* (2002).

116. See, e.g., James Q. Wilson, "Criminal Justice," in Schuck & Wilson, eds., *Understanding America*, 483–85.

CHAPTER 12: REMEDIES: LOWERING GOVERNMENT'S FAILURE RATE

1. Nelson W. Polsby, "The Political System," in Peter H. Schuck & James Q. Wilson, eds., *Understanding America: The Anatomy of an Exceptional Nation* (2008), 23.

2. Derek Bok, *The Trouble with Government* (2001).

3. See, e.g., Benjamin I. Page & Robert Y. Shapiro, *The Rational Public* (1992).

4. "Poll: Attitudes toward Gays Changing Fast," http://www.usatoday.com/story/news/politics/2012/12/05/poll-from-gay-marriage-to-adoption-attitudes-changing-fast/1748873/.

5. See, e.g., Robert N. Bellah, Richard Madsen, William M. Sullivan, Ann Swidler, & Steven M. Tipton, *Habits of the Heart: Individualism and Commitment in American Life* (1985); Mary Ann Glendon, *Rights Talk: The Impoverishment of Political Discourse* (2008); and Cass R. Sunstein, *After the Rights Revolution: Reconceiving the Regulatory State* (1990).

6. See, e.g., Stephen Breyer, *Breaking the Vicious Circle: Toward Effective Risk Regulation* (1993); Sunstein, *After the Rights Revolution*; Philip K. Howard, *The Death of Common Sense: How Law Is Suffocating America* (1994).

7. David S. Law & Mila Versteeg, "The Declining Influence of the United States Constitution," *New York University Law Review* 87 (2012): 762–858.

8. Sanford Levinson, *Our Undemocratic Constitution: Where the Constitution Goes Wrong (And How We the People Can Correct It)* (2006); Sanford Levinson, *Framed: America's 51 Constitutions and the Crisis of Governance* (2012).

9. National Conference of State Legislatures, "Gubernatorial Veto Authority with Respect to Major Budget Bill(s)," December 2008, http://www.ncsl.org/issues-research/budget/gubernatorial-veto-authority-with-respect-to-major.aspx.

10. Bruce E. Cain, "Redistricting Commissions: A Better Political Buffer?" *Yale Law Journal* 121 (2012): 1808–44.

11. See, e.g., Thomas Mann & Norman Ornstein, *It's Even Worse Than It Looks: How the American Constitutional System Collided with the New Politics of Extremism* (2012); and Bok, *The Trouble with Government*, chap. 11.

12. Norman Ornstein, "Congress Needs a Five-Day Workweek (Most of the Time)," May 26, 2009, http://www.rollcall.com/issues/54_136/-35207–1.html.

13. Mann & Ornstein, *It's Even Worse Than It Looks*.

14. See, e.g., Amy Gutmann & Dennis Thompson, *The Spirit of Compromise: Why Governing Demands It and Campaigning Undermines It* (2012).

15. See, e.g., Richard L. Hasen, "Why Washington Can't Be Fixed," *Slate*, May 9, 2012,

http://www.slate.com/articles/news_and_politics/politics/2012/05/thomas_mann
_and_norman_ornstein_s_ideas_won_t_solve_washington_s_gridlock_.single
.html#pagebreak_anchor_2.

16. "Processing Power," *Economist*, March 30, 2013, 63–64.

17. Beth Simone Noveck, *Wiki Government: How Technology Can Make Government Better, Democracy Stronger, and Citizens More Powerful* (2009).

18. Tom Baker, "On the Geneaology of Moral Hazard," *Texas Law Review* 75 (1996): 237–92.

19. Justin Gillis, "Rebuilding the Shores, Increasing the Risks," *New York Times*, April 9, 2013.

20. "Audit Says Katrina Aid May Have Been Misspent," *Wall Street Journal*, April 4, 2013.

21. See, generally, "Point/Counterpoint," Journal of Policy Analysis & Management 30 (2011): 381–400; and *Conclusions of the Financial Crisis Commission*, http://fcic-static .law.stanford.edu/cdn_media/fcic-reports/fcic_final_report_conclusions.pdf.

22. See Alex J. Pollock, "We Don't Need GSEs," testimony before the House Financial Services Committee, June 12, 2013, http://financialservices.house.gov/uploadedfiles/hhrg -113-ba00-wstate-apollock-20130612.pdf.

23. Dwight Jaffee & John M. Quigley, *The Future of the Government Sponsored Enterprises: The Role for Government in the U.S. Mortgage Market*, National Bureau of Economic Research Working Paper #17685 (December 2011).

24. Gretchen Morgenson, "Mortgages' Future Looks Too Much Like the Past," *New York Times*, March 24, 2012.

25. Bipartisan Policy Center, "Housing America's Future: New Directions for National Policy," http://bipartisanpolicy.org/library/report/housing-america's-future-new-directions -national-policy.

26. Morgenson, "Mortgages' Future Looks Too Much Like the Past."

27. See, e.g., Robert J. Schiller, *Irrational Exuberance*, 2nd ed. (2005).

28. Jesse Eisinger, "Overhaul Efforts Reflect Few Lessons of Housing Crisis," *New York Times*, June 13, 2013.

29. See, e.g., Robert Kuttner, *Debtors' Prison: The Politics of Austerity Versus Possibility* (2013).

30. See, e.g., Mark H. Moore, *Recognizing Public Value* (2013). See also the Brookings Institution's new Center for Management and Leadership, http://www.brookings.edu /about/projects/management-and-leadership.

31. Peter F. Drucker, *The Practice of Management* (1954).

32. Elaine Kamarck, *Lessons for the Future of Government Reform*, June 18, 2013 (testimony before House Committee on Oversight and Reform), http://www.brookings .edu/research/testimony/2013/06/18-reinventing-government-future-reform-kamarck.

33. John D. Donahue, *The Warping of Government Work* (2008).

34. Milton Friedman, *Capitalism and Freedom* (1962).

35. See, e.g., Paul Peterson, "First Systematic Study of School Vouchers and College Enrollment Shows Large Effects for African-Americans," August 23, 2012, http://www.hks .harvard.edu/news-events/news/press-releases/vouchers_college-enrollment.

36. Cancer Action Network, "Opportunities for Employees to Purchase Exchange Coverage," http://www.acscan.org/pdf/healthcare/implementation/background/Opportunities Employees.pdf.

37. Richard H. Thaler & Cass R. Sunstein, *Nudge: Improving Decisions about Health, Wealth, and Happiness* (2008).

38. Fedral Trade Commission, "FTC Announces Robocall Challenge Winners," http://www .ftc.gov/opa/2013/04/robocall.shtm.

39. Bipartisan Policy Center, "The Consumer Financial Protection Bureau: Measuring the Progress of a New Agency," September 24, 2013, http://bipartisanpolicy.org/library

/report/health-care-cost-containment; http://healthaffairs.org/blog/2013/07/02/compe
titive-bidding-in-medicare-a-response-to-the-bipartisan-policy-centers-proposal/.

40. Donahue, *The Warping of Government Work*, 115.

41. Robert H. Frank, "Heads, You Win. Tails, You Win, Too," *New York Times*, January 6, 2013.

42. Mariana Mazzucato, *The Entrepreneurial State: Debunking Public vs. Private Sector Myths* (2013).

43. Kauffman Task Force on Law, Innovation, and Growth, *Rules for Growth: Promoting Innovation and Growth through Legal Reform*, (2011).

44. *Theoretical Inquiries in Law*, volume 15 (forthcoming 2014).

45. John D. Donahue & Richard J. Zeckhauser, *Collaborative Governance: Private Roles for Public Goals in Turbulent Times* (2011).

46. Cass Sunstein, *Simpler* (2013), chap. 8.

47. Tyler Cowen, "More Freedom on the Airplane (If Nowhere Else)," *New York Times*, November 17, 2013.

48. Norman Ornstein & Thomas E. Mann, "If You Give a Congressman a Cookie," *New York Times*, January 19, 2006.

49. See, e.g., David Schoenbrod, "The Honest Deal: How to Get Our Politicians to Work for Us" (unpublished manuscript, 2013).

50. John Bridgeland & Peter Orzag, "Can Government Play Moneyball?" *Atlantic*, July–August 2013, 63.

51. Ibid., 65.

52. Michael Abramowicz, Ian Ayres, & Yair Listokin, "Randomizing Law," *University of Pennsylvania Law Review* 159 (2011): 931.

53. Ibid.

54. Jim Manzi, *Uncontrolled: The Surprising Payoff of Trial-and Error for Business, Politics, and Society* (2012), 146.

55. Ibid., 197–98.

56. See, generally, Judith M. Gueron & Howard Rolston, *Fighting for Reliable Evidence* (2013).

57. "Being Good Pays," *Economist*, August 18, 2012, 28.

58. William Alden, "Goldman Sachs to Finance Early Education Program," *New York Times*, June 13, 2013.

59. Viktor Mayer-Schonberger & Kenneth Cukier, *Big Data: A Revolution That Will Transform How We Live, Work, and Think* (2013).

60. Sunstein, *Simpler*, 216.

61. John Markoff, "Unreported Side Effects of Drugs Are Found Using Internet Search Data, Study Finds," *New York Times*, March 7, 2013; Peter Huber, *The Cure in the Code: How 20th Century Law Is Undermining 21st Century Medicine* (2013).

62. See, e.g., Yochai Benkler, *The Wealth of Networks: How Social Production Transforms Markets and Freedom* (2006).

63. See, e.g., Timothy D. Lytton, *Kosher: Private Regulation in the Age of Industrial Food* (2013); and Ross E. Cheit, *Setting Safety Standards in the Public and Private Sectors* (1990).

64. John M. Broder, "Environmentalists' Complaint Exposes Rift between 'Green' Certification Groups," *New York Times*, June 1, 2013.

65. Sam Roudman, "Bank of America's Toxic Tower," http://www.newrepublic.com/article
/113942/bank-america-tower-and-leed-ratings-racket?utm_campaign=tnr-daily
-newsletter&utm_source=hs_email&utm_medium=email&utm_content=9771660.

66. Stephanie Strom, "Seeking Food Ingredients That Aren't Gene-Altered," *New York Times*, May 27, 2013.

67. Bok, *The Trouble with Government*, 166–67. Bok wrote a decade before the NCAA's

more recent failures, chronicled in Taylor Branch, *The Cartel: Inside the Rise and Imminent Fall of the NCAA* (2011).

68. Caroline Hoxby & Sarah Turner, *Expanding College Opportunities for High-Achieving, Low Income Students*, SIEPR Discussion Paper 12–014, http://siepr.stanford.edu /?q=/system/files/shared/pubs/papers/12–014paper.pdf.

69. James R. Hagerty, "Tapping Crowds for Military Design," *Wall Street Journal*, August 17, 2012.

70. Cogressional Budget Office, "Fair-Value Accounting for Federal Credit Programs," http://www.cbo.gov/sites/default/files/cbofiles/attachments/03–05-FairValue_Brief .pdf.

71. Glenn Kessler, "Elizabeth Warren's Claim That the U.S. Earns $51 Billion in Profits on Student Loans," *Washington Post*, July 11, 2013.

72. Peter H. Schuck, "Against (and for) Madison: An Essay in Praise of Factions," *Yale Law & Policy Review* 15 (1997): 589–91, nn 135 and 138.

73. Office of Management and Budget, "The Statutory Pay-As-You-Go Act of 2010: A Description," http://www.whitehouse.gov/omb/paygo_description.

74. Matt Cover, "U.S. Government's Ex-Im Bank Gave 44% of Its Financing to Just 3 Companies," http://cnsnews.com/news/article/us-governments-ex-im-bank-gave-44-its -financing-just-3-companies.

75. Dani Rodrik & Richard J. Zeckhauser, "The Dilemma of Government Responsiveness," *Journal of Policy Analysis & Management* 7 (1988): 601–20.

76. See, e.g., *Motor Vehicle Manufacturers Assn. v. State Farm Insurance Co.*, 463 U.S. 29 (1983) (invalidating agency policy change); and *Permian Basin Area Rate Cases*, 390 U.S. 747 (1968) (upholding agency policy change).

77. Michael Abramowicz & Ian Ayres, "Commitment Bonds," *Georgetown Law Journal* 100 (2012): 605–656.

78. Peter H. Schuck, *Suing Government: Citizen Remedies for Official Wrongs* (1983), 188–89.

79. Paul C. Light, "The Sequester Is an Overhaul Opportunity," *Wall Street Journal*, March 21, 2013.

80. See, e.g., *Tax Notes*, April 29, 2013, 488–89.

81. David Freeman Engstrom, "Whither Whistleblowing? Bounty Regimes, Regulatory Context, and the Case of Workplace Safety," *Theoretical Inquiries in Law* 15 (forthcoming, 2014).

82. Peter H. Schuck, "Legal Complexity: Some Causes, Consequences, and Cures," in Peter H. Schuck, *The Limits of Law: Essays on Democratic Governance* (2000), chap. 1; originally published in *Duke Law Journal* 42 (1992): 1–52.

83. "Fixing the Republic," Schumpeter, *Economist*, April 20, 2013, 72.

84. See, e.g., Michael J. Graetz, *100 Million Unnecessary Returns: A Simple, Fair, and Competitive Tax Plan for the United States* (2007).

85. PR Newswire, "Nationwide Survey Shows Large Majorities of U.S. Voters Want Federal Government Simplified," December 11, 2012, http://www.prnewswire.com/news -releases/nationwide-survey-shows-large-majorities-of-us-voters-want-federal-govern ment-simplified-183002071.html.

86. Ibid., 4–6.

87. See, e.g., Martha Derthick, *Keeping the Compound Republic: Essays on American Federalism* (2001).

88. See, generally, Carl E. Van Horn, ed., *The State of the States*, 4th ed. (2006).

89. Thaler & Sunstein, *Nudge*.

90. For a less benign view of this form of regulatory paternalism, see Donald J. Boudreaux's review of Sunstein's *Simpler*, *Wall Street Journal*, April 24, 2013, emphasizing the risk of perverse consequences and reduced liberty.

91. Sunstein, *Simpler*, chap. 5.

92. George Loewenstein et al., "Consumers' Misunderstanding of Health Insurance," *Journal of Health Economics* 32 (2013): 850–62.

93. Sunstein, *Simpler*, introduction.

94. See, e.g., Thomas C. Leonard, "Richard H. Thaler, Cass R. Sunstein, Nudge: Improving Decisions about Health, Wealth, and Happiness" (review), http://www.princeton.edu /~tleonard/reviews/nudge.pdf; Alan Schwartz, "The Rationality Assumption in Consumer Law," unpublished ms., October 2013.

95. Sunstein, *Simpler*, chap. 8.

96. See Exec. Order 13,563, 76 Fed. Reg. 3821 (January 18, 2011).

97. Philip K. Howard, *The Death of Common Sense*.

98. Peter H. Schuck, "The New Judicial Ideology of Tort Law," in Walter Olson, ed., *New Directions in Liability Law* (1988), 4–17; Peter H. Schuck, "Why Regulating Guns through Litigation Won't Work," in Timothy Lytton, ed., *Suing the Gun Industry: A Battle at the Crossroads of Gun Control and Mass Torts* (2005), chap. 9. For more systematic critiques, see Stephen D. Sugarman, *Doing Away with Personal Injury Law* (1989); and Jeffrey O'Connell, *The Blame Game: Injuries, Insurance, and Injustice* (1987).

99. Paul C. Light, *A Government Ill-Executed: The Decline of the Federal Service and How to Reverse It* (2008), chap. 8.

100. Ibid., 215–16.

101. Ibid., 224–38.

CHAPTER 13: CONCLUSION

1. James Q. Wilson, *Thinking about Crime* (1975), 198–99.

Index